good reading
essay on HOPE R-O

101 !

D1571998

reinforce

by praise
not critisium

FIVE CLASSICS
BY TRUMAN G. MADSEN

FIVE CLASSICS
BY TRUMAN G. MADSEN

EAGLE GATE

SALT LAKE CITY, UTAH

Library of Congress Control Number: 2001093359

ISBN 1-57008-720-2

Printed in the United States of America   72082-6856
10   9   8   7   6   5   4   3   2   1

CONTENTS

꤮

ETERNAL MAN

꤮

FOUR ESSAYS ON LOVE

CHRIST AND THE INNER LIFE

THE HIGHEST IN US

THE RADIANT LIFE

PUBLISHER'S PREFACE

Truman Madsen is a man of great faith, broad learning, and compelling intellectual power. But it is his distinctive and illuminating vision, his great gift for seeing patterns of the Gospel everywhere, that makes his work so uniquely memorable. He sees the God-given design in our lives and our environment, and seeing that design, he can embody heavenly ideas, concepts, and principles in the solid stuff of everyday life. Truman helps us to see that Christ is central to *all* things, and that truly "all things . . . are a typifying of Him" (2 Nephi 11:4). Thus through Truman's explanations we are led to more than intellectual comprehension; we come to see and feel—to recognize—in such a way that we can experience Christ's influence in all the world around us. And because we see the "seeds" and "trees," because we feel the weight and pressure of the olive press in the context of the Gospel, we come to better appreciate and know the meaning of Gethsemane and Calvary and the empty tomb.

To put it another way, Truman may have the intellect of a

genius but he also has the sensitivity of a poet. Consider for example how he joins images of water and currents to help us understand an important principle in this following passage (chosen from the pages of this collection). He says, speaking of certain continuing doctrines, "I can bear you a testimony that these currents and many more are part of the flowing fountain of the Church. If we do not drink, if we die of thirst while only inches from the fountain, the fault comes down to us. For the free, full, flowing, living water is there."

In Truman's metaphors we not only recognize allusions to Christ's self-identification with the "living water" (John 4:7–14), we also see that life-giving stream as part and parcel of the Church itself. Furthermore, we hear in Truman's syllables a concern for the sounds of the words themselves; the very enunciation ("*free, full, flowing,*" and so on) effectively emphasizing and connecting the adjectives together for the ear as well as the eye in a beautiful representation of the qualities of that divine water. These are not mere rhetorical flourishes. Truman's love of words ultimately derives from his obvious love of Him whom John refers to as *The Word.*

Finally there is an unusual sincerity in these essays reflecting qualities of the author himself. Truman not only writes from a deep level of his own belief, he strives to live the principles he talks about; one recognizes the exhortations of these pages in the behavior of the man. To shake hands with Truman is to be pulled into the warm circle of his love. To travel with him is to see his concern for the "least among you." I remember, for instance, his careful, thoughtful, kindly support of an eighty-year-old travel-weary tourist up the uneven steps of Old Jerusalem, making sure that she too, in the last years of her life, could "walk today where Jesus walked."

As he cared for this silver-haired lady so he cares for his students. Though tall in stature, Truman never stands "above" his class nor his audience. He is one with his students, rejoicing with them in their coming to understand and know, as all are edified together (D&C 50:22–24). His sensitivity to all those who seek and strive to learn extends far beyond the lecture hall. Consider, for instance, one very small but telling example: a young family with seven children recently moved into the ward where Truman Madsen is a Gospel Doctrine teacher for the Sunday School. On the first Sunday there, the mother—tired and a bit frazzled by the chaotic challenge of unpacked boxes and trying to help the family find and unwrinkle Sunday clothes and get ready and get to the church—finally got her little brood settled into their respective Sunday School classes. She then slipped as quietly as possible into the back row of the already-in-progress Gospel Doctrine class. But her coming to Sunday School did not go unnoticed. Back home after church, she was surprised when, responding to a knock at her front door, she saw the teacher standing on her front porch. Truman had come to her door to welcome her into the ward. He saw her effort and presence in class that day as a compliment and thanked her for coming to Sunday School.

So it is with these pages. If we feel the welcoming presence of a genuine Christian, it is because of the true effort and the true faith of this true man. In what follows we are, indeed, well-taught. We have before us not just inspiring instruction, but an inspiring individual who loves the Savior. We are indeed fortunate in having these essays so attractively and conveniently brought forward again in this collection.

Neal Lambert
Professor Emeritus
Brigham Young University

ETERNAL MAN

Preface

*Sometimes during solitude I hear truth spoken with clarity and
freshness; uncolored and untranslated it speaks from within
myself in a language original but inarticulate, heard only with
the soul, and I realize I brought it with me, was never taught it
nor can I efficiently teach it to another.*
—President Hugh B. Brown

The story behind these essays is still a matter of wonder in
me. To a topic and title—"Whence Cometh Man???"—*The
Instructor* editors added a hope. "It has been suggested," their letter said, "that you explain the meaning of premortality for some
of the ultimate issues of human existence." Their intent was that I
sketch in outline form the singular Mormon theme of preexistence
on the canvas of present-day philosophical approaches to man. So
the effort was made.

The response was, to me at least, quite unforeseen. Not just
teachers, whom we had expected to nudge toward wider application of their topics, but a variety of persons wrote for sources and
further comparisons. Soon the editors asked that this article be the
introduction to six others, around the issues barely broached

within it: personal identity, creation, embodiment, freedom, suffering, and self-awareness. The query followed: "Will these be published in book form?" Till now I have answered, "No," convinced that interest would diminish. Instead it has increased.

Here, then, is the series, written as a kind of "midrash," a commentary on a theme. It can justly be said that they are not more than this, but not, I hope, that they are less. Letters of praise for their "objectivity" (which usually means that I have named and highlighted some of the live alternatives) miss my feeling that such merit as they have is in their subjectivity. Their primary gesture is toward inner echoes, toward, as it were, the nerve endings of the spirit. For this reason, likewise, I am surprised at comments which assume I have proved or refuted this or that. The goal has been to clarify rather than to verify, with little room for argument, except an implicit appeal to introspection.

The concept of eternal man, with its refinements in the prophets of this new era, has an immense philosophical and theological strength which is only beginning to be recognized. But this, when presented adequately, will sponsor a tome which is not pressed for abbreviation.

It has been said more than once that the essays are hard to understand. If this reflects a struggle with the terms and the heavily packed style, my own children prove that these yield to repeated exposure. But another anxiety is involved here. Those who believe, as I do, in the magnificence of simplicity and the hazards of speculation wonder whether the statement of contrasts should be reduced or simply avoided.

Now it goes without saying that though the master writings of the Prophet are authoritative, my commentary is not. Concern for absolute fidelity to his intent has pushed me to original sources and to all the checking procedures I know. But if there is distortion I am not only open, but eager, for correction. Similarly, I must be alone responsible for interpretations of the other materials alluded to throughout.

But nothing here is wilfully obscure. And it should be recognized that simplicity is not superficiality. The idea of a forever forward is not more or less simple than that of a forever backward. Yet, in our culture, one idea is commonplace, the other startling, even "unthinkable." (This retreat, it seems to me, is unavailable to those who say they understand the idea when it is applied to God.) My point is that there are depths in man, and in the attempt to plumb him, depths which tax the most disciplined of minds, as also, which is much more, the most enlightened souls. I am with those who wish for a larger cup to grasp the ocean. But the Prophet, who was superb in making "the broad expanse of eternity" intelligible, warned that we do not enlarge the cup by a snap of the finger nor by a "fanciful, flowery and heated imagination"; only, he said, "by careful and ponderous and solemn thoughts." "By contrarieties," he added, "truth is made manifest."

A related kind of authority is needed in this realm. It is what, in the vernacular, is called "room to talk." It is hard to come by. Academies help some, but life helps more.

The difference was all too graphic when I sat in the surgical chair of a Cambridge oculist. He asked me searching questions about the article on evil and suffering while he scraped at my eye. The pain was sharper than his instruments, and as I concentrated, or tried to, the thought recurred (familiar to most of us?) that I could stand both kinds of thrusts anywhere but there and then.

Personally, I think that any view of man that does not make a difference in such an ordeal, or in those compared to which this was a fleeting pinprick, is worthless. But it is only a rootless preju- dice of our time that morbidity is profundity, and that any insight that seems consoling is bound to be a wishful and vagrant bromide. (The crutch of the immoralist is often his wishful disbelief.) It doesn't matter that I have had enough experience to be safe from confusing the Garden of Eden and the Garden of Gethsemane. What matters is that Christ and his prophets are, in all history, those most immersed in these realities and therefore in ours. If I had not known that self-understanding on the scale Christ had it, and through Him others, can endow life—all of it—with glorious meaning, these articles would never have been begun.

—Truman G. Madsen

5

Chapter One

WHENCE COMETH MAN?

The great thing for us to know is to comprehend what God did institute before the foundation of the world. Who knows it?
—Joseph Smith

Modern revelation, said the Prophet Joseph Smith, establishes "a foundation that will revolutionize the whole world."[1]

No insights, no set of flashes, are more revolutionary to the axioms of religion in the Western world than these three:

A. Man and woman are not derived from a void. They are beginningless. Their primal existence, as uncreated and indestructible intelligences, is everlasting.[2]

B. The "creation" of spirit or soul is not a fiat act at the time of

---

Opening quotation: Joseph Smith, *Teachings* (1938), 320.

1. Ibid., 366.

2. "The intelligence of spirits had no beginning, neither will it have an end. That is good logic" (ibid., 353). "Intelligence is eternal and exists upon a self-existent principle" (ibid., 354). Compare D&C 93:29, 30.

mortal conception or birth. It is really Divine procreation in a world of glory.[3]

C. Physical birth in mortality is not totally at the initiative of God the Father. It is in part the result of premortal, individual election and foresight which are in harmony with uncreated law.[4]

Within the Church two opposite positions sometimes prevail about such ideas. One position assumes that they are so remote and incomplete that a "practical" man avoids thinking about them. The other assumes that by mere reference to pre-existence one can "explain" all events and eventualities.

The acceptance of these statements as ultimately true has immense consequences. To illustrate, here are several puzzles in philosophy and theology, along with glimpses of implied answers and their bearings:

1. The problem of human identity posed by Heraclitus and Hume, and by modern biology and physiology.[5]

2. The paradoxes of creation posed by Augustine and Thomas Aquinas.[6]

3. The mind-body problem posed by Descartes and by present-day cybernetics.[7]

4. The problem of human freedom posed by Greek fatalism and teleology and by present-day psychoanalysis.[8]

5. The problem of evil or suffering posed by Job, Leibnitz, and so-called existenz-philosophy.[9]

---

3. "Element had an existence from the time He had. The pure principles of element are principles which can never be destroyed; they may be organized; and reorganized, but not destroyed. They had no beginning and can have no end" (ibid., 352, 301).

4. Ibid., 325. "The organization of spiritual and heavenly worlds, and of spiritual and heavenly beings, was agreeable to the most perfect order and harmony; their limits and bounds were fixed irrevocably, and *voluntarily subscribed* to in their heavenly estate by themselves . . ." (italics added).

5. Guthrie, *Greek Philosophy.*

6. See *Basic Writings of St. Augustine.*

7. N. Smith, *Philosophy of Descartes.*

8. See "Free Will and Responsibility" in Hospers and Sellars, *Readings.*

9. See Book of Job. Leibnitz solution or "Theodicy" is presented in *Theodicy,* 123.

6. The problem of self-awareness posed by Plato, and in our day by Jung; and all approaches to the "depth self."[10]

These are issues with complexities foreign to the layman. But each of us has convictions on these questions under less technical labels. And our whole life, conscious and subconscious, is colored by them.

Let us turn now to patterns of ordinary reflection and put them in personal terms, as if they arose (as they do) from some of the abiding anxieties of life:

1. **The Problem of Identity** (Developed in chapter 2)

Might I cease to be? Is there anything permanent in me? Am I, as Hume had it, "a bundle of perceptions," or as Russell says, "an accidental collocation of atoms"?[11]

Your conscious and purposive existence is guaranteed forever. The elements composing your intelligence, your begotten spirit and mortal body, are indestructible. Through stages, either of growth or degeneration, selfhood remains. Both utter extinction and permanent regression to a prior state are impossibilities.

Hence we are not, contrary to literary lamentations about the "predicament of man," suspended over "the abyss of nonbeing."[12] Kierkegaard, Sartre, and Marcel are mistaken.[13] The only sense in which one can fail to *be* is in not realizing his full potential. His fundamental existence is not, and never will be, in jeopardy.

2. **The Paradoxes of Creation** (Developed in chapter 3)

How can I be anything except what God made me? How could an unchanging, immaterial First Cause bring a tangible me into being "ex nihilo" (from nothing)?

---

10. See Plato's dialogue *The Meno* where the pre-existent knowledge of the soul is demonstrated by a slave-boy's recollection of mathematical knowledge which he could not have apprehended in this world.

11. Russell uses this phrase in his famous essay, "A Free Man's Worship." See "Russell's Philosophy of Religion" in *Philosophy of Bertrand Russell*.

12. This is one of the recurring themes of existentialism—the threat of nothingness. See Reinhardt, *Existentialist Revolt*.

13. Kierkegaard pleads for a leap of faith to the Absolute. Sartre pleads for the recognition, with Nietzsche, that "God is dead." Marcel turns to the Thomistic answer.

There is no creation "from nothing." There *is* ordering of elements: movement from simple to complex; growth from one degree to a greater degree, and from part to whole.

You are not just a product; you are an originator. In space you are coexistent with God. In time you are coeternal with God.

This view contradicts not only Sartre and Berdyaev on self-creation,[14] but also the Calvinistic concept of absolute pre-causation of all realities. It vitiates the dualism of material and immaterial, of firsts and derivatives.[15] (We are all "firsts.") It invalidates all of Thomas Aquinas's classical arguments for God based on "contingency."[16] And it solves Augustine's difficulty, bristling with contradictions, about when and where time and space were created. (Answer: They were not created but have always been in existence.)

3. **The Mind-body Problem** (Developed in chapter 4)

Which part of me is dominant or most important? Is mind reducible to matter, or matter to mind?

All three modes of your being—intelligence, spirit, and body—are essential to your self-fulfillment. Perfection of any one requires inseparable union with the others. God Himself is God because of His tripartite perfection.[17]

Gilbert Ryle's attack on the idea of an evanescent "ghost in the machine" is well-taken, but for reasons that he does not

---

14. Sartre's idea of freedom is sketched in his *L'Etre et le Neant,* 127–130. Berdyaev's is outlined in *Zeitschrift fur philosophische Forschung,* 6:86ff. Calvinistic predetermination is taught in *The Institutes.* See *Calvin Theological Treatises,* 179.

15. The view that the immaterial is utterly different from the material, and that the latter is utterly dependent on the former pervades almost every book on Christian theology or philosophy. Thomas assumes both that there must be a First Cause and that there can only be *one* First. Joseph Smith rejected these assumptions. See *Saint Thomas Aquinas.*

16. The difficulties of Thomas' position are summarized in "The Existence of God," in Flew and Macintyre, *Philosophical Theology.* See Madsen, "Joseph Smith and the Ways of Knowing," in *Seminar on the Prophet* (1961), 36–37.

17. See Madsen, "The Nature of the Good Self" in "Joseph Smith and the Problems of Ethics" in *Seminar on the Prophet* (1962).

understand. The spirit is not a ghost, but a material entity.[18] The body is not a machine but an organic, purposive being. Interaction of these self-elements is far less problematic if (as is the case) they are similar in nature and not, as Descartes assumed, radically different.

Hence disparagements of intellect, mystical denials of the reality of the material world and religious or ethical castigations of the human body as utterly evil, here show up for what they are: extremes and delusions.[19]

4. **The Problem of Human Freedom** (Developed in chapter 5)

What are my capacities? Am I victimized by the circumstances of being badly born or badly conditioned?

Your autobiographical thread leads backward through the lineage of Deity and on to the original individual unit called "intelligence." In it, in miniature, is the acorn of your potential oak, the unsculptured image of a glorified personality.

Freedom was not created. You are, and always will be, independent in that stage of development to which your voluntary decisions and divine powers have led. There are limits all along the way to what you can be and do. But you are not a billiard ball. No power in the universe can coerce your complete assent or dissent.

This thesis on capacity dissolves the absolute wall that Western theologians have erected between Deity and man.[20] It increases the awe one feels in the superlative motives that led God the Father and Jesus the Christ to glorify not "things" of their absolute make, but persons who were part of their everlasting environment. It translates Bergson's metaphor into breath-taking fact, "The universe is a machine for the making of gods."[21]

---

18. Ryle, *Concept of Mind.*

19. Today the constant phrase is that God is "wholly other," "utterly transcendent," or "absolutely unconditioned." Whenever religion has moved in this direction it has tended, likewise, to minimize man. "Finite," demonic," "depraved," are typical of dominant trends.

20. Is there not a deeper root of love in us for a Father who lifts us by His own love and power, than for a Fiat Creator who brought us into being from nothing?

21. Bergson, *Two Sources,* 308.

The freedom thesis undercuts the causal dogmas of behaviorists, mechanists, fatalists, and predestinationists. John Wisdom has lately argued that one can only justify a belief in free agency by a belief in pre-existence.[22] The identification of freedom with primal intelligence does just that.

5. **The Problem of Evil, of Suffering** (Developed in chapter 6)

How can we account for inequalities? And how can God be good and powerful and yet permit human suffering?

God is responsible neither for the innate limits of uncreated element nor for the eternal and inviolate principles within which the Gospel plan is instituted. By application of these, not by a cosmic accident, He became what He is. Likewise He aids all of us in reaching our fulness.

Thus, it is not a "decree" that stress and pain are part of growth and enlightenment. The universe and the selves within it simply operate that way. It is enough to know that God the Father and His Son Jesus Christ, though not the source of tragedy, yet have power to enable us to climb above it, into everlasting joy.

As to present ills, we anticipated them. Yet we chose, and chose with knowledge, these very conditions and risks. In a word, we were not, contrary to French nihilists, "thrown" into the world. Every mortal, to reverse the popular statement, did "ask to be born." (And those who say they are in their second childhood unwittingly speak the truth.) We might have avoided mortality. Billions did, and thus drastically limited their possibilities.

This position abandons the classical dilemma of the nature and meaning of the soul's creation. It does not rest, with Edwards, on "the inscrutable will of God."[23] It exonerates God from "man's inhumanity to man." It parallels Brightman's notion of "the Given" with which God is struggling, willing the ultimate

---

22. Wisdom, *Philosophy and Psychoanalysis*.

23. The phrase is also central in Calvin. Not only is God inscrutable but we sin if we seek to understand God. God is "essential mystery," not simply a not-yet-known but an unknowable. In contrast Joseph Smith wrote, "The day shall come when you shall comprehend even God, being quickened in him and by him" (D&C 88:49).

happiness for all His creatures.[24] It refutes the view of a Bradley or a Buddha that evil is illusory.[25] It breaks out of the triangle argument that God cannot be both all-good and all-powerful, by showing that God is Himself operating within eternal limits.[26]

6. **The Problem of Self-awareness** (Developed in chapter 7)

How can I know my real self?

Your maximum unfolding depends partly on not yet knowing your infinite past; but also it depends on knowing what is deepest in you, while in mortality.

Such a learning process recollects more than it researches. It is the opposite of amnesia. It is less discovery than recovery. (And every religious teacher should, in this realm, conceive his role as the Master Teacher and Socrates did: as a midwife of ideas, not as their transplanter.)

One begins mortality with the veil drawn, but slowly he is moved to penetrate the veil within himself. He is, in time, led to seek the "holy of holies" within the temple of his own being.

The dawning of the light has three main sources:

First, there is inspired introspection. As we move through life, half-defined recollections and faint but sometimes vivid outlines combine to bring a familiar tone or ring to our experience.

One feels at times at home in a universe which, for all that is grotesque and bitter, yet has meaning. Wordsworth called this a

---

24. Brightman, *Philosophy of Religion.* Brightman is also convinced that God must be a personal being, and that the greatest coherence of human experience and observation confirms this. In this he stands with a minority of present-day writers on religion.

25. Both Christian Science and Oriental thought affirm that evil is appearance, not reality; that suffering is an illusion. Joseph Smith taught that suffering is real, but meaningful and purposive. His view is "instrumental" (see D&C 122).

26. The argument is that if God permits suffering because he cannot prevent it then he is not all-powerful. If he permits suffering though he could prevent it, then he is not all good. The standard reply is that God must allow suffering in order to allow freedom. But, again, if he were *all*-powerful, he could guarantee freedom without suffering. Joseph Smith revealed that God is himself surrounded by everlasting law, eternal intelligences; hence eternal conditions. He became God by abiding these conditions. He did not create, neither can he destroy them.

"presence that disturbs me with the joy of elevated thoughts. A sense sublime of something far more deeply interfused."[27]

One recognizes as Fromm and Rogers and others describe it, "What one authentically *is*."[28] At times he feels, with William James, like "the real me," "most alive."[29] One feels he is on a path anticipated or prepared for, in part a prefabricated path. Rufus Jones calls this "the luminous trail."[30]

One has sacred moments in relation to persons, places, and situations which bear the subtle stamp of prior awareness, however elusive. Rudolph Otto calls this (in Latin) "*a priori* numinousness."[31] One hears truths expressed, "hidden from before the foundation of the world," and is pulled to them with overwhelming gratitude. Jesus Christ, who promised He would bring all things to our remembrance, defined all this and more when He said, "My sheep know my voice."[32]

Second, beyond these inner hints recognized by poets and philosophers are the revelations of the prophets. Like a physician to a patient who has "lost" his memory they say:

"You were at the first organization in heaven.[33] You saw the Savior chosen and appointed, and the plan of life presented; and you sanctioned it.[34] You were a participant in a grand council when specific mortal missions were assigned and 'were ordained to that very calling.'[35] You were present at the creation of the earth and

---

27. "Tintern Abbey," in *Complete Poetical Works.*

28. Rogers, *Counseling and Psychotherapy.*

29. James, *Principles of Psychology,* 1:299. See also Grattan, *Three Jameses,* 225. "At such moments there is a voice inside which speaks and says: 'This is the real me.'"

30. Jones, *What Is Vital.*

31. Otto, *Idea of the Holy.* The word "numinous" is a derivative of "luminous." It depicts, for Otto, the deep and latent response to sacred things.

32. Joseph F. Smith, "Spirit Memories," in *Gospel Doctrine,* 13. "All those salient truths which come home so forcibly to the head and heart seem but the awakening of the memories of the spirit."

33. Joseph Smith, *Teachings* (1938), 181.

34. Ibid., 181, 308.

35. Ibid., 190, 220, 365.

took your place in the organization of the human family."[36] Illumined, these statements can change from cold conceptions or thoughts to warm realities.

But, *third,* there are the concrete and individual pronouncements of the patriarch who has been called to stand between heaven and earth. His inspiration may reach from the celestial hearth to earthly heritage, and from the vital promises of mission to the morning of divine reunion—and beyond. No "Whence came I?" and no "Who am I?" receive such a transforming answer as this leaf from the eternal diary.

Now, none of these "ways" is scientifically operational. Even if, as Jung thought, most psychic illness is rooted in religious maladjustment; even if glimpses of the "collective unconscious" can help resolve it, these glimpses are not laboratory-induced.[37] Traces of ourselves show up in inkblot tests, in free association, in dreams, in parapsychology. But always there is more, awaiting the visitation of the Perfect Psychiatrist.

Enough has now been said to establish the point that not only does awareness of the pre-existence make a difference, but that it is a prodigious difference.

For it follows from all this that no philosophy or psychology of personality, no attempt to speak accurately about the nature of the mental, the spiritual, or the physical, no solution to questions on the meaning of life, in sum, no approach to any question bearing on the origins or destiny of man (and all questions eventually lead to these), can be adequate without taking account of these six answers.

Modern man has penetrated the self and found much that is shocking and unspeakably dark. By a Freud, a Niebuhr, a Heidegger, the viper within man has been widely heralded.[38] But this, for all its professed depth, has been too shallow.

For deeper still, *in* and not just *below* all in man that needs

---

36. Ibid., 158.

37. See Jung, *Modern Man.*

38. Heidegger in philosophy has shown the depths of a man's guilt and "angst" (anguish). Freud in psychology has uncovered the riotous impulses of

healing and redeeming, are the remnants and rudiments of glory. As one uncovers that level he recognizes not one but two; not just his depths but his heights, not just himself but God.

And that is a syllable of meaning in one of the most profound statements ever made about man. It was given by Joseph Smith:

If men do not comprehend the character of God, they do not comprehend themselves.[39]

What, then, of the man who really comprehends himself?

<hr />

the subconscious. Niebuhr in theology has shown man victimized by the "Fall," the symbol of sins of pride and self-assurance.

39. Joseph Smith, *Teachings* (1938), 343.

Chapter Two

IDENTITY
OR NOTHING

*When things that are of the greatest importance are passed over
by weak-minded men without even a thought, I want to
see truth in all its bearings and hug it to my bosom.*
—Joseph Smith

If the ancient saying "Know Thyself" is a primary human aim, then "Seek Thine Origins" is surely a part of it.

Regarding the ultimate identity of man, the Prophet Joseph Smith taught that man as a primal intelligence is eternal. Likewise the spirit-elements that compose his Divinely-sired spirit and the matter-elements that compose his physically-sired body are eternal. Except in procreation, these elements of the total self never become an *essential* part of any other self. Once united, their destiny is to be glorified and "inseparably connected" throughout all eternity.

Opening quotation: Joseph Smith, *Teachings* (1938), 374.

My task is not to argue for or against this concept of personal eternalism.[1] Nor is it to examine the credentials which would be presented if the questions were raised, "Why is this believed?" or "How is this known?" Instead: Suppose this *is* the truth about man—what does it mean, and what follows? What are some important consequences of accepting this idea in the contemporary world?

FOUR CHARACTERIZATIONS

To begin with, what does Joseph Smith's affirmation about intelligences really say? Let us agree at the outset that much is left indeterminate.[2] But does not a careful reading require at least these four characterizations?[3]

Individuality. Man as a self had a beginningless beginning. He has never been identified wholly with any other being. Nor is he a product of nothing. "Intelligence is eternal and exists upon a self-existent principle. . . . There is no creation about it."[4]

---

1. The term "eternalism" was coined by B. H. Roberts to describe the Mormon position. See Roberts, *Comprehensive History,* 410.

2. Fascinating questions, for example, immediately arise about the unoriginated status, differences, "gifts," talents, and capacities of intelligences. On these issues there are only hints in the Prophet's teachings.

3. Another attempt to do this is in the paper, Truman G. Madsen, "Joseph Smith and the Problem of Ethics," *Seminar on the Prophet* (1962).

4. Joseph Smith, *Teachings* (1938), 354. Individuality is difficult to picture. That has led some to the view that "intelligence" is a name given to a primal stuff out of which, perhaps, the spirit personality is constructed, but that individuality does not really emerge until then. The doctrine of the Church, however, is clearly a doctrine of individual, separate intelligences. This is required by the original statements of the Prophet in Nauvoo. *The Journal of Wilford Woodruff,* for example, shows that the phrase "a spirit from age to age" refers to an entity, a person, an individual. (See footnotes to the sermon in Joseph Smith, *Teachings* (1938), 354.) It is required by the logic of the Prophet "Anything that has a beginning may have an end." It is required by the use of the plural "intelligences" in many passages in the Standard Works. Finally, it is required by official pronouncements of the Church. The issue became a matter of wide discussion in the early 1900s. B. H. Roberts's *Seventy's Yearbook,* volume 4, assumed the co-eternity of individuals. The book was read and approved by the First Council of the Seventy. Later controversy resulted in an article titled "The Immortality of Man." By assignment, Elder Roberts read this article first to President

Autonomy. The self is free. All intelligence " . . . is independent in that sphere in which God has placed it, to act for itself . . . otherwise there is no existence."[5]

Consciousness. There is no inanimate intelligence or unconscious mind. These are contradictions in terms. Selfhood and individual consciousness are unending. "The intelligence of spirits had no beginning, neither will it have an end. That is good logic. That which has a beginning may have an end."[6]

Capacity for Development. "All the minds and spirits that God ever sent into the world are susceptible of enlargement."[7]

THE SHAKING OF FOUNDATIONS

Few of us may realize how radical these theses are in contrast to dominant assumptions of our time.

I once presented to some graduate students the idea that man's intelligence was unoriginated and indestructible. That was in a Harvard Seminar on Augustine.[8] The entire class was violent in its outbursts. For some minutes the professor's anxiety to keep the peace was futile.

Why is the idea so staggering? Because it not only challenges established religious dogmas about man, but also leading secular viewpoints. It uproots in one fell swoop presuppositions that are lodged in billions of minds and millions of books. The notion

Francis M. Lyman, then to the First Presidency (President Joseph F. Smith was President) and seven of the Council of the Twelve. It was thoroughly discussed. The article was published with their encouragement and endorsement. (*Improvement Era,* April 1907). This article teaches the "existence of independent, uncreated, self-existent intelligences" which, though they differ, are "alike in their eternity and their freedom" (419). This is a doctrine, Roberts often said, "from which spring most glorious and harmonious truths."

5. D&C 93:29. I interpolate cautiously that the meaning here is "Otherwise there is no existence of *selves*" distinct from inanimate reality. If *all* existence depends on the independence of intelligence we have idealism instead of realism.

6. Joseph Smith, *Teachings* (1938), 353.

7. Ibid., 354.

8. The question arose in discussing the issues of predeterminism in Augustine's conception of creation.

today is more revolutionary than would be the revision of all mathematical operations of men and machines on the discovery that one and one do not make two, but infinity.

Likewise, as I have said elsewhere,[9] these ideas are so pervasive in their implications that every question that pertains to man is related to them.

REWARDING REWORDING

Even Latter-day Saints, when the idea is put in ways that break out of routine phraseology, may find that it shakes their ordinary ways of thinking. Here, for example, are some of its meanings and entailments:

The quantity, though not the quality, of selves is fixed forever. It is infinite.

There is no beginning to our "beginning."

Mind has no birthday and memory has no first.

Age is relative only to stages, not existence. No one is older, or younger, than anyone else.

We have always been alone, separate from, and always together, coexistent with, other intelligences.

Creation is never totally original; it is always a combination of prior realities.

Immortality is in no sense conditional. It is inevitable and universal, even for sub-human intelligences.

Whatever may be said of the spirit and body, death does not destroy the self, but only delimits it.

Death, like all events, is lived through. It is comparable to the loss of an arm, and that is temporary.

Suicide is just a change of scenery.

Through all transformations of eternity, no self can change completely into another thing. Identity remains.

In an ultimate sense, no existent self ever loses his mind nor his consciousness.

In sum, nothing is something we never were and never can be.

---

9. In "Whence Cometh Man," *Instructor,* June 1963.

THREE CONTRASTING OUTLOOKS

Let us turn now to three contrasting outlooks:

1. *Orthodox Christendom*

For the traditionated Christian, man is derived from nothing or from nonbeing by the fiat act of God. The Divine created *ex nihilo*[10] (out of nothing) both the soul and body of man, which is to say, the whole of man. Indeed, everything except God is derived from nonbeing.

Man, in this view, becomes the proof of God, for since man is absolutely contingent (he would not be except for something outside himself), we must conclude that something created him and that something must be absolutely necessary or self-existent. St. Thomas and his heirs, with faith, not, as claimed, with logic, move from that something to Something and from Something to the Christian God.[11]

Allied with this view is the notion of God's continual creation. God is the "sustainer" of man and of all reality. Without God there would be no other being; hence, He is "being-itself." This has tended repeatedly in Christian theology to limit or even deny man's freedom and certainly his enlargement. For if God is directly responsible for all that man is, He is indirectly responsible for all that man does.[12] Calvin faced this consequence squarely. Denying freedom, he held that all acts of men are acts of God, even the sinking of the murderer's knife into the victim's back.[13]

---

10. The official definition of "creation ex nihilo" is, "God brings the entire substance of a thing into existence from a state of nonexistence. . . . What is peculiar to creation is the entire absence of any prior subject-matter," Appleton, *Catholic Encyclopedia*, 4:470.

11. See *Saint Thomas Aquinas*, 709. That God is self-existent is correct enough. But, asks the Prophet, "Who told you that man does not exist in like manner on the same principles? Man does exist on the same principles" (Joseph Smith, *Teachings* (1938), 352).

12. And this is the problem of God-and-evil (theo-dike, theodicy). It remains the strongest secular objection to belief in a purposive and worthy Deity.

13. See critical commentary in Anthony Flew, "Divine Omnipotence and Human Freedom," in Flew and MacIntyre, *Philosophical Theology*.

Others have held that God created man totally for His purpose, yet that man is responsible for his salvation and is not a pawn.[14]

Christian theology qualifies the individuality and consciousness of man. Man may be swallowed up in the "Absolute Principle";[15] or his consciousness may cease at death;[16] or he may be subject to a conditional resurrection; or, (as in Eastern religion) he may be cast in a radically different form into a more ethereal realm.[17]

In sum: creation is the absolute mysterious act of God; freedom is foreshortened or denied; and consciousness and enlargement opportunities are focused on mortality. (Few Christians believe either in a premortal self or in salvation opportunities beyond mortal death.)

The orthodox Christian attitude toward life is a faith-state submission to the inscrutable will of God and faith in a purposeful fulfillment beyond the grave. He trusts that God is good and His creation of man meaningful. He is willing, whatever he may be, to be.

2. Existentialism

For existentialism, man is a derivative of nothing, is now almost nothing, and is destined for nothing.

"Existentialism" is the unpronounceable name of a doctrine advanced by a group, some religious, some a-religious, of European origin.[18] It is now one of the most influential movements in the Western world. These writers are in the lineage of Job, Augustine, and Pascal.[19] After the most agonizing studies in

---

14. Modern and liberal theology have emphasized the intrinsic worth and dignity of man and significantly have reinstated purpose, creative personality, heightened consciousness, and expanded opportunities in the life to come. But the present trend is a landslide toward a pessimistic disparagement of man. See Dillenberger and Welch, *Protestant Christianity*.

15. See an outline of different positions in Brightman, *Philosophy of Religion*.

16. This view for some sects is called "soul-sleeping."

17. Eastern religion, for example, Buddhism, aspires to absolute annihilation of the soul. Many Christians hope for the annihilation, or at least escape from, the body; hence do not believe in the resurrection.

18. Barrett, *Irrational Man*.

19. See Madsen, "The Contribution of Existentialism," in *BYU Studies*. (A synopsis is in the *Proceedings of the Utah Academy of Arts and Sciences*, 1959.)

self-scrutiny, they conclude that man is a phantom, a "useless passion," to use Sartre's phrase.[20]

Some of these writers account for man as self-creating. (It requires tremendously complex analysis to show how a nonexistent self can create an existent self; and then lack the power to perpetuate it.)[21] The main approach is not to man viewed from the outside, but from the inside. Such inner realities as anxiety, dread, guilt, suffering, monotony, nausea, despair are portrayed in excruciating detail.[22] The starkest, darkest threat of all is, paradoxically, nothing. Man is under the "threat of nonbeing," the ontological shock of "I might not be." Man is absolute finitude; and life, as Kierkegaard states it, is "the sickness unto death."[23] This is the "abyss" beneath the surface, the "limit-encounter" to rephrase Jaspers, which destroys security, destroys meaning, and haunts our identity until we are swallowed in its chasm. More than the fear of death, this is the anguish of absolute negation.[24]

In sum: creation is a mystery of self-propulsion; freedom is absolute except in overcoming the "limit" of being; consciousness is agony; and "enlargement" is meaningless.

The existentialist attitude toward life is utter pessimism. Suicide is its most consistent outcome. Answerable to nobody and estranged from everybody, these people suffer through the disease of "nihilism." Even those who follow Kierkegaard or Marcel or Tillich and "leap" to God, leap in the dark and are convinced that "Before God we are always in the wrong."[25] At best "eternal life" is a symbol for enduring in the present sordid world.[26] This is a religion of much nothing and nothing much.

---

20. See Marcel, *Philosophy of Existentialism.*

21. Berdyaev and Sartre are among the number. Sartre's great tome, *L'Etre et le Neant* (Being and Nothing) treats this subject at length.

22. The very titles of their books reflect chronic melancholy: Kierkegaard's, *Fear and Trembling;* Sartre's, *Flies, No Exit, Troubled Sleep;* Unamuno's, *Tragic Sense of Life.*

23. See Tillich's account in his "Introduction," in *Systematic Theology.*

24. Collins, *Existentialists* presents this under "Five Existentialists Themes."

25. So says Kierkegaard. See Emmet's treatment of this in connection with Barth, Brunner, and Niebuhr in chapter 6 of *Metaphysical Thinking.*

26. So Desan titles his treatment of Sartre, *The Tragic Finale.*

3. *Humanism*

For Humanists, man comes from something and returns to something. But this something is "cosmic dust," which is almost nothing.[27]

In close alliance with present scientific method and findings, humanists try to account for man as an "epiphenomenon"; man is to the cosmos what a train whistle is to the train.[28] If "explanations" are necessary, a blend of Darwin and microbiology may be invoked.[29] Matter or matter-energy came first, then one-celled organisms, then consciousness and the so-called "higher" human traits. Mind is an accident. It will not last long before its reduction to matter. The body is a collection of atoms whose turnover is complete every seven years, and whose disorganization is imminent.[30]

Man, on this view, is a temporary event, a fleeting figure in the blind careenings of the cosmos. (There is, of course, no reference to God.) His identity is soon to be obliterated, and with it all of his expressions of beauty, goodness, knowledge, and love. All will be swallowed up in what Russell calls "the vast death of the solar system."[31] So when Wernher von Braun tries to bolster hopes for personal immortality by saying "nothing disappears without a trace,"[32] the humanist agrees; but the trace will not be conscious. As Montague has it, the things that matter most will ultimately be at the mercy of the things that matter least.[33]

In sum: creation is a shifting of molecules; freedom is a name for our ignorance of the causes that determine us; consciousness is a flicker; and "enlargement" is a start before a final stop.

The humanist attitude toward life is, unlike the existentialist,

---

27. See Lamont, *Humanism.*
28. The point of the comparison is that the train whistle has no substantial character of its own, but disappears even if the train does not.
29. See, for instance, Wald, "The Origin of Life," in *Physics and Chemistry of Life.*
30. See Lamont, *Illusion of Immortality.*
31. Russell, "A Free Man's Worship," in *Mysticism and Logic.*
32. Von Braun is featured in the BYU Science and Religion film and restates what he said in a feature article in the *This Week* magazine section.
33. So Montague says in *Belief Unbound.*

affirmative. But unlike the Christian, it is altogether "this-worldly." He lives prudently, grateful for pleasures, patient in pain. He is not an absolute pessimist. There are still worthwhile dreams, hopes, and achievements. He is a kind of stoic, pursuing ends he believes will soon come to nothing.

Now, with these viewpoints as background, let the Latter-day Saints re-read and contrast Joseph Smith's theses on identity. Let him trace their incompatibility with these prevailing outlooks. And let him ask himself how they color his attitudes toward life, in ways far more numerous than this outline conveys.

THE NOTHINGNESS OF NOTHING

To speak logically and summarily, if the New Dispensation doctrine be true, then these three positions on the origins and identity of man are false. The orthodox Christian, the existentialist, and the humanist are asking themselves, with Hamlet, a pseudo-question: "To be or not to be?" That is *not* the question.[34] No one can choose to be or not to be. Nor can anything in the universe make anyone be or not be. Everyone simply and eternally *is* an individual, free, conscious, enlargeable self.

If the question is pointless, then so is the colossus of anxieties and efforts that revolve around it. *Nothing* is not the source of, not a threat to, and not the destiny of man. Any religion or doctrine of man that is haunted by *Nothing* is really haunted by nothing at all.

It necessarily follows that the orthodox Christian worships (and some Christians condemn) God for an impossible ex nihilo creation. This He did not and could not do. The existentialist laments in total anguish the threat of nonbeing. But there is no such threat. The humanist lives with hasty heroism to achieve a few satisfactions before cosmic oblivion. But such oblivion will never come.

All three movements hold theses on man's individuality,

---

34. Hamlet, of course, was really speaking of the choice between living and dying. He found the alternative of death, and the unknown beyond it, less desirable than facing his "sea of troubles." With many men today, it is the other way around.

freedom, consciousness, and enlargement that cannot be logically squared with the Prophet's teachings.

What *is* the question? The question is not one of being, but of becoming. "To become more or not to become more." This is the question faced by each intelligence in our universe. At this point, and not before, the absolute and inescapable need for God and His Christ arises. And those who choose are, in the declaration of the ancient prophet, Abraham, and in the language of the modern prophet, Joseph Smith, those who are "added upon."

Chapter Three

CREATION AND PROCREATION

*The immortal spirit. Where did it come from? All learned men
and doctors of divinity say that God created it in the beginning;
but it is not so: the very idea lessens man in my estimation.
I do not believe the doctrine; I know better. Hear it, all ye
ends of the world; for God has told me so; and if you don't
believe me, it will not make the truth without effect. . . .
I am going to tell of things more noble.*
—Joseph Smith

In his poetic rewriting of one of the sublime visions of all
time, the Prophet Joseph records:

And I heard a great voice bearing record from Heav'n,
He's the Saviour, and Only Begotten of God—
By him, of him, and through him, the worlds were all made,

Opening quotation: Joseph Smith, "King Follett Discourse," *Teachings*
(1938), 352. B. H. Roberts suggests that "immortal spirit" in this quotation refers
to intelligence. Nevertheless, the remarks apply also to the begetting of the spirit.

Even all that career in the heavens so broad.
Whose inhabitants, too, from the first to the last, Are sav'd by
    the very same Saviour of ours;
And, of course, are begotten God's daughters and sons,
By the very same truths, and the very same pow'rs.[1]

Eternity is here sketched in eight lines. We select two marvelous themes: First, the worlds, world-systems, and galaxies, dazzling in brightness and dizzying in number, move under the creative mastery of Jesus Christ. Second, all spirits of the inhabitants of these worlds, including the spirit of Jesus Christ Himself, were not gotten from nothing but begotten of God; not created but procreated, sired by the supreme personality of our universe, God the Father.[2]

In a world of glory that could not be endured by mortal man; in realms, indeed, that " . . . surpass all understanding in glory, and in might, and in dominion, . . ."[3] the eternal intelligence of man was merged with eternal spirit-elements and began its enlargement in the presence of the Divine.

THE FAMILIAR AND FAMILIAL

But is Divine fatherhood in any sense similar to human fatherhood?

The analogues are more profound than any Christian writer since the first century has dared to examine.[4] For our purpose one all-important likeness must be named. It is unequivocally taught by the Prophet.

---

1. *Times and Seasons,* 1 February 1843, 82–85.
2. See D&C 76:24.
3. Ibid., 76:114.
4. Some of the early Christian fathers clearly recognized the distinction between creation and generation, between a thing created and a self-procreated. Athanasius, for one, says, "Let it be repeated that a created thing is external to the nature of the being who creates; but a generation is the proper offspring of the nature" (of him who begets it). "Every son," he observes, "is co-essential or co-substantial with his father." But in later theology man is held to be "external to the nature of the being who creates," *not* a son (see Shedd, *Christian Doctrine,* 1:322).

28

In mortal birth, inherent physical and personality traits of the father and mother are transmitted to their son or daughter. (A thimbleful of chromosomes accounts for the physical makeup and qualities of the billions who have so far inhabited this globe.) More, one's bodily inheritance and then his environment mold him and largely condition his destiny.

It is exactly so with man's spirit. Long before mortality, in a process of actual transmission, there were forged into man's spirit the embryonic traits, attributes, and powers of God Himself! And in the surroundings of that realm man was nurtured in the Divine image.[5]

Before we trace the transcendent religious power of this truth, let us consider it from the center of critical theological analysis. There are two entrenched objections to it. Rarely have they had such an array of influential advocates. Both of them have been impressed upon most of us.

First, anthropomorphism. The idea of fatherhood is objectionable because of its primitive and naive approach to biblical language. Phrases like Jesus' "My father" and "your father," or Paul's "offspring of God" and "Father of our spirits" must not be interpreted as literal.[6] To apply such manlike qualities to the Divine, and Godlike qualities to man, is to abase and abuse the message. Since the time of Maimonides in Judaism and Dionysius in Christianity it has been a commonplace that we must not ascribe finite categories to Deity.[7] "Fatherhood" connotes materiality, subjection to space and time, and other absurdities. It destroys the dignity, majesty, and unconditioned ultimacy of God.[8]

Second, psychologism. The idea of fatherhood is objectionable

---

5. See Joseph Smith, "King Follett Discourse," *Teachings* (1938), 342–62.

6. There are over a hundred occurrences of "father" and its variants in the four Gospels. See Paul's phrases in Acts 17 and Hebrews 12.

7. On Maimonides see Bokser, *Maimonides*. See also Clark, *Vesman Mystics*.

8. See Tillich, *Biblical Religion*. See the near best seller by Robinson, an Anglican Bishop, *Honest To God*. It predicts the "end of theism" and the triumph of "being-itself."

because, as Freud tells us, all men tend to project (invent rather than discover) their "father-image."[9] "God the Father" is a paternal pie that is a lie in the sky. Alder says our inferiority feelings; Feuerbach, our childish wishes; Marx, our economic frustrations, are at the root of the projection.[10] We thus "personify" our subjective hopes to avoid reality.

Now quite apart from Joseph Smith and the modern prophets, there are telling rebuttals to these anxieties.

Milton saw the real issue. He was aware of the subtleties of language. And though he could not escape a whole canopy of now discredited assumptions in the 17th century, he claimed to be inspired in his poetry. The Bible, he says, is seriously literal in what it says about the fatherhood of God. There is no radical distinction between spirit and matter, and there is a point-by-point analogy between heaven and earth.[11] God is the actual sire of the souls of men. Why, he asks, should we be afraid to ascribe to God what He ascribes to Himself?[12]

Why indeed? The fear is especially inept in Christendom, which, by its most central thesis, is committed to the idea of Divine fatherhood. Every orthodox theologian must maintain that God was the immortal Father of Jesus. Jesus' actual Sonship accounts for the fact that He was, or became, "the express image of His (the Father's) person."[13] Mary, a human being, was the mother of the body of Christ.[14] Why should not God, a Divine

---

9. Freud, *Future of an Illusion.*

10. Alder, *Individual Psychology.*
Feuerbach, *Essence of Christianity.*
On Marx, see Fromm, *Marx's Concept of Man.*

11. See Milton, *Paradise Lost* and Whale, *Christian Doctrine,* beginning line 168.

12. See Whale, *Christian Doctrine,* book 1, chapter 2.

13. See Hebrews 1:1–3.

14. But the idea of a radical dualism between Divine and human has led Roman Catholicism to first qualify and then deny Mary's humanity. By papal decrees she was held immune to original sin, then given the graces of the Spirit, then called "co-redemptress" or "co-mediator" with Christ, then declared to be "assumed" bodily into heaven without death; now the Vatican Council is deliberating on whether she shall be decreed a member of the Godhead. See Sheed, *Mary Book.*

being, be the father of the spirit of man? If one is unthinkable, so is the other. In principle it is absurd to maintain that God could, without losing His dignity, majesty, or ultimacy transmit a divine nature through a mortal being, and then say that He could not transmit spirit traits, in His likeness, to immortal spirits.[15]

THE CONQUEST OF PARADOX

But the problem of the theologian is complex.

Behold the paradoxes that he presents as an alternative concept of creation:

The immaterial Trinity elicited from nothing both material and immaterial substance. The unchanging and unchangeable Deity yet changed and changes the whole of reality. A nontemporal and nonspatial being, literally nowhere and "nowhen," yet created and infused everywhere and "everywhen." The All-powerful and All-good simultaneously and yet continuously brought into being not only mankind, but the angels, the demons, and Satan. Moreover, like did not create like. Between the Divine and all other natures there was and is and always will be an absolute gulf.[16] Because man is utterly other than the Divine, his creation required mediators. Thus, through emanation or through angels who are "pure form" (bodiless and more than man yet less than God) or by the speaking of a cosmic word, man came into being.[17]

It is in vain to protest that these are radical contradictions. The creed-upholding Christian will reply, "Of course they are." They belong to the mysteries of the Divine, and obviously the finite intellect cannot understand. Thus it is often held that to be mystified is to be edified, and that intellectual confusion is a religious virtue.[18]

---

15. See note 4.

16. See Whale, *Christian Doctrine*, chapter 1.

17. Gilson summarizes the standard view: "The revealed notion of creation, (is) understood by believers and theologians alike as the absolute production of being from no other pre-existing condition than the free will of its creator" (see *Christian Philosophy*, 181).

18. See Hook, *Religious Experience* in which some logic-minded analysts confront the religious defenders of paradox, especially part 3.

The teachings of Joseph Smith, like those of the ancient prophets, are involved in *none* of these paradoxes.

REVERENCE OR IRREVERENCE

But what is the religious appeal of this outlook?

Significantly, the doctrine of an utterly transcendent God usually flourishes most in an era when humanity is shocked at its own demonic or depraved conduct. We live in such a time. Anything so tinctured with corruption, it is said, cannot be Divine. True enough. But almost without exception Western theologians have taken this insight and pushed it to conclusions not only mistaken, but contrary to their original intent. Weighed down by the fact of degenerate parenthood, they are unable to conceive of Divine parenthood. Inveighing against the corruptions of mortal personality, they are unable to conceive of Divine personality. Hence, they conclude that God is neither a parent nor a person.

What is left? "Being-itself"; what Buber, Marcel, Barth, Niebuhr, and Tillich, representing the Jewish, Catholic, and Protestant traditions call "The Transcendent."[19]

But nothing in the universe is loftier than personality. All who look outside of it in quest of the Divine will find something lower. Calling it the "Unconditioned" in capital letters fails to deify, though it does idolize. Only by covertly ignoring these theological restrictions and investing the concept with personal meaning can the words *dignity, majesty,* and *holiness* even begin to be appropriate.[20]

The charge of projection now arises anew. What is projected in this notion of Divine Being which, by definition, can never intersect finite experience? Guilt in the wretchedness of humanity? But

19. See Buber's, *I and Thou.*
Kegley and Bretall, *Reinhold Niebuhr.*
Weigel, "Myth, Symbol, and Analogy," in *Religion and Culture.*
Bultmann, *Kerygma and Myth.*
Tillich, *Systematic Theology.*
20. The ordinary layman *does* ignore such theological restrictions because, as Whitehead once said, "Aristotle's God (First Cause) is not available for religious purposes."

that is the worst form of anthropomorphism. Traits that exalt the *ground* or *power* of the cosmos by debasing personality? But that is blasphemy. Worship of a Something instead of a Someone? But that is idolatry.

Whatever the motives of the theologian, let every person ask himself: When Jesus says, " . . . I ascend unto my Father, and your Father . . ." (John 20:17) what does He mean? And if there is revulsion at His meaning, does the revulsion come out of reverence based on the revelation of God? Or is it really irreverence based on tradition and guilt which one cannot but project to "God"? The sword of anthropomorphism and psychologism cuts two ways. Which way?[21]

"THINGS MORE NOBLE"

Now let us abandon this mode of analysis and turn to an entirely different question, using the language of the heart.

What is the religious power of this idea? What are its effects as it moves along the threads of the inner life? Let us mark only one of the needs of man and gesture, at least, toward its glowing realization.

There is in all of us an apparently infinite, and certainly, ultimate, need for a rich, abiding, undergirding, trustworthy love. This is a love that reaches in and through the self, outward to others, and upward to the highest in the universe. In the ordinary world, even the world of religion, this craving finds extremely rare fulfillment, though it is talked about ceaselessly. But a dawning understanding is the key to its creative source and the beginning of its increase and transformation: that man was known and loved profoundly even prior to mortal birth; that love, indeed, drew him

---

21. The psychologist can at most remind us that we often tend to believe what is emotionally satisfying and to disbelieve what is austere and forbidding. What he cannot do is decide, by examining men's psyches, whether their projections really correspond to reality. That can only be settled by examining reality; and if it be said that we cannot know reality, that is simply another (projected?) decision about the nature of reality. For the Mormon the question of God can only be decided by revelation.

and his Eternal Father together in a sphere of perfected light and glory; that he, distinct from all other beings, animate or inanimate, in the universe, is a chosen and begotten spirit of the Divine; that this sonship, as well as the "second birth" through Jesus Christ, is at the core of any question about the meaning of life.

Of this sweeping awareness the Prophet Joseph spoke to a multitude of 20,000 enthralled under his voice:

"This is good doctrine. It tastes good. I can taste the principles of eternal life, and so can you. They are given to me by the revelations of Jesus Christ. . . . and when I tell you of these things which were given me by inspiration of the Holy Spirit, you are bound to receive them as sweet, and rejoice more and more."[22]

Man has always believed that somehow God could be in his heart. Now he realizes that godliness is veritably engrained in him through a divine lineage. And the whole of his soul lights up.

A child orphaned and cuffed about in a hostile world craves the lifting power of a person who radiates every cherished aspiration. Now comes the recognition that this is *inspiration,* that a real, living parent is here announcing, arms outstretched, "I am yours! And you are mine!"

A mother and father look down at their sleeping infant, in communing touch with what is sacred to both. Parental love, they see in this illumined moment, is not a shadow but a light of divine love in which splendor we became spirit children and by which we were enveloped.

These, with a wealth of poignant insights that follow in their wake, reveal meaning in human existence. In relationship to the divine they replace the grosser emotions of fear, distant awe, dread, bitter solitude, and even despair, with the subtler and finer feelings: gratitude, virtue akin to virtue, lightness of spirit, embracing sympathy, peace of soul, and motivation to share. They uncover layer after layer of worldly facade. They electrify, inspire, and ennoble. They are, in truth, the source and power of love.

---

22. Joseph Smith, *Teachings* (1938), 355. This was the last major address the Prophet delivered in the Nauvoo Grove prior to his death.

To the degree that Christendom denies the genuine fatherhood of God and the genuine sonship of man's spirit (and both Christendom and the major world religions do deny them) they have lost the image of man's real origin and therefore the image of his real destiny. They deny the "power of godliness."

All the rapturous things that are said about the love or *agape* of God who sent His Only Begotten in the flesh are hollow when coupled with the dogma that He did *not* so love us that He distinguished us from the rest of creation by implanting in us the potential of His own likeness. The dogma "lessens man." But, as any reference to a contemporary book on theology will show, it also lessens God, even while claiming to dignify Him. Shall we reject the shining truth because it is so shining?

Many of us in the modern world are prodigal sons. We have not only left home, we have forgotten it and the Father who still waits to unfold to us not only "all that I *have*" but also, "all that I *am*."

But only our actual sonship can account for this miracle: that an inner flame apprehends and affirms what the creeds and our own darkened thoughts solemnly deny. This flame is not quickened, but neither is it quenched when, asking for the bread of the living Father, we are given the stone of dead "being-itself."

This is the flame that is rekindled when a Prophet testifies in the 20th century as Jesus Christ did in the first, "God is our Father." An intuitive flash dissipates theological and psychological speculation. A luminous nostalgia arises in us. And as if from a far-off center, the glow of an evanescent past reawakens responses of awesome love we find it impossible to describe. And that is why, from the millions who listen to the strains of the Mormon Tabernacle Choir annually, a frequent request is for the music and words of a simple Mormon hymn. This is a hymn that expresses the heart of "Latter-day Saintliness." It is "O My Father."[23]

---

23. Of this hymn President Wilford Woodruff said, "That hymn is a revelation, though it was given unto us by a woman, Sister Eliza R. Snow. There are a great many sisters who have the spirit of revelation. There is no reason why they should not be inspired as well as men" (*Discourses of Wilford Woodruff*, 62).

Chapter Four

THE SPIRIT AND THE BODY

*Nor hath God designed to show Himself elsewhere more
clearly than in human form sublime; which,
since they image Him, alone I love.
—Michelangelo, from "Heaven-born Beauty"*

We came into this world that we might receive a body and present it pure before God in the celestial kingdom.

The great principle of happiness consists in having a body.

All beings who have bodies have power over those who have not.[1]

THE SPIRIT AND THE BODY

One of the all-time bafflements of life is this: Why is man embodied? Has the body a lasting purpose in nature or in the plan of God?

The question and typical answers have been badly blurred, due in great measure to the dogma of immaterialism. This assumption

---

1. Joseph Smith, *Teachings* (1938), 352, 181.

36

born in Greece now dominates both Judaism and Christianity and infiltrates the thought of the entire Western world.[2] The assumption is that there are two utterly different divisions of reality, one immaterial and the other material. Mind or soul or spirit are immaterial. Body is material.[3]

The dualisms that result tend to become radical: the soul has none of the qualities of the body and vice versa. Mind or soul is really real, the body is unreal or less real. The soul is eternal; the body temporal. The soul is good; the body is evil.[4]

In our time the focus shifts to the dualism of "finite reality" and "infinite reality," or of particular beings and being-itself, or of the objective-experimental and the Transcendent-existential. But in some form the old disjunction remains. And the mortal body is deemed inferior or demonic.

And thus arise a vast array of puzzles. How can two entities that have nothing in common, not even existence in space and time, be conjoined in any sense? How can one influence the other? Why would an unembodied God create an embodied man to achieve a disembodied immortality?

In reaction to the dogmas of a "ghost in the machine," modern naturalistic and scientific outlooks take the position of physicalism.[5] Physicalism denies that there is evidence for the shadowy entities,

---

2. For a dualistic approach to eastern religion see Stace, *Time and Eternity.* For a summary of the dualism in Christian thought of our time see Davidson, *Search for Meaning,* section 5.

3. The work of St. Thomas and the Scholastics revolved around this issue, with Platonic and Aristotelian premises—the relegating of the "heavenly" to immateriality, (the angels, for example, are "pure species") and of the "earthly" to materiality or corporeality. The "double truth" concept grew in this area as well as the distinction, still basic to Roman Catholic theology, between metaphysics and physics.

4. The tendency to call the body evil was manifest most sharply in the Manichees and this, in turn, is supposedly derived from Persian dualism. Common distinctions still lead, and mislead, our thought in religion; e.g. sacred vs. secular, spiritual vs. temporal. Modern revelation dissolves the distinction. See D&C 29:31–35.

5. See, for example, Alston and Nakhnikian, *Twentieth Century Philosophy,* parts 7 and 8.

"mind" or "soul," of traditional definition. Whatever the body is, it is all there is. Man is "nothing but" nucleic acids, cell structures, nerve nets, and the complicated phenomena called "mental."[6]

Thus immaterialists try to live as if there were no body, and physicalists try to live as if there were no soul or spirit.[7]

Almost universally today it is assumed that only if immaterialism or Transcendence be defended can God and religion be salvaged, and that if it be rejected both are disposed of. Over this issue major Catholic, Protestant, and Jewish faiths contend with Marxists, humanists, and many natural scientists.

THE ELEMENTS OF SELFHOOD

Here again Joseph Smith faces a confusing colossus. And with revelatory insight he replaces it. It turns out that deception is on both sides of the controversy. Without full awareness of its philosophical undercurrent, modern man is caught in a riptide. Forced by his environment to favor one side or the other of a traditional "either-or" he rarely recognizes that neither side is a safe guide to the nature of man.

The revolution, which brings a sunburst of self-understanding, is this:

Mind, spirit, and body are all material, in varying degrees of refinement. They have equal status in spatio-temporal existence and are, in their perfected state, of equal worth. Spirit and body are dissimilar enough to require each other in full selfhood. But they are similar enough that when our bodies are purified we shall see that "all spirit is matter." Embodied spirits *always* "have an ascendancy" over unembodied spirits.[8]

---

6. See Ryle, *Concept of Mind.*

7. It is, of course, impossible to live "as if" there were no body. Yet the view of absolute idealists, Christian Scientists, and certain mystics is that all materiality is illusion. The view tends to quietism, asceticism, and "other-worldliness." Physicalism is a scientific approach and is compatible with various ethical outlooks or ways of life. But typically it leads to hedonism, to an attempt to maximize the natural satisfactions of the body. See Russell, *Not a Christian.*

8. The word "ascendancy" is the Prophet's. He taught repeatedly that it is punishment to be denied a body. See Joseph Smith, *Teachings* (1938), 297, 306, 312.

Thus the immaterialist is wrong in what he affirms (immaterial entities), and the physicalist is wrong in what he denies (spirit entities). And thus a thousand dualistic puzzles and dilemmas collapse.[9]

This is not, as some may suppose, just an issue of word usage. It leads to a revision of attitudes and aspirations that affect the very breath of mankind. To illustrate, here is a cross-sectional comparison of the Prophet's teaching and dominant alternatives.

Immaterialists, e.g., Plotinus, Thomas, Calvin, teach that man was created in a body to prepare for a nontemporal eternity. The Prophet taught that we are living in a temporal eternity. Our co-eternal intelligences were first given spirit bodies and now, as a climax of our development, physical bodies which will have permanence in the resurrection.

Physicalists, e.g. Ryle, Morris, Lamont, teach that there is no "spirit" in combination with body. The body, including its so-called personality traits, reduces to physical genes.[10] The Prophet taught that the spirit-personality was developed long before our physical embodiment and profoundly affects it and that there are real and unmistakable spirit needs as there are body needs.[11]

Extreme immaterialists, e.g. mystics like St. John of the Cross and ascetics like Ghandi, despise "body, parts, and passions"and define God as lacking them.[12] They tend not only to disparage the body but to torment and renounce it. Extreme physicalists, on the other hand (e.g. Russell), teach that since the body is all, it is the sole source of happiness. They tend to define happiness without regard for quality, at least without spiritual modes.[13] A pig satisfied at the trough is better than a Socrates unsatisfied at the trial.

---

9. The mind-body problem and a variety of solutions is sketched in Castell, *Modern Philosophy,* topic 2.

10. The Prophet taught that the spiritual creation preceded and was in the likeness of the physical creation. See Moses 3:5 and D&C 77:2; 131:7, 8.

11. See Joseph Smith, *Teachings* (1938), 255, 381, 296, 297.

12. See D'Arcy, introduction to *St. John of the Cross.* See also *Ghandi's.*

13. The controversy of "quantitative vs. qualitative hedonism" carries over into religion under different labels. The issue is this: are there satisfactions of the self that are more intensive and inclusive as one approaches the likeness of God?

Joseph Smith taught that man's body is the marvelously per-fectible instrument of his likewise perfectible mind and spirit. "That which is without body, parts and passions is nothing."[14] There are levels of consciousness, powers of expression, ways of fulfillment in thought, feeling, and action that come only when the threefold nature of man is harmoniously combined.[15] To cultivate the soul is to cultivate both body and spirit.[16]

Nietzsche, speaking for physicalists, maintains that "we are what we eat" and that the body has a total "turnover" every seven years.[17] The Prophet taught that our identity is not simply a thread of memory or a bundle of impressions. None of the eternal ele-ments of our person (even during the temporary disorganization of the body) becomes an essential part of another body.[18]

Boehme, speaking for immaterialists, teaches that our mental and spiritual powers and our communion with God are impaired by the body.[19] The Prophet taught that our mental and spiritual powers will ultimately be enhanced by the body. Thus:

> And if your eye be single to my glory, your whole bodies shall be filled with light, and there shall be no darkness in you; and that body which is filled with light comprehendeth all things. (D&C 88:67)

And do thy involve withdrawal from the senses? The Prophet answered "yes" to the first question and "no" to the second.

14. Joseph Smith, *Teachings* (1938), 181.

15. This point is put in a near-classic form by Parley P. Pratt who, after con-version to Mormonism, wrote an essay (almost unknown to our generation) enti-tled, "Intelligence and Affection" (see Robison, *Parley P. Pratt*).

16. Indeed the Prophet records in Doctrine and Covenants 93 that the "spirit and the body *are* the soul of man." The soul of man is the whole of man.

17. See Nietzsche, *Modern Library Giant.*

18. This statement was made in response to a question by Orson Pratt. Recent biology suggests that it is almost as if our own "identification tag" is on each constituent cell of our bodies.

19. See Boehme, *Personal Christianity.* "That which is of the earth and must return to it is not merely the visible physical body, but also the carnal mind and the astral man with his earthly desires. There is nothing immortal in man, except that which is divine in him." Like-minded writers deny that there can be anything divine about the physical (265).

Immaterialists tend to believe that the body is the product of sin or error. (In the Orient it is the evil aftermath of "Karma.") Flesh is utterly depraved, and man's ills began with the body and will end with it.[20] Some, like Buddha, long for annihilation.[21]

The Prophet taught that the body is the product of righteousness. We will look upon the temporary absence of our spirits from our bodies as bondage, not as freedom. (See D&C 45:17.) "Even here," he taught, "we may begin to enjoy that which shall be in full hereafter."[22] But only when the spirit and body are "inseparably connected" or resurrected, in a celestial condition, will we receive a fullness of glory and thus a fullness of joy. (See D&C 84, 88, 93.)

OF THE FALLEN AND THE FAILING

What is good and what is evil about the body?

The three modes of man's makeup, the Prophet taught, are related so intimately that they delimit or exalt each other together. One cannot say to the other, "I have no need of thee." There is not just parallelism but interaction and fusion through the life-giving power of Jesus the Christ.

Is the failure to complete one's nature an evil? Then mind and spirit may be evil as well as the body. Is refinement in knowledge, power, and glory a good? Then the body may be good as well as mind and spirit. In this sense heaven is as secular as earth and the body as sacred as the spirit.

But is not mortal man "fallen" and "carnal, sensual, devilish"?[23]

---

20. See Blakney, *Meister Eckhar.* Compare Happold, "Coinherence of Spirit and Matter," in *Mysticism.*

21. "Nirvana" is thought by Western Minds to be a kind of heaven. But many Oriental writers speak of absolute extinction and certainly mean the loss of all consciousness.

22. Joseph Smith, *Teachings* (1938), 296.

23. The Prophet taught that man was fallen and in need of the "second birth." But he did not teach "total depravity"; he did not teach "original sin" if that means *we* participated in Adam's fall metaphysically or symbolically; he did not teach that corporeality was a curse. Man may be not only unfulfilled; but a rebel, shot through with tendencies that lead to further corruption. But the degenerate

Did not the ancient apostle say to "crucify the flesh with its affections and lusts"?[24] Yes and yes.

But the way of sanctification is *in* the body not *out* of it. And to a marked degree the effects of the purifying process or "new birth" are visible. The inspired way of Christ is not utter renunciation but regeneration, not emasculation but inspired expression, not the way of death but the way of life, not to nurture the poisons of corruption but to replace them with the powers of godliness.

> The nearer a man approaches perfection the clearer are his views and the greater his enjoyments till he has overcome the evils of his life and lost every desire for sin.[25]

The joy that accompanies wholeness is a rich and inclusive joy, of a quality that resounds through the total being. Thus, for Joseph Smith, even the processes of purification are life-giving. They are not, as ironically named, "mortifying." One meaning of fasting and prayer, for example, is "rejoicing and prayer." (See D&C 59.) The body is sensitized to deeper awareness of the subtler realities of God and His Spirit. But the experience of rejoicing includes, as it were, the sense-spectrums of both spirit and body.

THE PRICE OF ANGUISH

Today an avalanche of case books on psychotherapy chronicles the miseries of what Menninger calls "Man Against Himself."[26] There are pathetic victims, worshipping in vain one or the other of the two omnipresent gods, immaterialism and physicalism. In anguish millions still refuse to believe that negation is futile, dissipation is futile, and escape is impossible.

The attitudes surrounding these religions distill like plasma into

---

can become regenerate. For Joseph Smith the problem is worse (it includes mind and spirit in the fall) and regeneration better (it leads to a condition exactly akin to that of the Divine), than traditional views.

24. See Paul in Galatians 6. Paul has been credited (or blamed) with a flesh-spirit dualism. But this is a moot question. He clearly saw the difference between corrupt flesh and godly flesh. But he did not teach a doctrine of escape.

25. Joseph Smith, *Teachings* (1938), 51.

26. See Menninger and Hillner, *Constructive Aspects.*

the veins of all of us. It is no surprise that Gabriel Marcel says with horror, "I am my body,"[27] and that we walk the streets aware of the body's degenerate dirge unbelieving that anyone really achieves its transformed symphony.

Psychologists, committed only to the superiority of sanity, go on telling us that we must learn to "live with ourselves," some times in radical disagreement as to the nature of self. They have the almost desperate hope that there *is* something meaningful, wholesome, spiritual, sublime about the body at its best, and that somehow self-unity is within reach. (We can vision this when a lovely being shines through the face of a child, when what the Prophet called his "glory, bloom, and beauty" is vividly forecast.)[28] But how long can we hold to this when our pulse thunders with opposite ideals—that the flesh is a "nasty, brutish" shack, or that it is a supersensual castle? Where in heaven or earth is the power to make the body what an ancient disciple of Christ said it was: a living Temple of the Spirit of God?

This *is* the Truth and Power re-revealed through the Prophet Joseph Smith. And it is the restoration of wholeness.

Modern man is not imprisoned in his body but imprisoned in a set of distortions of it. Man, not God, has turned his body into a perpetual torture chamber.

The feeling truth is that the body is the crowning stage of progressive unfoldment toward celestial personality.

The redeeming truth is that Jesus Christ lived and died not only to heal, lift, and fulfill all men but *all of man*—intelligence, spirit, and body. And He exemplified magnificently the possible final outcome.

The glorifying truth is that the transformation of the Spirit of God that emanates through Christ in His perfected condition reaches to the very cell structure and bloodstream, to the very affections and tendencies of our composite nature. The only

---

27. See Marcel on the "limit situation" the body imposes in Wild, *Challenge*.

28. Speaking of the resurrection, the Prophet says "they glory in bloom and beauty. No man can describe it to you, no man can write it" (Joseph Smith, *Teachings* [1938], 368).

lasting sorrow will be in the measure we fail to receive the power of His promise: that some day we may be fashioned like unto Him!

This philosophy of embodiment is destined not only to conquer the world, but to redeem and sanctify it under the feet of radiant sons and daughters of God. These, in the likeness of God and through the power of Christ, will be embodied light and enlightened bodies—forever.

Chapter Five

EVIL AND SUFFERING

*. . . Know thou, my son, that all these things shall give thee
experience, and shall be for thy good. The Son
of Man hath descended below them all.
Art thou greater than he?*

The most staggering objection to belief in a personal God is the ugly, tragic, overwhelming fact of human inequality and suffering.

Dare we uncover this stark reality, not as an academic toy, but at its worst?

As a beginning, let us walk into a hospital.

Here. This newborn infant with the lovely face. She could not have had worthier parents. But she was born in total paralysis and is blind. The doctors do not know whether she will survive. And if she does. . . .

This bed is empty. Its occupant, a quivering psychotic with a wild stare, is upstairs undergoing shock treatment. He collapsed

---

Opening quotation: D&C 122:7, 8. These words were received and written after the Prophet had languished four months in the darkness of Liberty Jail.

when his wife and two children were maimed in a fire, one beyond recognition.

Over here is a surgeon who had a rare brain disease and asked his closest friend to operate. The operation failed; and he has been, for nearly three years, a human vegetable. His friend has since committed suicide.

Somewhere tonight the families of these souls are crying themselves to sleep.

Now, if your arm will hold out, write as many zeros after a "1" as will portray similar reenactments of these scenes that are, or have been, or may be, on this planet. And that will be one thread in the tapestry of human misery.

Come next to the roof of the hospital and gaze up at the order and design of the stars. Do they prove that God is there? What, then, is proved by the utter disorder, the cruel indifference, the fantastic meaninglessness of life below us? Does God care more about the stars than about His children?

Traditionally, the last resort (if not the first) of the believer in God, under this twisting knife, is: "Strange and inscrutable are the ways of the Divine."

But this retreat to mystery, even for its advocates, leaves gnawing anxieties. So have arisen two major efforts at reconciliation. One approach says that evil is not really real. It is privative, or perspectival, or illusory.[1] The other approach says that evil *is* really real, worse, even, than the enemies of religion have said.[2] The one supposes to exonerate God by denying evil. The other supposes strangely to placate man by exaggerating it. The one says there

---

1. That evil is "privation," absence of good, not a positive reality, is the official view of Roman Catholicism. That evil is in our "perspective" but disappears under the eternal perspective is the view of Leibniz, Spinoza and Josiah Royce. That evil is illusory is the view of Christian Science, Buddhism, and some forms of spiritualism.

2. This is the approach of "crisis theology" and existentialism. Instead of minimizing evil their ruthless portrayal of its modes maximizes it. So desperate is the plight of man that futility dominates. Religion reduces to stoical endurance and/or despair.

is no problem, the other implies that there is no hope. Both are mistaken.

Let us summon, now, a prophet-son of modern times.

We will require that he know, in the very marrow of his bones, the excruciating anguish of mortal life.[3] For nothing is more barren, to one in agony, than pat answers which seem the unfeeling evasions of a distant spectator who "never felt a wound."

Let us introduce the Prophet Joseph Smith to the mother of a blind baby. Listen to the queries of her heart in this imaginary dialogue.[4] And mark how these, the merest kernels of his prophetic grasp of man's origins, radically alter typical reflections on suffering.[5]

MOTHER: Is what I am going through "illusion"? Is it "all in my mind"?

THE PROPHET: Suffering often results from illusions. But whether or not we face reality as it is, suffering is still real and none escape it. Christ did not.

MOTHER: But why did not God prevent what has happened to me? Why should I or my child be the victims? What have we done to deserve this?

THE PROPHET: You assume suffering is always a form of Divine punishment. It is not. You are convinced by Job's "friends" instead of by Job.[6] But let us go further back. It is true that God can prevent (as He can induce) some kinds of suffering. But not all.[7]

---

3. Rarely, if ever, has so much of relentless trial and soul struggle been crowded into one life as in Joseph Smith's.

4. The dialogue is imaginary, but the ideas are not. The "Mother" poses questions that have been raised numberless times. For every sentence in the Prophet's "replies" there is a first-hand counterpart in his writings or sermons.

5. This is only an outline of the Prophet's teachings, some ways in which the backward look to premortal life affects the question.

6. See Job 38 where, the Prophet taught, there is a display of the human tendency to conclude that suffering is always the wrath of an angry God. This is an "unhallowed principle" (see Joseph Smith, *Teachings* (1938), 162).

7. If, for example, evil be defined as delimitation in growth, conflict of wills, refusal to receive the love and power of God, seeking to become a law unto oneself, then evil is eternal. For always there will be intelligences, spirits, and resurrected beings in these conditions.

MOTHER: What do you mean? Is not God all powerful? Are not all things possible with Him? How can we have faith in a limited God?

THE PROPHET: The question is rather how we can have faith in the "unconditioned" God of the Creeds. The Creeds say that God, being Absolute in power, could have created the universe and its creatures in a utopia of happiness and without pain. They say that with Absolute foreknowledge our "freedom" would be hopelessly abused. He elected not to return this mass of humanity to nothing, but to thrust it into a worse, and endless, torment.[8]

Non-Christians call such a God "monstrous." Many Christians call Him (or "It") "inscrutable" and live, for all their talk of love, in terror. Thank God the living God has revealed that no such god exists.

MOTHER: But if God is not behind all our suffering, what is? Are you saying there is some other ultimate explanation?

THE PROPHET: Yes. You have been taught that God is the total cause of everything. The truth is that He is not the *total* cause of anything.[9]

MOTHER: What, then?

THE PROPHET: God is forever surrounded by us, by co-eternal intelligences, and by the self-existent elements and principles of reality. These are as unoriginated as He is.

Now the Creeds say that God has always been God. But this well-motivated expression of reverence is a solemn travesty. The truth is infinitely more inspiring: that God Himself *became* God (whose power now extends in and through all things) by the mastery of the same ultimate and unchanging conditions to which you and I are subject. So, likewise, did His Firstborn Son, Jesus the Christ.[10]

---

8. See Aiken's latest treatment of the classic argument that evil proves God does not exist: "God and Evil" in *Reason and Conduct*.

9. See Joseph Smith, *Teachings* (1938), 158, 181, 350, 351, 354.

10. See the "King Follett Discourse," and footnotes by B. H. Roberts, ibid., 342. The rare notion that God is in a sense finite, limited by the nature of His environment, has been taught in some form by such men as William James,

In His relationship to us, "all things are possible" that are possible. But some things are impossible. We cannot have crucial experience without having it. We cannot unfold into His fulness except in His way. We cannot develop without stress nor be perfected without suffering. The belief that we can write "God" in front of these statements and thus remove the "nots" is an illusion that will only end in disillusion.[11]

MOTHER: But why do some suffer so much more than others? Are we not created equal?

THE PROPHET: We are equal as far as the concern, and the pure, glorious, fatherly love of God are concerned; for we are all spiritually begotten of Him. And no superlative in our present language can describe this love. We are also equal before the law, eternal law.

But in our original natures we are *un*created and *un*equal. Individual differences (and therefore needs) predate mortality and even our beginnings as spirits. They are "gnolaum" or eternal.[12] God did not create them so. Thus, no waving of a Divine wand can transform a Satan into a Christ nor a Christ into a Satan. In nobility, and in response to the sanctifying powers that emanate from God the Father, they differ. And so do all the spirit sons and daughters of God.

MOTHER: But what has this to do with me? Why has God thrown us into this world with these horrible handicaps? Why? Why?

THE PROPHET: Again, you assume that God alone accounts for your being here and that handicaps are all necessarily final and horrible. Instead, you and the child of your bosom counseled

A. N. Whitehead, Charles Hartshorne, E. S. Brightman, and A. C. Garnett. See also Macquarrie, *Religious Thought,* chapter 17.

11. Traditional theology has taught that God's "all-powerfulness" is limited only by the laws of contradiction. Yet, theologians continue to maintain that it is impossible for God, being infinite, to manifest Himself to man in literal revelation, and likewise impossible for God to transform man into His literal likeness. It turns out, therefore, that in these and other ways, the living God of modern revelation is *more* powerful than the "god" of the classical creeds.

12. See Abraham 3:18, 19, 22, 23. See also Roberts, *Seventy's,* vol. 4, lesson 4.

intimately with God the Father. Freely, fully, and with a courage that astonishes mortal imagination, you elected and prepared for this estate. The contrasts of the flesh, its risks, its terrific trials were known to you. More than that, you comprehended your actual appointed mission in this world, designed to meet your individual needs, and those who would depend upon you. Perhaps you anticipated these exact circumstances.[13]

Why did you make an irrevocable covenant to enter the flesh? You recognized that, whatever the price, the increasing glory, light, and power of the Divine was in every way worth it!

MOTHER: But that seems so cruel. Did not Christ come to relieve suffering? Are not His disciples to be blessed?

THE PROPHET: Christ came that suffering might result not only in good, but in its perfect work, which is perfection. He did not live to end all suffering, but to end all needless suffering and to turn suffering into joy, even in this world.[14]

Let me explain.

In our own inner experience we can trace the opposite products of pain. At this hour life seems blinding, devastating. Yet it is a measure of our discipleship of Christ that even sorely grievous hours have yielded enlightenment, a budding knowledge of self and others, and ennoblement. When we search ourselves, it is no mystery that good, the purifying force of godliness, may arise out of affliction. (Looking back we may wonder whether anything we really prize comes without it.)

---

13. "The organization of the spiritual and heavenly worlds, and of spiritual and heavenly beings, was agreeable to the most perfect order and harmony: their limits and bounds were fixed irrevocably, and voluntarily subscribed to in their heavenly estate by themselves, and were by our first parents subscribed to upon the earth. Hence the importance of embracing and subscribing to principles of eternal truth by all men upon the earth that expect eternal life" (Joseph Smith, *Teachings* (1938), 325).

14. Latter-day Saints tend to ignore the context of the oft-quoted passage of Lehi's: " . . . Men are, that they might have joy" (2 Nephi 2:25). Lehi teaches that joy could not arise except through contrasts of mortality. Mortal life is sweet, but it is bittersweet.

This should caution us in judging what is and what is not a blessing in this life.

MOTHER: Yes. I recognize that precious things of mind and spirit cannot come from ease, nor from evasion of struggle. But such suffering as this, so meaningless, so destructive, often leads to worse suffering, and that, in turn, to worse. Why so vast a sum in the world?

THE PROPHET: We are on the threshold now of a sum you may rarely have contemplated. The premortal relationship we had with Jesus Christ was a prevision of our descent and ascent.[15] Then, as now, we shrank from innocent suffering. For this is of the essence of love.

But what is left to the Tender Parent who *cannot* (not simply, *will not*) force His spirit-child into the path of self-realization? What lifting power exceeds all others in our stages of deficiency, ignorance, and then a corrupt nature?[16] It is the completely voluntary, and completely undeserved, suffering of "the Lamb slain from before the foundation of the world." Somehow that is infinite. The innate mercy of our spirits was heightened in the presence of His compassion.[17] And in this world, often through pain, we are reawakened in our spirit to the Christ who really was and is. Only the most darkened soul can flout the profound inner craving that His suffering, and all else, even the tremors of your infant, may yield power and purity, and not finally be in vain.

---

15. "The Father called all spirits before Him at the creation of man, and organized them."

"At the first organization in heaven we were all present, and saw the Saviour chosen and appointed and the plan of salvation made, and we sanctioned it" (Joseph Smith, *Teachings* (1938), 158, 181).

16. C. S. Lewis argues in his *Problem of Pain* that God is Omnipotent, yet insists that God *cannot* make us susceptible to His grace without pain, and adds that some are incapable even then. The Prophet taught that experience itself is invaluable, and that our individual callings involve suffering in the service of humanity. The widest experience in trial is the most desirable. (See Roberts's comment on "Sweet are the uses of adversity," *Gospel,* 290.)

17. "For intelligence cleaveth unto intelligence; wisdom receiveth wisdom; truth embraceth truth; virtue loveth virtue; light cleaveth unto light; mercy hath compassion on mercy and claimeth her own . . ." (D&C 88:40).

51

MOTHER: Was His sacrifice necessary to enable us to rise into a life like His?

THE PROPHET: Yes. But the warm and overwhelming miracle is this: the more we approach Him and His likeness, the more we come to love as He loves, and the less we suffer needlessly.[18]

These physical losses and tribulations, if endured in His name, have their limits and are refining. The apparently, but not really, limitless mental and spiritual anguish that arises from life's buffetings takes on meaning. Pain becomes a laboratory of soul-nurture, and we may "count it all joy." The darkest abyss has its own revelations, its own chrysalis of higher promise. This is not myth! I testify it is the deepest secret of life.

MOTHER: It is all so hard, so hard.

THE PROPHET: Yes. Yet strangely beautiful. In your present nightmare a voice whips you with *why,* and *if only,* and *how long,* and *what might have been.* All that I have said may seem empty. But that fever will pass.

And as it does, you will be newly sensitive to the flashes of revelation that are your privilege in the quiet soundings of your soul. They alone can give you individual testimony of this hour's actual meaning for you. They alone can convincingly witness what seems now so utterly unbelievable. You are in the very hollow of the hand of God, a hand that will not, by your premortal request, remove you from the furnace; but will see you through it.[19]

---

18. We need not suffer further for our sinfulness, for through Him we may be redeemed. We need not suffer further from false expectations, for as we increase in righteousness, His revelations replace error with truth. Eventually, we need not suffer in the threat of final failure and condemnation. For as we prove that we are "determined to serve the Lord at all hazards" we can receive the assurance of eternal life, "an anchor to the soul, sure and steadfast." "Though the thunders might roll and lightnings flash, and earthquakes bellow, and war gather thick around, yet this hope and knowledge would support the soul in every hour of trial, trouble and tribulation. Then knowledge through our Lord and Saviour Jesus Christ is the grand key that unlocks the glories and mysteries of the kingdom of heaven" (Joseph Smith, *Teachings* [1938], 298).

19. "I assure the Saints that truth, in reference to these matters, can and may be known through the revelations of God in the way of His ordinances, and in answer to prayer" (ibid., 325).

Whatever the Lord's individual word to you may be, there are two abiding certainties.

The awful tragedy of this life, as of the next, is not suffering. It is "suffering in vain." Or worse, it is suffering that could have been the elixir of nobility, transforming us into a godliness beyond description which, instead, has become the poison of bitterness and alienation.[20]

But this is equally certain: from the smoldering rubble of our lives, stricken and agonized though they be, there can arise, through Christ, an incredible shining joy, a joy in the image of Christ who is the image of God who overcame all things.

"All your losses will be made up to you in the resurrection provided you continue faithful. By the vision of the Almighty I have seen it."[21] For you, your child, as for the Father and Christ, there was, there is no other way.

---

20. The Prophet was counseled in his youth, "Be patient in afflictions for thou shalt have many" (D&C 24:8). "If I obtain the glory which I have in view, I expect to wade through much tribulation" (*Juvenile Instructor,* 27:173). And toward the end he said, "Every wave of adversity has only wafted me that much closer to Deity." Brigham Young observed that the Prophet was more perfected in 38 years with severe trials than he could have been in a thousand years without them.

21. Joseph Smith, *Teachings* (1938), 296.

Chapter Six

FREEDOM AND FULFILLMENT

*All is voluntary. . . . God will not exert any
compulsory means and the Devil cannot.*
—Joseph Smith

Any approach to the nature of man leads to the question of freedom. In what sense, if at all, is man free?

Paradoxically, this is a question we are not free to ignore. We agonize over it daily. The impact of life upon us, or, if we prefer, our impact on life compels us to ask ourselves—What is "within my power" and what is not? Did I have to happen? Does anything or everything have to happen? Given the same conditions could I have been or done otherwise?

The central issue, put loosely, is whether or not man can upset the causal chain? The determinist answers, "No." The indeterminist

---

Opening quotation: Joseph Smith, *Teachings* (1938),187.

answers, "Yes."[1] In our time there is a certain freshness to the stalemate as three developments have given birth to new searches and researches.

1. *On the side of determinism.*

Some forms of psychology and psychoanalysis point to the immense domination of man's subconscious which, in turn, is fueled by traceable stimuli. These, apparently, are in no way separable from prior causation. Hypnotized, to illustrate, a person may be told that on awakening he will take off his shirt and stand on his head, but that he will forget the instruction. He does so, then invents the most ingenious but clearly false "reasons" for his behavior. Question: Is not all our conduct thus controlled and is not "freedom" just a name for our ignorance of hidden causes?[2]

2. *On the side of indeterminism.*

The so-called Heisenberg principle in quantum physics affirms that inanimate particles at the sub-atomic level behave in unpredictable ways. Neither their position nor velocity can be charted accurately. Explanation, therefore, must be statistical. By analogy, we can predict the approximate number, but not the exact identity, of persons who will be killed or injured on a Labor Day weekend. The logic of the point, at least for Eddington and Born, is that being indeterminate, the particles are therefore undetermined, therefore "free."[3] Question: If inanimate matter behaves "freely," why reject the belief that man does?

---

1. Some sentence definitions: The determinist says all events are caused. The indeterminist says some events, namely acts of free will, are uncaused. The fatalist says some or all events are predetermined or "fated" by forces beyond man. The predestinarian says that man's salvation, and/or damnation, was unconditionally decided by God's from eternity. The behaviorist says all behavior is due to man's reaction with environment. The mechanist says the world, and man, are machines moving like a computer. Mormonism fits in none of these pigeonholes (see note 9). See for a discussion of the controversy: Morgenbesser and Walsh, *Free Will.*

2. See discussion on this issue in Hospers and Sellars, "Guilt and Responsibility" in *Readings.*

3. See Eddington, *Physical World.* An answer to this argument from the point of view of a determinist is in Blanshard, "The Case for Determinism," in *Determinism and Freedom,* 19–30.

3. *Then there is existential analysis.*

Writers on man's depth awareness, from Nietzsche to Sartre, from Berdyaev to Heidegger, find freedom an invincible datum in our inner consciousness. They uncover an inferno of guilt toward the past—what I might have done; another inferno of anxiety (not just suspense) toward the future—what I might yet be. In dramatic ways they show that no one, not even the most hardheaded determinist, is able to relieve himself of the sense of personal, and admittedly dreadful, freedom. If we could really believe in a thoroughgoing way that what we are and do is unavoidable, we could not consistently feel guilt for we could not sincerely feel responsible. Question: Why not acknowledge on the surface what we all profoundly encounter in the depths?[4]

IN THE BEGINNING

In classical and contemporary debate, one supposition passes unquestioned. Determinists and indeterminists alike suppose that man had a beginning over which he had no control. There are different versions, e.g., "First Cause," "Nature," "Chance," and "God." But, in any case, the view maintains that self-awareness and freedom, whatever they are, came with or after this creation.

Modern revelation not only undercuts this assumption but in an all-important way reverses it. To say that "Man was also in the beginning *with* God," and that "All intelligence is independent in that sphere in which God has placed it to act for itself," is to say that man never has been totally a product.[5] His uncreated intelligence is active and self-propelling.[6] The process of generation

---

4. For a contrast of the scientific and existential approaches to freedom see Truman G. Madsen, "The Contribution of Existentialism," in *BYU Studies.*

5. D&C 93:29. Compare the Prophet's statement, "Intelligence is eternal and exists upon a self-existing principle. It is a spirit from age to age and there is no creation about it" (Joseph Smith, *Teachings* [1938], 354).

6. This, at least, was the Prophet's understanding of uncreate intelligence. See the relevant quotations and comments of Roberts in "The Atonement" in *Seventy's,* vol. 4, lessons 1 and 2. Roberts concludes from scriptural statements, and the later discourses of the Prophet, that reason, imagination, and volition are among the innate qualities of intelligence.

and combination of elements that developed spirit and physical bodies followed, instead of preceding, his independent existence.[7] In this sense man is an eternal co-cause through all stages and all sequences of existence.

MAN'S DESTINY

But with this doctrine of freedom is a doctrine of destiny. Man's nature includes not only the innate possibilities of prime intelligence, but also the embryonic nature of his Eternal Father. In the unfolding process he has already made decisions that are irrevocable and eternal in scope. These, with an everlasting environment, condition him. And from these conditions there is no retreat.[8]

To outline the extensive philosophical implications of this view and its bearing on a hornet's nest of puzzles is impossible here.[9] I turn instead to a close look at some of our everyday reflections on freedom. For when these views are accepted as true, some of our most common and cherished notions are immediately revised.

WHAT IS FREEDOM?

We ordinarily define and defend freedom as the yearning to breathe free, free from pushy parents, blustery policemen, the fetters of red tape, etc. We are so defensive that often we refuse to do what we had decided to do when someone tells us that we

---

7. The view that freedom is only explicable if we assume man's premortal existence is defended by Wisdom in *Philosophy and Psychoanalysis*. The difficulties of reconciling the evidence both for causation and freedom are outlined in Ross, "Determinism and Indeterminism," in *Foundations*.

8. The decision to enter mortality in a physical body, for example, is final. Not just in the sense that consequences will extend forever. But in the sense that the embodied condition will be everlasting.

9. There are puzzles, for example, such as Augustine's—what God was doing before He created man and how man can be blameworthy for acts which follow inevitably from the nature which God created. Another is how the indeterminist can establish responsibility when he says that "free will" events "just happen."

The "Gordian knot" is cut not by indeterminism, but by self-determination. Cause-effect relationships, apparently, are universal. But man is, and always has been, one of the unmoved movers, one of the originating causes in the network.

57

"must" do it. (The suspicion may haunt us that we are not really upholding our freedom but exhibiting our slavery to pride.) Many have died for the "four freedoms," for rights of "freedom from." But more precious still is "freedom for," freedom for turning external pressures into internal gains, freedom for becoming what we have it in us to become, the emergence of our authentic selves. Such freedom can flourish or flounder independent of the "inalienable rights." It is the kind of liberty Joseph Smith could not be denied, even in the darkened squalor of Liberty Jail.[10]

FREEDOM AND LAW

We talk as if freedom were opposed to law when we say, "There ought to be a law against that"; or when we speak in timid lament about "the long right arm of the law."

But whatever may be said of the laws of men, in the eternal scheme, law is the guarantor of freedom. The continuities of our existence, the exceptionless conditions of life, give freedom its lasting power. If, when we flip a coin, it can be both (or neither) heads or tails, if *anything* can really happen following any action, then the freedom of both coins and men is meaningless. The power of man's agency, because of the greater power of God's, can turn the "bounds and conditions" of action into good. And when we seek to become "a law unto ourselves," we are not masters of law, but victims of it, forced to remain unfulfilled.[11] We do not chortle about "getting away with murder" when we recognize that what we are killing is our own potential.

FREEDOM AND
RESPONSIBILITY ARE BROTHERS

We talk as if freedom is incompatible with foreknowledge, as when we say of a spontaneous act that it was "just on impulse" or

---

10. See Frankl, *Man's Search,* 206–210. Frankl survived two years in the most incredibly loathsome conditions in the death camps of Auschwitz. His approach to freedom is unusual on the present scene.

11. There are, to every kingdom, certain "bounds and conditions." All beings who "abide not" those conditions are not justified. Law enables us to be perfected and sanctified (D&C 88:34–61; 130:20, 21).

58

"just for the dickens of it." But is it not apparent that the fullest exercise of freedom requires foreknowledge, knowledge of our actual possibilities, of reachable ends and effective means? Lacking it, we are at best moles in a maze in pointless quest of survival, for what? The disillusion of our time is largely the effect of lost moorings and the terrible suspense of the unforeseen. "Men's hearts fail them" thus. And hence arise a dozen forms of fatalism invoked because it is apparently more bearable to believe the future is all fixed, than to believe it still depends—on us. Thus religions of grace-alone and psychologies of adjustment-alone perpetuate imprisonment. They encourage us to accept our soul-sicknesses in the conviction that there is nothing we can do.[12]

We often recite glibly the chain of blame, making excuses in a way that does not separate the sheep from the scapegoats. Everyone can blame everyone else, who, happily, can blame others still. Even the devil comes in for his undue share.[13] But the logic, or rather psychologic, of the position is that since the devil shows signs of being a compulsive sadist he should not be held responsible, certainly not punished. He no doubt had delinquent parents!

The truth is that any chain-tracing will eventually lead us to ourselves, and some sovereign decision. Addictions of character, for example, may justify the cry, "I can't help it." But it can always be said truly, "You could have helped it."

WE ARE FREE TO CHANGE

On the other hand we talk at times as if freedom were a constant, available whenever we want to use it. "I could do it (or stop doing it) if I wanted to." When praise is in order, it is customary to

---

12. Indeed, some writers on freedom are convinced that most doctrines of causal necessity have been invented subjectively by men to cover up their needling sense of responsibility. Determinism is an intellectual tranquilizer. But William James says lucidly why another part of us finds determinism intolerable, though he does not prove the existence of free will. See his essay, "Dilemma of Determinism," available in many paperback collections.

13. "There are three independent principles: the spirit of God, the spirit of man, and the spirit of the devil. All men have power to resist the devil" (Joseph Smith, *Teachings* [1938], 189).

claim to be "self-made," as if, for example, according to our own fancy, we can live without breathing and breathe without air.

Actually, the most frightening power of freedom is to freely give itself up to forces that stunt it. An acorn can become an oak or less than an oak, but not something else. So with us. In an acorn there are indispensable elements of nurture. So with us. Unlike the acorn, we have intelligent initiative that can go astray. In this realm the role of Christ is to break the bonds of our diminishing freedom and reenthrone our becoming. In crucial ways only He can do this.[14] But here again, He *can*not if we *will* not. We must will and seek and apply His powers with the measure of control that remains to us. The measure is always more than zero. "There is never a time when the spirit is too old to approach God."[15]

FREEDOM INVOLVES COMMITMENT

We talk as if freedom consisted in having the greatest variety of options and that a "once-and-for-all" decision coerces our initiative. But is freedom increased by every new flavor of ice cream?

Actually, it is only when we rise above trivial options and ask ourselves in the depths, "What do I want *to be?*" that we emerge from the bondage of a flitting and faceless mode of life.[16] The most majestic wonder of our freedom is that we can make all-time binding decisions, eternal covenants.[17] Once made, once "renewed

---

14. This is the true version of predestination, namely, that the means of our redemption were predetermined in harmony with eternal law and as sanctioned voluntarily by us. But our own agency was not "predetermined" except as its exercise carries over into our present tendencies. "God did predestinate that all who were saved would be saved through Jesus Christ, but unconditional election was not taught by the ancient apostles" (ibid., 189).

15. Ibid., 191.

16. This is the difference between choosing between separate acts, and choosing between whole ways of life. In this realm none of us can act, without blindness, except by revelation. The Prophet said, "A man can do nothing for himself unless God directs him in the right way and the priesthood is for that purpose" (ibid., 364).

17. According to the Prophet we already have made such a covenant "before the foundations of the earth were laid." Now, as we mature in the flesh, this "new and everlasting covenant" is "renewed and confirmed" upon us "for the sake of the whole world" (D&C 84:33–40, 48; 86: 8–11).

and confirmed," they free us from the life-wasting torment of "bringing it all up" over and over. The decisions, as it were, reverberate through the whole galaxy.[18] And even the lesser roles of life, its distractions and setbacks, take on color and creativity as instruments of the larger "becoming."

Why is it, we may ask, that the Father and the Son "cannot" break their eternal compacts?[19] Because they are "unfree" in attitude? Just the opposite. Because they have made everlasting covenant that they will express freedom in the fullest way, to the resounding blessing of the whole human family.[20] For us, such a decision requires incalculably more intelligent use of individual talent than does shrinking postponement of decision. Made in imitation of the Divine, man's free agency is the boldest, most powerful, most sweeping, and most exciting commitment possible.

Freely we must face it. Out of the eternities we chose and were chosen for light and Divine sonship. Only if we become determined against such a glorious destiny will we avoid the over-arching decisions of direction that bring total freedom. For if we will, our destiny is to become more and more free in the widening circles of fulfillment called Eternal Life.

---

18. "The Lord God will disperse the powers of darkness from before you, and cause the heavens to shake for your good, and his name's glory" (ibid., 21:4–6).

19. This is a "cannot" that reduces to an eternal "will not." It is impossible because He has so chosen, not because external forces prevent it. Another remarkable power of freedom.

20. "Everlasting covenant was made between three personages before the organization of this earth, and relates to their dispensation of things to men on the earth; these personages, according to Abraham's record, are called God the first, the Creator; God the second, the Redeemer; and God the third, the witness or Testator" (Joseph Smith, *Teachings* [1938], 190).

Chapter Seven

REVELATION AND SELF-REVELATION

There is surely a piece of the Divinity in us. Something that
was before the Elements and owes no homage to the Sun.
Nature tells me that I am the Image of God as well as
Scripture. He that understands not this much hath not
his introduction or first lesson and is yet
to begin the alphabet of man.
—*Sir Thomas Browne,* Religio Medici.

Intensive self-analysis is the preoccupation of our time. Many methods are employed to probe the mysterious regions below the consciousness, regions "sheer, frightful, no-man-fathomed." Out of this has arisen a variety of attempts to define and explain man's religiousness. And thus, for example, there are "reductions" of religion to folk-psychology, or primitive taboo, or flights of wish, or emotional purgation, or aesthetic ritual, etc.

On one point there is surprising agreement among writers otherwise opposed. It is recognition of a wholly unique spread of awareness in man—that is called, by Otto, the "numinous" sense—deep innate sensitivity to something sacred, an underived feeling for the holy, with responses of wonder, awe, and reverence.[1] This, it is claimed by many, is primary, a given fact of human consciousness that cannot be traced to rational or empirical sources. We do not learn it. It is somehow, and strangely, innate.

For this and a vast spectrum of related phenomena, the Prophet Joseph Smith gave a seminal explanation: the heightening sense of light within is rooted in man's spirit. It is not something magically created at birth. It permeates our cumulative heritage of individual awareness and extends infinitely into the past. Its composition is actually derived from a Divine nebula of elements "in which," the Prophet taught, "dwells all the glory."[2]

EXPLAINING THE INEXPLICABLE

Attempts to account for the bases of religious consciousness that are "this-worldly," therefore, often leave a great deal unexplained or inadequately explained away. But the recognition that religion is more involved in *re*covery than discovery, that our destiny is not union with Divine realities, but *re*union, opens up a whole new perspective.

Within the framework of Judaeo-Christian assumptions, for example, it aids immensely.

This recognition explains, to begin with, the Prophet's classic

---

1. See Otto, *Idea of the Holy*. Otto was a German Protestant theologian. Others of varied persuasions who nevertheless agree that the "sacred sense" is the core of religious experience are Huxley, a Humanist, in *Religion Without Revelation;* Jones, the "mild mystic" of the Society of Friends in *What Is Vital;* Schweitzer, who has become the living conscience of the 20th Century, in *Out of My Life.* His code is "reverence for life." Jung, psychoanalyst, speaks of the "collective unconscious" or "symbol-making factory" in man that leads us to religious expression reflecting a kind of "racial memory" in *Undiscovered Self.* Chardin, a Catholic scientist, in *Phenomenon of Man,* speaks of a kind of knowledge-sphere which is hidden in us. John Wisdom and Ronald W. Hepburn, both in the positivistic tradition, agree on this sense of holiness. See the latter's *Christianity and Paradox.* The "depth-theologians," e.g. Tillich, Marcel, and Buber, speak of "intuition" and in various ways hold that "unconditional concern" in man is the foundation of all religion.

2. Joseph Smith, *Teachings* (1938), 351.

statement on religious knowing. Whether written, spoken, or directly presented within, the "word of Jehovah" has such an influence over the human mind, the logical mind, that it is convincing without other testimony.[3] When it comes, he later said, as a flow of pure intelligence attended by a burning in the center self, it is of God.[4] Our search for external warrant is really the confirmation and application of what is already, and more certainly, known.

It aids in comprehending the essence of faith. Faith or trust in the Divine is not a blind leap nor desperate gullibility, not "being crucified on the paradox of the absurd."[5] Faith rests on knowledge and self-knowledge and cannot survive without them. It is the expression of the inner self in harmony with a whole segment of one's prior experiences. These experiences, however hidden under mortal amnesia, are indelible in their effect on our affinities, kinships, and sensitivities.[6]

Understanding our religious destiny clarifies the apparent requirement, which may be said to underlie the whole of the scriptures, that we are expected both to believe and respond. To the query, how can you believe what is utterly unevidenced, the question may be returned, how have you managed to repress the ingrained evidence within? The caution, often justified in religion, that one should not say he knows when he does not know is to be matched with the caution that it is equally deceptive to claim one does not know when, in fact, he does know. Both errors betray and disrupt the self.

This understanding of our relationship to God gives meaning to the theme of modern revelation that the forces of darkness

---

3. Roberts, *Comprehensive History,* 5:526.

4. See Joseph Smith, *Teachings* (1938), 151; also D&C 9:8, 9.

5. This is one of Kierkegaard's descriptions of the nature of the "leap of faith" to Christ.

6. Plato's notion of "knowledge by recollection" of a former existence was mainly conceptual or mathematical. For the prophets the awakening of "spirit memories" is also concrete, pictorial, personal. The present world is a grosser duplicate of the heavenly order, whereas Plato's heaven was a realm transcending space, time, and materiality.

operate by subtraction more than by addition. "That which was from the beginning is plainly manifest unto them," and "every spirit of man was innocent in the beginning." Then "one cometh and *taketh away* light and truth, through disobedience, from the children of men, and because of the tradition of their fathers." (D&C 93:31, 38, 39.) The love for darkness which follows on the flouting of the inner light often goes under apparently praiseworthy disguises: objectivity, intellectual integrity, precision, strength to resist one's "mere feelings," etc.

This understanding exposes the structure of testimony and the nature of judgment. "Every man whose spirit receiveth not the light is under condemnation. For man is spirit. . . ." (D&C 93:32, 33.) This is to say, as B. H. Roberts puts it, that the spirit is "native to truth"; that as a flame leaps toward a flame, the soul's very nature is to reach toward and embrace the light. One who thrusts down or represses these sovereign impulses sunders himself. He eventually falls victim, as Jung maintains, to some of the worst forms of psychosomatic illness and misery. (Contrary to the Freudians, Jung believes one can healthily suppress his more superficial desires, however compulsive, but not these.)[7] Of all the laws of spiritual life, this may be the most fundamental. He who welcomes truth and light, on the other hand, moves toward "a perfect bright recollection" and "receiveth truth and light until he is glorified in truth and knoweth all things," growing "brighter and brighter until the perfect day." (D&C 93:28. Compare 50:23, 24; 88:67.)

THE UPRUSH AND THE DOWNFLOW

To move from interpretation of the sacred inner life to adequate description is notoriously difficult. Nevertheless, here is an attempt to capture the flavor of the Latter-day Saint "experiment in depth," revelatory touches with the self that seem to disclose the longer-than-mortal sense. (Inevitably we veer into the oblique but

---

7. Jung, *Modern Man.*

somehow more expressive language of simile and metaphor.) There are:

—*Prayer flashes,* when our words outreach thought and we seem to be listening above ourselves, completely at home while we are surprised at hints of hidden spirit memories within.

—*Familiarity of persons,* immediate luminous rapport—this face or that gesture or motion—that elicits the sense of recall, a premortal intimacy, especially in the environs of teaching and being taught.

—*Haunting sensations,* usually visual, sometimes auditory, of a landscape of life or a bitter predicament in the soul, that call up simultaneous feelings of "again" and "for the first time"; like being thrust, as leading actor, into the last act of a play without knowing, and yet almost knowing, what occurred in the first two.

—*Numbing protests* from below sometimes of unrelievable urgency or guilt, that are ruthless in unmasking our pretense. These are not simply the yeas or nays of "conscience" about acts, but bell sounds of a whole self that will not be muffled, that ring with presentiments, thrusting us toward ends that seem tied to an elusive but white-lighted blueprint inside.

—*Shades of consciousness* that occur just at awakening or just before sleep, unpredictably impressing while they express, in images or silent words or free association. By the sanctity of their feeling-tone, these are different than our usual helter-skelter menagerie of thought.

—*Dreams and illusions* that seem not to be mere dreams or mere illusions, catching us quite off-guard and lingering in their after-effect, as if life were a game of internal hide-the-thimble and we were "getting warm" to our own potential.

—*Unaccountable reverberations* (e.g., in tear-filled eye or tingling throat or spine) from a phrase or sentiment (which, for the speaker or writer may be merely parenthetical), or from a strain of music, or some trivial stimulus in the midst of drudgery, bearing a holy atmosphere of spontaneous and total recognition.

—*Reflections of our faces* in the mirror when we look in and not just at, our eyes. As if light were coming to the surface, and a curious recovery, and even awe, of the self occurs. There lurks an autobiography, a soul-story that is foreign, yet intimate, unfolding a more-than-I-thought-I-was.

—*Right-track feelings,* the sense of the foreordained, like emerging from a fever to find that roughshod or happenstance trials have been presided over by some uncanny instinctual self who knows what he is about. Just before or just after turning a crucial corner, this someone nearer than you, that *is* you, holds a quiet celebration that injects peace into the marrow of the bones.

Such flashes and drives are tied to the whole gamut of complex mental life and may have neat and utterly mundane naturalistic explanations (such as the chemistry of the occipital lobe). Yet the joy that comes from these uprisings, rooted, as they seem to be, in some more primal creative being and that, in turn, in God, supersedes any of the pleasures of human possession or external manipulation.

CLEANING THE LAMPSHADE

Much of modern life is a darkening process, cutting us off from the uprush of the fountain at our center. The lives we live and the demands of environment to which science and technology and strategy are admirably adapted, tend to lead us toward self-estrangement.

Becoming more out of alignment with our inner selves, straining to present faces that are acceptable to the world, we suffer a shallowing effect. And what William James called "the Energies of Men" are trapped and suffocated, because we are afraid of being deluded, we have a revulsion at many forms of religion, and a kind of psychological hypochondria which makes us suspect our subconscious is solely inhabited by snakes and spiders.

Was it a sort of ancient hoodwink the Master recommended— these strange sentences about "becoming as a little child"? Are the virtues of the childlike more obvious than the vices of the childish?

Maybe He was saying more, saying that we are not, as empiricists assert, born an empty tablet on which the chalk of childhood writes. Maybe He was saying that a child has swift, untinctured

67

affinity and response to his own burning deeps. He is exemplary not, as is so often said, in vulnerable readiness to believe others' voices, but in soul-unity that prevents disbelief of his own. He has whole, happy, healthy relationship with the core of creativity and spirituality which is his glory-laden spirit.

If so, the explicit and expansive messages of Messiah, "bringing all things to their remembrance," would shine more clearly through the boy Samuel, the boy Nephi, or the boy Joseph, and likewise the childlike Adam who, though he was centuries old when the human race was in its infancy, vibrated with prophetic vision. That would explain the verse, added by the Prophet, to the biblical account of the youth of Christ Himself: "He needed not that any man should teach Him."[8] God, to reveal Himself to Christ, needed only to reveal Christ to Himself, in "the glory he had with Him before the foundations of the world." Is it really different with us?[9]

---

8. See Joseph Smith's Inspired Version of the Bible, Matthew 3:24–26 (he adds three verses). "And it came to pass that Jesus grew up with his brethren, and waxed strong, and waited upon the Lord for the time of his ministry to come. And he served his father, and he spake not as other men, neither could he be taught; for he needed not that any man should teach him. And after many years, the hour of his ministry drew nigh."

9. In his greatest discourse the Prophet testified of the interdependence of knowledge of God and knowledge of self. "If men do not comprehend the character of God, they do not comprehend themselves" (Joseph Smith, *Teachings* [1938], 343).

FOUR ESSAYS ON LOVE

Chapter One

JOSEPH SMITH AND THE SOURCES OF LOVE

My brothers and sisters, today we reach into a realm that is subtle and intricate, all intertwined with feeling. More than usual I pray that you will be forgiving if my own feelings are apparent. As we drove past the Logan Temple this morning, I could not recall ever hearing the word "love" in the endowment ordinance, that summation of eternity presented there. But does love have on earth a more glowing demonstration? If so, the Prophet is profoundly articulate on the sources of love in ways that transcend words.

Some first vital words came when Joseph was a lad of only fourteen summers, kneeling in a shaft of light. They are both a divine indictment and an imperative, and we should take them personally. Said the voice, "They draw near to me with their lips but their hearts are far from me" (Joseph Smith—History 1:19). Late in his short life, the Prophet stood in the midst of a multitude and said, "People ask, 'Why is it this babbler gains so many followers, and retains them?' I answer: It is because I possess the principle of love" (Joseph Smith, *Teachings* [1938], 313).

What principle is this? Return to a scene at Harmony, Pennsylvania. Here two young men (the Prophet was then twenty-three), immersed in poverty, living on mackerel, are translating "a great and marvelous work" on scratch paper. Oliver Cowdery sits and struggles to make readable ink marks.[1] The words Joseph dictates are these:

All things must fail . . .

But charity is the pure love of Christ, and it endureth forever; and whoso is found possessed of it at the last day, it shall be well with him.

Wherefore my beloved brethren, pray unto the Father with all the energy of heart, that ye may be filled with this love, which He hath bestowed upon all who are true followers of His Son Jesus Christ. (Moroni 7:46–48)

Have you ever wondered how the Prophet felt in such moments? We do not often reflect that translation (no matter how it be "explained") was a learning process for him, often tinctured with first-time wonderment. One day, Emma Smith records, she was writing for him and he dictated the phrase, "the wall of Jerusalem." The Prophet paused and then said, in effect, "Emma, I didn't know there was a wall around Jerusalem" (*Saints Herald*, 21 June 1884, 396–97). Perhaps a similar exclamation came from him when the passage above was given on the source of pure love.

The characterization of "pure love" as "bestowed," something with which we may be "filled," becomes personified in the portrait of Jesus Christ in the "Fifth Gospel," Third Nephi. This picture, in fact, is more than a sufficient answer to the query, "Why another book?" For here, surely, is the heart of the Book of

---

1. The original manuscript is on a variety of kinds and sizes of paper. Oliver Cowdery's handwriting is almost without punctuation, as if the whole book were one long dictated sentence.

Mormon. In this segment of the life of Christ, otherwise unknown, He is a resurrected, composite self (3 Nephi 11–26). He has received "the glory of the Father" and dares to apply the word "perfect" to Himself. His is not an abstract, or metaphysical, or "utterly other" perfection. He is, in all the highest senses of flesh and spirit, a personality. He can be seen, felt, embraced—loved. He is the revelation of the Father, not because "two natures" are combined but because He is now exactly like the Father in nature. He is the revelation of man, not because He has condescended to act like one but because He has now become what man may become. He is still "troubled" by the degradations of Israel. He ministers and responds to a multitude who have great spiritual capacities. His heart is "filled with compassion." He kneels with them in prayer, consumed by "the will of the Father." He calls down upon them the powers of the Spirit, first its purifying, then its glorifying, and then, I believe, its sealing powers. He weeps and then weeps again as he blesses their children. He prays in ways that reach beyond mortal grasp, and yet "their hears were opened and they did understand in their hearts the words which he prayed" (3 Nephi 19:33; see also 17:14–17). This is the highest possible order of existence.

Although they profess monotheism, our Christian creeds actually teach two kinds of God. They retain only shadows of Christ's personality, or, if they seriously affirm it, they likewise affirm that there is an unconditioned, non-spatial Something that is the "real" and "ultimate" Deity. They permit us, of course, to think of God in personal terms, provided we do not assume our images to be literally true.[2] But through Joseph Smith's recovery of this portrait in the Book of Mormon and its confirmation in his own experience, we know that the Living Christ is a Christ of response, who not only feels all we feel, and by similar processes, but wills us to feel all He feels. The spectrum of affection, presently limited

2. A few contemporary writers have described a more immanent, personal God, but the usual emphasis is still on the transcendence of Deity.

73

in us, is filled out fully in Him, not because He is less personal than we but because He is more.

In the same vein, the Prophet recorded, before he was twenty-five, a central pearl of the Pearl of Great Price, the vision of Enoch. Here the Father (as the Son did later) suffers the anguish of our sleepy, ugly indifference, an anguish that issues in tears. When Enoch, appalled, marveled and cried out, after naming all the perfections of God, "How is it thou canst weep?" the answer came,

> Unto thy brethren have I said . . . that they should love one another, and that they should choose me, their Father; but behold, they are without affection, and they hate their own blood. (Moses 7:33)

Millions have said we need God, but that God "has no needs." Joseph Smith witnessed that there is a sense in which God and Christ need us and our love.

Now it seems clear that we do not (and cannot) love because of walls we ourselves have erected, which can only be eradicated from mind and heart when "we see as we are seen" of God. Rufus Jones (*What Is Vital*), Alfred North Whitehead (*Religion in the Making*), and Henri Bergson (*Two Sources*) dared to speculate, in this century of abysmal alienation, that God is closer to man and man closer to God, in possibility, than the old dualistic theology would allow. They have convinced very few. Love is defined in one contemporary statement as the "reunion of the separated" (Tillich, *Love*). But its advocates work with assumptions which make reunion impossible.

It is common to suppose that in love "opposites attract." This may be a motive of much popular writing about the transcendence of God—as if the more unlike two beings are, the greater the power of love. Love, for Joseph Smith, however, is a relationship of similars. "Intelligence cleaveth unto truth, virtue loveth virtue, light cleaveth unto light, mercy hath compassion on mercy" (D&C 88:29–40). Even the opposites within us must merge and harmonize before we can truly love. The "pure love of Christ," then, is Christ's love for us as well as ours for Him. Actual kinship is the core of it. The commandment to love is a hopeless request until we begin to encounter those qualities in fulness in Him and in embryo in ourselves. That presupposes individual revelation.

There is in most of us a hidden apology for the lack of love. We tend to identify love with action, to credit ourselves with it when we do a good turn hourly, when we serve in the sheer constraint of obligation. Joseph Smith turns us from that stone to bread. Going the second (or the first) mile grudgingly, or even habitually and numbly, is not Christ's way. Love becomes a fountain even "unto the consuming of our flesh" in the growing person—not a source of drudgery but a captivating awareness that pulls us even in our most miserable hours (2 Nephi 4:21). Until our duty-sense merges into this "energy of heart," until love is the feeling-tone at the root of all our feelings and actions, we are still spiritual infants trying to get credit for our moral strength. In religion, this heroic vanity can lead eventually to a sort of insanity.

It is also typical to say we must purge our love of self from our love of God. Hence many a sentimental sermon about an "unselfish" love for God that would cheerfully go to endless torment if it pleased Him. The Prophet drew the thin, precious line here. Am I selfish when I care so little about my total self that I push some fragment of it to fleeting satisfaction, disease, and death? No. In a sense, I am not selfish enough. God, taught the Prophet, loves Himself in an inclusive way and hence "everything God does is to aggrandize His kingdom" (Joseph Smith, *History of the Church,* 5:286). Such love expands to the "self" to include all selves, all life; and God, therefore, cannot be happy except in the happiness of all creatures. Call that "selfish" if you like. But notice that the opposite is a selfishness which seeks something in indifference to or at the expense of others. We are commanded to be selfish as God is. Joseph Smith taught that there is a law (not, if I understand him, of God's making but in the very nature of things) that "upon no other principle can a man permanently and justly aggrandize himself" (Joseph Smith, *Teachings* [1938], 297). This is the meaning of the Master's cryptic phrase: "Lose yourself . . . and find yourself." Expand your caring to include all carings

and you begin to overcome destructive selfishness. It is the shrinking awareness of self that leads us to hate ourselves that is most
agonizing to the Father.

We have thought that we must separate our love of God from
our love of the world. In one sense, yes. But the Prophet taught
that God, who formed and beautified this world, will enable its
sanctified sons and daughters to inherit it in its eventual full-
flowering re-creation.[3] Again, like has affinity with like. When
John the Beloved said, "Love not the world, neither the things that
are in the world," he meant the corruptions of men in the world.
The Prophet clarified the preposition and thus the proposition. His
version reads, "Love not the world, neither the things that are of
the world" (1 John 2:15, Inspired Version). The lights and shadows of Eden in all color and variety are in this world, not just as a
fading racial memory but as a prophecy.[4] We must love the world,
and what is in it, as we love all that feels and all that moves. Once
again a withdrawal doctrine is transformed into a participation
doctrine. The World itself is a composition of the love of God.

These instances suggest the close interrelationship of love and
knowledge. Our hearts cannot get closer to God than our minds.
And here, once more, an assumption is uprooted. We all quietly
suspect that love may destroy "objectivity" and the perception of
truth, if not man to man at least man to cosmos. The Prophet
taught the exact contrary. The tensions, and they are sometimes
traumatic, between our struggle for God and our struggle for truth
are due to our ignorance of both. We cannot apprehend nor comprehend reality as it is save through the love of God. And the
Prophet taught that any imposed limitation on our pursuit of either
is a limitation on love. For himself he wrote, "It feels so good not
to be trammeled." Thus, in one breath he could say that we want
all men to "drink into one principle of love," and in the next add,
"One of the grand fundamental principles of 'Mormonism' is to

---

3. Christ said the beatified shall "inherit the earth." Small comfort for those
who despise it.

4. The "end of the world" for Joseph Smith is the end of rampant wickedness,
not the destruction of the earth (Joseph Smith, *Teachings,* [1938] 98).

receive truth, let it come from whence it may" (Joseph Smith, *Teachings* [1938], 313).

Often love is described as something that "covers" sins, a sort of "blindness" to our own or others' defects. Says the scripture, "Charity covereth a multitude of sins." Perhaps so. But the Prophet strengthened the verb. "Charity," he wrote, "preventeth a multitude of sins" (1 Peter 4:8, Inspired Version). In us and in others, love is the Lord's preventive medicine; and, as we are now learning, it is the only lasting foundation for powerful therapy, whether for sin or for suffering.

But does not love for God separate us from those who love Him not? The Prophet replies, writing from a damp, submerged dungeon, that God-like love, the unique love of those who walk uprightly, is "without prejudice." "It gives scope to the mind which enables us to conduct ourselves with a greater liberality toward all that are not of our faith than what they have for themselves" (Joseph Smith, *Teachings* [1938], 147).[5] He taught, in fact, that it is a mark of our unfamiliarity with the principles of godliness when our affectionate feelings are "contracted." The closer we come to our Heavenly Father, he told some huffy sisters in Relief Society, the more we look upon perishing souls with compassion. "We feel that we want to take them upon our shoulders and cast their sins behind our backs" (Joseph Smith, *Teachings* [1938], 241). It follows, and he gave it as a lasting key, that we know something in us has passed from life to death when we hate the brethren (Joseph Smith, *Teachings* [1938], 136, 137, 193; 1 John 3:14; *Junvenile Instructor* 27:42). Any brethren.

Millions in the world today believe that the love of God, or agape, must be finally separated from the love of our mates, or eros. The latter "we know" will end. From the Greek distrust of matter and the flesh comes this attitude (if not the explicit doctrine) that religious love, when pure, is "purely spiritual," and anything physical cannot be as pure. Conclusion: the lyrical joys

---

5. We love others because of their partial or potential loveableness, not in spite of its absence.

of the body are of this world only. The Prophet Joseph, in contrast, teaches that there is no unholy love (though there is much unsanctified lust). Romantic and marital love are approved of God here and now (which most Christians will allow). But he taught far more: agape and eros merge as modes of the ultimate nature of God! Whole-souled love includes the love-expressions of a glorified body even for Him. In us the seed of such love is not only blessed rather than cursed by God, but "visited with my power" and "without condemnation on earth or in heaven" (D&C 132:48).

Thus Joseph's teaching heals a malaise that plagues men to this hour. An innocent child might ask, "Why did God make us creatures but never to be Creators-like-him?" The reply is either that He could not (and that is embarrassing for theologians who insist on God's power to make anything from nothing) or that He loves us—but not that much! Joseph testified He did and does love us that much. The chasm which religious etiquette says we must not attempt has been bridged, not by an arrogant man but by the God of life and love. If men would receive the doctrine (but guilt and terror yield slowly), it would cure many of the psychological and social maladies of our age.

Let us turn now to one of the "hows" of love. We are living in the midst of what is called a "liturgical revival." Many of the wings of Christianity, with cues from psychology and art, have sought to find again what they earlier abandoned. They have seen the vision of reaching men, in a deeper way, through the impact of liturgy, ceremony, and sacramental act; extensive research is uncovering patterns of worship, old and new, that might heighten this mode of contact.

The Prophet (violating, by the way, the whole thrust of New York revivalism) introduced a concept of ordinances which is unequivocal. "Without the ordinances of the priesthood and the authority thereof," a revelation says, "the power of godliness is not manifest unto men in the flesh" (D&C 84:21). For him the function of baptism, confirmation, sacrament, temple worship is not only psychological, but to teach and remind us of principles and to lead us to renewed commitment. Ordinances are also divinely

78

appointed "channels" and "keys" of divine awareness. To receive them, to cultivate their influence within our very inward parts, is to encounter the Divine and to be ennobled and sanctified into His very image. "Being born again," said the Prophet to the Council of Twelve, who were about to undertake foreign missions, "comes by the Spirit of God through ordinances" (Joseph Smith, *Teachings* [1938], 162).

One can have the forms without the power but not the power without the forms. Of course ritual may be "empty." But so it may be full, full of godly power.

Moreover, ordinances require the upward reach from below. The Prophet was commissioned to establish at the center of every ordinance a covenant, an "everlasting covenant." By such enactments we do not essay to try or experiment or hope. We say we will do and will not do certain things—forever. This, the Prophet taught, opens the buds of our nature in a decisive act that reverberates through the heavens. Until that takes place, in sacred places in the presence of witnesses and under the influence of God, we do not deeply feel the nurturing spirit sunshine that increases love.

Let us look now at the Prophet's own makeup, stressing aspects that carry an element of surprise. Note first that his was a masculine love, combined with a robust and muscular faith. Love led him, for example, to strong rebukes of his brethren. Virtuous men grew; others became almost demonic. "I frequently rebuke and admonish my brethren," he wrote, "and that because I love them." Over the long haul he had ample, yes, crushing reason to know that, as the Master learned, "the higher the authority the greater the difficulty of the station" (Joseph Smith, *Teachings* [1938], 112, 113).

Love led him to test and try men's love for Christ, and for himself, to the core of their being. In some ways the Church's survival in that first generation required it. Thus he could walk into a Nauvoo store and say, "Brother Wooley, we want all of your goods for the building up of the Kingdom of God." Brother Wooley (with what inner turbulence we can only guess) set about loading his merchandise into boxes, excepting only some goods on consignment from St. Louis. Calling the Prophet, he offered to pack them also. The Prophet asked searchingly, "Are you really willing, Brother Wooley, to give us all your store goods?" "Yes." Joseph, with deep feeling, embraced his shoulder and said, "Then replace them on your shelves" (Jenson, *Biographical* 1:632).

Filled with the love of God, the Prophet yet knew, to his depth, that suffering and stress like unto Christ's are inevitable elements of life. Love cannot obliterate pain. It can give it meaning and redeeming power. In one of his bleak hours, crying out, he asked like Job, on behalf of his people and himself, "Why this horror? Why us? How long will it last?" He received assurances, under a wave of Spirit, which belong with the great religious consolations of all time:

> If thou endure it well, God shall exalt thee on high . . . all these things shall give thee experience and shall be for thy good.

> The Son of Man hath descended below them all.

> Thine adversity and thine afflictions shall be but a small moment. (D&C 121:7, 8; 122: 7, 8)

For him that "small moment" was five more tempestuous years.

Yet this kind of love led the Prophet to an exhilarating outlook on life, in all its aspects. He was other-worldly but also this-worldly. Call him an intellectual, a contemplative, but add that he was a statesman, a thoroughly active leader. If you say he enjoyed drama, music, poetry, you must add that he also delighted to wrestle, play ball, jump to the mark, pull stakes. Note that he was a dignified, serious, ponderous man, but add that he was gifted in social animation, was cheerful, both playful and warm, incapable of ignoring the child, the laborer, or the aged friend. He could turn a phrase, swing an ax, cut a caper. Most traditional distinctions we make in defining the "religious man" break down in him and in those who caught the vision through him. As Divinity intended, temporal and spiritual fused in him.

Read, for example, about the day a group of the Saints met in

80

the Nauvoo Temple. Part of the morning was spent in sweaty, gritty cleaning and painting. Then came a study class. Later, bathed and dressed in their temple robes, they participated in temple worship. A prayer and testimony service followed in which the Spirit of God was so intense that many spiritual gifts were manifest. The group next adjourned to the upstairs rooms and relished a feast of raisins and cakes. And then, until late in the evening, they enjoyed music and dancing. What? The whole of life—even dancing—surrounded by a temple of God? Yes. And why not? For the Prophet, every attempt to withdraw "religiousness" from some part of living, including recreation, was a blow against both God and love, and therefore the self (Richards, Diary, 17–18).

Joseph exercised an almost irresistible influence on the lives that surrounded him. Parley P. Pratt, for one, after interviews with the Prophet which, he says, "lifted a corner of the veil and gave me a single glance into eternity," burst into a rhapsody of words:

> I had loved before, but I knew not why. But now I loved—with a pureness—an intensity of elevated, exalted feelings, which would lift my soul from the transitory things of this groveling sphere and expand it as the ocean. I felt that God was my heavenly Father indeed; that Jesus was my brother, and that the wife of my bosom was an immortal, eternal companion: a kind, ministering angel, given to me as a comfort, and a crown of glory forever and ever. In short, I could now love with the spirit and with the understanding also.

These "glorious principles concerning God and the heavenly order of eternity" are, Parley wrote, such that "none but the highly intellectual, the refined and pure in heart, know how to prize, and . . . are at the very foundation of everything worthy to be called happiness" (Pratt, *Autobiography,* 297, 298). They grew in him until his own martyrdom.

Remember that some of the Prophet's own brethren, including ten of the original Twelve Apostles at one time or another, out of the lust for power or pride of life or base transgression, came to betray him. (Of the original Twelve, only Brigham Young and Heber C. Kimball remained constantly faithful.) But over the following ten years there grew around him a group of men and women who were a marvel of united power and love.

We can read whole volumes in a sentence or two. To Jedediah M. Grant, who had "dyspepsia," the Prophet one day said, "If I could always be with you I could cure you" (Young, *Journal of Discourses,* 3:12). Gauge the love-meaning in that!

Why did Willard Richards, weary after thirty days of penning affidavits in that final period of tragedy, offer to be hanged in the Prophet's stead? Why did John Taylor, blasted in the same volley of bullets, but not fatally, write the hymn, "Oh, Give Me Back My Prophet Dear"? Why did Wilford Woodruff write such extravagant things as this in his Journal: "There is not so great a man as Joseph standing in this generation. His mind, like Enoch's, expands as eternity, and God alone can comprehend his soul" (Cowley, *Woodruff,* 68).

Brigham Young, for the first thirty days after the Prophet's death, could not be comforted. At Winter Quarters there came a renewed revelatory touch with the Prophet. And for the rest of Brigham's monumental life, there was no forgetting. He died saying, "Joseph, Joseph, Joseph."

It is easy to conclude that these are the product of insipid and sentimental blindness. But will we someday realize that only such persons imbued with the Spirit of God, could have really loved and therefore really known the Prophet as he was? If so, these are, indeed, touches of the "pure love of Christ."

A prevailing need for love, even in its most unenlightened forms, is the uncontested finding of the contemporary study of man, one of the things we know for sure. But we live in a strange time, for the very experts who tell us this warn, and wisely, that often the thing we most want is projected instead of discovered and that much that we call "love," especially in religion, is make-believe. It follows that the religion that has the greatest power to answer our thirst is, by this logic, the one of which we should be most suspicious. Sometimes too, like atomic fallout, the influence of the despairing philosophies of our culture gets through to us. We sincerely tremble as if the whole house of love is a house of cards—just too good to be true.

Introspection moves in a similar circle. Who does not feel that life without love is a life of diminishing fervor, for children as for those of us who pretend to be adults? Who doubts that the raw, fragmental love of the world is not enough? We see something of ourselves in the plays and on the screen. It is a time of terrible disillusion. Thence comes the groan in literature: the themes of loneliness, monotony, boredom, nausea, anxiety, dread, troubled sleep, death.

This cultural moan was anticipated by the Prophet, or rather, by Him who inspired him.

> I the Lord knowing the calamity which should come upon the inhabitants of the earth, called upon my servant Joseph Smith, Junior. (D&C 1:17)

Is there a way out, or, at least, up? The Prophet said, "All will suffer until they obey Christ Himself" (Joseph Smith, *Teachings* [1938], 357; see also 321, 323).

And so we return to the beginning, to the real Christ, the living Christ, the Christ who manifests himself now, not a mythical Jesus who was, but the Christ who is. "The Savior," the Prophet said, "has the words of eternal life. Nothing else can profit us" (Joseph Smith, *Teachings* [1938], 364).

In all history there may not have been, except for David and Jonathan, a pair of men more closely bound by brotherly and godly affection than were Joseph and Hyrum. William Taylor, describing how they looked whenever they met each other, says it was deep looking to deep, "the same expression of supreme joy." When Joseph craved the privilege of pioneering the Rocky Mountains and was turned by the clamor of his own to the road to Carthage, Hyrum was first to volunteer to go. "If you go, I will go with you," said Joseph, "but we shall be butchered." Later, having predicted with certainty his then imminent death, Joseph at least three times pled for Hyrum to leave. "I want Hyrum to live." But each time Hyrum could only reply, "Joseph, I cannot leave you" (Joseph Smith, *Teachings* [1938], 364).[6]

Mother Smith came on that fateful day to view the inert bodies of her two sons (unaware that her son, Samuel, as a result of a related mobbing, was on his deathbed); she says she seemed to hear them speak. Mere motherly delirium? Perhaps. But listen to what she seemed to hear:

> Mother, weep not for us. We have overcome the world by love. We carried to them the Gospel that their souls might be saved. They slew us for our testimony and they have placed us beyond their power. Their ascendency is for a moment. Ours is an eternal triumph. (Lucy Mack Smith, *History,* 325)

Every man must make up his mind whether Hyrum's lifetime closeness makes him the most creditable witness the Prophet had—or the least. He knew him from his birth to a few seconds before his death. (It was Hyrum who held Joseph as a boy through weeks of bone pain when there were no sedatives or anesthetic.) This, in a sentence, is the testimony he has left for mankind to ponder.

> There were prophets before. But Joseph has the spirit and power of all the prophets. (Joseph Smith, *History of the Church* 6:346)

The spirit and power of all the prophets is the spirit and power of Jesus Christ, and His Spirit is the spirit and power of pure love, "the chief characteristic of Deity." It is the mission of Jesus Christ to bring into the world again and again the sunshine of light and warmth that is love. By our literal descent and by our redeemed ascent through Christ, we are fully begotten and loved of God the Eternal Father. If we will only respond to what He has given and now gives, we will grow in the nurture of perfected love.

---

6. The grandson of Hyrum Smith, President Joseph Fielding Smith, believes that if Oliver Cowdery had been faithful, he, not Hyrum, would have died at Carthage, a joint witness to the death with the Prophet. But all the promises and keys and gifts once conferred on Oliver were conferred on Hyrum. (D&C 124:95)

I cannot close without a personal testimony. I know what those who despair are talking about, those who say with Bertrand Russell, "Such a thing as Christian love is impossible." I know the arguments. But I have witnessed refutation in experience. I bear testimony that the Prophet Joseph Smith and his heirs have lived to love and died to love, and that because of them we have capacities and privileges for love beyond our present conception. I bear that testimony in the name of Jesus Christ. Amen.

Chapter Two

HOW TO BE
LOVED AND BELOVED

*In the midst of the stresses of youth there is a secret:
how to find and express romantic love.
It is exciting.
It is consuming.
But it is also uncommon. Few know it at its actual source
and still fewer are able to communicate it, even in poetry
or music.
Meanwhile we give our immoral support to stars who
throw dust in our eyes.
Let's start with one.*

I

You all know the initials of the handsome man who pays millions in alimony. He is a superb actor, and for widely screened reasons he is big box office. No matter whom he is married to this week, he says he cannot perform on stage or camera without a "powerful love interest" in his leading lady, an interest which, apparently, goes all the way. In sacred books this sort of "interest" is not described as love. But if we are disposed to stone Mr. B, let us learn at least this much from him: Even make-believe love, even diseased and perverted love, is a powerful force.

II

Now to another model. Wouldn't it be fabulous (if you are a girl) to be a vision of beauty, a symbol for all the world, a lush embodiment of female allure? The question brings up, or maybe it is down, the blonde that gentlemen were supposed to prefer.

Much has been said of the causes of her suicide, her desperate reach for the lethal overdose. Her ex-husbands are silent. Mr. Priestly says she was drowned in a wave of erotic illusion, or perhaps disillusion. Mrs. Luce says the American public killed her. All agree that she was not the girl who had everything. But what would a spiritual post-mortem show? Not, perhaps, that no one loved her but that she, like so many of us, lacked the power of love; that she was still-born in an atmosphere that neither her conscious mind nor her spirit-self ever really breathed? Anyway, MM is something to ponder. Her sleeping pills awaken us to the futility of the fiction that when you get right down to it love is just animated glands.

III

Let us move now eastward toward Eden.

I cite the voice of an unknown man from a scene that is somehow unforgettable.

It was an anniversary banquet. A four-generation family gathered to honor their silvery grandfather and his sweetheart. It seems to me it was their sixtieth, but, as you will see, it doesn't matter which. This slight, hallowed woman sat, very close, I thought, to her husband. He was an oak, 81, and his body had the measuring lines and circles of his long, hard pull. You would say he was an ugly old fellow, except for the clearness of his eyes. He stood and made some comment about the flamboyant way love is advertised these days. Then he said,

"When I was a boy, it thrilled me just to touch Lucy's arm."

He turned, smiled in her lifted face and said, most softly, "And it still does."

So far we have illustrated one provable point: Whatever it isn't, one thing love surely is—a matter of life and death.

IV

That leads to three stark paradoxes, designed to jar you a bit, though no one over four is shocked these days.

First, the prevention and murder of love is the most highly paid occupation of our time. Yet it is billed in bright lights as the worship of love.

Second, yielding to this feverish idolatry is more deadening than the Mafia. Yet the healthiest response is not to take it seriously but lightly.

Third, the way to overcome the fake fires that are omni-present in our culture is neither wet blankets nor cold water. It is to burn with a brighter, richer flame.

V

We're on the verge of the secret now.

(And please don't assume that I am just playing with metaphors.)

Love is Fire.

That is the great secret.

It is Fire with a large F. It is Divine Fire. When it is in you it lights you, all of you. And transforms. No self-induced flicker can compare with it.

Modern revelation has several words for the emanation that conveys this Love. They are not exact synonyms: Life. Light. Spirit. Power. All are "sent forth by the will of the Father through Jesus Christ His Son."

Thus you cannot "make" love. You cannot love until you are

loved. You cannot be loved until you are Beloved, Beloved of God. His flame burns and encircles reaching the self at its core, its spiritual center, and then moving outward to physical fingers and toes.

Such love, over long periods, becomes diamond-like. A real diamond, being pure carbon, burns up in split seconds surrounded by flame. Yet there are other fantastic pressures and refinements that give it luster and sheen until it can cut and endure through almost anything. Love in you is both that destructible and that durable.

A little unreachable and ethereal, you say? Agreed. Let's relate it to some fashionable attitudes about love. Some of them are exactly upside down.

VI

"Love is a special way of feeling." Rather, it is a special way of being, of which feelings are a rich and intense part.

"Love is doing what comes naturally." Yes, when combined with doing what comes supernaturally.

"There is love at first sight." More accurately there is sight at first love, a widened world, not just for the eyes but for mind and spirit too. Only fake love is "blind."

"Falling in love is sudden. It can happen to anyone." Maybe. But rising in love, which is a lot more exciting, is something else again. The brighter and more illumined the mind, the more profoundly expansive the spirit, the more sensitive (which is to say, pure) the body, the greater your whole shimmering response to the Flame in you and your beloved. But the rise is a slow, aching, anything-but-sudden process.

"The most intense love is wild, unbridled, explosive passion." A grotesque myth. The demons must be in stitches as we dance their little tawdry tune!

No. The most intense love is described by Alma who said:

"See that ye bridle all your passions that you may be filled with love."

Love, like anything that is harmonic and beautiful, requires endless discipline, terrible periods of the self at war with the self, tortures of involvement (you vastly increase your capacities for pain when you identify with someone else), and an infinite patience. Is it worth it? Well, millions have compassed land and sea to reach the shrine of far lesser satisfactions.

You think profligates know more about it than prophets? Then you are a child who thinks a rag doll is more beautiful than a friend. Worse. You fancy surface contact with a corpse (and all due disrespect for corpses, there are many of them walking around advocating the diminishing thrill) is more attractive than the whole-souled love with a god or goddess made a little higher than the angels.

"But religion condemns love, it is against romantic and marital fulfillment." Yes, there are well-intended and often badly distorted dogmas against love. Some are gray, stupid, hypocritical and uninspired. But so, often, are the "enlightened" present-day reactions against them in movies and magazines. The religion of the living God, who has the distinction of being the only one in the theological catalog who exists, is a religion of perpetual creation, of freeing, ever-renewing, increasing love, love that burns with His clear, gem-like flame. Christ has spoken in modern revelation against too little of this love, against its extinguishing. But He has said nothing against too much, for, at this level, there is no such thing. He has said that there is a kind of love and a kind of marriage which

> "shall be visited with blessings, and not cursings, and with My power, said the Lord, and shall be without condemnation on earth and in heaven." (D&C 132:48)

VII

This, then, is the pattern within which anguished questions of youth find answer. For ultimately all our turbulent heart askings will lead us to look up:

> Why is unchastity in any form a dulling, dimming, damning thing?

Is "making out" wrong?

Why modesty in dress and dance?

If there is little honest love in my home is there hope for me to find it elsewhere?

What is really phony about pornography?

What is amiss in the Victorian, the prude, the view that marriage is Satanic?

Can I pray about my most secret feelings?

Should I?

Is it better for me to walk in the desert (for years if necessary) alone, rather than accept the proposal of someone who lacks the Spirit of love?

When is romance secure? How can I know?

Who knows whether my dream-life and fantasies are warping me, or deepening my capacities for the real thing?

These, and all queries like them, can be translated into burning questions about the brighter Flame . . . and you.

VIII

And now one of you may react:

"If all this is really true, if there is no preparation for the Fire of love except through self-control and transformation, if there is no hope for youth except through purging the acids of sin in their flesh and the stupefying settle-for-less tendencies of their minds, if no matter how impatient or eager their desires are, love cannot come to life except through the Spirit of God, if, before sweethearts are really close to each other they must be close to the Lord Jesus Christ, well, then, all I can say is, heaven help us."

Exactly.

Much has been taught me by the reactions of those who have read this pamphlet. This is my opportunity to reply to some of the questions they have raised not because I am in any sense an "authority" on the topic but because I am convinced that by this process many of us may think more deeply and reverently about love. And that, in any degree, is gain.

I. WHO ARE THE PERSONALITIES YOU ONLY INITIAL? WHY THEM?

This is, in a way, irrelevant. They are already dated. But in every generation there have been and will be celebrities who are as famous for their flouting of convention as for their considerable talent.

These persons are only symbols of three different riptides felt in youth. First, the notion that love is lust and that "it is all;" "nothing but seething glands." Second, the notion, traceable in part to the Puritan tradition, that it is really a very nasty business. And third, the notion, for which religion has too often been responsible, that love and marriage are of the Fall and even of the Devil and that the really religious person avoids them in their romantic modes.

These attitudes are not always explicitly voiced. But they are "in the air" and they drench us, and they mislead us.

My own experience was the tendency to jump from one superstition to another and only slowly did it dawn on me that my own heritage was that love was of the Spirit. And Christ's Spirit is what you seek to build love, to repair it, and to heal it when it is sick. The Temple, more than anything, confirmed this insight which, I then realized, had been in and between the lines of all the prophets.

II. WHAT DO YOU REALLY MEAN ABOUT THIS "FIRE" IMAGE AND THE IDEA THAT YOU CAN ONLY LOVE WHEN YOU ARE BELOVED OF GOD?

Love is with some justice described variously as a quality, a feeling, a relationship, a virtue, an attribute. The prophets get to the root of it by making it a substance-power. As a remarkable and radiant mother once said to me, "Love is a wave on the ether." She meant that it flows, pours, saturates and, like light, can be described both as a wave and a "corpuscular" thing. Love centers in God and radiates from Him.

To be less abstract, I rejoice in the wonder of the Prophet who sought words to designate the glory and brightness of God: His later key sentences such as: "Our God is a consuming fire." "Our Father dwells in everlasting burnings." "His eyes were as a flame of fire." This is not a glaring, nor unpleasant kind of fire, not the fire that scorches and lays waste. Instead, it is heightening, shadowless, intensifying. It melts and refines and hallows. So when Nephi says, "He filled me with his love unto the consuming of my flesh," he is also saying he has been filled with the Spirit of God. When Joseph Smith says, "My soul was filled with love for many days, and I could rejoice with great joy, and the Lord was with me," he is basking in the reflected glory of the Lord's love. And when President McKay says love is "the divinest attribute of the human soul" he is saying we can become love-receptive, so much akin to God that we individually generate and call down such love by our very nature.

III. WHAT DO YOU MEAN BY NATURAL AND SUPERNATURAL?

In Latter-day Saint writing, "soul" means "whole," the whole man, body and spirit. Sometimes the word "natural" is used as a synonym for "evil." But Parley P. Pratt taught me the distinction more clearly. He says:

> Some persons have supposed that our natural affections were the results of a fallen and corrupt nature, and that they are "carnal, sensual, and devilish," and therefore ought to be resisted, subdued, or overcome as so many evils which prevent our perfection, or progress in the spiritual life. In short, that they should be greatly subdued in this world, and in the world to come entirely done away. And even our intelligence also.

> So far from this being the case, our natural affections are planted in us by the Spirit of God, for a wise purpose; and they are the very mainsprings of life and happiness—they are the cement

of all virtuous and heavenly society—they are the essence of charity, or love; and therefore never fail, but endure forever.

There is not a more pure and holy principle in existence than the affection which glows in the bosom of a virtuous man for his companion; for his parents, brothers, sisters and children.

These pure affections are inspired in our bosoms, and interwoven with our nature by an all-wise and benevolent being, who rejoices in the happiness and welfare of his creatures. All his revelations to man, touching this subject, are calculated to approve, encourage, and strengthen these emotions, and to increase and perfect them; that man, enlightened and taught of God, may be more free, more social, cheerful, happy, kind, familiar, and lovely than he was before, that he may fill all the relationships of life, and act in every sphere of usefulness with a greater energy, and with a readier mind, and a more willing heart.

What then is sinful? I answer, our unnatural passions and affections, or in other words the abuse, the perversion, the unlawful indulgence of that which is otherwise good. Sodom was not destroyed for their natural affections, but for the want of it. They had perverted all their affections, and had given place to that which was unnatural, and contrary to nature. Thus they had lost those holy and pure principles of virtue and love which were calculated to preserve and exalt mankind; and were overwhelmed in all manner of corruption, and also hatred towards those who were good. (Pratt, *Writings*)

IV. YOUR QUOTE FROM ALMA SEEMS TO BE A CONTRADICTION. YOU ADMIT LOVE IS FULL OF FEELING YET ALMA TALKS AS IF PASSION IS OPPOSED TO LOVE.

Alma knew whereof he spoke. "See that ye bridle your passions." Focus on the word "bridle." What is a bridle for? To kill, to diminish, or even to limit the spirit and power of the steed? Never. "What's the matter with that horse?" asked the farmer of a wild pony that rammed into trees, fences, and barns. "Is he blind?" "No. He just doesn't give a rap!" Youth are pulled by all the connotations of "wild" and depressed by all the connotations of "refined." But we are given our bodies and our emotions not to destroy but to ride. They magnify our feelings and increase enjoyments. The body is a step up in the scale of progression. Indeed all that is in the earth has been given for the "blessing and benefit of man." There will never come a time when sensuous (which is different than sensual) awareness will be separated from us. Ultimately we need not lament the use of physical art forms for the presentation of our message for this earth itself is the future heaven. Once you have trained your pony you can direct him with the merest nudge and ride with a "confidence that waxeth strong in the presence of God." Eventually you can "give him his head" and ride free, bareback like the wind.

The bridle warns you that to "get excited" without listening to the voice of the Spirit (the rider) will bring a complaint, "Hey, wait for me!" More often, the Spirit will speak, before, during and after, "That is not what I really want—it is not even what you really want. Let's go this way." The body, on the other hand, rarely complains at the Spirit. Somewhere Brigham Young pleads that when you are full of evil passion "let" (he does not say "make" because the spirit is already powerfully motivated) the spirit take the lead. When the body is susceptible to the Spirit, it can always catch up to the Spirit. But I defy anyone to get the Spirit in harmony with the runaway body. It will warn, throb, and enwrap you with a sense of loss: "Why did you do that?"

V. BUT WHAT DO YOU MEAN TO "BURN WITH A BRIGHTER, RICHER FLAME?"

Nowhere in Holy Writ do I find a blanket condemnation of passionate love. The attempt to disentangle love from passion is ingenious and persistent but in my judgment a complete failure. The scriptures are full of a belief in increase . . . expanse . . . intensification. Laws describe the effects of its abuse. There are always impulses in us that try to trick the laws: Some supposing that love is all of the flesh end with ashes. Others supposing it is all of the spirit end with deprivation and despair. Actually, the Lord pleads for us to feel all we can and the Prophet Joseph promised that the nearer we approach perfection, "the clearer are our views and the greater our enjoyments." But he added that this was a condition which we do not arrive at in a moment and that only slowly do we overcome the evils of our life and lose every desire for sin. But we do not lose desire. Instead, we increase in it. The "rules" or "laws" of mature love are not just in a college handbook. They are written in the constitution of man and woman. Like those of a tennis game, they are what make the game meaningful, and fun. There are no rules on how powerful is your swing, how rapid or intense your volleys and returns; only on where is in bounds. If you go out of bounds in tennis you lose a point. If you throw your racket, you may lose a friend. In love, if you violate the laws of the nature of love, you harvest a kind of hell. And the hell is in you.

VI. ISN'T IT A STRETCH TO SAY THAT "THERE IS SIGHT AT FIRST LOVE?" PEOPLE DO SOME VERY STUPID THINGS WHEN THEY ARE IN LOVE.

Granting that under the title "love" many absurdities are celebrated. But youth should know that the real thing improves their very eyesight. Years ago Elder Harold B. Lee in YOUTH IN THE CHURCH spoke of the story of the "enchanted cottage" and said that "lovers are beautiful to each other." He implied that there is an enchantment that others do not see. Time vindicates him. I have learned that love not only opens new discoveries of the world and the self, it creates a beautiful secret, it brings out the loveliness of the loved one.

If you doubt this, I suggest a long-range experiment. In your school yearbook mark the pictures of five "pretty girls." And five ordinary or even unattractive girls. Years later compare the "pretty girls" who have ignored or flouted the Gospel and family love and the "ordinary girls" who have lived it. In every case you will find, on my hypothesis, that those who have been in touch with the circuit of righteousness will carry a bloom and beauty missing in their friends. Couples, in fact, who magnify such love come to look like each other. It has been said that the Spirit, "contributes to beauty of person, form, and feature." Yes, literally and in the long run, inevitably. The marks of a life of cheap aversion, perversion, and inversion also show vividly. Both are especially potent around the eyes.

VII. HOW MANY OF US REALLY HAVE THE POTENTIAL FOR THIS KIND OF LOVE?

Love is a kinship of likenesses. "Intelligence cleaveth unto intelligence, virtue loveth virtue, light cleaveth unto light, mercy hath compassion on mercy." We only come to see ourselves and others when we have a measure of revelatory love. In fact, if we view mankind through our mole hole of pettiness and spite, we can hardly see them at all. With the eyes of love one can, at times at least, recognize that we are mingling with potential gods and goddesses. How tempering is the recognition that someone that today "galls on you" is a person who, if you could see him in eternity would bring out your deepest tendency to kneel and worship. Christ may have been the only one who kept that measure of intelligence and kinship constantly. He never saw anyone as a no one. He saw all as immortals capacitated for everlasting splendor.

After three decades of counselling, Elder Spencer W. Kimball says the most basic problem in courtship and marriage is "selfishness." And in our time, I interpolate, it is the sicker selfishness. What we want for ourselves is not good but often, a second-and-third-nature-kind of bad. In a society where, "anything goes," everything goes . . . down the tubes. Studies show that victims of this sickness not only cannot love "all mankind"; they cannot love even one other person. Which means, of course, they cannot love themselves.

The truth is that the soul of every child of God comes with an overwhelming need and an overwhelming capacity for such love. When we settle for less, we settle for a flute. But what the Father would have us have is the whole symphony. Even in our darkest moments we are really preparing for it. (And "prepare" is the way we should spell "wait.") To lose the vision of the possibility is to lose the motivation to live for it. And that, in the counsel of those who have heard the Divine music, is to lose all.

Chapter Three

THE LANGUAGE OF LOVE AT HOME

 One day an executive exploded into his office building, slammed his brief case down on a chair, and let out an irritated moan.

"What is it?" we said.

"My wife. That woman wants the sizzle more than the steak."

We were all puzzled, and no doubt looked it.

"I got up at 5:30 this morning, I washed, waxed, and polished the floors, cleaned the garage, cut the lawn, planted flowers. At 12:00 I showered and was about to leave. As I walked out the front door, my wife said: 'John, the least you could do is kiss me good-by!'"

Now, switch the scene. A woman sat on the other side of my desk. She was pretty, smart, and utterly indignant.

"It's hopeless," she said. "Just hopeless. My husband is so supersensitive to everything I say. The merest little word and he sulks, or walks out, or takes it out on me some way. Why can't he understand? Women nowadays are to be heard as well as seen."

99

FOUR ESSAYS ON LOVE

These two stories may suggest on the surface that the fly in the marriage ointment is what men don't say, and what women do. It seems to be a problem of language, and almost entirely that. Professor Higgins posed the question: "Why can't a woman be like a man?" One answer is for the same reason a man can't be more like a woman. Higgins and Liza were reconciled when they learned to communicate. But they are a rarity. Apparently, man and woman by their nature have learned to hear different languages and to refuse to speak the language of the other. And in no realm is the more disastrous than in the communication of what matters most to both of them . . . their love.

Are we willing to consider the possibility that neither of us knows the language of love; that we are cramped, as it were, by our native tongue; that we have a kind of blind spot which is a matter of pride? But if man learns the native woman language and if woman learns the native man language, even a few sentences of it, the response can be overwhelming. Not just meaning develops, but power. Our words help recreate the very love they "express" and it comes back in return waves with a "purr."

So what should John have said? And what should Mary have said?

Well, wait just a minute. Let's first consult the experts on the wondrous power of love, best traced in its effects, not in abstraction. Everyone knows there is a lot of silliness and nonsense in people's heads about love and that in no area do we prove ourselves more gullible. But every parent has known the utter frustration of having a budding son or daughter say, "What is love? How do I recognize it?" After some clumsy sentences about what it is not, and what it is like, we usually end by saying, "Well, I just can't tell you. But I can promise you that when you are in love you will know."

In short, we can define and describe love no better than we can define atomic fallout. But they are quite similar in that their transmission reaches to the most minute processes of the most tiny cells in the total human self. But there is a difference. Nuclear fallout is the most quietly destructive force we presently know. But

100

love is the most quietly creative force we have ever known. Does this sound like a poetic overstatement? Let's turn to the scientists.

Did you know that many bodily ills can be definitely traced to the absence of love? Loved and loving people are measurably healthier (and far better able to cope with pain). Did you know that among orphan newborn infants if mother love is not replaced in some degree with nurse love, two out of three infants will die? Did you know that a loving personality is almost magic in his effect on animals like collies or spaniels—who seem to wag their tails and long to do good in response; on plants like roses or carrots which seem to bloom and grow more luxuriously (the real meaning of the "green thumb"); and even on inanimate objects like washing machines which seem to sing and whirr in response to the delicate hand? The explanations are complex, but the fact is verifiable.

Some will reply, "You just mean that love leads people to do things, to act with greater care. It is the painstaking concern, not the love, that has these effects." Have it your way, if you insist. But whether the effects are direct or indirect, (and my own view is that they are both) love is the indispensable element. Did you know that therapy for mental illness is almost impotent unless one first establishes the tokens, at least, of love: acceptance, willingness to listen, and unconditional concern with the core of the person, not just to his maladies or defects. One reason psychiatric aid does not heal better and faster, is that radiant love cannot be created at each office call—not even for a fancy fee. Did you know that the love quality in a home is as tangible to the perceptive person (and especially children) as temperature, humidity, and the color of the drapes? Infants spot this more quickly than children and women more quickly than men. Did you know, finally, that one out of three people, according to some studies, walks down the street surrounded by an emotional moat, defying anyone to cross it? He would rather count on hate, and often unconsciously generates it, because he has never been able, with anyone, to count on love.

Now, porpoises communicate. So do robots and telstars. But

love — roots in soul

until we get into the area of imagination, of creativity, of esthetic sensitivity, of joy and laughter and sacred silence, our communication is all on the surface . . . and still not in the service of love. It goes deeper still.

Love is spiritual in content and portent; its roots are in the soul and, beyond the soul, in the very soul of the living God. Some will admit that there are facets of love that are "spiritual" which they consider to be the more-or-less inexpressible center of man—his depth self—his heart. Such persons may not believe in God or immortality. Fewer recognize love to be Spiritual (with a capital S), a derivative influence of the Spirit of God. Those who do still tend to say love is earthbound, that God makes marriages only to finally break them. Fewer still see it as Divine . . . that the love of man for woman—the love we know most powerfully in heart and hearth—"emanates from the fountain of Eternal Love—God . . ." Emanates from because it centers in. Strangely, those who insist "God is love" utterly deny that He is a Lover. But we say He is— the highest personage capable of the most soul-inclusive and harmonious love in the galaxy.

Husbands by and large glut themselves on techniques and talk to many good and wise "plain men" who claim to know how to deal with wives. But they miss this. The most common complaint I hear as an amateur marriage counselor is that "We don't communicate; we don't talk things out; we just go our separate ways." Assumedly, the cure is "talk to your wife more often." My notion is that the deeper thirst is not communication. It is communion. An infinity of things may remain unsaid or on the other hand said. But what is wanted—indeed needed—or else love suffocates, is the swifter and often non-verbal relationship; being in soul touch, when you are at the same depths or heights, or just in ordinary old-shoes comfort. You are aware of each other at the core. Talk alone can conceal as well as reveal. Much of the banter and pleasantry of our conversation does. But not if we are in the same inward rivers together.

Thus, being soul to soul, even for a brief time, goes a long way. A taste is quite enough to put a new color on the world; make the drudgery worth it and still worth it. Memory and the anticipation merge in your consciousness. It is amazing how much else you can lack or never get around to; how little else you actually need. It keeps the ship of marriage afloat and moving. But I submit that if this is lacking (or as it lags or slumps toward zero), the oil of gladness is gone. The frictions groan and stick and jam up, and then words are quite impotent.

Now, a woman who is a woman delights in being thought a woman. She is "romance conscious," and in the deeper sense love-anxious most of the time. The language she understands includes a lot of little (and in the opinion of many husbands, disgustingly trivial) things . . . the tender touch, the kiss good-by, the kiss hello. A morning of robust yard work is not as eloquent to her as the quiet smoothing of little hurdles, the gallantry of an open door, helping her with a chair or a coat and these mean a hundred times more to her feelings of response than the salary you bring home. Having an eye for the new dress or even the old one, saying the word, however inept or inadequate, about this salad or that gravy, remembering and repeating utterly trivial sentiments and events which no grown-up man can remember unless he wants to, no woman can forget even if she tries.

After a couple were married on one February 23, the husband said, "I'll never forget our anniversary. It is the day after Washington's birthday." The wife replied, "I will never forget Washington's birthday. It is the day before our anniversary." This is not a difference of memory. It is a focus of concern. Any man can remember to speak his love through an anniversary, if he cares enough.

Universally, woman is made rich by the man who knows that these touches mean everything. This language speaks to her being. She will respond to it and give.

Now, turn to the man. A man who is a man delights in being thought a man. He is "authority conscious." The language he understands includes a lot of little things, the language of her listening even to his nonsense, the language of biting her tongue instead of lashing with it when his decisions are finally made, the uninterrupted phone call, the restraining of curiosity, the controlling of the disposition to inquisition. (A wife who insists on knowing nothing will eventually have everything, but the wife who insists on knowing everything will eventually have nothing.) The man understands the language of flexibility in a wife who respects his final decisions (even the decision of not to decide), or even so trivial a matter as when we leave the party. The man comprehends the exhilaration of a woman who, when his delays bring him home late, offers a brighter welcome instead of a dismal doghouse.

Universally, a man is responsive to these little matters which mean everything to him. He will rise to them and give in kind.

It is easy to say that we should prize other languages. If a man brings home the bacon and doesn't complain at the wife's food, and shows sympathy for her lot, then why all this emphasis on the romantic sizzle? "If I don't like your cooking, I'll say so; otherwise you are doing fine," said one. On the other hand, if the wife works day and night to tend his kids, to keep his home, and put up with him, then why all the childish emphasis on the authority sizzle? Does a woman have to pander to this desire of a man to have the last word?

Well, it may be strange, as some cynics say (a weird kind of insecurity which mature people ignore), it may even seem ridiculous. But the cost is so little and the results so vast that it is tragic to work against the grain. You can't speak without speaking a language. And this language is magic. Why not master it and speak it?

One hesitates to cite examples of this, to select some "butterfly wings and honey" and ignore (or suppress) the warfare of soul that is no doubt behind the achievement.

But in President David O. McKay and his companion we see a man and woman who show how intimate is the power of these languages and how fabulous the outcome.

Just look at some little-known little things:

> In his Temple marriage counsels (his son has published them in his *Home Memories*) the whole thing comes down to courtesy and

kindness . . . these he says are the instruments to keep charity—caritas—love (from Paul's Psalm of love in 1 Corinthians 13) alive. He says they are the product and the measure of soulful trust.

Through thick and thin he has always reserved Friday night for his wife, a time for her to anticipate, count on, prepare and dress for (and, I suspect, save up for). This is not just a time for "going out" but a time of communion. It is astonishing how much drudgery a woman can endure if she can vision and depend on such a time to break out.

He has the charm to concentrate. "I have noticed," says one close to him, "that when he looks at you with those blue eyes he gives you his whole attention, never wavers." When he is with you he is with you. So it is with his wife.

In his eighties, as his legs began to fail, it sometimes took him a full minute to help her with her chair taking tiny shuffling steps. But he insisted. He still insists on rising to meet guests, and it is a huge struggle.

"Never shout at your wife," he counsels, "unless the house is on fire."

He treats all women as ladies with the same invincible resolve of tenderness. I saw him, at eighty-five, kneel at the side of a car and pick up a pair of gloves that a young lady had dropped. He draped them over his left arm as he returned them.

His wife in return, has cultivated the language of support. There is very little truth in his twinkling comment on board ship once, "I am President of the Church: all except Sister McKay." He dares to write to his children (who know), "Never to this day have you heard your mother say a cross or disrespectful word."

In his nineties, he stopped President Tanner who was pushing his wheelchair into a Temple corridor and said, "We must go back." Back through elevators and halls they went. Why? He hadn't kissed his Emma Rae good-by.

To daughters and granddaughters who are in the awkward and gangling stage of growth, instead of embarrassing comment he says, "What a queen you are becoming."

105

He has given a wise clue to all leaders as to all parents: credit before blame. Instead of pouncing on what has been done wrong, he awaits the opportunity to praise what has been done right—maybe the first or only time.

He reinforces by praise.

One can no doubt be syrupy and sentimental about all this. The example may seem too good to be true, unbearably sweet. But it is true. And that should move us to be better instead of worse.

When we turn to children, we find the same point. Children have a language they understand, intuitively all languages. They hear the intent inside words. It is important to speak it. We know a couple who saved for many months to make possible a full week vacation for their family in exciting places. They purchased a new car, bought special camp equipment, then decked their children out in sports equipment and swim suits. As they traveled, they stayed in plush motels, ate the finest food, visited luxurious places and elaborate zoos, amusement parks, and resorts. The trip was a real production from beginning to end. As they were approaching home, the father said to one of his daughters, "What will you remember as the best part of the trip?" She answered immediately and with tears, "When you, Daddy, got out of the car and walked with me along the beach to find sea shells." That was the one sentence of love she really heard . . . the language of being with, being for, being hers.

Children, too, are somewhat a mirror of their parents. Much of the present confusion and misery of our time is the constant "who's who" battle that is going on. The child wants to know the head and the heart of the home. And what are the parents really saying to each other? Their own impressions of the way to act and how to react are always in high fidelity. (Every scratch is recorded.) Children need first of all to see the way adults express love. Their language at its best will be the language learned out of the experience of consideration, kindness, courtesy, and trust. Children need to know what it feels like to have their parents not just be with them but all with them. There are books from anthropologists, sociologists, psychologists that say the first three years or so are the era when the light of love either reaches the child or does not, and the rest of their lives are made or mutilated by the experience.

Children illustrate, too, that the communication of love is at least 90 per cent not verbal. Even when pleasant words don't mean anything unless the tone, the face, the gesture, the touch, the subtle atmosphere is as tangible as a tub bath. The most constant plea of disturbed youngsters in our time is either, "My parents don't understand me," or "My parents don't care." But when the caring is deep felt, when there is a warm cloak in the home, understanding follows . . . enough understanding to be enough. We all have that thirst to be understood. But usually we mean that we want to be loved, understood or not. More security and power to cope with life has come through the mere holding of hands than through the Niagara of nagging that is part of many homes.

It is important to distinguish the outcries of children (including us grown-up children) in terms of their deeper need, not always at face value. When a child cries out that someone, say a brother or sister, has cheated or is selfish, etc., the proper answer sometimes is, "I am hungry, too, let's eat." (Most arguments, you notice, occur just before dinner when the blood sugar is down.) When there is a pandemonium in the playroom and tears over some trivial thing, the proper response may be, "It has been a long, hard day; let's all go to bed." When a child is trying desperately to do the opposite of what we say, he may be neither perverse nor rebellious but just thirsty—thoroughly thirsty for the light of love. Contention often reflects the absence of attention. And the proper response may be a silent, lingering, "let me hold you," an honest hug. After which, like a ship in the Panama Canal, we can be lifted to a higher watermark and embark on a new ocean of understanding.

By some uncanny innate gift women are alert to sounds that men do not notice. More remarkably, they detect multiple shades of meaning. Even a young girl asked for the first time to babysit can swiftly grasp the various messages of cry or outcry or whimper. She knows the sound of hunger and thirst and discomfort and fear and anxiety and all the subtleties of the churning of the infant life. She even knows the varieties of silence and what they mean. "Things are too quiet in there." Who taught her? There are no books on these themes because there are no rules. But there is deep-laden knowledge. Training and concentration can enhance this gift but its tacit promise seems to be within the soul of every woman.

By exact analogy a woman sensitized by love can hear the strains at every level in her husband, and marvelous is the woman who knows when and how to answer them; who can open the purse of her emotional riches and match or modify or mellow or magnify—as the flash of the moment makes need—every one appropriately. If she can, she is a poetess however halting may be her use of words. Her language is the richer and infinitely more flexible and effective language of reaching out.

Has some choice friend ever rung your doorbell in the midst of a family furor, when each was set against the other, dagger-eyed and menacing, and has the person entered with the fresh air, quite unaware of the strains and therefore untroubled by them, and has not the whole complexion of the home, your hearts, life itself changed? Everyone notices that. And the ability to throw that aura around misery is one of the greatest household skills in the world. And one of the rarest.

With all this in mind, here are two specific suggestions. First, if I were newly or oldly wed, in the spring or autumn of life, I would have a time set apart every day as dependable as tropical rain when I could be in some sense really with my companion. It would be a time when we both could concentrate on nothing but each other and speak to each other sometimes in complete rapport, telegraphing the sense of being supremely important to each other. This I would take as a religious ritual. The closer to worship, the better.

Second, if I were a parent, I would set a time at some stable point in the schedule, when each child could count on my drawing a curtain and giving my whole attention to a concentrated review of his feelings, his present struggle. My leading question might be, "What has been your happiest moment, and what your saddest, today?" It may surprise me what strains weigh him down, and what things have lifted him up. I would hold this time so sacred that the child would be aware that short of terrible emergencies I would be his and his alone for this time, and whatever we said or didn't say my goal would be a kind of X-ray treatment—to relieve him of the blight of indifference.

Finally, and in summary I would remember—remember constantly—that we live in a world of massive dehumanization when most of the sounds we are paid and encouraged to make are machine sounds. Our lives are about as booming and crowded and frenetic as a steaming New York subway at rush hour. It is a world of automation and mass productions—a world where, outside the home, we are mere cogs and where we often treat each other as things, not as feeling persons. It follows that the one thing left to be produced at home and by hand is LOVE. And right now our gross national product is at an all-time low.

Chapter Four

HUMAN ANGUISH
AND DIVINE LOVE

The subject of this chapter is not a question or problem, not an academic toy. It is the human predicament, as we can show with three illustrations:

1. An irreverent but it seems to me downright honest critic of Christianity argues, in effect: "If a child is born to me healthy and bright-eyed, you tell me, God loves you. If a child is born without a spine, or hopelessly paralyzed, you tell me, God still loves you. Frankly, that kind of love I can do without. If God causes or permits events that my worst mortal enemy would not permit, then the idea of both 'God' and 'love' are absurd."

2. One day my family sat watching the big screen production of *The Greatest Story Ever Told.* There you see a sinister Herod send his soldiers to Bethlehem. Then come the screams of mothers, glimpses of blood-smirched swords pulled from children's bodies. Then you see Mary and Joseph, who have received divine warning, walking peacefully with their Babe toward the safety of Egypt. As this scene closed, the hand of my little girl came into

mine and she whispered, confused and frightened, "Daddy, didn't
Heavenly Father care about those other children?"

3. Third is the universal outcry of our own souls in tribulation.
"Why?" and "Why me?" We speak much of worthiness and
blessedness—and of keeping the laws that result in both. But there
is, in this cry, the sense of what some call "frustrated entitlement."
We have, in measure (not perfectly, but close enough), kept the
law; and we aspire through dark and dawn to do better. We feel a
certain inner worthiness, a sense of "deserving better." But no
better comes. Only worse. And still worse. Others we think of as
less worthy seem to prosper. We do not demand ease. But we
sense injustice, and we crave, alas, a little mercy. And how long
can we hold on to this slipping rope and pray in faith, let alone in
love?

All this supposes that God both can and should prevent such
misfortunes; that, indeed, a good and loving God would.

Let us look at the "can" before we look at the "should."

In a seminar at Harvard we were devoted to the analysis of
St. Augustine's writings. And if you've read any of Augustine's
confessions, you're aware that his early life, to say the least, was a
traumatic and guilty one (much more so, incidentally, than Joseph
Smith's). In his doctrine of creation, Augustine begins with a
premise that God is all-powerful. To him that means that all
things—all else beside God, including space, time, and the souls
of men—were created by God from nothing. The puzzle arises as
to why a being of unlimited power should have chosen to create
such a universe as this: of pain, torment, and (on some views) endless damnation. Specifically, evil and the devil were among the
realities God chose to create. Why, being good, could He—would
He—do such a thing?

This eventually led Augustine to the topic of freedom. How
was it that God could make us from nothing and yet condemn us
or reward us for actions? Why hold us responsible when He alone
is responsible? "For," said one student in the class, "a God who is
totally the cause of what is, is indirectly the cause of everything
one does." At this point I raised my hand and said with a measure

of restraint, "Isn't it at least conceivable that man is not totally the creation of God?" There was a roar of disapproval, and students began to hammer at me from both sides. When things quieted down, the professor said, "Well, the idea cannot be ruled out arbitrarily." But the idea is ruled out by the major wings of Christianity. Otherwise, on their view God would not be absolute.

Actually, as soon as it is recognized, as in modern revelation it is, that there is more than one eternal will in the universe—indeed, an infinity of such wills or autonomous intelligences—we have cut the thread that supposes God can "do anything." In all-important ways even He, the greatest of all, can only do with us what we will permit Him to do. Our center selves can agree or disagree, assent or resent, cooperate or oppose. To say, as the scriptures do, that God has all power and that He is almighty and that with Him all things are possible is to say that He has all the power and might it is possible to have in this universe of multiple selves.

And as soon as it is recognized, as in modern revelation it is, that there are eternal inanimate things which are subject to laws, to "bounds and conditions" which God did not create but himself has mastered, we have cut another thread of illusory omnipotence. For on the extreme view of His power, whatever purpose He may have had in creating everything from nothing, those same results could have come if He had created nothing from everything. To say "that is impossible" is to say with the Mormon that God cannot "do just anything." He can do only what our wills and eternal laws will permit. In short, He did not make us from nothing, and what He makes of us depends on us and the ultimate nature of a co-eternal universe.

Thus we make it too simple when we say in an hour of stinging misfortune, "Couldn't God have prevented this?" The related issue is, ought He to? The "bounds and conditions" mean that if He prevents this He cannot achieve that.

For example, growth, expansion, development. We can only grow with stress and distress. There is no muscle without strain, no character without the fiery trials of action and conflict. "There must needs be opposition" not only implies an eternal resistance in the nature of things; it also implies that man needs opposition in order to become what he has it in him to become.

So much on the "can."

Now on the "should."

Our outcry supposes that if we really were in charge, these things would never happen. But is that completely the case? Did we come into the world "without our own permission"? On the contrary.

We chose knowingly to enter our present state or sphere of existence. That's a fascinating idea. You may have heard a teenager who says shiftily, "I did not ask to be born," to which it can be truly replied, "Oh, yes, you did." There's another answer you can indulge for comic relief. When your child says, "I didn't ask to be born," you can say, "If you had, the answer would have been no."

We did knowingly elect, and not only choose and elect but also prepare for this world with its real risks, its real opportunities, and its real promises. And those who say they are in their second childhood are unwittingly speaking the truth.

The question thrown upward, "Why did you get me into this?" needs translation: "Why did I get me into this?"

Imagine, for a moment, what it might be like to have a close, intimate friend who is sworn to stand by you and protect you, and maybe even die for you. Suppose he is a native of a foreign country and has never heard of modern surgery.

If he were ushered into a room where you were undergoing an appendectomy, saw the doctors and nurses cutting away and the evidences of blood and pain, he would likely jump to three conclusions:

1. That these persons were trying to torture you, perhaps take your life.

2. That all this was being done against your will.

3. That the highest service he could render you would be to pull them off.

But, you see, he would not only be mistaken; his assumptions would, in fact, be the exact opposite of the truth. These highly trained persons are intent on helping you. Truly, they could spare you the pain of the operation; but only at the cost of your life. It is at your request; and your willingness, even anxiety, to "go through with it," however you might shrink, led you to sign a statement justifying any medical action they deemed proper while you were still incapable of further instructions. (You might even have cautioned them: "Don't pay any attention to my groans. Do what you have to do.") And third, the worst thing he could do would be to prevent or even to interrupt their carrying out their task.

Life is an obstacle course. And sometimes it is a spook alley. But the before was a time of visioning the after. And some of our prayers are like the gamblers,' "Give me the money I made you promise not to give me if I asked for it." What does a true friend do in such a case? God will honor our first request, to let us go through it; and He will provide us (let Him) with the way to make it bearable. More, to make it productive.

THE PUNITIVE THEORY

Now, let me mention the theory about evil that we all theoretically reject. In practice it often still clings to us. We deny it of others, suspect it of ourselves. It's the so-called "punitive" theory of evil, to the effect that whenever someone suffers, it is because he deserves to. All misfortune is the product of sin. We "had it coming."

To be autobiographical for a moment, I recall an early clean-cut instance of temptation and submission. As a small fry, by jimmying my bank with a screwdriver I recovered my small fortune of seventeen cents, went to the store, and bought fig newtons. (You know, Augustine worries about the fact that he once stole pears. He spends a whole chapter on the question, what motivated him to steal? "Why did I do it?" My problem was figs.) While I was riding home on my tricycle—I must have been five or six—a hose or something in the sidewalk upset my bike; I tipped over and badly scuffed my knee. What was my first thought? Yes, you know very well. So with all of us. And I submit that though you are now mature and no longer believe that all mishaps and

114

suffering are retribution, still the thought lingers. "What have I done to deserve this?" Sometimes that is an appropriate question, and there is an answer. But I want to talk about the instances where the answer is not that you have in fact deserved it, but something else.

Now, since I've mentioned a classical theory, let me mention three others, which, as I believe, are misleading, even or especially when they contain a kernel of genuine insight.

IS EVIL "ALL IN YOUR MIND"?

One theory which arises and is motivated by supreme reverence for the perfection of God is what is called the illusory theory; that all we call "evil" is but the phantom of our minds. It is not real. God, this view reasons, is perfect. Therefore, His creation is perfect. But there is nothing He did not create. Therefore, everything is perfect. This is the nerve of Christian Science, and is characteristic of certain kinds of absolute idealism and certain strains of Buddhism. All concrete suffering is addressed with: "It's all in your mind. You are a victim of error. If you saw aright, you would know that this world is perfect."

One reason why this will not hold up is that in a perfectly good universe even the illusion of evil would not be present. We are imperfect in seeing it otherwise. Admit that imperfection and then why not others? Some of us, in moments of puppy-love, may have heard impatient people say: "But you're not really in love. You just think you're in love." And we may have walked away saying to ourselves: "Maybe so. But to me it could not have more impact if it were real." Haven't you ever wanted to say in response to, "It is all in your mind," "I would rather have it almost anywhere else"? Some mental illness is more resistant to treatment than physical.

Now, there may be certain things we call evil that are not, and vice versa. But that theory is not adequate.

IS IT "THE POINT OF VIEW"?

A second theory is the perspective theory, especially evident in Leibniz and satirized by the Voltaire of *Candide,* a book that is painfully funny. What does Leibniz say? He says, as Browning does at the end of his poem, "God's in his heaven, all's right with the world." Under the aspect of eternity, the view of God, the "evil" is acceptable because this is the "best of all possible worlds." Evil is "compossible" with good to achieve a greater good. To which Bertrand Russell replies, "How do we know that good is not in the world to achieve a greater evil?" This theory differs from the illusory theory because it implies that if you get out of perspective, evil is really there. There is common sense support for this. If the Venus de Milo was on a stand in your home, and you walked up to it and put your nose right against the base, you would see something, but it would hardly be beautiful. On the other hand, if you recede too far in the distance, you only see a gray cylinder on the horizon. Again, beauty is lost. But from the proper perspective the Venus de Milo is beautiful, even without her arms.

By the same token, a man with a magnifying glass can look at the nose of his girl. But he shouldn't, unless he wants to see a volcanic field. In aesthetics there is a famous theory by Bullough which talks about psychic distance. He uses a clever analogy. Suppose you suddenly see a fire on the dark horizon. You drive closer. The clouds hang over it in a majestic way, and the eerie colors of the flames play on people's faces and on the firemen with their hoses and ladders. This calls for a camera. It's magnificent. But if you happen to be the owner of the uninsured house, all of that beauty is lost on you. Perspective does make a difference.

One problem is: We don't have God's perspective. And Leibniz offers us few suggestions on how we can come closer to it.

THE PRIVATIVE THEORY

Another view is the official theory of the Roman Catholic Church. It's called the privative theory. Essentially, it's an attempt to exonerate God from creating evil. It says that evil is not a positive reality, but is the absence of good. Now, that is a bit puzzling until you realize that the absence is not in vacuo, it is an absence in something. If, therefore, I call you evil, what I really mean on this theory is that you lack or are deprived of certain kinds of goodness. The devil is a privative being. He just isn't any good.

How satisfactory is that? Not very, I'm afraid, if what one wants is either comfort or conquest. For if anyone had said to me, as I lay in the hospital on one occasion, that I was not really experiencing pain but only the absence of pleasure, I would have wanted to throw him out as a mockingbird.

Evil does have positive effects, positive force in the world, like it or not. Hate begets hate, just as love begets love.

Privative evil (for example, ignorance) is only one kind of real evil.

THE INSTRUMENTAL THEORY

This leads up to a view which, I think, is at the center of the restored gospel. It is sometimes technically called an instrumental theory. It does not say all pain is the result of transgression, nor deny its reality, nor resort to perspective or privation. Evil, suffering, and stress are seen as eternal. They will not be destroyed, but can be utilized. They can be instruments to something good. Indeed, the highest work of suffering is a work of perfection—godliness.

THE LORD'S WAY

But let us bring this insight down to loam soil.

In the original of the letter Joseph Smith wrote from Liberty Jail (it belongs with Psalms—a masterpiece of religious writing) are several moving insights which precede the deeper one. For one thing, the Prophet is told that "thine adversity and thine afflictions shall be but a small moment" (D&C 121:7). That "small moment" turned out to be five more years of incredible struggle. But comparatively, it was a small moment. That, I submit, is a real force in facing suffering. To believe—better, to know—that this lonely or crushed or deprived or painwracked condition won't last forever, that it will somehow, somewhere be over, is a balm of comfort. Without it, certain kinds of suffering would indeed be unbearable.

Then the Lord says, "Thou art not yet as Job." Here we have the "It could be worse" appeal. Always it could be. Says a Persian legend, "I complained that I had no shoes until I saw a man who had no feet." A little bit of chiding comes through in the Lord's reminder and promise that, unlike the situation of Job, "Thy friends do stand by thee, and they shall hail thee again with warm hearts and friendly hands" (vv. 9, 10). Some friends are the wrong kind and add to our burden. They come in and say: "All right, Job. Let's have it! What have you done wrong?" "Job's comforters," they're called. No comfort. Job didn't have the memory of awful transgressions. The roof fell in on a loving, righteous man. That was redramatized in MacLeish's modern play *JB*. A literary critic said, "The thing that amazed me was to see JB, after it's all over, say, 'All right, let's start again,' not knowing but what the whole roof would fall in again." That is the tingle and threat of Job's life. And of ours. But those of us with faithful friends are always better off than he.

Nietzsche is often classified as an anti-Christ. But Nietzsche saw some things more clearly than his religious friends. For several years he had a continual toothache. He talked about "eternal recurrence." And his attitude was heroic. He arose each morning, set his jaw, and said, "Once more." He had the courage to go on. He would not be weak, would not yield to it, and was "grateful for small mercies." That is Jobian trust.

There is an "if" clause in the Lord's answer. "If" what? "If thou endure it well" (D&C 121:8). The original, I'm impressed to say, says "If thou art faithful and endure it well." Faithful. Faith-full. That makes a great difference. "If thou art called to pass through tribulation" (D&C 122:5).

I know many people who comfort themselves with what technically is "Deism"—the absentee landlord conception of the Lord; that He "wound up" the universe and then turned His back on us, and consequences fall without intervention.

If that outlook helps anyone, I would be the last to seek to overturn it. It does seem to me that the message of this letter qualifies it, for the Lord says, "their bounds are set, they cannot pass"

(v. 9). Who were bound? Joseph's enemies, his betrayers, his "false brethren"—all men. They could only go so far. Some will say such a promise is not made to us. But it is.

Indeed, promises have been given (yes, many are conditional) that require the Lord to be very close. One day when I was on an airplane we hit some terribly rough air. The wings were swaying, it seemed, like seagulls. Even the flight attendants became alarmed, and that only distressed the passengers more. I was reading, feeling very calm. When I asked myself why, it was because of a promise given me in a blessing that, in effect, while in the path of duty I would travel safely, "whether on land, sea, or air." Musing about that, it seemed to me apparent that either the Lord had adequate foreknowledge that no airplane (which must include this airplane) would crash with me aboard. Or, lacking that foreknowledge, He yet had such power that in the event such a disaster were imminent He would somehow intervene and prevent it.

Take either or both of those alternatives and apply them to the thousands (millions?) of inspired promises made to the Lord's covenant people (even scriptural generalizations such as "If you will . . . then I will"). It means His power and knowledge in our lives are much more intimate and ever-present than we tend to dream. He may, indeed, be closest when we suppose Him to be farthest away.

THE GLORIFICATION OF EXPERIENCE

The most vital and, in some ways, miraculous insight of all (and the most trying, perhaps, to our faith and love) is this: that after describing a whole catalog of anguish which, either previously, then, or later, the Prophet faced, including betrayal, and having his young son thrust from him by the sword, and having "all the elements combine to hedge up the way" (have you ever felt like that, when everything goes wrong?), and seeing the heavens "gather blackness," and having "the very jaws of hell gape open the mouth," the Lord reveals the pearl of great price:

> Know thou, my son, that all these things shall give thee experi-
> ence, and shall be for thy good. The Son of Man hath descended
> below them all. Art thou greater than he? (D&C 122:7–8)

What good, we may ask, could possibly be served by such affliction?

Brigham Young said of Joseph (and leaving out the fact that, as John Taylor wrote, he has done more, save Jesus only, for the salvation of man than any other man who ever lived) that he suffered more in thirty-eight years than many men could in one thousand; that loosing one thousand hounds on Temple Square after one jackrabbit "would not be a bad illustration of the situation of the times of the Prophet Joseph" (Young, *Journal of Discourses* 10:315; see also 2:7); but that he was more perfected, more sanctified, more glorified because, in Joseph's words, "I have waded in tribulation lip-deep; but every wave of adversity which has struck me has only wafted me that much nearer to Deity."

The Prophet teaches and embodies this marvelously. Hence, it is not enough to endure stoically. Many religions and individuals have based themselves primarily on stoicism. Spinoza did. Under that discipline you endure only because you're saying to yourself, "It had to be." Why? "Stark necessity." That can keep you alive in a prison camp or in the loss of vital organs. It has been known to. "It has to be. Face it. It's necessary." That is resignation, a kind of fatalism. But it's not enough. The greater thing is to endure suffering with faith in the Son of Man, which enables it to yield its perfect result, which means the fulness of the powers of godliness.

Now, let me briefly address two immediate objections. It has been said that too easily this view of suffering slips into asceticism; that is, to the notion that the more one suffers, the better he is. Soon he is led to take the initiative: to deny himself, to sit on nails, to refuse himself normal appetites. Elements of asceticism can be found in both Catholic and Protestant traditions, and even more in Eastern religions. Hence the *New Yorker* magazine cartoons showing emaciated men reclining on stones or nails. Do we take the position that this is desirable? No. Mormonism is not ascetic. It does not recommend that you suffer by your own hand.

I want to mention one anecdote: A brother, who shall remain nameless, during the Zion's camp episode deliberately sought to be bitten by a snake, thus to exercise faith and fulfill the promise of the New Testament that if believers should take up any deadly serpent it would not harm them (see Mark 16:18). He was rebuked by the Prophet. The point that emerged was that if, in the line of one's calling, one is in fact bitten, he can expect relief. But one who deliberately seeks it is entitled to no such promise. And so it is, I submit, in all forms of human affliction. Suffering ought to be the by-product of purposeful service, not a self-obsessed way of life.

A second objection, more difficult to remove, is that if this is the purpose of mortality, this coping with opposition, how is it that so few really do triumph? How is it that so many are themselves overcome? Instead of their souls developing, they shrink; instead of their characters being made into steel, they are made into a tormented shambles; instead of taking on the fluids of godliness, they take on the acids of degradation. That is a hard, hard question. It is even harder if we point to innocent suffering. In children's hospitals, for example, some of the patients are well below the age of accountability, with congenital maladies—no arms, no eyes, and many other afflictions that few can bear to see. This is one of the most difficult realities to reconcile with meaning and purpose, and with God's love.

But regardless of purpose, I want to mention three solid facts that are worth remembering. I find them hidden in the Prophet's letter.

The first point is that there are limits to what we can suffer; there is a cut-out point physically and psychically beyond which we lose full alert consciousness. There are kinds of cancer that attack the bone which could persist to unbearable scales of pain except for the fact that there are other organs in the body that, eventually, almost like a fuse, break the circuit. I am among those who are grateful that that is so.

121

Second, pain does not compound. When it is over, it is over. That's not true of some other kinds of evil, but it's true of pain. Emily Dickinson years ago wrote a poem that fits here. I don't understand the words and yet I understand her. Two lines are indelible. She says: "After great pain, a formal feeling comes. / The nerves sit ceremonious, like tombs." In the next stanza is the phrase, "quartz-like contentment." She is describing the glory of relief. Pain once past does not compound. It is simply over.

Then third, as C. S. Lewis reminds us, it is important to remember that no one is suffering all the pain. We can talk about the fact that if we count right now the number of people in our office or other place of employment, each is suffering a certain amount. We'll call that amount X. If you multiply X by the number of people there are in the world, you come up with four billion X, shall we say. Then add the whole animate creation—the animals, the sparrows, and the insects. William James once said, "This universe will never be all good so long as one cockroach suffers the pangs of unrequited love." Now you have multiple billion X. The Prophet said God desires the happiness of all His creatures. And think of all that pain! But notice: no one is suffering multiple billion X. Each is only suffering his own X.

Only if we could see the outcome, even for the most bitter among us, could we estimate how wise—as well as brave—we were to enter mortality. The miracle is that the same thing— suffering—can have totally opposite effects, depending on how we respond to it.

I know a man who has received 3,200 blood transfusions. He is a hemophiliac, hospitalized with inner bleeding every three weeks. He tells me that each experience is like a "baptismal" . . . "I come out of the hospital feeling like the blackboard has been wiped clean, anxious that it shall not be filled again." He copes with pain with an expression on his face that would convince a child he was praying. He can inspire a depressed soul, whether in the hospital or out. He has not known a day or a night in fifteen years without pain—and I don't mean low-level aches like stiff muscles, pleasant pains. I mean the hydraulic pain of bone joints being forced apart by his own life-giving blood. Some other people I know have suffered far less but are bitter, cynical, hateful.

How can good and bad fruit come from the same experience? The divine and the devilish? It is the root of our spiritual nourishment that changes everything. That is the scale on which we came to be weighed.

Wrote B. H. Roberts, who identified with Joseph Smith as closely as did his blood brothers:

> Some of the lowliest walks in life, the paths which lead into the deepest valleys of sorrow and up to the most rugged steeps of adversity, are the ones which, if a man travel in, will best accomplish the object of his existence in this world. . . . The conditions which place men where they may always walk on the unbroken plain of prosperity and seek for nothing but their own pleasure, are not the best within the gift of God. For in such circumstances men soon drop into a position analogous to the stagnant pool; while those who have to contend with difficulties, brave dangers, endure disappointments, struggle with sorrows, eat the bread of adversity and drink the water of affliction, develop a moral and spiritual strength, together with a purity of life and character, unknown to the heirs of ease and wealth and pleasure. With the English bard, therefore, I believe: Sweet are the uses of adversity! (*Gospel*, 289–90)

Yes, sweet, but bittersweet. "No chastening for the present seemeth to be joyous, but grievous: nevertheless afterward it yieldeth the peaceable fruit of righteousness unto them which are exercised thereby" (Hebrews 12:11).

As a little boy, I watched a favorite uncle bring in willows with cocoons on them. Later, we saw the slight opening in one and, boy-like, put our ears up against it to hear the seemingly audible groans and strains of the moth. It wanted out. And we wanted to help. We did not ask our wiser uncle. We just found some scissors and with one decisive snip we shed that moth of its confining coat. It lay there, and we waited for it to fly. But it never flew. It quivered and finally died.

The mortal experience will enable us to fly if we will let it, help

123

it, use it with faith in the Christ who "descended below all." The message of the modern prophets, to a man (and none of them, if you look closely, has been spared any of the vicissitudes), is this: that there is meaning and purpose in all things we suffer; that "all these things" can be for our good, however empty and barren they now appear. The elements of truth in the classical theories have been caught up in a greater whole. The Lord is not playing games with us. The outcome will far exceed the price; the "chastening" will be visioned as our blessing, the fiber of soul-quality will leave no regrets, only infinite and eternal gratitude, and the partnership we forged with Him before we entered this refining fire will loom as marvelous to us as does the face of a loving mother in the eyes of a child who has just emerged from his fever . . . healed, alive, and prepared for life, eternal life, life like God's.

The Prophet Joseph Smith declared: "All your losses will be made up to you in the resurrection, provided you continue faithful. By the vision of the Almighty I have seen it" (Joseph Smith, *Teachings* [1938], 296).

CHRIST
AND THE
INNER LIFE

Preface to
Second Edition

In the aftermath of a series of lectures a young lady with hurt eyes waited patiently. When most of the others were out of earshot, she said: "The one thing that makes sense to me in your lectures is that sin is death. I know something in me has died. How do I regain it?" I answered in only one word: "Christ." Her whisper was almost desperate, "But how?" Because I have heard that desperate whisper from many, and in my own heart, I understood.

Near the close of the book of Malachi the Jehovah of the Old Testament who was to become the Christ of the New promised, "Unto you that fear [reverence] my name, shall the Sun [Son] of Righteousness arise with healing in his wings; and ye shall go forth, and grow up as calves of the stall" (Malachi 4:2). From his lips the promise came again at the end of his ministry among the receptive multitude in the Land Bountiful (3 Nephi 25:2). And again, at the beginning of the restoration of our day, this was one of the first about-to-be-fulfilled prophecies spoken from on high to a stripling boy-prophet (Joseph Smith—History 1:36, 37).

"With healing in his wings." The Hebrew root of *wings* is *kanaph*, which denotes extremity, or uttermost part; "healing," one might read it, "in his hands and feet." In another sense, by his own extremity—the most unfathomable time in a lonely place on the side of the Mount of Olives—Christ's healing and nourishing power were generated. It is, likewise, in our own extremity that we rediscover him.

But is Christ's way a way of sacrifice, self-denial and discipline? Or is it a way of adventure, fulfillment and joy? The answer to both of these questions is yes. Within each soul, as in his, it is both. The world is dying to righteousness and therefore to life. The Saints are dying to sin and therefore to death, "growing up as calves of the stall." One cannot experience the heights which Christ promises without knowing, by vicarious or actual experience, the depths. And repentance through Christ is complete when we would rather die (die physically) than sin (die spiritually).

In the conviction that we are, most of us, radically undernourished by his light and life and spirit, and that our need for that nourishment is continual and crucial, I have written these brief essays. Undergirding them all is the strongest assurance of my soul: Christ is indeed a matter of life and death.

TRUMAN G. MADSEN
MAY 1978

Chapter One

THE PREEMINENCE
OF CHRIST

The convert who inspired this essay (originally published in the Millennial Star) is John Heidenreich, now deceased. Often he related how he and his wife sat, during the period of their conversion, late into the night, saying over and over again, "It is so awesome, so marvelous. Christ is a personality." Here is an attempt to illustrate this magnificent Mormon insight: that Christ is both the revelation of God as He is and the revelation of man as he may become.

"If I ever joined that Church [The Church of Jesus Christ of Latter-day Saints] it would be for another reason: In their midst Jesus Christ has a place of preeminence as in no other Christian group."

So spoke a minister some years ago to other churchmen who were discussing the "temporal achievements" of Mormonism. Today he is a Latter-day Saint.

What, I asked him recently, did he mean? He had been for at least twenty-five years a careful student of the New Testament, of theology and of history. He had voiced with conviction the creedal statements that Jesus was "Very God, God Incarnate." In prayer, in worship and service, all, he had been convinced, "in His footsteps," he had not only been captivated by the personality of the Master but had experienced, as he witnessed to his congregation, the Spirit of Him. Christ, he often said, was not just a theological concept, but a "daily walk, a fellowship, and a present help." What of this had he now abandoned, and what had he deepened? What, beyond it, had he discovered? What difference did it make?

As we quietly discussed things sacred, clarity of thought and purity of feeling seemed to combine. Though much, we both knew, failed to get into words, we came to "understand one another, and both [were] edified and rejoiced together" (D&C 50:22).

This man had been pushed and pulled in the religious world between two competing conceptions. Neither had the full "ring of truth" to him, nor could he envision a combination or compromise of them. To take either of them seriously was, he felt, to dilute the events of Christ's life, particularly of Gethsemane and Golgotha, into mystery or meaninglessness.

At one extreme, Jesus Christ was viewed as substantially God the Father, the Triune God of Greek and Latin creeds. His earthly ministry involved all the contradictions of incarnation: the Immaterial became material, the Creator of man became a creature of man, the Non-spatial and Non-temporal became subject to space and time. Thus, though God and man would remain forever unlike, Divine Incarnation, by a miracle open only to the eye of faith, "reconciled" them. Today Christianity, either by its seven sacraments or by grace mediated through the biblical word, was supposed to achieve the end envisioned, salvation.

On this view Christ's "sufferings and death" were those of an Absolute Being. In spite of the paradoxical declaration (at the Council of Chalcedon) of both the Full Divinity and Full Humanity of Jesus, it was clear that ultimately the manhood of Jesus was only the clothing of his Godhood.

At the other extreme, Jesus was viewed as simply another man, unique in some matters of degree but certainly not in kind. He lived a remarkable, and at times inspiring, life. Like so many reformers of society, he estranged those he sought to aid; and he met death at the hands of the Roman authorities.

On this view Jesus' sufferings and death were tragic. The prayer of Gethsemane was simply an effort toward courage to face crucifixion. But events in the life of Jesus had little more significance than those in the life of Socrates. To talk of atonement, in legal, psychological, or spiritual terms, was to indulge in nonsense.

Unable, then, to deny that there was something divine about Christ, yet unable fully to believe that he came into the world either wholly God or wholly man, this man sought a more adequate answer.

The re-revealed insights of the restoration came to him, as to others, with a convincing power that was unspectacular but pervasive. He saw in these insights the drawing together of the truths of opposed conceptions, the overcoming of their errors, and a flood of light on the meaning of life, both of Christ's and of our own.

Jesus Christ was not God the Eternal Father. He was the pre-eminent Son of God. He was not "another man." He was the Firstborn in the spirit and the Only Begotten in the flesh. His past, which he had in common with God the Father, is the foundation of his role as Christ. To ignore or deny these insights would be to miss the power and promise of his mission.

Without detailing the vast effects of these promises, including the resurrection, let us focus on Gethsemane and view it through the manifestations of the Son of God in modern revelation.

Out of our own spiritual lack, our own darkness, there may be profound misgivings about the significance of Jesus' example and his relationship to us.

We may say, for example: "He was God from the beginning. He was not really akin to us." The truth is that he lived, as we lived, in the preexistent presence of the Father. He offered himself as the "Lamb slain from before the foundation of the world," and assisted in the organization of the earth. In these senses he was the greatest of all and was properly called God. But mortality was for him, as for us, a genuine second estate, a growth process, and in it

> he received not of the fulness at first, but continued from grace to grace until he received a fulness. (D&C 93:13)

We say, "But surely he was not subject to the conditions we face." The truth is that though by his divine inheritance he had power over death, he was tempted in "all points" as we are, yet without sin, suffering pains and afflictions and temptations of every kind. He did not "ascend up on high" until he had

> descended below all things, . . . that he might be in all and through all things the light of truth. (D&C 88:6)

> Behold I am the light; I have set an example for you. (3 Nephi 18:16)

> . . . What manner of men ought ye to be? Verily I say unto you, even as I am. (3 Nephi 27:27)

We say, "But because he did not violate the law of God as we do, he does not know the burden of guilt and alienation." The truth is that, because of his sensitive, uncompromising submission to the Father's will, he was the only one of the Father's family who did not transgress, who in no sense deserved the throes of sin and the withdrawal of the Spirit. Yet through his life, climaxed by those incomprehensible hours in a garden beyond the brook Cedron, he suffered "according to the flesh" (Alma 7:13) the pains and afflictions of all forms of human evil-doing. He participated, voluntarily, in the actual conditions that follow in the wake of deliberate transgression. He experienced the cumulative impact of our vicious thoughts, motives, and acts.

We say, "But it was easier for him because of his divine Sonship." The truth is that it was infinitely harder. He endured "even more than man can suffer except it be unto death" (Mosiah 3:7), a suffering how exquisite and hard to bear we know not, which caused him

to tremble because of pain, and to bleed at every pore, and to
suffer both body and spirit—and would that I might not drink the
bitter cup, and shrink—

Nevertheless, glory be to the Father, and I partook, and finished
my preparations unto the children of men. (D&C 19:18, 19)

We say, "But he was never left unto himself, as we are." The
truth is that few can comprehend his cry on the cross, "My God,
my God, why hast thou forsaken me?" Who can fathom his reit-
erated statement in modern times,

[I have] trodden the wine-press alone, even the wine-press of
the fierceness of the wrath of Almighty God. (D&C 88:106; italics
added)

We say, "But what he did twenty centuries ago cannot affect
me now." The truth is that the Christ who was is the Christ who
is. Out of his life came a full knowledge of righteousness and a
full knowledge of the effects of sin. This means that no human
encounter, no tragic loss, no spiritual failure is beyond the pale of
his present knowledge and compassion, gained

according to the flesh—that he may know . . . how to succor his
people according to their infirmities. (Alma 7:12)

No act in all history has united intelligence, virtue and mercy
in so complete an expression of love, a love which, even dimly
glimpsed, will "draw all men unto him"; a love which underlies
his present living roles as Mediator, Revelator, Savior, Redeemer,
and Advocate with the Father.

We say, "But his glorious triumph has no bearing on my own."
The truth is that, exalted now on high, Jesus Christ is he by whom
"the life and the light, the Spirit and the power" are sent forth by
the will of the Father (D&C 50:27). Through Jesus Christ, we may
come unto the Father. The pattern ordained is a pattern which
begins when the light of Christ is given to every man who enters
the world. It leads, if it is honored, into the first principles and
ordinances of the gospel. It includes sublime blessings—
knowledge, glory and communion, love, joy and peace, blessings

CHRIST AND THE INNER LIFE

even of personal visitation—which transcend the highest aspirations of martyr or mystic and of enlightened souls in every age.

But beyond these we are promised,

> . . . If you keep my commandments you shall receive of his fulness, and be glorified in me as I am in the Father; therefore, I say unto you, you shall receive grace for grace. (D&C 93:20)

Moved, as few who have tasted of his Spirit and love fail to be, with "a broken heart and contrite spirit" we may walk the path whereby to become, as President David O. McKay repeatedly testified with Peter, "partakers of the divine nature" (2 Peter 1:4). As Christ was begotten of God the Father both in spirit and in body, so by being begotten of Jesus Christ through his laws and ordinances we may be transformed into a like condition of complete fulfillment, sons of God in the fullest sense, like him.

> Wherefore, all things are theirs, whether life or death, or things present, or things to come, all are theirs and they are Christ's and Christ is God's.

> And they shall overcome all things. (D&C 76:59, 60)

Whatever else the "preeminence of Jesus Christ" means (and it means much, much more), this is the heart of it. Today, in testimonies of living witnesses and the radiance of lives endowed with his power, in the spirit and operations of his priesthood, and in the covenants and ordinances of his holy temples, the drama enacted in the land of Palestine is conveyed to our souls. As his sufferings and death brought man nearer to God and to each other, so individually, as we seek to comprehend him, he brings us ever nearer the realization of our own spiritual destiny, that the light in us may grow " . . . brighter and brighter until the perfect day" (D&C 50:24). No hour of life need be so despairing or so exalting as to blot out his voice:

> Listen to him who is [your] advocate with the Father, who is pleading your cause before him—

Saying: Father, behold the sufferings and death of him who did no sin, in whom thou wast well pleased; behold the blood of thy Son which was shed, the blood of him whom thou gavest that thyself might be glorified.

Wherefore, Father, spare these my brethren that believe on my name, that they may come unto me and have everlasting life. (D&C 45:3–5)

Chapter Two

THE COMMANDING
IMAGE OF CHRIST

*The fable which introduces this chapter was originally presented
at a devotional assembly at BYU. The central point is that honest
   doubt about spiritual realities must be open, else it becomes
   blind dogmatism; or, in other words, that darkness can only
   be removed by light. The related theme: until our image of
   Christ is compelling, until we rid ourselves of the images in
   our heads which make him a colorless, weak and, as one
   said, "vanilla-flavored" dreamer, we will not respond to his
   will. Hence the title "The Commanding Image of Christ."*

Aware of the contrast of light and darkness, I sat down one day
and wrote a fable. Have a little fun with this, because all too soon I
am going to be very serious. It is entitled "The Sunstriking Fox."

Once there was a young fox who lived on the dark side of the
moon. He associated with the other young foxes and took
for granted their outlook. They claimed to be influenced by a
moonlike orb on the other side called the Sun. No one had devised

a way of traveling there, but some testified of visionary glimpses. And all claimed to be subject to its warmth.

Eventually the fox went away to school. When he came back he was often seen talking to himself. That, on good authority, is normal for most foxes, in school or out. One of his friends followed him around until he knew what he was down to. The monologue went something like this:

"All this talk of sunshine is really moonshine. I am going on a sunstrike. I will dig a hole way down. Then I will say, 'I don't know.' If anyone tries to argue I will say, 'No young fox knows.' And if they push me I will say, 'No fox can know.'"

He had no more than finished his hole than his friend came up, or, rather, down.

"What do you mean," he began, "no fox can know about the sun?" He had to say it loudly three times, because when someone is that deep in a hole it is hard to hear.

"Just that," the fox replied. "Foxes are using the word 'Sun' and no one even knows what it means."

"Interesting," replied the friend. "But that means you don't know what the word means . . ."

"All right," said the fox. "What I am saying is that I don't think anyone, especially young foxes, can know about 'the Sun.'"

"I see," said the friend. "How do you know that no young fox knows?"

"They just don't," the fox replied. "They just think they know."

"A remarkable assertion," the friend replied. "To be sure of that, or even fairly sure, you must have looked up all the young foxes. That is quite a fox hunt."

"No," said the fox. "I haven't counted all the heads in that way. Let's just say I doubt that they know."

"That brings us to you," said the friend. "Which is where, I believe, you both started and ended on this subject. You say you don't know."

"That's right."

"What would have to happen in your life to enable you to know?"

"I am not sure. But something that I can really see and that others can too."

"Very good," said the friend. "The Sun's rays are, if not presently seeable, at least presently sensible. But let us pursue your test. Convince me of your doubts."

"That is tricky," replied the fox. "But in the case of my doubts there is evidence that even you can see. I act as though I don't know."

"But do you admit that people with belief in the Sun can support their beliefs by action?" asked the friend.

"No."

"It is curious, then, that you should expect me to take actions as evidence of your doubt. But if action is the test, I have noticed that you do not live down to your disbeliefs. Last week I saw you reading a book on the delights of sunbathing. And hidden in your hole is a sunlamp."

"Well," the fox said, feeling a little sheepish in his fox clothing, "at least I am not psychological. I am not guilty of wanting there to be a Sun."

"Granting that wishful belief does not make a thing true, nether does wishful disbelief make it false. Where are we then?"

"Yes, indeed," said the fox, "where are we?"

"We are to this point," suggested the friend. "You are required to admit, after all, that there may be a Sun. But by your own tests I would say that as long as you stay underground you are not likely to come up with much evidence on either side. You are the cause of your own eclipse.

"Anyway, for all your expressed doubts you haven't yet been around enough to know that young foxes don't know, therefore not enough to know that no fox knows."

Moral: There are no atheists in foxholes (Madsen, *Fables,* 18–20). (Though some may claim to be.)

Now I want to talk seriously about the sun. Modern revelation tells us that Christ "is in the sun, and the light of the sun, and the power thereof by which it was made" (D&C 88:7). I would remind you that your 20–20 eyes, of whatever color, are no good without light—no good at all.

There are three great statements that the Living Christ has made of and about himself in our generation. I would like to submit them to you with an example or two and then bear witness.

CHRIST'S INTELLIGENCE

One is the staggering statement, "I am more intelligent than they all" (Abraham 3:19). The late B. H. Roberts took that to mean that Jesus the Christ is more intelligent than all of us together—all of the inhabitants of the human family in this world and in all of the multiple worlds of which Christ was Creator.

Whether or not that be the correct reading, one thing is clear, that somehow—and it is the nature of that "somehow" on which I want to dwell—Christ came to a "fulness of the glory of the Father" (D&C 93:16). The glory of God *is* light and truth, or in other words, intelligence (D&C 93:36).

But how? Are you aware that in one experience the Prophet had, the Master approached him and said, in substance, "Joseph, I want you to read this. Then I want to tell you why I wanted you to read it. It is something John wrote about me." What does it say? It says something which is blasphemy in relation to the creeds of Christendom. Therefore, so much the worse for the creeds. It says, "He (Christ) received not of the fulness at the first." He became what he became—and it says it three times. But he was called *the Son* of God because he received not of the fulness at the first, but "continued from grace to grace until he received a fulness" (D&C 93:12, 13, 14).

Now we leave that context and refer to another one, this one from the witness of a man who considered himself hopeless, a man who knew the *Angst* of life (the German word that means more than anxiety), a man who had said at one point that he yearned for his own extinction. He didn't just want to cease to suffer; he wanted to cease to be. But something happened to Alma. And talking about it later to one he loved, his son, and others, he said he knew that though Christ could have looked upon mankind with the aid of the Spirit to behold what we are suffering, that wasn't enough. He (Christ) forever left the realm of spectator and entered the realm of participant. And, says Alma, he suffered in the flesh pains and afflictions and temptations of every kind. (See Alma 7:11, 13.) And any theology which teaches that there were some thing he did *not* suffer is falsification of his life. He knew them all. Why? That he might succor, which is to say comfort and heal, this people. He knew the full nature of the human struggle.

At this point a very large issue weighs us down and distorts the commanding image of Christ that we would otherwise have. It is this: "Yes, he may have overcome the world and temptations, but he does not know the meaning of failure. He does not know what I know—which is alienation, anguish, and knowing that the light has been withdrawn and that I deserve to have it withdrawn. These he does not know because he lived a sinless life."

But in modern revelation he has answered that.

I would like to tell you of one of the settings of the answer. It was within four walls, ironically named Liberty Jail, where the Prophet Joseph Smith spent four months without liberty—one of the few times (if there were any) when he was in despair. Much has been said of his physical suffering. It was terrible. But it is nothing compared to what he suffered inwardly, in the consciousness that his people were being whipped, house-burned, raped, and driven mercilessly, and he could do nothing—not even write to deny the faith by saying, "Forget Mormonism and go back home and refuse the word."

He said at one point, "If I had not gotten into this work I would back out, but I cannot back out. I have no doubt of the truth."

That sure conviction cost him the helpless awareness of hundreds upon hundreds of Saints in misery.

He cried out, and you know the answer. I select only this much: "If thou art called to pass through tribulation, . . ." and there continues a series of "ifs" (D&C 122:5).

I cannot help recalling that that is the way the adversary taunted the Master: "*If* thou be the Son of God . . ." (Matthew 4:3; italics added).

All of these "if" clauses in the description of section 122 were fulfilled in fact:

> . . . If they tear thee from the society of thy father and mother and brethren and sisters; and if . . . thine offspring, and thine elder son, although but six years of age, shall cling to thy garments, and shall say, My father, my father, why can't you stay with us? Oh, my father, what are the men going to do with you? and if then he shall be thrust from thee by the sword,
>
> . . . know thou, my son, that all these things shall give thee experience, and shall be for thy good. (D&C 122:6, 7)

Joseph might not have been able to believe such a statement from a distant observer, but then the Master said: "The Son of Man hath *descended below them all*" (D&C 122:8; italics added).

In Gethsemane he knelt and endured all the feelings that you have had or can have in the blighting experiences of this world, "that his bowels might be filled with compassion."

CHRIST'S POWER OF LIGHT

The second great statement of and about Christ is from modern revelation: "That which is of God is light; and he that receiveth light, and continueth in God, recieveth *more* light" (D&C 50:24; italics added).

More light! We have light that enables us to see objects here, but the light of Jesus Christ lights the *subject*. It illumines minds and spirits—yes, and bodies. Listen to his promise:

> And if your eye be single to my glory, your *whole bodies* shall be filled with light, and there shall be no darkness in you; and that body which is filled with light comprehendeth all things. (D&C 88:67; italics added. Compare D&C 84:33; Luke 11:34–36)

Then elsewhere in the scriptures we find the third great statement by Christ.

CHRIST'S NATURE AS OUR DESTINY

"The day shall come when you shall comprehend [it does not just say apprehend] even God, being quickened in him and by him" (D&C 88:49).

Men have stood at pulpits and elsewhere—great men—and have testified that their knees have never buckled, that as one said of another, "He had nothing to hide." We have had monumental men who did not need redemption as much as they needed power, and who never fell very far from the communing light of which I have spoken. I cannot bear that kind of testimony. But if there are some of you who have been tricked into the conviction that you have gone too far, that you have been weighed down with doubts on which you alone have a monopoly, that you have had the poison of sin which makes it impossible ever again to be what you could have been—then hear me.

I bear testimony that you cannot sink farther than the light and sweeping intelligence of Jesus Christ can reach. I bear testimony that as long as there is one spark of the will to repent and to reach, *he is there.* He did not just descend *to* your condition; he descended *below* it, "that he might be in all and through all things, the light of truth" (D&C 88:6).

If only one person who reads this can feel what I feel of the Spirit of God as I bear witness to the truth, this book is worth the effort.

Chapter Three

CHRIST AND PRAYER

We all have a crying need for intimacy in prayer—to be "on the level," to stop pretending. Such prayer is self-revealing. But it is also Spirit-giving. And "he that asketh in Spirit shall receive in Spirit" (D&C 46:28), the Spirit of Christ. We pray "in his name" as we pray through him, and with him.

YEARNING PRAYER

They say it in one way or another, those who really know about prayer: Only yearning prayer gets through.

But there are three kinds of yearning.

We yearn when we mean what we say. But is that enough when we are asking the impossible, or when what we are asking is, if we could only see, not for our good?

We yearn when we care terribly. But is that enough when what we care for, however desperately, is a fist-shaking fixation that presumes God visions less of what is needed than we?

We yearn, finally, when we do not only mean and care intensely, but when at the core we are as anxious to listen as to ask. We yearn when we will to abide counsels already given and to respond to him and his way in his way.

So long as we are set in our uninspired desires, not moldable, we must break our hearts before we can pray from them. So need we wonder why the heavens are often like brass over our heads?

Humble prayer is the beginning of communion with the highest of personalities—God and his Son Jesus Christ—of higher ways of seeing and feeling, as it were, through their eyes.

Achieving this is a life-process, not a five-minute thing. But it is sometimes closer in youth than in maturity. Youth may keenly grasp the truth: that even at our best we are like the blind boy who walks with his friend. He does not believe, nor bluff, that he is self-sufficient. Instead, he responds to the slightest nudge. (If you would know the power of God, try, early in life, to become just this dependable in your dependence.)

As this happens, the whole being becomes the instrument that vibrates upwardly. No special words are needed, no forced tone of voice, and no dramatic play-acting.

Then we begin to recognize the "first answers" to our prayers—the answers that always come before the others.

What are these?

They are subtle flashes that register within. And they are real. They center "in your mind and in your heart" (D&C 8:2) and are, therefore, a perfect blend of thought and feeling. They come with a serene flow of power that is light and warmth and liquid surety. They whisper a "Yes," or a "No," a "Wait," or a "Be still," a "Trust," or an "Act well thy part."

This is what a modern young prophet calls "breaking the ice" and "obtaining the Holy Spirit" which cause "the bosom to burn." He says that much emptying ourselves of unworthiness and much filling ourselves with concentration precedes it. He says we should strive to stay on our knees until it happens.

And how do you know that this burning is of God? Maybe it is just hope, guess, or wish.

You know by the quiet verdict of your own inner being. (And you know just as well when you don't know.) You know because the haunting "I doubt" and the painful "I fear" are swallowed up in living light. You arise this time, after many darkened times, tinctured with gratitude. With the glow comes a lingering love, a knowledge that forges resolve to do what must now be done, and a faith for next time.

Thus yearning prayer becomes burning prayer—burning-with-the-Spirit prayer.

Happy is the youth who prays for, and then until, and finally with, this subtle flame. For "he that asketh in Spirit shall receive in Spirit" (D&C 46:28).

FACETS OF PRAYER

My point is simple. The "how" of prayer is both the hardest and the easiest thing in the world. Enos proves it.

My inspiration is simple: I know a lot of twentieth-century lads just like Enos.

One afternoon Enos went to hunt beasts in the forest. He was not long in the wilds before he forgot all about hunting. He forgot because he began remembering. " . . . The words which I had often heard my father speak concerning eternal life, and the joy of the saints, sunk deep into my heart. And my soul hungered" (Enos 1:3, 4).

He went to his knees and began to cry unto God for relief from his backlog of evasion and cover-up.

How long did he pray? All the day long and on into the night. What could he possibly say in all that time? He tells us that his prayers were "many long strugglings," a searching and exposing of his own depths, a pouring out of his "whole soul."

The answers (and they came in what a present-day apostle calls "finished sentences") overwhelmed him. "Enos, thy sins are forgiven thee" (v. 5). He prayed on, and still on, for those he loved, for reassurance about the future. And when testimony came, here too he "knew that God could not lie; . . ." (v. 6), "wherefore [his] soul did rest" (v. 17).

And he returned home.

So what was unique about Enos's prayer?

THE HIDDEN SELF

It was a "wrestle which I had before God," a pouring of his real self into the cups of his words. But it was more than that. At one level we all indulge the daily cliches and more or less "mean" them,—"forgive us, help us to overcome our weaknesses." At a deeper level we voice actual present feelings, even when they are raw, ugly, miserable ones. "Father. I feel awful—I am racked with anxiety." But there is a deeper level, the inmost, which often defies words, even feeling-words. This level may be likened to what the scriptures call "groanings which cannot be uttered." Turned upward they became the most powerful prayer-thrust of all. There *is* a wordless center in us.[1]

Such, we may be sure, was the tone of Enos's prayer through those long hours. He learned that when we break the veil to our deepest self, we also penetrate the veil of heaven.

FAITH IN CHRIST

Some might say, "Well, maybe Enos just had more faith than the rest of us; most likely he was gifted that way—naturally religious."

Look more closely.

His words suggest that he was surprised to learn he had *any* faith. He knelt, mostly convinced of one thing: a weighty mountain of his own great need. That kind of mountain, incidentally, only faith can move. After many hours of pleading and receiving, he was in awe. "My guilt was swept away" (v. 6), he says. He did not doubt that it was gone. But marveling he cried out, "Lord, how is it done?" (v. 7).

Note the puzzling answer. "Because of thy faith in Christ, whom thou has never before heard nor seen" (v. 8). It was true he

---

1. "We know not," says Paul, "what we should pray for as we ought; but the Spirit itself maketh intercession for us with groanings which cannot be uttered" (Romans 8:26). The Prophet Joseph changed "groanings" to "strivings." Thus we can through the Spirit pray wordlessly and soundlessly.

had not seen Christ. But he had heard *of* him in the living words of his father.

But notice also that the instant he had a directing touch from the Lord, it brought a staggering inner influence. "My faith began to be unshaken in the Lord, . . ." (v. 11), he writes. Thus kneeling there, the mustard seed became a tree!

There is, in all of us, an eternity more of faith in God than we tap. Kneeling to reach for faith we may find we are reaching *with* it. That, Enos shows us, is another facet of real prayer.

Enos's response was total. He did not run away holding his ears. We have the hindsight (the record is clear) to know that Enos became a lifelong dynamo, that he was "wrought upon by the power of God" (v. 26) unto the end of his days and that he "rejoiced in it above that of the world" (v. 26).

That performance demonstrated the foresight of God. Surely the Lord knew the real Enos—that he had it in him to use divine power as the Lord himself would use it. That enabled the Lord to answer Enos without reserve. It must be a different problem for the Lord to answer cool, bargaining, curious, all-talk-and-no-listen prayers.

And isn't it true that, unlike Enos, we pray for God to change everything—except us?

We hear much today about an identity crisis—the ache that comes when one begins to ask in a lonely, anguished way, "Who am I? What do I really want?" A lot of fuzzy answers can be given. But what is needed is a change of question. If you are, as I happen to know, an embryonic Enos, then you can kneel in some forest or other and ask from the center of you, "Whose am I?" And I testify that when you expose your hidden self and latent faith and when you honor the quiet voice with total response, you will make a double discovery—yourself and God.

That is what prayer is all about.

Chapter Four

TWENTY QUESTIONS

"Reflect often upon thy past," is one of the profound counsels of patriarchs. The very remembering of spiritual things becomes, in a measure, a reliving of them, an antidote to dark days and self-doubts and a quiet form of worship. "Twenty Questions" was given at a summer school devotional at BYU. All will answer some of these queries with a "Yes." My hope was (and is) to evoke in the reader not just answers, but deeper and more personal questions like these about the influences of Christ in the life of the Church.

Some years ago on my return from the East, just after finishing my Ph.D., I had a phone call. A voice I hadn't heard before said, "Is your name Madsen?"

"Yes."

"You just finished your graduate work?"

"Yes."

"Was your field philosophy?"

"Yes."

"Philosophy and religion?"

"Yes."

148

"Are you still active in the Mormon Church?"

"Yes."

"How come?"

I played dumb, which isn't too hard for me sometimes, and said, "What do you mean, how come?"

"Well, anybody who has studied as you have—I don't see how you get these things together."

I said, "I'll be happy to talk to you about it." So he eventually invited me to dinner. It turned out—and I do not want to tell you too much about him because you might know him—that he was a fairly prominent young man who had graduated from a university which shall remain nameless, and that while at the university he had become seriously disturbed. He was now married, and, as we say, "married in the temple." He was curious still and wanted to know if there was a way of reconciling his former faith and his new discipline.

Well, it was an interesting evening, and it was not until we had spent nearly an hour merely sparring that I suggested we do something else. I said: "Look, I think we can get to the root of this if I ask you some questions and if you answer them with a simple yes or no. In advance, you should be aware that the questions are designed to see if you have really been subject to the dynamic currents of the Church. I think it will be easy for you to say yes or no. All right?"

"All right."

So began a series of questions, about twenty. He answered seventeen of them, "no," two of them, "maybe," and one of them, "yes."

OF BUT NOT IN

When we were through I said, "Well, now in all candor, if I had been on the witness stand and had been pledged to tell the truth, the whole truth, and nothing but the truth, and if those same questions had been put to me, I would have had to say yes to about eighteen of them. So the difference between you and me is not so much the various enterprises we have studied or sought to master in the world; the difference is that I have had some experiences that you haven't had. And that means that actually you are not about to leave the Church, as you say. You have never really been *in* it!"

Well, he resented that and told me that he had several standard quorum awards and other such "gold stars on his forehead" as evidences of being really *in.*

But I said, "No, the Church's flowing powers have not *really* been *in* you, whatever the geography of your Sunday afternoons."

SOME QUESTIONS

I have made an outline list of those queries I put to him. I intend to ask them of you as perhaps a fruitful way of looking at yourselves.

PRAYER

First about *prayer,* "Have you ever prayed and been lifted beyond yourself, both in the manner and in the content of your expression, so that it became more than a dialogue with yourself?"

He said no. He admitted that he had said prayers, though not recently; but so far as he could remember, he knew of no instance in which he was sure he was talking to anyone other than himself.

President Heber C. Kimball told his children that unless one feels before he finishes his prayer a certain wave of the Spirit of God, a certain burning in the center of the self, he can be fairly sure that his prayer is not heard under ordinary circumstances. If we apply that to our own prayers, I, for one, have to acknowledge a good deal of barrenness. But if any of your prayers are in that burning category, thank God and keep praying.

THE SACRAMENT

About *the sacrament.* "Have you ever had the experience that Elder Melvin J. Ballard decribes, 'feeling the wounds on your soul,' being soothed, being filled with the Spirit that warms, and thus being quickened in a hunger and a thirst to return to the sacrament table where you find healing? Has it been as if you were taking hold of a couple of electrodes and were subject to a current?"

He said, "No, I have always found sacrament meetings quite boring."

A PATRIARCHAL BLESSING

About a *patriarchal blessing.* "Have you ever had what President McKay would call the 'thin veil' experience? When a patriarch made promises to you, declaring your heritage and something of the promise of your destiny, was it as if you were surrounded by glorious, but somehow less tangible, persons?"

On that one he said, "Well, yes, I do acknowledge that I felt something; but I have since concluded that it was just my own wishful thinking."

THE SCRIPTURES

About *the scriptures.* "Have you had the 'before and after' experience of Joseph Smith, who speaks of reading the scriptures after receiving the gift of the Holy Ghost? He was astonished, looking back and comparing the experience with his previous readings:

> Our minds [his and Oliver Cowdery's] being now enlightened, we began to have the scriptures laid open to our understandings, and the true meaning and intention of their more mysterious passages revealed unto us in a manner which we never could attain to previously, nor ever before had thought of. (Joseph Smith— History 1:74)

"Another way of saying it is: There are times when the scriptures can leap up off the page and bomb you, hit you between the eyes and, as it were, between the ribs such that you know these phrases were written under inspiration, and you see clearly how they apply to you."

It was Brother Marion G. Romney who told of reading with his son, in the upper and lower berths of a train on one occasion, taking turns—a verse at a time. After a while, he read a verse and his son was silent. He assumed his boy had gone to sleep. But a little later his son said, "Dad, do you ever cry when you read the Book of Mormon?" Brother Romney said, "Yes, son, there are times when the power and light of this book so permeate me that I find myself in tears." His son replied, "I guess that is what happened to me tonight."

Well, if we have been awakened in that way—he said he had not—then we are not one of those who have read the Book of Mormon up to the Isaiah passages and quit. I have sometimes wished that the book could be reordered, starting with Moroni, then Ether, and maybe Third Nephi, and then moving on. I am afraid that there are hundreds of thousands in the Church who have been hung up on the Isaiah passages and missed the treasures.

ORDINATION

About *ordination*. "Have you ever, in receiving the priesthood, or an office within it, or a calling to serve felt what President Stephen L Richards calls an 'essence of power,' or what Elder Orson F. Whitney calls 'liquid fire,' or what the Prophet himself spoke about as 'virtue' which somehow passed from the person into you?"

He said, simply, no.

AN INSTRUMENT

"Have you ever been involved at the other end, *being the instrument* for setting apart or ordaining or baptizing or confirming? Moroni records the words of the Savior that, after calling upon God in mighty prayer, 'ye shall have power that to him upon whom ye shall lay your hands ye shall give the Holy Ghost' (Moroni 2:2). Have you ever had the experience of thus being a vehicle?"

"No, I have stood in a circle or two, but I would say it was a sort of mumbo-jumbo of remembered phrases."

TESTIMONY

About *bearing testimony*. "Have you ever stood up, not simply to express gratitude, which we often do, and not simply to parrot the trilogy of phrases (about the reality of God, the sonship of Christ, the prophetic mantle among us) that we often use, but stood up because there was an almost compulsive lift to stand? Did you have the sensation of being, as it were, outside yourself, listening to yourself, when your words came with a transparent clarity, running ahead of your ordinary thinking; and you felt the core of your soul coming to the fore with a glow of unqualified conviction?"

He said, "No, I have occasionally 'borne my testimony' but I did not have one really. I was just using the words."

"What about," I asked him, "others who have spoken in your hearing? Has there never been a case in a classroom, or in a meeting, or in a conference, have there not even been instances when you have listened to the 'living oracles' at the head of the Church, when you were sure the person was speaking beyond his natural ability, when *the power of his testimony* seemed to cut through all the fog and go directly to you?"

"BEYOND HIS NATURAL ABILITY"

I could have recalled the incident of President Heber J. Grant, who saw his brother enter the Salt Lake Tabernacle many years ago. His brother had been everywhere except in the Church, around the Horn, in mining camps, and oil fields. He had come to the point of suicide and then received, in ways I cannot detail, a strong feeling he should contact his brother, Heber. Well, he stumbled into the Tabernacle. President Grant did not know that he would be called on to speak, but he prayed that if he were he could say something to touch his brother. But he thought perhaps he had better check a reference or two. He pulled down his ready reference and began to look through it desperately. He wanted to speak beyond his own natural ability and so prayed.

Well, he was called on. He soon forgot that ready reference and simply bore his testimony to the power of Christ that led to the Restoration and that led the people of this Church across the plains. Specifically he bore witness to the prophetic glory of the Prophet Joseph Smith.

I have read that talk. There is nothing, as far as I can find, that is distinctive or unusual about it—it is on the surface a fairly ordinary collection of words. But when he finished and sat down, he heard George Q. Cannon quietly say, "Thank God for the power of that testimony." And President Grant bowed his head and wept.

Brother Cannon was asked to speak. He stood up and said, "There are times when the Lord Almighty inspires some speaker by the revelations of his Spirit, and he is so abundantly blessed by the inspiration of the living God that it is a mistake for anybody else to speak following him, and one of those occasions has been today, and I desire that this meeting be dismissed without further remarks." And so it was.

I will paraphrase somewhat the event of the next day when President Grant's brother came and said, "Heber, I heard you yesterday. Heber, *you* can't speak that well. You spoke beyond your natural ability." He used the exact phrase.

President Grant, who was pretty stark in his response, said, "Does the Lord have to get a club and knock you down? What does it mean when you know I can't speak that well when I talk about the Master and Joseph Smith?"

His brother said, "You win." He became an active Latter-day Saint and a powerful speaker in his own right (Grant, *Gospel Standards,* 369–70).

That kind of experience, occasionally at least, should have happened to all of us. It had not to my friend or if it had, he had long since forgotten.

SPIRITUAL GIFTS

About *spiritual gifts.* The Prophet said, in effect, that no one has faith in Christ unless he has something along with it. "A man," he said, "who has none of the gifts has no faith; and he deceives himself, if he supposes he has" (Joseph Smith, *Teachings* [1938], 270).

You can check the lists of spiritual gifts. There is one in Moroni 10, another in Doctrine and Covenants section 46, and another in Paul's writings, 1 Corinthians 12. You can check, if you want more carefully to go through all the Doctrine and Covenants, and you will find about thirty different ways in which gifts are manifest.

"Have you ever had such a gift, especially in serving others? Have you ever sensed, say, the gift of discernment—the gift for the word of truth or knowledge—or the gift to teach it, or of wisdom or the gift to teach that?"

He said simply, "No, I do not believe in these mystical gifts."

PURE INTELLIGENCE

About the more specific issue, the Prophet's "flash of intelligence" phenomenon. "Have you ever received what the Prophet calls *'pure intelligence* flowing into you,' or a quickening in your soul that binds you to a truth or a person or a sacred place; a drawing power toward something or away from something that you cannot trace into your ordinary environment? Or have you ever just known by the spirit of prophecy that a certain thing was going to happen? I am not talking about wishes, guesses, hopes, hunches; I am talking about the phenomenon of *just knowing.*"

Occasionally I have asked groups how many present have known at times, in *that* sense of knowing, that they were about to be called on to pray or to speak or to fill a particular office. All of these groups have ended up with two-thirds of the hands high, many others halfway up, not quite sure whether these "sudden strokes" came from a divine source or from somewhere else.

Again his answer was in the negative.

MUSIC

About the voice of God in *music.* "Have you ever sung a hymn, or is there a single piece of music in this Church that speaks to your soul in the way the others do not—like for example, 'O My Father' with Crawford Gates's French horns and the Philadelphia Orchestra; or 'Come, Come, Ye Saints' at its climax; or the Phelps 'Spirit of God' anthem?"

A girl was leading music in a sacrament meeting at BYU some time back. (Mormons cannot sing without a conductor; I have

155

often marveled at that. Maybe it is symbolic of the fact that we believe the script, but there has to be a living person handling the script.) She was leading in a fairly perfunctory way the Eliza R. Snow hymn "O My Father." Then for the first time, I think she began to understand the words. This time they were given with power. As she led, she soon was not singing anymore and then was in tears. Somehow that was catching, it moved through the congregation. By the time they reached the last verse nobody was singing, or at least not with their voices!

Well, he said he had never had that experience. The words meant nothing to him.

CONSCIENCE

About the question of *conscience.* We do a lot to suppress and even distort our consciences. It is not uncommon in a standard course having to do with environment, whether it is psychology, sociology, or anthropology, to say that all you have when you talk about conscience is the residue of your early experience, some no-noes and yes-yeses. But conscience is not reliable, so goes the argument. Everybody has claimed the conscience for having done something that you would consider an atrocity, and then not having done other things that you would consider right, so it is very relative.

I am not sure of this; I tend to agree with the view of Parley P. Pratt—that is, if you will go far enough back in your memory (and this is difficult because you have closed it off), you will find that at age four or five your first approaches to temptation and sin were attended by a fantastic burning. "No," was the sensation, "no." And if you persisted that sensation became a fever. Then if you went ahead and did it, you felt an after-burning of guilt. Had you hearkened to that, according to Parley P. Pratt, and honored it, you would have increased in light to the present day. Instead, you have smothered it and written it off as just some sort of psychological illusion.

This is an intrinsic awareness—all of us have it. We are loathe to admit it to anyone, last of all to ourselves, but it is here, in the heart. And as the Prophet put it, it "gnaws at us," and it seems to be particularly unimpressed with any of the arguments that we can advance. It is as if it were deaf. We say, "I couldn't help it, it was bigger than both of us." "Everyone is doing it, nobody will find out." But conscience has wax in its ears; it does not respond.

Well, he told me that he thought "conscience" was a wholly ambiguous concept and that we would do well to eliminate it from our vocabulary.

THE TEMPLE

About the *temple*—he had been there. He was not too impressed, or worse, he was impressed negatively. Someone had suggested to him in his earlier life that, in condemning "pagan ritual," Mormons were saying they did not believe in symbols. The person had also pointed out to him that what matters is conduct, not just sacramental acts. And so he was disturbed.

(We do a disservice to condemn ritual per se. There is nothing intrinsically evil about ceremony or ritual. It can be distorted. But so can everything else. It can become an end in itself, and we can and often do lose its power and its meaning, but neither of those are necessary.)

I asked him if he felt anything about the promise given at Kirtland referring to the House of God as "a place of holiness." I asked him if he was constrained to acknowledge as he entered the temple, regardless of the process within, that it was indeed "a house of glory, a house of order, a house of God" (D&C 88:119). I asked him, in other words, if he had a feeling or *sense of the sacred.*

He said no, not at all, and he had no desire to return there.

I could have borne him the testimony of President McKay (but did not) to the effect that he was disappointed—the audience gasped when he said it, he, President David O. McKay was disappointed—when he first visited the temple. He gave us the reasons, and they are the ones that bother us: that it was over his head; that he did not distinguish the symbol from the thing symbolized; that he saw the human elements—people, different personalities—not all of them appealing to him; that he had very strange expectations, few of them fulfilled; and that he was not yet ripe in spiritual things. But I heard him say, at age eighty after having been in the house of the Lord every week for more than fifty years, that there were few, even temple workers, who comprehend the full meaning and power of the temple. I felt his witness to my core and decided I would reserve my misjudgments, keep quiet, and listen. I have learned—and absorbed—quite a good deal since.

LOVE

About *love*. How do you feel about this? Elder Matthew Cowley said he had never lost a friend (he made up his mind in his youth that he wouldn't) over religion or politics. That is the Spirit of Christ. I think it is particularly needful in this Church at this time.

There is a spirit that can come to one who has tasted the flow of Christ's power that makes it impossible for a person to push you out of his reach. He may for the moment reject you, he may for years do so. But always you are there compassionate and concerned—unwilling, just because you disagree, to say, "I will never speak to you again," unwilling to breed distrust and suspicion, to nurture your own bad blood against him. If a person has not tasted that spirit, then by the Prophet's definition he has not yet begun to get close to Christ. For, said he, "The nearer we get to our Heavenly Father, the more we are disposed to look with compassion on perishing souls; we feel that we want to take them upon our shoulders, and cast their sins behind our backs" (Joseph Smith, *Teachings* [1938], 241). "Perishing"—that is a good word, it can mean a lot of things, any sense of perishing. When you find a spirit that wants to condemn, to attack, to pull down, you witness a spirit that is not of Christ. With love like his we are able to see others deeply, but seeing them, we are able to overlook the things that would otherwise antagonize us.

"I can't work with certain people," a man said once. He was being encouraged to do a task, a "dirty work" task, in his ward. "I can't work with these people, they're dumb, they're oafish, they're clumsy, they're not pleasant to work with."

And the person who had called him smiled and simply said, "Christ did."

The young man I was talking with found joy with only one or two of his Church associates.

3 NEPHI 17

In summary, I asked him whether he responded with anything unusual in reading Third Nephi. That happens to be a transparent book for me. I have a friend who says that the most sacred chapter of the Bible is chapter seventeen of John. For me the most sacred chapter of the Book of Mormon is the same number, seventeen, in Third Nephi.

THE TESTIMONY OF JESUS

I asked him if he had received *"the testimony of Jesus."* (See D&C 76:51–53.) I asked him if the most thrilling prospect of his life was not simply to imitate Jesus in behavior patterns, but *to become like him* in nature, in very attribute and appearance, and eventually, even though being begotten of him with all that means, *possessed of his power.*

He told me that he did not see the point of all this talk about Christ, and as a matter of fact, he doubted most of the theological utterances that Church members made about Him.

So much for the questions.

LIVING WATER

I have not reflected my own grateful experiences in each of these dimensions. I have talked instead of past worthies. But I can bear you a testimony that these currents and many more are part of the flowing fountain of the Church. If we do not drink, if we die of thirst while only inches from the fountain, the fault comes down to us. For the free, full, flowing, living water is there.

"COME YE TO THE WATERS . . ."

Perhaps more often than any other, the question is repeated today, "Why aren't there as many spiritual outpourings today as there were in the first generation?" This is a very revealing question, because there *are*. But those who ask seem always to assume that their lack of experience applies to everyone.

It is like the person who comes in and says, "How do I know that I have a testimony?" In flippant moments I have occasionally replied, "If you have to ask *me,* you don't!" That is pretty harsh. But it is true.

The living water is with us. If anything, *more* is available today because of the varied and expanding opportunities of the Church. But it becomes actual only when the individual who seeks has a clear sense of the possibilities and is then willing to pay the price. I find any number of youths who are, as I was, very anxious to say what they would do *for* such blessings, but less anxious to say what they would do *with* them if they came. After a little introspection, we should not be surprised that the Lord is hesitant to entrust more to us than we can carry.

Several years ago I went to Jerusalem. A wall is still there, parts of it the same as anciently. East of the wall is a valley called the Valley of Cedron; there once was a brook that flowed down from it. East of that is a mount. It is called the Mount of Olives. And somewhere up on the side of that mountain—no one knows exactly where, though some profess to—there was a garden. Not the kind of garden you may have imagined, not a beautiful, flowered garden, but a garden of trees—olive trees. Into that grove, after he knew that he had to accept the will of the Father, and knowing what it meant, Jesus Christ took three of his disciples. And then he prayed alone.

THE POWER OF CHRIST

I sat there and looked back at Jerusalem. You do not comprehend, I think, the fantastic power of the opposition of all kinds that he faced. You have been impressed in our generation with the war machines of the major nations. They are not comparable in any way, in lethal enmity, in ruthlessness, to what was beyond that wall. One walked into the clutches of Rome with the confidence you would have in the clutches of an octopus. Remember? Jesus did not answer all the objections of the learned, the canny, or the curious. In looking back and knowing what was ahead, he overcame them by his very life.

I say to you that when he said to the woman of Samaria and to others, "He that believeth on me, shall never thirst" (John 6:35); I say to you that when on the cross he looked down and back, under the searing sun, and said, "I thirst," he was reflecting both the promise and the need that all of us have. We, too, thirst until we ache. We, too, are living and dying on deserts. There is no alternative. Some of those deserts we are commanded to walk across without water just, I believe at times, to see what is in us. But when we struggle on, we find an oasis, and the living water, or what I have called the dynamic currents of the power of Christ. They flow into us.

A TESTIMONY

I bear testimony that those currents are here. I bear testimony that the problem of reconciling this or that philosophy of religion with commitment is not as technical as we often make it. These problems are easily worked out when the mind is clear. The solution is simple: it is being alive, fully alive to the flow and power of the living Christ. When we are, everything is better; when we are not, everything seems dark.

May God help us to walk in the light; and, when we do not feel that we have it, to walk in the memory of it *with integrity.*

Chapter Five

CHRIST AND CONQUERING THOUGHTS

If there is a sense in which we are what we think, and therefore inevitably the product of and accountable to our thoughts, then we need the power of the Christ to make such "weak things become strong unto us." The essay below (originally printed in the New England Advocate, a missionary journal) is concerned with practical ways of coping with unworthy thoughts.

My worst problem is that I have bad thoughts. What can I do?"

Associated with the house of the Lord is the symbol of an all-seeing eye.

It reminds us that Christ who lives is, as he told his young Prophet, "a discerner of the thoughts and intents of the heart" (D&C 33:1), and that as Paul says, "all things are naked and open unto the eyes of him with whom we have to do" (Hebrews 4:13).

At first that is a frightening perception. We shrink from it. We

162

think about wanting "mountains to hide us." But when we pursue it in depth, it is different.

Consider.

Are any of our conceivable evil thoughts beyond the Lord? If so, would there be any sound foundation for trust in him? How can a Christ who does not know or refuses to recognize our thoughts, one whose awareness is restricted to an utterly other realm of awareness, really help us now? This ethereal view of Christ (reinforced, I am afraid, by much traditional theology) also implies that venomous or unworthy thoughts could not be entertained by him during his mortal life, nor after.

But the power of his own voice in our era has brought that impotent idea to the ground. And thus given us power to rise above the ground.

He was "in all points tempted like as we are" (Paul), with "temptations of every kind" (Alma). How low then can we go in our thoughts? Not as low as he in the contemplation of evil. He was tempted through "the darkest abyss" and "descended below all things." Why? That he might be "in and through *all* things the light of truth." What? In and through *my* vagrant, aching, turbulent, unworthy thoughts? "Yes, my sons, yes." He has comprehended them all. His is the compassion of kinship (D&C 88:6).

A second flash.

An all-seeing personage sees all. That means that just seeing evil or contemplating it (however we may define evil) is not itself evil; that thoughts about evil are not necessarily evil thoughts. For Jesus Christ is now beholding the entire ugly spectrum of human experience. Is he therefore unholy? Was he in mortality? He is in a condition that enables him to "see through" all ideas, judgments and images to the truth.

Reread the oft-quoted passages about the thoughts. You will note that it is not the occurrence of ideas in the head but their lodgment in the heart that degrades. "As [a man] thinketh *in his heart* so is he" (Proverbs 23:7; italics added). The issue is not so much what thoughts occur in our minds, but how we nurture them in our desires—what we aspire toward and recoil from. Some worthy men of God reached a point, so we are told, at which they could "only look upon sin with abhorrence" (Alma 13:12). It was lusting (more than thinking) that the Master defined as committing adultery "already in the heart." He did not say lusting was identical with the act. He *did* say that it was the beginning of it. "Suffer none of these things to enter *into your heart*" (3 Nephi 12:29; italics added).

The heart, as the scriptures have it, is the combustion chamber of both the exalted and the degenerate drives in man's inner life, whether wrathful, envious, covetous, or erotic. Our minds may be bright and lucid in building idyllic palaces or contemplate, as the Prophet says, the darkest abyss. Our hearts settle the question as to whether something is good or bad. Therefore "blessed are the pure in mind" actually means "blessed are the pure in *heart.*"

It follows that what we call temptation really occurs in the life of the heart. If so, then so also must its overcoming. I submit that this is where we need Christ most and also where we admit him least. We think it sacrilege that he should somehow *leave* his throne and enter with us into the quagmire. Afterward we struggle to overcome it by not thinking about it. Thus we are driven in the wrong direction. We look down in shame instead of up in faith, while thought becomes intent, intent becomes obsession, and obsession carried out brings ashen despair.

What, then, is the way out?

Here are some standard and sometimes useful answers.

"Concentrate on work." Yes, but what do we do when feeling-drenched thoughts return? "Think of the consequences." Excellent, but when the pressure is really on, and we are blind to them, what then?" "Think of your mother, your honor, and the Golden Rule." Fine, but these often elude us. "Quote scripture," that helps sometimes. "Sing hymns to chase darkness." Good.

But what is ultimately needed, I witness, is something as dramatic (yes, and even traumatic) as the drama of life itself, an antidote as powerful as the poison. "He that *trembleth* under my power shall be made strong" (D&C 52:17; italics added).

Here, where it matters most because it is sacred and intimate, I can only be suggestive. But anyone who is buffeted will know what is involved. Who hath ears to hear will hear.

The atonement of Jesus Christ has unfathomed intellectual aspects. And it is astonishing how much time we spend (I do not say waste) struggling to get it through our heads, to understand it. But a beginning of real understanding is to stand under it, to permit his power to reach *beyond* our depths so that Christ's life can grasp, shake, and transform our own. *That* is the point at which we are living or dying.

So suppose a diabolical picture comes to mind, a thought of which we are ashamed (or is it the *feeling* we have toward the thought that makes us ashamed?). The force of it may blot out all that we ordinarily see and feel. Spiritual sensitivities are the first to go. We isolate this fraction of consciousness (I've got to have this out!), build up syrupy anticipation, convince ourselves that this is what we really want, and become numb to all else. Thus, it is fitting to speak of blind rage, blind greed, blind passion. In his *Screwtape Letters* C. S. Lewis has the devil say to a henchman, "It is funny how mortals always picture us as putting things into their minds; in reality our best work is done by keeping things out." We have forgotten that we would "always remember *him*" (which is more than remembering his teachings).

In such a moment of distress how can you pull him into your consciousness so that strength replaces weakness? I designate two ways from the prophets.

1. Picture Christ and remember how you are bound to him. In the crisis for example, when your temples thunder, imagine what you are tempted to do as if it were a large sledge hammer. See! See if you can stand at the cross and by this act or indulgence swing that hammer on the nail. That will break your compulsive pattern and restore enough to your consciousness to enable you to cry out and *mean*, "No!"

2. The other picture is positive. It is the more calm but daily vision to overarch all else.

It is the vision of the real-in-prospect.

Take, for example, carnal thoughts, the bubbling erotica which

165

imbue our environment and, mysteriously, the subconscious. Ask yourself what you *really* want. But as you ask, invite and invoke your spirit, the deepest and best in you, and the Master's Spirit. Search with him for the vision of love and marriage that can claim your whole being, to include, but not end with, the chemistry of the flesh.

Such a vision will bring into focus a queen or king, an anticipation of the real thing. You will be inspired by your righteous thirst for such kinships and excitements. You will envision love that glorifies a pathway through the temple of God, and finally the culmination in which there is whiteness and joy.

Thus you take raw subliminal impulses that corrode. You sublimate (literally make sublime) them into conscious, desirable pictures. You light corroding fire with redeeming fire. And Christ who is the exemplar of all forms of godly love becomes the revelator both of your own possibilities in the world of affection and of the pathway that will make them actual.

Without such a vision the heart is sort of a mixer of cheap poisons for our veins. But with it life takes on a deep-breathing color of godliness. But isn't it sinful or at least impractical to have such visionary fantasies? Listen to Orson Pratt: "There is no danger of loving too much, but only of loving too little." Lurid, lustful desires are a form of the "too little." But the effulgent dream of godly love is "at the foundation of everything worthy to be called happiness."

You doubt? You fear to open up your own caldron to the Christ?

Then go on pretending, if you must, that there is a way to hide. But hear in the distance what, if you will, you can feel in the marrow of your bones. It is a contemporary voice the Lord expressed in Doctrine and Covenants 6:36: "Look unto me *in every thought;* doubt not, fear not."

Chapter Six

CHRIST AND THE SACRAMENT

These reflections on the sacrament were presented to a Holy Land tour group as we visited in early morning the "Garden of Olives" (Gethsemane) and later held a special sacrament meeting at the "Garden Tomb" outside the ancient wall of Jerusalem and near the alleged place of crucifixion.

Perhaps the reason we have been given two set prayers for the sacred sacrament ordinance is that it is of paramount importance in this instance that we comprehend clearly what we are doing, what we are asking, and what we are promised in fulfillment of the conditions.

These prayers have been memorized by most of us. They are written in our heads and can be written in our souls as we hunger for the sacrament with the same constancy that fills our lungs with air.

The testimony of Melvin J. Ballard, a man I never knew personally, was, "I am a witness that there is a Spirit that attends the sacrament that warms the soul from head to foot. You feel the wounds of your soul being lifted." I testify to this reality also.

This ordinance—an ordinance that somehow connects with all other ordinances—is a way the Lord has given us of opening the portals of heaven. I know he honors it, just as he honors baptism or the laying on of hands. I know that when he spoke to one of the most righteous multitudes who have ever listened to his voice in this world (the Nephites), he taught them that through this pattern they could have direct communion with him.

The prayer petitions that we may "always remember *him*" (more than remembering his commandments). Sermons often suggest that we should think more consciously about him. That, I am sure, is true. But in a relationship of love, the beloved may not be every minute present in consciousness, but is in the hidden levels of awareness. Anything we do in a day has glory and meaning because under and over it all is our pull toward the beloved. Husbands and wives know. That is why Jacob could work seven years happily knowing that he would be given Rachel. That's why Nephi had the assurance of Christ, even while facing marauders and oceans and wilderness.

So we are always to remember him in our deepest motivations, in the core of our spirits. We are alive to his love in the deepmost part of us.

> And if ye do always remember me ye shall have my Spirit to be with you. (3 Nephi 18:11)

He asks of us in the first prayer (the blessing of the bread) that we be *willing* to take upon us his name and that we be *willing* to keep his commandments. Maybe I am straining at the word. But that is a little different than saying, "We are now perfectly *able* to accept you and live as you would have us." We are *willing* after we have come to him and, as Paul says, "examined ourselves" stripped of all the facades. We have acknowledged our need. From the Old Testament prophets he required the offering of animal sacrifices. To us he has said, "I require only [and it is a real only] the offering of a broken heart and a contrite spirit" (D&C 97:8; 20:37).

Any honest man who contemplates himself in the Lord's mirror is contrite; and submissive; and grateful to acknowledge, heart melted, that such spiritual blessings as he has are not all *earned* (except by this honest attitude of penitence), but have been given as a gift.

In the first prayer Christ asks us to remember *his body.* The great insight given through the modern prophets is that Jesus the Christ was indeed the revelation of God the Father. To know him as he is, a glorified personage, is to know the *exact* nature of the Eternal Father. That nature is officially denied by Christendom. Moreover, the Jesus Christ of the creeds (often pushed out of reach by doctrinal distortion) is shrouded in mystery by the notion that his physical presence is contained universally in the wafer and wine. No. We are to remember his body, and his body is glorified in space and time. More, it is the exact image of our own destiny if we will but glimpse it. Thus, the understanding of his glorification is the anticipation of our own. These emblems do not take his substance into them. The truth is unspeakably more. Because of these emblems and our inner attitude, his Spirit is *poured into us,* preparing us for his actual personal presence and the brightness of his glory. The human self is transformed; transubstantiation is, as it were, in *us.*

In the second prayer (the blessing of the water) we remember *his blood.* Why? Why blood? Is that not melodramatic? No. He is reminding us of more than blood from his side when someone threw or thrust a sword into him. More than the blood from the wounds in his hands and feet. He is reminding us of the blood that came from every pore of his body in those hours of the atonement, which to me are more inspiring than those on the cross. He is touching us with the power of recognition: that the blood he shed makes it possible for him to sanctify *our* blood. As modern revelation says, making us "clean from the blood of this generation" (D&C 88:138). Clean means more than exonerated from the shedding of blood by men who have killed the prophets and the faithful. It means clean—sanctified—in our own bloodstream through his power. "The blood which was shed." Why? For himself? No. He would not have had to suffer thus for his own salvation. He could have received the presence of God the Father without it—note the wording, " . . . the blood of thy Son which was shed *for them.*" In an agony of compassion of which our worst pains are but a small taste, he bled for us.

> And he said unto them: He that eateth this bread eateth of my body to his soul; and he that drinketh of this wine drinketh of my blood to his soul; and his soul shall never hunger nor thirst, but shall be filled. (3 Nephi 20:8)

It is thus that we are removed from the recognition of what he did to the reception of what he *now does* for us.

Chapter Seven

YE ARE MY WITNESSES

Though fiction, this story is based on the narratives in Third Nephi. (It was printed first in the New England Advocate.) It springs out of a concern that has haunted me ever since I began to understand the New Testament. What would Christ say, what would he do, what more of himself would he unfold if he were surrounded by persons whose love for him was as intense as the hate of those who crucified him? The Nephite multitude provided such a setting.

Timothy, his ankles bound with leather, was a crumpled figure against the gray and merciless wall. Here, on the outskirts of the city, the fury of the mob was increasing. They were stripping him now, denying even the protection of cloth between him and the small stones they were throwing. Their pellets had been shrewdly chosen—sharp, cutting, intended by their size and speed first to torment, then to gash and bruise, and finally to kill. They wanted him to die; but he must die slowly, wincing and writhing. He would suffer until a rock to the temple or just above the eyes crushed his last breath.

Down the narrow roadway, behind a sagging wall of an abandoned house, Nephi, brother of Timothy, was watching. His own
life in jeopardy, he had followed the conspirators here, burning
with indignation that they were violating the public pact of the
Chief Judge: Stoning required the full review and sanction of the
Zarahemla Governor. Yet here, now, were judges goading the mob
to violence.

For thirty years, ever since the commission of their aging
parent, Nephi and Timothy had labored in the cities of the land
Bountiful, teaching and witnessing of the coming Messiah, repeating the prophetic saying of their forefathers. And in thirty years
the hostility, even of some who first befriended them, had turned
into murderous intent. Now, in a well-planned scuffle near Nephi's
home, they had singled out Timothy for torture.

Nephi was watching, but then he could not watch. The ghastly
spectacle of their leering faces, the off-blows of the rocks, the
swollen face of his brother, the crescendo of their curses staggered
him. In waves the terrible sense of his own utter helplessness went
over him. He was unbelieving as he hid his face in his hands. Was
it happening? Could it happen? Was he really here? And where
was God?

For an instant there was a lull. Were they satisfied and would
they leave Timothy wounded but alive? No. It was over. He knew
from the sound of the mob. They were receding now, scattering to
their preappointed places to establish their alibis. They would
abandon the body for others to discover. The word would travel
fast to the Governor, but not fast enough to bring any justice.

Sickened and reeling Nephi waited, waited for the silence that
meant the street and his brother were abandoned. How long it took
he couldn't tell. Time was strangely elusive. But with only the
sound of his dust-muffled sandals on the roadway, and his uneven
breath, he came to the limp figure. For a moment he felt revulsion
and horror at the heap of stones stained with blood. He could only
look by sheer will at Timothy's body, cold in death. Then, his eyes
closed, and he sank to his knees and moved in a spontaneous
gesture of his soul.

"Timothy," he murmured, placing his hands on his head. "Timothy, in the name of Christ return to life. By his authority I command you to rise."

At the sound of his own voice his faith seemed to spring up anew. He sat back in a penetrating gaze. There was no motion. But he watched and waited with full expectation. Then it began. There was a stir in Timothy's lips, a flutter in his eye. He groaned and moved slightly. It seemed forever before his eyes opened and he looked up but without sight. "Timothy!" Nephi said, again the sound of a miracle in his voice. At last Timothy not only looked but saw. "Nephi!" he said.

Two years had passed since then. Reports of this miracle and of other manifestations of divine intervention were circulated throughout the land Bountiful. But they brought no one to faith. They were viewed by the lawyers and the learned and the luxurious as a legend to trick others into this delusion about Christ. "Obviously," they said, "Timothy had never died."

Like an evil wind, a secret political combination gained power. The Governor was stabbed in his chamber, several worthy judges were poisoned, and the civil government was in ruins. In every city the halls and courts of law were abandoned. The only order in the land grew out of families grouped for their own protection, many of them desperately afraid there would be bloodshed even among themselves. And the only unity was found among those who had made a secret pact in a Cain-like conspiracy to be "united in hatred" against those who continued to talk of the traditions of the fathers about a Messiah and the so-called "signs" of his coming.

To Nephi and his brethren this meant that there was little safety and less hope.

They were marked men. They could not so much as teach their children of the prophets without risk that one day, in a school or dooryard, someone would set off explosions of violence. Travel, for any purpose, was an open invitation to marauders who preyed upon the caravans and on each other. The house and family of any

173

man who expressed belief in the prophets, especially Samuel, was threatened with fire or ransacking or something worse.

And as for the conduct of the people. A sodden, sensual syrup had filled them. Their learning was cunning, not wisdom, and that cunning insulated them from anything sacred. They were motivated by position, power, and riches. Few, terribly few, cared for honor. Rape was as common as drunkenness; and murder, as common as both.

Traveling in various disguises, meeting in caves and sometimes underground, Nephi and Timothy and a few others continued to testify. The baptism of repentance (which, in secret, they still read about in the accounts of "The Waters of Mormon") was given to those who were touched by the great power which attended their prophets' words. Sometimes when Nephi spoke there was such a demonstration of the Spirit of God in his testimony that none could disbelieve. Yet belief was followed, too often, not by love and prayer but by bitter anger. And even some who listened fell into the patterns of those who didn't, saying of the prophets:

"Some things they may have guessed right among so many."

"But it is not reasonable that such a being as Christ shall come."

"If so, why will he not be born in this land instead of the land abroad?"

"This is a deception of the fathers to keep us in ignorance to believe some great and marvelous thing."

"They want us to be slaves to their words."

"They want to possess our lives."

"They hide in ignorance, for there is no way that our own eyes can see that what they say is true."

Then came disasters.

One evening, as Nephi rose from a table and was turning around, the floor suddenly became a dizzying, rippling monster. There was nowhere to go, nothing to do. In a matter of seconds the children were nauseated and panicked. Convulsion after convulsion, each one worse than the last, tore away at every desire for relief. The family groaned as they crouched in doorways. Thunder

174

and lightning, such as they had never seen, seemed to have entered the very earth, intent on destroying it and all life with it.

It was an ordeal such as even Nephi had not really foreseen. He had tried to picture how Jesus might be put to death, to understand what the prophets meant when they spoke of Christ's suffering and death being signalized by tremors in the earth and leading to the exclamation, "The God of nature suffers." But this! Three hours for destruction to reign! And then darkness, thick suffocating darkness.

Nephi was soon to receive word that Gilgal and Jacob, large and notable cities, were utterly buried; that Onihah and Mocum had been swept into the tidal swirl of the sea; that fire and crags and gaping fissures had wiped out the people of Gad and Josh and Kishkumen.

In all, sixteen cities were either destroyed or gutted!

But while others mourned in abject misery, Nephi knelt with his loved ones and gave thanks, again and again, that his family had been spared! And his house! And the temple!

Around that temple in the land Bountiful the fugitive survivors gathered, to count the cost and recount the holocaust, gathered in response to Nephi's request to all the faithful.

And there, while they marveled, twenty-five hundred of them heard a voice from the heavens.

What had they expected? Nephi wondered as he listened. They had known the shock-power of earthquake; every one of them had been buffeted by the turbulent forces from without. Now they were to experience the far more moving power within which was neither loud, brash, nor dinning in their ears.

Instead, it was as if the earthquake and the fire and the lightning and the sea were pulled together into a liquid burning and then released into the marrow of their bones. It pierced their souls. To the depths of their aloneness and anxiety and estrangement and even despair it penetrated. And their hearts were on fire!

That was the beginning of a day that transcended Nephi's most inspired anticipations.

For as the voice spoke the third time, it was understood.

175

"Behold, my Beloved Son, in whom I am well pleased, in whom I have glorified my name—hear ye him."

The Christ descended before them and the multitude fell to their knees. He bade them arise and come forth. And they touched him. Then the Lord spoke to Nephi, calling him by name, and singled out eleven others who were to receive his ministry.

Through that entire day Nephi listened enraptured while Christ ministered with overwhelming power, and counseled and ordained, and expounded with a visionary sweep of all time at his command, and reviewed the prophets with breathtaking light and healed the sick one by one, and blessed their children, and then prayed with the entire multitude in a way that filled their souls with inconceivable joy.

Then as the multitude wearied, he promised to return to them on the following day and withdrew.

By morning the multitude had swelled. All night the report had been carried throughout the land. And many, even of the halt and injured, found ways to gather to the spot where Jesus had been seen and heard.

As Nephi stood in the early dawn and looked out over the multitude it was a strange, but welcome, sight. He saw persons almost faint from the effort to cross the rude bridges over swollen rivers and athwart awesome cracks in the earth; aged men and infirm women, strong and eager youths, mothers with child. He saw makeshift garments, shoes that did not match and some with no shoes at all. There were many small children, some, no doubt because parents were anxious to bring them, others because the memory of the earthquake made them cling to their families.

Nephi recognized the faces of many who had risked their lives to be baptized unto repentance, some he had not been able to visit for years. It was a reunion that melted his heart.

Nephi gathered the Twelve near the temple and instructed them to divide the expanding multitude into twelve groups. Each disciple was assigned a group to teach, reliving the experiences of the day before.

In his own teaching Nephi felt spiritual exhilaration. It was so real that it seemed unreal: That he should be here recounting to his brethren what it meant to him to kneel at the Master's feet and to recognize the prints of the nails in his feet! What it meant to embrace the Redeemer after he had opened his robe and led Nephi's right hand to the wound in his side. As Nephi spoke of his vivid remembrance of the teachings of the Master, there rolled through his soul the phrase of Alma, "O, then, is this not real? Yea, because it is light." All the heaviness of the past, the years of anguish were instruments of the light, a light that seemed now to defy gravity as well as disperse darkness. And the response of the multitude was almost smothering—no shouts of derision, no anger, no stones. There was faith here. And hunger for the things of God.

After the formal counsel, the Twelve went to the water's edge, and the multitude followed. Nephi fulfilled the Master's charge that they kneel in mighty prayer and seek the Holy Ghost. Then he took his brethren one by one, baptized them, and came forth out of the water.

As they emerged from the water the Spirit of God flowed down upon them. The multitude watched (did they all see it?) while an actual conduit of light and fire descended. It became, as it were, high noon at mid-morning. The moist air appeared as bright fire, and the quiet clouds and silent trees seemed a sacred sanctuary. And while they stood thus filled with the eternal burnings of high heaven, Jesus stood in the midst of them.

He commanded the disciples and the multitudes to kneel down again.

And then it happened.

They had been praying, only minutes before, to the Father in the name of Christ. But now Nephi and his brethren, lifted and lured by the divine fire, found themselves praying directly to the Lord Jesus Christ. "My Lord, my God," Nephi said in a barely audible voice. Gratitude and confidence and intimate rejoicing poured out of him.

In this act Nephi felt sure release. He had known the Spirit at times in his ministry, but not as he knew it now. In touch with the present personage of Christ, Nephi felt like his spirit enveloped his body, open to a flame that was both his own and yet not his own. There was no labor to think of words, no striving for their expression. Desire sprang up in him from below all the surfaces of his nature. And he knew as he prayed that he prayed according to the will of the Father.

He could not take his eyes from the radiant Christ who seemed to stand between heaven and earth. Yes. Nephi knew him. His superlative manliness and matchless tenderness were beautiful, overwhelming. His height and nobility and serenity and aura combined in his movements to make them sublime. Nephi felt he was remembering what he had, in some primeval awareness, known, as if his eyes were apprehending now what his spirit had always intuited.

In a moment the Savior locked him in his gaze. And Nephi sensed, felt, knew that he was being seen as he was, that the pulsings and aches of his center self were clear to him. Jesus was not looking at him but into his soul. Faith rekindled in Nephi with the longing for complete worthiness in Christ's presence.

As if by preappointment Jesus took a few steps from Nephi and the kneeling disciples. Then he himself bowed to the earth. With face upturned so that Nephi could see his profile, he said:

"Father, I thank thee that thou hast given the Holy Ghost unto these whom I have chosen; and it is because of their belief in me that I have chosen them out of the world.

"Father, I pray thee that thou wilt give the Holy Ghost unto all them that shall believe in their words.

"Father, thou hast given them the Holy Ghost because they believe in me; and thou seest that they believe in me because thou hearest them, and they pray unto me; and they pray unto me because I am with them."

Witnessing these words from the lips of the Savior, Nephi felt new flashes of intelligence in the prophetic writings that had become part of him. He could see now what he had not fully seen before, the glorious answer to those who said that the life and sufferings of Christ made no sense at all.

178

For here before him knelt the Son of God, the eminent Son of all sons. One could read his life in his countenance. Had he not lived through the frail hours of infancy? Had he not known the fiery darts of mortal temptation? Had he escaped any of the struggle with the blood of the family of man, the blood which, without divine power, blasts man's dignity and turns evil into worse evil? None. And he had over-mastered all! The glory of godliness now was his in magnificent justice. All of Nephi's strivings for worth were engulfed in this sacred moment.

Jesus arose and returned to his Twelve. In unison they continued to pray with steadfast assurance.

Then, as Jesus looked upon them, he smiled. And such a smile! As Nephi studied the lines and sweeping comprehension of that smile, he saw a transfiguring light. The Savior's face, his robes, his whole person seemed to become near-transparent, as if a coursing power of illumination had burst into brilliant flame. Through and through, his robe was white, his hair was white, not a blanched shade, but a living, fulsome, vivid white. And it was as if the place where he stood had been put at the center of a prism.

Wondering if others likewise beheld, Nephi turned to Timothy. And beheld that his brother and the disciples, all of them, were likewise aglow! They were transformed! In an instant Nephi knew that he too was full of this light, and that he shone above all brightness.

Thus enveloped, Nephi felt cleansed. A molten purging power along his veins and arteries seemed to heal him of the residues of his past and its poisons. He could taste the rapture of being clean. Purity was not numbness, he thought in a flash, but the ringing and singing of every fiber of his flesh. He almost choked in conscious aliveness.

Resolute, the Savior said to his disciples, "Pray on!" But Nephi only wondered how any of them could wish to cease.

Jesus went again a little way away and knelt.

"Father, I thank thee that thou hast purified those whom I have chosen, because of their faith, and I pray for them, and also for them who shall believe on their words, that they may be purified

179

CHRIST AND THE INNER LIFE

in me, through faith on their words, even as they are purified in me."

Then the Redeemer said:

"Father, I pray not for the world, but for those whom thou hast given me out of the world, because of their faith, that they may be purified in me, that I may be in them as thou, Father, art in me, that we may be one, that I may be glorified in them."

Again the Savior returned to his chosen ones and smiled upon them. Then he returned to his kneeling place. "Father," he said. And then came words no human tongue could utter.

The language of Jesus soared beyond any Nephi had ever heard in mortal life. Was it an unknown, a foreign tongue? No, because he understood it at the core of his being. Yet he did not know the words. He listened and it was as if the expressions of the Master swallowed up distance and separation. Word, thought, and feeling were all one, A comprehensive vision emerged through the tatters of the clumsy words Nephi had learned to know and use. Such an outpouring, such perfect grasp! It was the language of the Divine! From the moment of its utterance, Nephi felt he had been ushered into the presence of the Eternal Father.

Hearing and seeing in this way Nephi was pulled to the inner love of Christ in what was, at the time, a flood of self-awareness. He grasped (had he ever before?) the perfect bond between the Father and the Son and the sons of men. Layers of obscuring doubt and confusion were lifted away. It was more than experiencing the Holy Ghost, more even than the joy of its sanctifying power.

In the depths of him he was seeing a visual prophecy. For in the prayer of the Christ he saw the visage, the visible image, of Christ's eternal nature. He could visualize, picture the personage of the Eternal Father. And in that comprehension he received the sealing testimony, the indelible promise of his own glorification.

That was what Christ meant—"that they may be one in me as thou, Father, art in me." He beheld it! The precious promised transmission of the divine nature, from the Father to the Son to the sons, by the lawful miracle of light upon light.

He saw. And felt.

Then Jesus arose. This time as he approached the Twelve there was an air of release in his step as if he, too, had been measured and fulfilled, as if some long-waiting chord in him had found attunement. Nephi, studying the Savior's face, saw again, attended by transcending whiteness, the same expression of compassion as on the evening before when having healed so many children he had said, "Behold, your little ones." One of them was Nephi's. Named after Grandfather Alma, he was small for his four years. His left leg had been withered from birth. Many times the family fasted and prayed that Nephi might heal him. But though he had often blessed others, these efforts for little Alma were vain. The boy had never learned to walk even with a crutch. At his instant recovery under Jesus' hands, he and his sisters had danced a circle of joy, hugging and tugging at the leg of the Master, and singing, "Oh, I am so happy." Did Jesus know that once home and asleep Alma kept crying out in a nightmare of fear that he was still crippled? His mother awakened him and helped him again to his feet. And then tried to laugh through her tears, as he sprang all over the bed saying, "Look! Look what I can do!"

Jesus had wept yesterday. Nephi was weeping now. And feeling all the honest unutterable gratitude of a little child.

Jesus spoke:

"So great faith have I never seen among all the Jews; wherefore I could not show unto them so great miracles, because of their unbelief.

"Verily I say unto you, there are none of them that have seen so great things as ye have seen; neither have they heard so great things as ye have heard."

All was silent. It was a rich, warm silence; the serenity of it seemed charged with peace, and more of love wafted through the air than any sound of motion could carry. This was communion in the manner of the angels. This was holy ground.

Impulsively, still on his knees, Nephi reached to Timothy and embraced his shoulders. In the security of that gesture something passed between them. Both were vividly aware that the sores and

181

scars of their long labor seemed now the tokens of rejoicing. They marveled that they could ever have been wearied, that any strand of their mind or body could have felt the costs too great. For their enemies, even those of murderous intent, they felt a well of forgiveness. Without looking at each other they knew, knew now a whole renewal to endure and to overcome . . . for him . . . like him. An invincible wish pulled at their throats. And as they lifted their heads they wondered if the Savior knew their thoughts.

He knew.

THE
HIGHEST
IN US

Preface

There are no ordinary people," C. S. Lewis writes. Instead we "live in a society of possible gods and goddesses. The dullest and most uninteresting person you talk to may one day be a creature which, if you saw it now, you would be strongly tempted to worship, or else a horror and corruption such as you now meet, if at all, only in a nightmare" (*Weight of Glory,* 15).

The nightmare is all about us. And as we peer out at the world, whether by the aid of television or not, there is much of horror and of corruption. Yet, on occasion, quiet voices remind us, against all evidence to the contrary, that there are "overwhelming possibilities" locked within mankind.

What we see of potential in others we see only dimly in ourselves, in spite of much that is in the air about attitudes and positive thinking. One of our own classic LDS sources says we must view ourselves, in our carnal state, as less than the dust of the earth. Whatever else that abysmal self-appraisal means, it is at least clear that, unlike those of us who go on postponing response to our better selves, the dust is subject to the will and power of the Master. But what would dust, filled with life and consciousness and glory, be? The very nature of the Master. And here we must see upward in order to see inward. "No being can thoroughly learn himself, without understanding more or less of the things of God;

185

neither can any being learn and understand the things of
God without learning himself; he must learn himself, or he never
can learn God" (Young, *Journal of Discourses* 8:33). Modern
prophets, who had not only the image but the vision of the things
of God, say, like the Prophet Joseph Smith struggling to describe
the majesty of the resurrection, "No man can describe it to you,
no man can tell it." Yet, expressible or not, a glimpse is overwhelming. Brigham Young, addressing disillusioned wives, testified, "The transcendent beauty of person, the God-like qualities of
the resurrected husband that she now despises, even if she could
see but a vision of him," would lead her to "feel like worshipping
him, he is so holy, so pure, so perfect, so filled with God."

This collection of essays revolves around the quest to unleash
the "highest in us." Its undergirding theme is that the power of
God is in places we consistently neglect—in the spiritual sense of
our divine origins, in flashes of spirit memories, in the Master's
call to expanded and intensified living, in the sacramental
approach to daily life, in soul-probing responses to tests like unto
Abraham's, in the lucid and time-tested pronouncements of our
own conscience, in the privileges of intimate prayer, and in the
environs of the link between heaven and earth, the temple.

None of these sources and resources are exhausted in our
lives—some remain almost untouched. But the possibilities are
there.

On hostile college campuses, as I have learned in recent years,
there is much resistance to the Latter-day Saint understanding of
man: that he embodies more than a spark of the divine—that he
is, in his potential, the complete flame of God. All the counter-
arguments reduce to one: It is a self-serving "stretch" beyond
reality; it is too good to be true. Nevertheless, it is true. And this
awareness of self in doubt-consuming light, brings what one
writer has called the sense of winning the sweepstakes. It releases
powers of love and healing and energy and creativity that can be
found in no other way.

Needless to say, the readings and interpretations herein, in matters both of history and of doctrine, are my own. I do not speak officially.

My thanks to Paul Green of Bookcraft, who encouraged me to bring under one cover these presentations, and to a continual flow of students who demonstrate to me that, beyond all the justified pessimism, cynicism and skepticism of our times, there is a way up and out.

—Truman G. Madsen

Chapter One

THE HIGHEST
IN US

We begin with an incident from our LDS history which, when I first read it, inflamed me and changed my life. In the 1830s there was a student at Oberlin College, Ohio, whose name was Lorenzo Snow. He was disillusioned with what he saw of religion in general and Christianity in particular. He wrote a letter to his sister who had become a Latter-day Saint, Eliza R. Snow, and confessed his difficulties. She wrote back and invited him to Kirtland. He came. Within a few moments, as I read the story, he was inside the temple, the building which at that time served, as many of you know, more than one purpose. It served *all* of the fundamental functions of the Church. As he entered, there was a small meeting in progress. Patriarchal blessings were being given by the Prophet's father, Joseph Smith, Sr. He listened, first incredulous, then open, and toward the end inspired. He kept saying to himself, "Can this

---

Based on an address given at a ten-stake fireside at BYU, March 3, 1974.

be simply a man or is there something divine involved?" More and more he felt that the Spirit was in it.

At the end of the meeting, the Prophet's father took Lorenzo's hand (there had been no introduction as I read it) and, still filled with the light of his calling, said two things to him. "You will become one of us." Lorenzo Snow understood that but didn't believe it. But now the staggering statement. "And you will become great—even as great as God is. And you could not wish to become greater." Young Lorenzo Snow did not understand that. Shortly the first prediction was fulfilled. His conversion, his baptism and confirmation left him somewhat stillborn. But then came his immersion in the influences of God so that for several nights he could hardly sleep, burning, he says, with a "tangible awareness" of God in a way that changed him.[1]

Move now to a later period in his life. He had served; he had become one of our great and dedicated missionaries. He was sitting discussing the scriptures with a brother in Nauvoo. At that moment something happened to him which in later life he called an impression; sometimes he spoke of it as a vision, and always as an overwhelming revelation. He came to glimpse the meaning of what had been said to him. And he formed it in a couplet which all of us hesitate, and I think wisely, to cite in discussion or conversation but which is a sacred, glorious insight. It's a couplet; he put it in faultless rhythm: "As man now is God once was. As God now is man may become." He says he saw a conduit, as it were, down through which, in fact, by our very nature, by our being begotten of our eternal Parents, we descend and up through which

---

1. "When the Book of Mormon was first read at my father's, I was struck with favorable impressions; and afterwards on hearing Joseph Smith bear his testimony by the power of the Holy Ghost to its truth, a light arose in my understanding which has never been extinguished" (Lorenzo Snow, Journal, 1).

"I was baptized by John Boynton in June, 1836, and confirmed by Hyrum Smith. I received a knowledge of the divine authenticity of the gospel in the most happy and glorious manner. The heavens were opened and the Holy Spirit descended upon me and I tasted the joys of eternity in the midst of the power of God. Those manifestations have never been effaced from my memory" (Lorenzo Snow, Journal, 3).

we may ascend. It struck him with power that if a prince born to a king will one day inherit his throne, so a son of an Eternal Father will one day inherit the fulness of his Father's kingdom.

Suddenly he recovered the New Testament verses, repeated but without depth, in which we are commanded to become perfect. (Then, lest we should relativize that, the Master had added, "even as your Father.") The verses in 1 John vibrate with John's comprehension of love: "Behold, what manner of love the Father hath bestowed upon us, that *we* should be called the sons of God. . . . Beloved, now *are we* the sons of God, and it doth not yet appear what we shall be: but we know that, when he shall appear, *we shall be like him;* for we shall see him as he is" (1 John 3:1–2; italics added).

The concept became a guiding star to young Lorenzo Snow. It went with him through other callings and sacrifices. He hardly dared breathe it—even to his intimates—except to his sister, Eliza, and later during a close missionary discussion with Brother Brigham Young. Not a word had been spoken by the Prophet Joseph specifically giving that principle, but Lorenzo knew it. And you can imagine how he felt when, in the Nauvoo Grove in April 1844, the Prophet Joseph Smith arose and said with power, "God was once a man as we are now."

Now may I take you elsewhere to sympathize for a moment with the outlook others have on this and to understand why our concept is sacred and must be kept so. In a discussion at a widely known theological seminary in the East, I was asked, "What is the Mormon understanding of God?" I struggled to testify. Then three of the most learned of their teachers, not with acrimony but with candor, said: "Let us explain why we cannot accept this. First of all, you people talk of God in terms that are human—all too human." (That's a phrase, incidentally, from Nietzsche.) "But the second problem is worse. You dare to say that man can become like God." And then they held up a hand and said, "Blasphemy."

Well, that hurts a little. I was led to ask two series of questions. (Mind you, I'm telling you the story. I'm not sure they would tell it the same way. I've had a chance to improve it in the interim.)

The first was a series of questions about the nature of Christ. "Was he a person?"

"Yes."

"Did he live in a certain place and time?"

"Yes."

"Was he embodied?"

"Yes."

"Was he somewhere between five and seven feet in height?"

"Well, we hadn't thought of it, but, yes, we suppose he was."

"Was he resurrected with his physical body?"

"He was."

"Does he now have that body?"

"Yes."

"Will he always?"

"Yes."

"Is there any reason we should not adore and honor and worship him for what he has now become?"

"No," they said, "he is very God."

"Yes," I said, "what then of the Father?"

"Oh no, oh no!" And then they issued a kind of Platonic manifesto—the statement out of the traditional creeds which are, all due honor to them, more Greek than they are Hebrew. "No, no, the Father is 'immaterial, incorporeal, beyond space, beyond time, unchanging, unembodied, etc.'"

Now, earlier they had berated me because Mormons, as you know, are credited—or blamed—for teaching, not trinitarianism, but tritheism—the idea of separate, distinct personages in the Godhead—and denying the metaphysical oneness of God. I couldn't resist at this point saying: "*Who* has two Gods? You are the ones who are saying that there are two utterly unlike persons. The religious dilemma is, How can I honor the Father and seek to become like him (for even the pronoun *him* is not appropriate) without becoming *un*like the Christ whom you say we can properly adore and worship and honor?" Well, the response at that point was that I didn't understand the Trinity. And I acknowledged that was true.

But now the second set of questions: "Why," I dared to ask—and it's a question any child can ask—"did God make us at all?" There's an answer to that in the catechisms. Basically, it is that God created man for his own pleasure and by his inscrutable will. Sometimes it is suggested that he did so that he might have creatures to honor and worship him—which, if we are stark in response, is not the most unselfish motive one could conceive. Sometimes it is said that he did so for *our* happiness. But because of the creeds it is impossible to say that God *needed* to do so, for God, in their view, is beyond need. And then the bold question I put was "You hold, don't you, that God has and had all power, all knowledge, all anticipatory wisdom, and that he knew, therefore, exactly what he was about and could have done otherwise?"

"Yes," they allowed, "he could."

"Why, then, since God could have created co-creators, did he choose to make us creatures? Why did God choose to make us his everlasting inferiors?"

At that point one of them said, "God's very nature *forbids* that he should have peers."

I replied: "That's interesting. For us, God's very nature *requires* that he should have peers. Which God is more worthy of our love?"

Now, as Latter-day Saints we know that prophets have lived and died to reestablish in the world in our generation that glorious truth—that what the Eternal Father wants for you and with you is the fulness of your possibilities. And those possibilities are infinite. He did not simply make you from nothing into a worm; he adopted and begat you into his likeness in order to share his nature. And he sent his Firstborn Son to exemplify just how glorious that nature can be—even in mortality. That is our witness.

In all things, Lorenzo came to wonder why others did not wonder at this. "Nothing," he said about three months before his death, "was ever revealed more distinctly than that was to me. Of course, now that it is so well known, it may not appear such a wonderful manifestation, but when I received it the knowledge was marvelous to me" (*Church News,* 2 April 1938). Modern revelation, in ways even Latter-day Saints take for granted, had taught clearly that Jesus the Christ exceeded mankind in every way and was unique in that he was the Firstborn, and the Only Begotten in the flesh, and the only sinless man and therefore "wrought out the perfect atonement through the shedding of his own blood" (D&C 76:69). The atonement was and is perfect because it empowers mankind for a perfect work: perfection. Christ's mission was to overcome the vast difference between his nature and blessedness and our own. Thus he came to accomplish, in the language of a modern scholar, "the universal divinization of man." That we might understand how to worship and know what we worship, the following great kinships of destiny are taught in the Doctrine and Covenants. (I have made some minor modifications of wording in the quotations given.)

I was in the beginning with the Father. (93:21)	Ye were also in the beginning with the Father. (93:23)
I am the Firstborn. (93:21)	All those who are begotten through me are partakers of the glory of the same [the Firstborn], and are the church of the Firstborn. (93:22)
[I] received not of the fulness at first, but continued from grace to grace, until [I] received a fulness. (93:13)	Ye must grow in grace and in the knowledge of the truth . . . you shall receive grace for grace. (93:20)
I . . . received grace for grace. (93:12)	
I . . . received a fulness of the glory of the Father. (93:16)	You may come unto the Father in my name, and in due time receive of his fulness. (93:19)
[I] received a fulness of truth, yea, even of all truth. (93:26)	He that keepeth [my] commandments receiveth truth and

light, until he is glorified in truth and knoweth all things. (93:28)

The glory of the Father was with [me] for he dwelt in [me]. (93:17)

If you keep my commandments you . . . shall be glorified in me as I am in the Father. (93:20)

[I] received all power, both in heaven and on earth. (93:17)

[You are] possessor[s] of all things; for all things are subject unto [you], both in heaven and on the earth, the life and the light, the Spirit and the power, sent forth by the will of the Father through Jesus Christ his Son. (50:27)

[I] . . . ascended up on high, as also [I] descended below all things, in that [I] comprehended all things, that [I] might be in all and through all things, the light of truth. (88:6)

The day shall come when you shall comprehend even God, being quickened in him and by him. (88:49)

[My] light shineth in darkness, and the darkness comprehendeth [me] not. (88:49)

If your eye be single to my glory, your whole bodies shall be filled with light, and there shall be no darkness in you; and that body which is filled with light comprehendeth all things. (88:67)

Glory be to the Father, and I partook and finished my preparations unto the children of men. (19:19)

[Ye] shall be priests of God and Christ, and shall reign with him. (Revelation 20:6)

[I] shall reign for ever and ever. (Revelation 11:15)

King of kings and Lord of lords. (Revelation 19:16)

[He] hath made us kings and priests unto God and his Father. (Revelation 1:6)

He that receiveth me receiveth my Father; And he that receiveth my Father receiveth my Father's kingdom; therefore all that my Father hath shall be given unto him. (84:37–38)

[Ye] are priests of the Most High, after the order of Melchizedek, which was after the order of Enoch, which was after the order of the Only Begotten Son.

Wherefore, as it is written, they are gods, even the sons of God—

Wherefore, all things are theirs, whether life or death, or things present, or things to come, all are theirs and they are Christ's, and Christ is God's.

And they shall overcome all things.

Wherefore, let no man glory in man, but rather let him glory in God, who shall subdue all enemies under his feet. (76:57–61)

Christ, Paul testified, "thought it not robbery to be equal with God." Modern prophets thought it not blasphemy to be "joint heirs" with Christ.

But how can all this relate to the pronouncements of scripture that man is, in his raw and rudimental state, "carnal, sensual, and devilish"; that man must come to see himself as "even less than the dust of the earth"? (The dust, at least, abides the measure of its creation. Not the earth but the inhabitants thereof pollute and abuse and "hate their own blood.") Is not the tenor of the scriptures ancient and modern that we must become as little children and, in the depths of humility, "consider ourselves fools before God," and that otherwise we are "despised" and the Lord will not open unto us?

More than once in heady circumstances such statements have been thrown up to us, especially from those of the "neoorthodox" tradition in theology which holds, in the spirit of Augustine, Calvin, Barth, Brunner, and Reinhold Niebuhr, that Mormons are afflicted with a triple and fatal pride—a pride of Church status, a pride of self-righteousness, but worst of all a pride of aspiration.

Lorenzo Snow found his answer in Christ the Exemplar:

Jesus was a god before he came into the world and yet his knowledge was taken from him. He did not know his former greatness, neither do we know what greatness we had attained to before we came here, but he had to pass through an ordeal, as we have to, without knowing or realizing at the time the greatness and importance of his mission and works. (Lorenzo Snow, Journal, 181–182)

Lorenzo Snow had no doubt that we are dependent upon the Lord for life itself and utterly dependent upon the Lord Jesus Christ for eternal life. Yet he could say, "Godliness cannot be conferred, but must be acquired" (Eliza R. Snow Smith, *Biography,* 193).

And cannot such aspiration be selfish? Not for him. No man understood better than he that in order to be and become like the Master one must submit and surrender. Thus he wrote, "The Priesthood was bestowed upon you, as upon the Son of God, for no other purpose than that through sacrifice you might be proven, that, peradventure, at the last day, you might stand approved before God, and before perfect and holy beings, and that in order to merit this divine approval, *it may be necessary to forget self and individual aggrandizement and seek the interest of your brethren*" (Eliza R. Snow Smith, *Biography,* 376–77; italics added).

When the Prophet first presented to him the law of eternal marriage, Lorenzo shrank and said he felt to fear that he could not live this principle in righteousness. The Prophet Joseph replied (confirming what Lorenzo Snow had wondered about in his own spirit): "The principles of honesty and integrity are founded within you and you will never be guilty of any serious error or wrong, to lead you from the path of duty. The Lord will open your way to receive and obey the law of Celestial Marriage" (Eliza R. Snow Smith, *Biography,* 70). And so he did. There is something autobiographical in his comment, "I have known individuals who have trembled at the idea of passing through certain ordeals who after they were through the temptation said they could approach the Lord in more confidence and ask for such blessings as they desired." And then he added:

Every man has got to learn to stand upon his own knowledge;
he cannot depend upon his neighbor; every man must be independent; he must depend upon his God for himself entirely. It
depends upon himself to see if he will stand the tide of trouble and
overcome the impediments that are strewed in the pathway of life
to prevent his progress. A man can get information by the operations of the Holy Spirit and he approaches to God and increases in
his faith in proportion as he is diligent. (Gems of Truth, *Millenial
Star*, 10 December 1888, 806)

The light of the Holy Spirit, as Brigham Young once said,
lighted up his weaknesses as well as his strengths. (It is no contradiction to say that the greater our vision of possibilities, the
greater our consciousness of present weaknesses.) During the
"reformation" era in the Church, when all the Brethren were asked
to reexamine and probe and purify their lives, Lorenzo Snow with
his friend Franklin D. Richards finally came to feel that they were
unworthy of their high callings. The two went together to
President Brigham Young and offered to give up their priesthood
and their standing in the Twelve. "I guess there were tears in his
eyes when he said, 'You have magnified your priesthood satisfac-
torily to the Lord'" (see *Southern Star*, 2:39).

As the demands of discipleship descended upon Lorenzo he
recapitulated the struggle of righteous men of every generation.
The "why me?" that many ask in the hour of tragedy was coupled
with "why me?" in the presence of great blessings. He heard the
Prophet witness that the nearer one comes to living celestial law
the greater the opposition to be expected.

But instead of seeking to become a man of Bunker Hill (as in
the children's game, "I'm the boss of Bunker Hill, I can fight and
I can kill") in an unlicensed will to power (in some dominant,
Hitlerian sense) it was for Lorenzo Snow just the other way:

There is just one thing that a Latter-day Saint, as an Elder in
Israel should never forget: it should be a bright illuminating star
before him all the time—in his heart, in his soul, and all through
him—that is, he need not worry in the least whether he should be
a deacon or President of the Church. It is sufficient for him to

know that his destiny is to be like his Father, a God in eternity. He will not only be President but he may see himself president of a Kingdom, president of worlds with never-ending opportunities to enlarge his sphere of dominion.

I saw this principle after being in the Church but a short time; it was made as clear to me as the noon day sun. . . .

This thought in the breasts of men filled with the light of the Holy Spirit, tends to purify them and *cleanse them from every ambitious or improper feeling.*

This glorious opportunity of becoming truly great belongs to every faithful Elder in Israel; it is his by right divine and he will not have to come before this or any other quorum to have his status defined. He may be a God in eternity; he may become like his Father, doing the works which his Father did before him and he cannot be deprived of the opportunity of reaching this exalted state.

I never sought to be a Seventy or a High Priest, because this eternal principle was revealed to me long before I was ordained to the Priesthood. The position which I now occupy [he was then President of the Church] is nothing as compared with what I expect to occupy in the future. (At a meeting of the First Presidency and the Council of the Twelve, recorded in BYU Special Collections, Microfilm Reel number 1, page 209; italics added)

My testimony to you is that you have come literally "trailing clouds of glory." No amount of mortal abuse can quench the divine spark. If you only knew who you are and what you did and how you earned the privileges of mortality, and not just mortality but of this time, this place, this dispensation, and the associates that have been meant to cross and intertwine with your lives; if you knew now the vision you had then of what this trial, this probation (what in my bitter moments I call this spook alley) of mortality could produce, would produce; if you knew the latent infinite power that is locked up and hidden for your own good now—if you knew these things you would never again yield to any of the putdowns that are a dime a dozen in our culture today. Everywhere pessimism, everywhere suspicion, everywhere the denial of the worth and dignity of man.

I have faith that if we caught hold of God's living candle on that truth and went out into the world—I don't care if the vocations concerned are sensational, spectacular, or brilliant—just out in the world being true to the vision, we would not need to defend the cause of Jesus Christ. People would come and ask: "Where have you found such peace? Where have you found the radiance that I sense in your eyes and in your face? How come you don't get carried away with the world?" And we could answer that the work of salvation is the glorious work of Jesus Christ. But it is also the glorious work of the uncovering and recovering of your own latent divinity.

I know that idea is offensive to persons whom I would not wish to offend. I know that it goes against the grain of much that is built into our secular culture. I know that there are those who say there is no proof. But I bear witness that Jesus Christ, if there were none else, is the living proof, and that, as you walk in the pattern he has ordained, *you* will be living proof. I bear that witness in the name of Jesus Christ. Amen.

Chapter Two

FREEDOM TO BECOME

My wife, Ann, and I had the privilege not long ago of visiting Hong Kong, that little, jutting segment of China which does not really belong to the new China but which is still under British rule, and where many Chinese have come for political asylum. We met many of some four thousand who had recently become Christians—Latter-day Saints—most of them under the age of thirty. Not a few of them had come from Red China. They first came for only one reason—freedom.

As we stood at that border, which is carefully marked, and saw the small river that separates the two realms, we inquired quite naively: "Well, why don't people just walk over? We don't see anything to prevent it." (We'd heard of the bamboo curtain but we couldn't see any bamboo.) It was explained to us that no one, not even a mouse, could cross there. It was mined; it was watched; it was guarded like a prison yard. And if anybody thought that he could get out of Red China and into Hong Kong there was only

Address given at an investigator fireside at Oakland Interstake Center, July 28, 1973.

201

one way today—a marathon swim. He had to go out into the ocean a great distance in cold and sometimes shark-infested water, and then he had to make a kind of a moon-shaped swim and come back in—sometimes swimming as much as twenty-five miles. No sane person would begin that swim unless he knew he could stay in the water for at least a day and a half. That's why those who made it were young.

The week we were there we met a man whose relative had made that attempt only a week before. This man started with thirteen others. People know before they begin that their odds for survival are one in ten. When patrol boats spot them, they're simply shot. (The bodies roll up onto Kowloon Peninsula every day.) The men in this particular group went without food for five days before they began to swim. (That was because if they had asked for food it might have been suspected what they were about.)

Of the thirteen, three made it, one of them the man whose relative we met. We learned from him that there had recently been a couple who set out for freedom and the Communists had shot the husband when they were four miles away. Apparently the patrol unit didn't recognize that there were two swimmers. So the wife, in the manner of lifesaving swimming, then pulled her husband's body the rest of the way so he could be buried on free land!

Now, I believe in freedom and I believe freedom is worth sacrifices. And I believe America is great, if it *is* great at all, because blood has been shed not only to buy freedom here but to hold to it elsewhere. But that's freedom *from*. That's freedom *from* intimidation; freedom *from* a police state; freedom *from* external pressures and dominations.

There's another kind of freedom. That is freedom *for* something. Freedom to *become* what you have it in you to become. Sometimes you don't have to be free *from* in order to be free *for*. Christ became what he is while being denied most of the freedoms you and I have in this country. The Prophet Joseph Smith grew most at times when he had the least freedom *from*. He experienced a tremendous soul growth during a six-month period when he was in jail—much of that time in a jail ironically called

Liberty. Freedom to *become* matters even more than freedom *from*.

Now, will you forgive me if I confide in a personal manner a story which has gripped me more than I can say? It is a story by James Hilton, the author of *Goodbye, Mr. Chips* and of *Lost Horizon*, the man who created the beautiful myth of Shangri La. James Hilton wrote another book called *Random Harvest*. Many years ago a film version of that book was made starring Ronald Coleman and Greer Garson.

The story is about a wealthy and titled Englishman who goes to war and in the midst of a battle is, as they used to say, "shell-shocked" by an explosion. His memory is blotted out. He doesn't even know his own name. And further, his speech is impaired to the point that under any pressure he can hardly say a word. They bring him back to England and put him in an asylum. He stays there in the hope that his parents—he doesn't know *who* they are—will come and inquire and tell him who he is. He yearns to belong to someone. Many couples come. All turn away immediately, disappointed.

The war ends and in a pea-soup fog he walks out of the asylum—no one guarding, all are celebrating—finds himself hustled and bustled in the crowd, and comes into a little shop. There he meets Paula, a beautiful woman who immediately recognizes that he is from this hospital. Out of sympathy and with a certain amount of courage she cares for him. In due time his stutter passes a bit and he begins to find himself. He aspires to be a writer on a shoestring and they marry and subsequently have a son.

One day (you feel a little ominous about it as you see the movie) he's saying good-bye to her, their first parting since marriage. He's going into the big city to deliver a manuscript. In Liverpool he is struck by a cab, and all of his former memory of his identity comes back. But he is blank from the moment of shell shock; which means he cannot remember meeting Paula or any of the subsequent events.

Now what? Well, that's the rest of the story. The point here isn't just that this is a great love story (for it is that); it's that it is the symbol—the allegory—of our lives. And I'll explain in a moment how deeply the allegory applies.

He goes back to his family home, Random Hall, becomes successful in business, and runs for Parliament. The doctors advise Paula that there is no way she can jog or shake him into remembering her, but she loves him so deeply that eventually she applies successfully to be his secretary. There are moments when he stares at her and asks questions. She *knows* he's on the verge of recall, but always, disappointingly, he turns away and says something like, "Well, you know how people have feelings that they have known someone before."

Then the plot thickens; he proposes marriage—but only a state marriage, only a social-secretary arrangement, what he calls "a merger." "No emotional demands," he says. Again the doctor advises her "No," ("You're going to be hurt") but she can't help herself, and she becomes a kind of wife. The climax of their difficulty is the night that he presents her with an incredibly beautiful emerald, but as she goes into her room and opens the drawer, there is the little bit of cheap jewelry that he had given her as "Smithy" (that's what she called him). Somehow the value of the those beads over the value of the jewel pierces her heart and she cries out, "Smithy!" He discovers her in this condition and wonders aloud if he should have "interfered in her life." Paula laments: "The best of you, your capacity for loving, your joy in living are buried in a space of time you've forgotten." She is resolved to leave him, perhaps for good.

Just before her departure he travels on business to Melbridge, the same community where the asylum is. He assumes he's never been there before. He takes care of his business, but, walking with a friend, he says, "Let's go into this little shop." And the friend asks, "How did you know there was a little shop of this description?" "I don't know, I . . . I *did* know! But I don't know how!" Memories begin to flow. Shortly he finds his way back to the asylum. "I remember I was here. I came out of these gates." His friend says, "Let's retrace your steps, then."

Now comes the climactic scene. (And I have read somewhere

that Greer Garson says that of all the parts she ever played in life as well as in Hollywood, no scene overwhelmed her as did this one.) He goes back to the cottage where he lived with Paula as Smithy. All the time in the interim he has carried the key in his vest pocket. Now he is back to the door where he had waved good-bye that morning. He walks to the gate; it still squeaks in the same way. He walks under the buds of a tree; they have a familiar look. The key fits, and the door swings open. Now Paula, who has heard that he is in the area and is hoping against hope that he will remember her, rushes up to the gate. He turns around. The question is, will she say, "Smithy," or will she say, "Charles"? She risks it. She says, "Smithy." He looks confused. She says it again and breaks into tears. He still looks confused. And then the camera comes in close and you see in one radiant wave the whole past come to his face. In an instant he recovers himself, his past, and his beloved. "Paula!" And they rush into each other's arms. That's the end. It's also the beginning.

What does that story have to do with freedom and fulfillment? What does it have to do with *you?* So much! So much!

We, too, are wealthy and titled "Englishmen." We once dwelt in the scintillating presence of the Eternal Father. So rich, so exquisite was our condition there (though it was not without conflict), that we can hardly endure remembering. Wilford Woodruff heard the Prophet Joseph Smith remark that were it not for the strong biological urge in us to survive, to hold on to the slipping rope even when we are in pain and suffering, and, in addition, were it not for the veil of forgetfulness, we could not stand this world. Our mortal amnesia is the Lord's anesthesia. We must stay in this condition to work out our possibilities, undergo the stress and distress that lead to perfection.

One role of Christ, as of his prophets, is to remind us—to "bring all things to our remembrance." (See John 14 and Laub, Diary, 9–16.) Brigham Young taught that we are totally familiar with God the Father, but that knowledge is "locked up" within us. Nothing, he said, will so much astound us "when our eyes are open in eternity, as to think that we were so stupid in the body."

205

(See Lee, *Youth*, 50.) Lorenzo Snow taught that "according to our preparation there"—and he taught that our preparation was exactly suited to our anticipated missions—"our flesh was to become acquainted with our experiences in the spirit."

Like Sir Charles Rainier in the story, we were sent into the mortal world clear in the vision of how high were the stakes. (There is a real evidence that some shrank from that momentous decision.) And we, too, have been shell-shocked. We do not now know our own name, rank, and serial number. Even the memory of a perfect language, with its grace and ease and instant communicative power, is gone. Here, we do indeed stammer and stutter in speech as in conduct, groping our way to self-understanding and feeling at times, even in the midst of helpful people, "strangers and foreigners." We yearn to belong. Only when we are touched by the Spirit do we overcome, for a fleeting time, our memory imprisonment. Then, as Joseph F. Smith puts it, "we are lighted up with the glory of our former home."

And there are other wonderings. Why are we drawn toward certain persons and they to us, as if we have always known each other? Is it a fact that we always have? No matter if the "parties are strangers," Parley P. Pratt observes, "no matter if they have never spoken to each other. Each will be apt to remark, 'Oh, what an atmosphere encircles that stranger. How my heart thrilled with pure and holy feelings in his presence. What confidence and sympathy he inspired'" (*Theology,* 96). "If the ties of this world will extend to the next, why not believe," Orson F. Whitney asks, "we had similar ties before we came into this world . . . some of them at least?" "I have this belief concerning us," says George Q. Cannon, "that it was arranged before we came here how we should come and through what lineage we should come. . . . I am as convinced that it was predestined before I was born that I should come through my father as I am sure that I stand here" (*Utah Genealogical and Historical Magazine,* 21:124.) The Prophet Joseph Smith confided to his intimates that we had some choice as to the time and the family of our mortal sojourn, he having chosen his parents.

"I believe that our Savior is the ever-living example to all flesh in these things. He no doubt possessed a foreknowledge of all the vicissitudes through which he would have to pass in the mortal tabernacle. . . . If Christ knew beforehand, so did we" (Joseph F. Smith, *Gospel Doctrine,* 13). Through the perceptions of prophetic men we are told the day will come when we shall recognize, as Orson Pratt wrote, that every spirit of man saw Christ in the premortal councils. And in the resurrection: "Then shall ye know that ye have seen me, that I am, and that I am the true light that is in you, . . . otherwise ye could not abound" (D&C 88:50).

The language of the literary world preserves something of the premortal sense. Plato's classic myth in the *Symposium* teaches (some think only playfully) that the soul lived in a perfect world, directly aware of the true, the good and beautiful; that lovers were there entwined in a metaphysical unity. In this present world, learning is but recollection. We search in vain for self-understanding until we encounter our exact counterpart, our "other half," our mate. Then our capacity for love expands and we relive the intense passional echoes of that relationship. In finding our companion or companions we literally find ourselves.

The myth is contained, with profound Christian overtones, in the newly discovered apocalyptic writings of upper Egypt. We know now that there were many forms of Gnosticism, but some of them contained elements of New Testament truth. It is taught in one form of Gnosticism that the fall of man was estrangement from woman and the glorification of man is sacred marriage, the reunion of the separated in the mergings of the "bridal chamber," which is the highest sacrament. Eve, whatever her role in man's fall, is a partner with Christ in his redemption.

We have flashes—the French phrase is *déjà vu,* which literally translated means "already seen." We cry out, " I have anticipated this." And there are other wonderings—haunting landscapes, the sounds of music that are echoes of eternity, a love for the truth ("my sheep know my voice"), and spiritual acquaintanceship. We only skim the surface in our seekings, yet we do not trust the psychologists who tell us that we use less than 5 percent of our potential. We doubt the studies of aptitude and talent that show that we are, each one of us, in a unique way, geniuses. In the struggle to communicate, to decide, to plan, to express creative talent, to forecast, to cope with learning challenges, we often consider ourselves "behind," "backward," and "just average." But the prophets teach us that "to every man is given a gift," and, as Orson Pratt put it, no one is left destitute. Joseph Smith taught that we cannot receive more until we honor what has already been given. We have great gifts, greater endowments, and the greatest of destinies. The gold is in the mine. But the power of Christ must sink a shaft to bring it out. In the end our becoming depends on pretastes or, quite literally, after-tastes.

A morning is ahead when there will be brightness and glory exceeding all prior mornings, and a "perfect bright recollection." Then, we are promised, we will be given back our lost memory and with it our selves. The key will fit the door. As the earth will become an instrument of truth whereby "all things for our glory, past, present and future" will be manifest, so we will become living Urim and Thummim. We will not just begin to see. We will see it all. "The day shall come when you shall comprehend even God, being quickened in him by him." To comprehend God is to comprehend all that God comprehends, to "see as [we] are seen and know as [we] are known" (D&C 76:94). If in this world our spirits still sing in the afterburn of that exposure, how, "with spirit and element inseparably connected," we shall sing a new, more glorious song in his eternal presence! Surely a climactic scene awaits all of us.

Chapter Three

I AM THE LIFE

Education Weeks are a baptism of fire. The instructions seem easy enough: Just condense a whole semester's course into three hours, expect an average of three hundred students per class, teach three to four classes in a row, live out of a can, and, oh yes, teach like Karl G. Maeser! I recall overhearing a colleague of mine discussing the resurrection. He made the point that many prophets have said that there are essential elements in our bodies which will never become an essential part of any other and which will be reunited with our spirits in the resurrection. Someone asked him, "What are the fundamental elements?" He thought for a moment and said: "Go and see Truman Madsen. He's down to them already."

In this and other ways I've been accused of being undernourished. In self-defense I have said that there is nothing in the scriptures that provides for the survival of the fattest. Seriously, I have on occasion wanted to say to these many choice people who come to Education Week—come hungering and thirsting, some of

---

Address given at BYU Education Week devotional, 1973.

them giving up vacations, sleeping in cars, going without—a sentence spoken by Christ himself anciently: "I have meat to eat that ye know not of." The most exhausting and most exhilarating teaching challenge of my life has been Education Week.

The spirit may be strong even when the body is weak. A few blocks from here is a home and a bedroom where, even as I speak to you this morning, there is a boy sixteen years old, slowly dying. In his infancy he was normal, healthy, bright-eyed, promising; but then the processes began to reverse in him. (There's a technical name for the affliction—Herler's Syndrome.) Since eight-and-a-half or nine he has been bedfast, and he has long been immobile. It is inadequate to say he is only skin and bone—he is hardly that. He has not enough muscle left even to clear his throat, and only enough consciousness to recognize his mother, she thinks. The fading vital signs diminish the hope that he will live much longer. Asked to administer to this youngster, I faced the strange dilemma as I placed my hands upon him: to whom am I speaking? And there came over me a feeling that locked within this racked body was a giant of a spirit. Almost the feeling of a musical genius struggling to perform on a battered, stringless instrument. And as I sought to make promises, and then, trembling, left the home with the bishop, I became conscious in ways I cannot put into words that there is meaning in the sentences, "I am the life," and "I am the resurrection and the life."

The Lord Jesus Christ in all his teaching presupposes that he has somehow gained power over all the powers of life, that all things, both in heaven and in earth, are subject unto him. Professor Hugh Nibley, who has just read a thousand books in order to write one, tells us that in most ancient world religions—Greek, Roman, Oriental, Phoenician, Hebrew—the temple was symbolic of the very navel of the universe, the life link between heaven and earth. The temple is the house of the Lord Jesus Christ. That insight becomes exponential when you think that he has also told us in modern revelation "man is himself a temple—a living temple." To cut or to poison that channel is to begin to die. To have health, wholeness in it is to begin to live.

A graduate student and a lover of comparative literature was assigned recently to go through the Doctrine and Covenants and look for what we called "image families." His quest: To what illustrations does the Lord over and over resort in revelation? You who have read the book, could you guess? There are three that dominate all others. They are: light and darkness, planting and harvesting, and lifting and raising up. The biological analogues are photosynthesis, growth, and fruitfulness. And at the very center of those images used so often is the image of birth and rebirth. The Lord says in that glorious prose poem, Doctrine and Covenants 93, "All those who are begotten through me are partakers of the glory of the same." He is the Firstborn. We, through him, though we be lastborn, are yet partakers of the glory of the Firstborn. The word *glory* itself has a constellation of connotations—life, spirit, power, light, fire.

It was the Prophet Joseph Smith who taught us that we must have a kind of new birth even to *see* the kingdom of God and recognize that we are somehow out of it. Then we must be born of water and of the Spirit in order to *enter* it. And just as that is central to all his teaching, it is central to all the ordinances of the gospel which take the life-giving elements—for example, the water, the bread, the oil—and enable us to participate in the process of divine nourishment.

Students constantly corner me and ask, "Dr. Madsen, do you believe there are any absolutes in this universe of ours?" (They have been taught that all absolutes are obsolete.) I answer, "Yes." They challenge, "Name one." Here is one: Life can only come from life. That is an eternal law. There is no other way. You can only be born by having parents. (Any of you who were born in some other way can be excused from genealogical research.) The Lord chose the image of begetting to remind us of that central and glorious truth.

Recently I stood in a translating room where words that have been written heretofore in English are now being put into Chinese characters. The mission president confided that he had a real problem with the Doctrine and Covenants. The trouble is the word *quickened.* It is used frequently in modern revelation. But it has no Mandarin or Cantonese synonym. They can come close. There are words that imply motion or function or speeding up. What is missing in any of the attempted words is the idea of animation, of life. It is the word *quickened* that the scripture uses to describe what happened to Adam when he came up out of the water and the power of God centered in him and he was "quickened in the inner man" (Moses 6:65). "Quickened," the source of life. The Chinese have the life without the word. Perhaps we Americans have the word without the life.

May I apply this insight to some of our ordinary thinking about life in the Church? The Prophet Joseph Smith once compared life to a wheel that each of us move around. There are times when we are up and someone else is down. But in due time it is the other way around. In that setting he added, "Every man [every woman, too] will fail sometime." Hence the need of the Church, that some who are alive and high can lift those of us who are more or less barren, numbed, deadened. If this perspective begins to sink into us, many things take on a different light.

One supreme compliment to a member of the Church is, "He is active." But so are falling rocks and billiard balls. The word the Lord uses, and the question derived from it is, "Are you a *lively* member?" Are you alive?

It's no longer a question of whether you have been through the standard works, but whether the life and light in them has somehow passed through the very skin of your bodies and enlivened you.

It isn't whether you *say* your prayers in a proper fashion and position and time, but whether you open up honestly what is alive and more or less dead within you to the Source of life and stay with it and with him until the return wave of life enters you.

In recent years the Church has set many new attendance records. But how nourished are those who are within the Church buildings?

It's not a question of whether you can show the leaves—go through the motions, if you will—of the religious life. Christ, in what seems to some a most severe act, saw those leaves on the fig tree near Jericho and was convinced thereby that there were figs, whereas actually there were none. And the tree was cursed and henceforth was good for nothing but to be burned. Are you fruitful? Do you bear fruit? That is the question.

"Is he a good speaker or teacher in the Church?" we often ask. How little do our students, our classroom members, understand that most of what happens depends on them. If they come hungering, thirsting, centering their concentrated faith in the person who seeks to speak or teach, they pull out of him the seeds of life and spirit which are then planted in them and grow. This I've come to know as people come forward and thank me for teaching them things that I myself did not know. It is the Spirit that nourishes growth. The teacher only plants.

We stand and testify and speak well about the Lord's menu. But do we deliver the Lord's food—and feed his sheep with heavenly manna?

Are we programming each other (programming can be to death as well as to life)? Or are there dynamic currents flowing through these programs into us?

We "sustain" the Brethren by "voting" for them periodically. But the question is, Do we give them our sustenance? Do we seek assurance that the Spirit of the Lord called this man to his position? Are we willing to exercise our faith and prayers that he may be magnified? If so, both he and we are vitalized.

We have a teacher training program that has been preoccupied, in recent years, with the idea that the classroom experience should change behavior. But the Lord Jesus Christ is far more ambitious for us than that. He wants to change us, to produce celestial personalities. And if we will let him, he has the power. How can any mortal teacher do that? He cannot—unless he has an unimpeded channel to the generator of life, who is Christ. A teacher's greatest success is when his students are tied to Christ. Too many of us are tempted to win *our own* disciples.

Some of us do a "100 percent home teaching." But do we leave in the home a living atmosphere?

What good is a woman, I am sometimes asked, who has done almost nothing for years "except hold a family together"? That is all. The Lord's answer is that if she has created and transmitted the nutriments of spiritual life in her home (and in the early days the Saints always dedicated their home to the Lord), then she has been the purveyor of life. And nothing is more crucial!

Suppose we go to the temple and (how impotent the phrase!) "do names." Actually we are bringing new birth and life to spirit personalities whose exquisite gratitude, according to the Prophet Joseph Smith, will be such that they will fall to our knees and embrace them and bathe our feet with their tears. That is what we are about. And in the well-chosen phrase of Arthur Henry King, we ourselves return again and again to the temple to be born and reborn again and "to resacramentalize our marriage" and our home.

The time may come when we don't just "say a blessing" on the food but when we, in effect, seek to make every act of our lives life-giving and done in the Lord's name and with his Spirit. Then the whole earth and the whole day and the whole of our lives will be the temple within which we labor with and for him.

In short, worship of the Lord Jesus Christ is more than being attracted by his personality, fascinated by his teaching, even desirous of imitating his conduct. That's only part. It is a matter of our coming unto him with all of our life faculties open and receiving his glory—receiving his power and his life.

President Marion G. Romney has borne witness that when section 88 says that there are three different degrees of glory, those degrees are more than orbs or worlds. They are you—your own body. And your glory is to be that glory by which you are quickened *in the present life*. There is therefore a sense in which, as we sit here today, there are three kinds of personality—three different circuits, right here and now—some who are attuned to the celestial life and nourished by it breathe a better atmosphere, sing a richer song, express more powerful forces, and drink and eat a stronger and more heavenly meal. Others of us are still on a lesser circuit, eating husks. Our ultimate glory will depend upon our circuit here.

Now may I take you to a sacred place. There is a garden near some fruitful olive trees in Jerusalem. To it Jesus was wont to go. (The Prophet's verb is "accustomed to go.") On a given night anciently the power of his compassion, the power of his identifying imagination, the power of his sacrificial love began its awful work in his system. As he knelt under the ravages of all the forms of spiritual dying, he cried out for help. Even he? Yes. But was he not one who had moved "from grace to grace," one who had honored always the will of the Father? Did he not have sufficient strength to go through it? Thank the Lord for the message still in the record and left unchanged in the Inspired Version, that even he reached the limit.

Luke records, "And there appeared an angel unto him from heaven, strengthening him." This was the same Christ who had only within days been on the Mount of Transfiguration, having undergone divine manifestations so great that we have not yet been trusted to know all that took place. Yet now the burden became unbearable. And who was the angel? We know there are none who minister to this earth (minister or administer) but those who do belong or have belonged to it. Who was he? And can we believe, though we know not, that the strengthening, the life-giving touch (for it must have been that) was infinitely more than the placing of a moist, cool cloth on a fevered and bleeding brow?

How many of us have been stillborn, are stunted, staggered, barely holding on? But Christ went through what he had to in order to generate in his own center self compassion for us. And to earn everlastingly, and make real to every bit of consciousness throughout all space and time, the power of life!

Now, I pray that we will not be, as were the Jewish leaders and the Romans who stood looking up at the cross, unable really to see, taunting him with words like these: "Come down, you who are so high and mighty; you who have claimed so much; you who have said you could save men and now cannot save yourself. Come down! Prove you are God." Here is the ultimate absurdity of sign-seeking, saying in effect, "We will only believe if you will come off the cross and do external magic." The whole message was that he was willingly *on* the cross to prove forever, and lift us forever toward, the inward power of love and life.

To those of us, then, who thirst, I plead, Come to him. He turns no penitent one away. Would you, if you had paid so much in suffering? Would you ever give up? All doors that are locked against the Lord are locked by us. He is always waiting, promising life where there has been death, healing where there has been sickness, forgiveness where there has been sin. And sin is poison. He sets us all an inversion of our own example. We say to people who have hurt us: "If you will change, I will forgive you—but not until. If you deserve forgiveness, you shall have it." But Christ said to the woman taken in adultery, as he wrote in the sand in the outer court of the temple (the only writing of his that is mentioned in the four Gospels), "Where are thine accusers?" You remember her reply. He said: "Neither do I condemn thee; go, and sin no more" (John 8:10–11, Inspired Version). The Inspired Version adds a sentence: "And the woman glorified God from that hour, and believed on his name." The offer of forgiveness *before* we have changed in order that we may change—that is the power of Christ. And it brings flowing, living water to the famished soul.

It was John the Beloved (who according to a recently discovered manuscript likely was the youngest of the ancient apostles), a mere boy not yet weathered into cynicism, who stood, you recall, with the mother of Christ before the cross. The only one of the Twelve. Later, having filled a great mission—weathered, but not withered—and having received the revelation that closes the New Testament, he cites the voice of the Lord Jesus Christ in power in the spirit of eternal truth and in glorious poetry. He says: "And the Spirit and the bride say, Come. And let him that heareth say, Come. And let him that is athirst come. And whosoever will, let him take the water of life freely" (Revelation 22:17).

How more could the Lord have taught us this than when he identified himself over and over with the elements of life?

"I am the living bread."

"I am the true fountain."

"He that believeth on me, as the scripture hath said, out of his belly shall flow rivers of living water. But this [says John] spake he of the Spirit."

"I am the vine."

"Ye are the branches."

"I am the life."

"Without me ye can do nothing."

May God bless us to come hungering and thirsting and receive the birth and rebirth that is in Jesus Christ until we, like him, are "quickened in the inner man."

Chapter Four

THE SACRAMENTAL LIFE

Let me begin with a kind of cross-disciplinary statement about religion. There is a remarkable convergence of ideas about the aspect of religion I want to discuss. Borrowing a phrase from an anthropologist, Clifford Geertz, I speak tonight of "consecrated behavior." What he means by this is so obvious it may elude us:

> It is in some sort of ceremonial form, even if that form be hardly more than a recitation of a myth, or the consultation of an oracle, or the decoration of a grave, that the moods and motivations which sacred symbols induce in men and the general conceptions of the order of existence which they formulate for men, meet and reinforce one another (see "Religion As a Cultural System," in *Anthropological Study,* 28).

What he is saying is that in ritual (or what we would call ordinances), our deepest motivations and deepest understandings merge. In all discussions of morality this, I take it, is the source

BYU James E. Talmage Lecture, 1971.

of power most often underestimated. And this is so even in our own midst. We need to recognize that ceremony is indispensable. And the most unanswerable evidence of the necessity of ceremony (notice I didn't say "desire" or "need," but a stronger word still—*necessity*) is that even those most hostile to it end by participation in it.

Look for a moment at worldly analogues. In student life, we see purportedly unstructured youth very structured indeed: the proper smudge on the shoes, the proper purr words (*neat, all right, swinging, grooving*), photographic imitation of rebuffs and greetings and departures, and even of the gesture that pushes the hair back. I am saying nothing against this; I'm not prescribing, only describing manifestations of symbolic gesturings—to show that there is no ceremonyless human being.

A friend of mine describes a laughable situation in which a group of men had banded together in a kind of social fraternal group. They all knew each other by first names and also in the Church by "brother." But they spent the evening in verbal stumbles, correcting themselves from "brother" to "worthy highmaster" and other such terms, trying to learn the new acceptable system.

The question then is not whether we will express ourselves in ceremonies. Inevitably we will. The question is, Which ceremonies are most powerful in motivating us in *becoming?*

The answer is, Those revealed from heaven.

Depth psychologists are telling us that touch, a handshake, the way we use space (to quote Edward Hall) has much to do with our balance in life. (You are only comfortable in conversation if the person is at a "proper" distance.) Scientist Polanyi speaks of the "tacit dimension" of life—what he calls "indwelling"—an intuitive, implicit consciousness of meaning which transcends "common sense," scientific method, or rational analyses; for example, recognizing (as we all do) the expression of puzzlement on a human face. There is Jung's notion of "the collective unconscious" which he elsewhere calls the great "symbol-making factory." He is convinced that each of us inherits not only our own

219

parents' chromosomes but also a cumulative set of responses to symbolic forms.

Recognizing the power of symbolic ritual, many theologians today clamor for what they call a "liturgical revival." Protestants who whittled the seven sacraments to two (baptism and communion) and then decided they could get along with none at all now often wish they hadn't. They seek a new vital contact with the originals: "What did Jesus really do at the Last Supper?" "Would it help if we put a rock band in the St. John's Cathedral?" "Should there be a laying on of hands in confirmation?"

Semanticists today talk about how words often have roles or functions quite different than their dictionary meanings (for example, "I do" in a marriage ceremony). In their ritual functioning they take on something of the character of the thing they symbolize. C. S. Lewis alerts us to "semantic halos" and how they influence us beyond usual definitions. And J. L. Austin speaks of performatory utterances such as "I christen this ship," and "I baptize you," and describes these not as statements of fact but as ceremonial enactments—a doing of something through words. And he finds them immensely strong.

Formal mathematicians such as Tarski, Hempel, and Max Black have analyzed the nature of mathematics, which is the language of science, and have concluded that where mathematical definition is certain it has nothing to do with reality and when it is applied to reality it is misleading. Some acknowledge that personality, and especially religious expression, is not amenable to exact mathematical measure. And so (as a student of mine put it) the key to the universe may not be mathematics but metaphor, the language of compared qualities, the language of feeling. Ordinances are living metaphors or, as Orson F. Whitney put it, "poems in action."

The next step (to those of us who have not yet discovered this, I offer it as a hypothesis) is to recognize that ordinances in the kingdom—from baptism to anointing to sealing—are the most intensively loaded and extensively applicable metaphors of the universe.

Let me pause here to warn against a certain hostility that I find in myself and assume may be in some of you. It arises not because we have correctly read the Restoration but because we have misread the Apostasy. We see remnants of ritual; we see them elaborated or embellished and also abandoned or reduced to things that are mystical or hollow or merely aesthetic. All of this we call "pagan ceremony." Thus, on guard against distortions, we are on edge about ordinances themselves. But when ordinances have been renewed, when their beauty has been revivified, when their appropriateness and significance has been reestablished, they are not pagan and they are not empty.

We turn then to two functions that ordinances can and ought to have in our daily lives.

It is Mircia Eliade, famous for his studies of the "symbolic structure" of religion, who says, "For the religious man, the cosmos lives and speaks" (*Sacred,* 165). And he supposes that this is so because for *all* religions God or the gods have created the cosmos. But that, for Mormons, is a misstatement. Note two distinct propositions that stand behind our whole relationship to the earth and therefore to the ordinances:

First, the earth and the cosmos were not created. The elements are uncreate; the earth has been ordered, given form. The earth is not only the handiwork of God but it is somehow alive and is to be reverenced; the earth's destiny is to become a celestial body. The implication is that the earth is not to be escaped but transformed. And it pleases God that "the fulness of the earth is yours" and that "he hath given all these things unto man" (D&C 59:16). It is not merely a bleak shadow of a higher world, it is on the way to *becoming* one.

Second, therefore, the distinction characteristic of all religion between sacred and secular—between what is holy and what is earthly—is finally artificial. We are taught, "All things unto me are spiritual" (D&C 29:34).

Thus, modern revelation teems with assurance that every earthly human experience may be lived not only on a *higher* plane

221

but eventually on the *highest*. Eternity is the extension—not the replacement—of the patterns of this earth.

Now, I suggest that ordinances as they have been reestablished in our midst are signs of reality, full-freighted with meaning. They are eternal teaching mechanisms. In confirmation, consider these three statements:

> God has set many signs on the earth, as well as in the heavens; for instance, the oak of the forest, the fruit of the tree, the herb of the field, all bear a sign that seed hath been planted there; for it is a decree of the Lord that every tree, plant, and herb bearing seed should bring forth of its kind, and cannot come forth after any other law or principle." (Joseph Smith, *Teachings* [1938], 198)

In the Book of Moses the Master teaches Adam that "all things bear record of me" (Moses 6:63).

And again, "All things which have been given of God from the beginning of the world, unto man, are the typifying of him" (2 Nephi 11:4).

At the core, then, of all ordinances and all divinely revealed ceremonies are these signs of God and Christ which center in the source of life, the power of *becoming*. And this awareness with all its ceremonial enactments is the drive shaft of "consecrated" behavior.

Comparative religion tells us that many cultures have had rituals of fertility and their various offshoots: worship of the seasons, sun worship, the isolation of any and every kind of creature—scorpions, serpents, cows, and trees—to which are ascribed the powers of life, of generation, even of human regeneration. But these can and often do become idolatric. We are not to look *to* them but *through* them. They are signs of the ultimate source of life—Christ himself.

It is interesting to me that the word *ordinance* has the same root as *ordained* and *order*. Those connotations are appropriate. But it also has the same root as *ordinary*. That, too, is relevant. An ordinance takes the most ordinary of elements (for what is more commonplace than water, bread, olive oil?—kneeling, clasping hands, lifting of arms are ordinary things) and gives them or receives them or consecrates them as holy, as somehow focusing our mortal upreach and an immortal response. Ordinances make possible the transformation of the ordinary. Our ordinary work, ordinary breathing and speaking, ordinary pleasures, become extraordinary when they are consciously sacramental.

The later sermons of the Prophet Joseph Smith (who, until the Restoration, was taught that no sacrament is essential) abound with concern that the Saints understand this. One sees some frustration in him that the Saints—even they—are slow to understand. One statement, by the way, is itself a remarkable figure which time has blurred. He said getting this idea into the minds of the Saints was (here comes the simile) like "cutting hemlock knots using a corn-dodger for a wedge, and a pumpkin for a beetle." That is meaningless until you go back to his usage. Hemlock knots are tough to split, among the toughest. If your "wedge" were a cornmeal pancake and if the "hammer" with which you drove it in were a pumpkin you would know the difficulty of the task.

Some of Joseph's anxiety shows in a comment he made when the brethren were inquiring (after all, they had no precedent experience), "Why sacrifice to build the Kirtland Temple?" What did "endowment" mean anyway? The Prophet replied that he could not answer yet. "Nor could Gabriel explain it to the understanding of your dark minds" (Joseph Smith, *Teachings* [1938], 91). I'm afraid that means (and this is a frightening thought) that even God cannot explain fully until we open to him and his light.

But sparks of insight come out of the Prophet's teaching about ordinances, "that they may be perfect in the understanding of their ministry" (D&C 97:14). Aren't there better ways of teaching than ordinances? "Who can I teach except my friends?" Plato asks. We can only learn some things in an environment of love—consecrated space and time—where we are approved and embraced. I'm a professional educator aware of lecturing, case method, class participation, summary, role playing, story, repetition, examination, personal reports, group dynamics, maps, audio-visual aids, dial access. Yet the kernel of worth of all of these is improved and enhanced by intelligent participation in ordinances. I wish we had another word for the blending of thought and feeling that takes place in an ordinance, a word perhaps like *compre-feel*. In modern thought, brain and heart are separated and often detached from the subtler aspirations of the spirit (sometimes the psychologists are responsible). But in ordinances, a symphonic combination of all aspects of the self occurs.

Again, the Prophet said ordinances combine the beautiful and the true. Those are my words, but listen to his. He is talking here about the ceremony for greeting one another to welcome them into the School of the Prophets. "I salute you in token or remembrance of the everlasting covenant" (D&C 88:133). "Behold, this is beautiful that he may be an example" (D&C 88:130). Again he tells us that ordinances are the triggering of memory—our infinite memories—for ordinances were established "from before the foundation of the world" and reveal things which have been "kept hid" until now. And we were there. Another scripture does not say that the Lord has given them for the first time, but that he has "renewed and confirmed" them (D&C 84:48). He does not say that we thus *begin* to share in his goodness here, but that we "*continue* in his goodness." The Prophet teaches further that these ordinances take away our facades, the many faces of Adam and Eve which we have constructed to mask our real selves. Face-to-face communion with God requires more than an arrival at a level where we can see his face. The problem is for us to decide which face to show him, which face is really authentic.

Some of you may be asking, "Can one develop a skill, an approach, a way of thinking that would help him understand more what is being taught in these rich signs and ordinances?" Here I am going to express a paradox.

On the one hand we sometimes need to leave behind logical, practical thought. There is a parallel here to the process of developing creativity, which has become the new universal value. (Nobody is against creativity today. But we know very little about it, especially about the "how" of it.) We know that it has something to do with the deeps, with spiritual respiration, with being on friendly terms with our subconscious, and that it flourishes best in an atmosphere of approval. (Nothing turns creativity off faster than for somebody to say, "Oh, no!" Then we wither.) In the same sense, I suggest we can open up to an even deeper than subconscious realm in us—the thirsting of the soul—and in silence that yields to Powers greater than our own, we can be filled.

On the other hand we need to remain practical. To me it is interesting that a man of great scholarly achievement (he had a Ph.D. in agrarian chemistry) found an answer to one of his chemical problems while in the temple. Paradox? I've just said, "Abandon the practical"; now I am saying, "Take your most worldly problems with you" into the ordinances. I quote him:

> The endowment is so richly symbolic that only a fool would attempt to describe it. It is so packed full of revelations to those who exercise their strength to seek and see, that no human words can explain or make clear the possibilities that reside in the temple service.

What is true of the temple service is true of all the ordinances. Who am I quoting? John A. Widtsoe, the apostle. ("Temple Worship," *Utah Genealogical and Historical Magazine,* 12:55–64.)

There is something about ordinances that combines the universal and the particular. Not only are they tangible instruments of our own intimate spiritual need, they are themselves archetypal. Nothing about them is merely abstract in the old Platonic sense. Latter-day Saints know that we are closest to God when we are most personal, most intimately specific. Yet the whole thrust of western religion since Plato has been to glorify the abstract and even beyond that to introduce a premise of an utterly different order beyond this world which is both unknown and unknowable. Ordinances pull both worlds together for us until we come to know they are one.

Now the second great function. I've spoken of meaning and teaching, now I speak of power. Listen to these sentences:

In the ordinances thereof [and "thereof" refers back to the priesthood], the power of godliness is manifest. And without the ordinances thereof, and the authority of the priesthood, the power of godliness is not manifest unto men in the flesh." (D&C 84:20–21)

A related statement: "Being born again, comes by the Spirit of God through ordinances" (Joseph Smith, *Teachings* [1938], 162). And another:

All men who become heirs of God and joint heirs with Jesus Christ will have to receive the fullness of the ordinances of his kingdom; and those who will not receive all the ordinances [and I interpolate that "*all* that can be transmitted *through* the ordinances"] will come short of the fullness of that glory, if they do not lose the whole. (Joseph Smith, *Teachings* [1938], 309)

Our hesitancy to recognize ordinances as co-eternal with eternal principles is reflected here:

Ordinances instituted in the heavens before the foundation of the world . . . are not to be altered or changed. . . . There are a great many wise men and women too in our midst who are too wise to be taught. (Joseph Smith, *Teachings* [1938], 308–9)

In the Doctrine and Covenants we are told we can discern "the spirits in all cases under the whole heavens" by one pattern or test—"if he obey mine ordinances . . . and . . . bring forth fruits of praise and wisdom" (see D&C 52:14–19).

Somewhere George A. Smith, while Church Historian, described the difficulties the Prophet faced (in Kirtland) with the pre-Relief Society relief society. They hadn't yet organized. Some of the women received garbled accounts of what was taking place in the temple, and some were indignant, thinking it could only be mischievous. Elder Smith described how some members were disappointed that so little power was manifest in the temple and some were disappointed that so much—too much—was given. And this fine line between openness and receptivity and being closed was characteristic of our people then as it is now.

Ordinances in this setting are a form of prayer ("Ye receive the

Spirit through prayer" [D&C 63:64])—perhaps the highest form. Krister Stendahl, one of the world authorities on the Book of Matthew, tells me it is conceivable that the Lord's prayer has been offered and sung these many centuries by millions with hardly a glimpse of its original intent. His study convinces him that the entire prayer was rooted in the expectation of the coming kingdom, therefore a new-making process. And for him, every sentence in it is to be translated into that invocation. Thus the phrase "Give us this day our daily bread," which I had supposed was a plea for physical survival, was really intended to say (according to Stendahl): "Give us today a foretaste, a sacramental touch with thee. Let us sit at table anticipating the day when we sit down together and partake of newness in thy presence."

Interestingly enough, such a sacrament meeting, when all worthies come together—all worthy—in the presence of the Lamb, who is the "worthy-Maker," is promised in modern revelation— the revelation on the sacrament. It is taught that the sacrament is both a remembering and an anticipation. "For," says he, "the hour cometh that I will drink of the fruit of the vine with you on the earth. . . . And . . . with all those whom my Father hath given me." This is the preface of the later passages which I had never thought to connect to the sacrament of lifting up our hearts to rejoice, of girding our loins with truth, of taking on the whole armor of God, and of receiving what the Lord calls the "sword [sceptre] of my Spirit, which I will pour out upon you." This welding and wedding feast, of which Christ is the Bridegroom, is the preface to his final promise: "Ye shall be caught up, that where I am ye shall be also" (D&C 27).

The language of Matthew and what I have cited from Doctrine and Covenants 27 is also clear in the omissions of 3 Nephi. Have you ever noticed that two phrases are there missing from the Lord's prayer as given in Matthew 6? They are "Thy kingdom come," and "Give us this day our daily bread" (3 Nephi 13:9–13). Surely Joseph Smith, knowing the worldwide familiarity with this prayer, would not have omitted them without reason. May we assume that Christ omitted them among the Nephites—and for the best of all possible reasons: The kingdom had come; *he* was with them. They had received the initiatory ordinances in a splendor that imparted to them also the brilliant whiteness of the Savior (3 Nephi 19:25). The Beatitudes were not taught then as challenges to the will, a set of separate virtues; they came as a description of the tangible fruits that follow from receiving Christ, that he might baptize them all "with fire and the Holy Ghost." What we see in 3 Nephi (the phrase occurs "neither can it be written") is what Elder Talmage called "an ineffable outpouring of prayer." It was prayer that took them into the water and into the ordinances of fire, that led them to the touch of his very person and the healing of an entire multitude. That fire burned for four generations among a people (the Prophet Joseph later said) who were unusually persevering either in righteousness or in wickedness.

Did you know that the word *active* does not occur in the Doctrine and Covenants? The word *act* occurs fifteen times, but interestingly enough ten of these are verb forms: "acting in my name," "acting in concert," "acting in the office" to which one is appointed. If we need a word to describe a man who is admirable in the Lord's eyes the Doctrine and Covenants provides one: He is a "lively" member. One can be active and comparatively dead. But a lively member is something else. Alive! Elsewhere the book speaks of "plants of renown"—those who are planted "in a goodly land by a pure stream," and who bring forth "much precious fruit."

We speak in the Church of attending the sacrament table to renew our covenants. We should also speak of making covenants thus to receive Christ's renewal. We speak in the Church of being severed in other ways simply by dimming our own minds and refusing to care and reach. We should remember the comment of one of the Council of the Twelve who, after his excommunication and then rebaptism and laying on of hands, looked up and said, "Light, light after fourteen years of darkness." Without the ordinances, I submit, we often act without life, have friction without fire, motion without emotion, and forms without the power thereof.

Now a few implications. First, a word about drugs. "Yes,"

228

Al Capp said to hostile students, "the drugs expand consciousness just like the bomb expanded Hiroshima." The very anxiety to be "turned on" is but the distorted concern for godly power. The fever and fervor, which is not always selfish, to "blow one's mind" is often an attempt to escape the emptiness, the absurdity, the hell that fills all too many homes and hearts. Huston Smith, an expert on world religions, has argued that there is a common element of certain drug-trips and certain religious experiences. (He is not fully aware of what *we* mean by religious experiences.) But he adds that drugs do not freshen our faculties, do not expand creativity. You cannot get admission into Harvard Graduate School if you use drugs. Experience has proved that such students just can't hack it. Drugs don't produce a whole and happifying personality. Drugs can produce kicks, bruising and destructive kicks, but not persons. They are a backfiring shortcut.

Second (strange subject), demonology. The same concern for power is manifest in our time in a widespread new interest (and it is a religious interest) in the occult, in Satanism, in demonology and witchcraft. More Ouija boards were sold in this country last Christmas than games of Monopoly. Astrology and its variations are taking as much energy as church service. One in five believe there is "something to it." The history of religion is replete with invented rituals for exorcism to ward off, to protect from, to put down, the evil ones, but just as often to invoke them. We have no such set in Mormonism. The ordinances that bring you closer to God by that same process give you increased power over the adversary. Tampering with the occult can begin with idle curiosity. Then one develops a pathetic preoccupation with the works of darkness. People start out, in boredom, to scare themselves. All too soon they hear a real footfall in the darkened hall.

Third, a word about aesthetics. To me it is strange that traditional religion (I have in mind both Catholic and Protestant wings) in the West—setting out with the premise that there are two radically different orders, this world and an "utterly other" higher world—has concluded that any earthly art must be at most a feeble gesture toward the divine order. Yet Catholicism

229

(predominantly) has been the greatest harbor of the master artists of the West. To stand until your neck hurts looking up at the Sistine Chapel ceiling is to be impressed with this gift. But the Catholic theologian must say: "No, these are not pictures of realities! They are at most analogies—the finite and material for the infinite and immaterial. Nothing there corresponds to Divine Reality."

In contrast, we have a doctrine of "immaculate perception." The senses are eternal. In fact, we define the soul as "spirit and body inseparably connected," or what President Joseph Fielding Smith delightfully calls "a fusion." That means that the seeable, touchable, hearable realm is forever. The senses will never be replaced; they will only be enhanced. And it follows that we, of all people, have a foundation for superb art, the expression of great insight in the tangible levels of reality available on this earth.

If we are suspicious of this, it is partly because we can see the futility of art for art's sake. But we should be open to art—for man's sake. That approach will again obliterate the ordinary distinctions between sacred and secular art. At root all music, all painting, all artful motion—even the art of conversation or baking a loaf of bread—can have an eternal significance. It is the individualizing of ordinances. "Nevertheless thy vows shall be offered up in righteousness on all days and at all times" (D&C 59:11). We may infuse them with our own individual creative talents. If we are to acknowledge the hand of God in all things, an indispensable first step is to summon him into all *our* things. Intrinsic in the outlook of our forebears was the view that their lives sanctified the earth itself, increased the water, softened the climate, tempered the frost, and brought fruitfulness to what was barren. Today as we have moved toward the city we must attempt the new challenge of doing this with steel and glass and machines. Then we may realize how much power—even sacred power—our created environment exercises in and through our lives.

And now a final comment. There is much talk today about the "loss of community," about loneliness and isolation. There is a unifying power that derives from ordinances—unity within the self, unity among selves—that is available in no other way. Today the word *power* has become a chant often symbolizing, though not admittedly, a craving for divisive or dictatorial or destructive power. But we are taught that Christ yearned to gather the world "as a hen gathereth her chicks" (a beautiful figure). Third Nephi adds, "that I may nourish you" (3 Nephi 10:3). He wants to gather us "to receive the ordinances of his house and the glories of his kingdom" (Joseph Smith, *Teachings* [1938], 308). You can only perform an ordinance *with* someone and in relationship to a higher Someone. (Otherwise your performance is not an ordinance but an imitation). As the Prophet looked back over his life (near its end), he said, "If a skillful mechanic, in taking a welding heat, uses borax, alum, etc., and succeeds in welding together iron or steel more perfectly than any other mechanic, is he not deserving of praise?" (Joseph Smith, *Teachings* [1938], 313). My answer is: He is. Christ, through his eternal ordinances, is the welding heat. "For the presence of the Lord shall be as the melting fire that burneth" (D&C 133:4).

In summary, it is in ordinances that the power to *become* is generated. Morality is lifeless unless it is rooted in Christ's ordinances—for they are rooted in him. This is where the truth is. This is where the life is. All substitutes are husks, if they are not also poison. It is tragic for any of us to starve to death. It is even more tragic to starve to death in the midst of plenty.

Chapter Five

POWER FROM ABRAHAMIC TESTS

I would like you to go for a moment to a place where President Hugh B. Brown and I were together—just he, his doctor, and I—in a valley known as Hebron, a place now beautifully fruitful and where tradition has it that there is a tomb to father Abraham. As we approached, I, the guide—but in need of guidance—asked, "What are the blessings of Abraham, Isaac, and Jacob?"

Elder Brown thought a moment and answered in one word, "Posterity." Then I almost burst out, "Why, then, was Abraham commanded to go to Mount Moriah and offer his only hope of posterity?"

It was clear that this man, nearly ninety, had thought and prayed and wept over that question before. He finally said, "Abraham needed to learn something about Abraham." That is my text this morning.

Address given at BYU devotional, October 12, 1971.

You are aware that the record speaks of the incredible promise that Abraham, after years of barrenness—which in some ways to the Israelites was the greatest curse of life—would sire a son who would in turn sire sons and become the father of nations. This came about after Abraham had left a culture where human sacrifice was performed. Abraham was then counseled, and if that is too weak a word he was *commanded,* to take this miracle son up to the mount.

We often identify with Abraham; we sometimes think less about what that meant to Sarah, the mother, and to Isaac, the son. If we can trust the Apocrypha, there are three details that the present narrative omits. First, Isaac was not a mere boy. He was a youth, a stripling youth on the verge of manhood. Second, Abraham did not keep from him, finally, the commandment or the source of the commandment. But having made the heavy journey (how heavy!), he counseled with his son. Third, Isaac said in effect: "My father, if you alone had asked me to give my life for you, I would have been honored and would have given it. That both you and Jehovah ask only doubles my willingness." It was at Isaac's request that his arms were bound, lest involuntarily but spontaneously he should resist the sinking of the knife. Though many have assumed it to be so, only the Book of Mormon records a prophet's words saying that this was in "similitude of God and his Only Begotten Son" (Jacob 4:5).

As we later ascended the mount traditionally known as Mount Moriah—it is just inside the east wall of Jerusalem—we remembered a statement of Brother Ellis Rasmussen of BYU: one can believe that it was to that same mount that another Son ascended. And this time there was no ram in the thicket.

Scholars are widely split over this account. At one extreme are those who say that it could not be, that it did not happen, that the account is an allegory; that we have here a description of the internal struggle that Abraham went through in trying to leave behind his boyhood training in human sacrifice; that God would not require such a thing. One man put it to me this way: "That is a terrible way to test a man. A loving God would not do it."

At the other extreme are those who have held that the story, if not true to history, is nevertheless true to life. However, they go further. They almost rejoice in the contradiction. They say this story illustrates that faith must do more than go beyond reason. Faith, if it is genuine, pulverizes reason. We must, as Kierkegaard puts it, be "crucified upon the paradox of the absurd."

My testimony is that both the rationalists and the irrationalists have misread. For in modern times we have been taught that this story does not simply lie in our remote past but in our own individual future. As modern revelation states, we must be "chastened and tried, even as Abraham" (D&C 101:4). Do you remember after that more than nine-hundred-mile march from Kirtland to Missouri—a march that from all mortal appearance was a failure, for it achieved nothing—someone came to Brigham Young and said, "What did you get out of that fiasco?" He replied, "Everything we went for—experience." He could say that because he had only within hours been with the Prophet Joseph in a meeting where the Prophet had declared in substance: "Brethren, some of you are angry with me because you did not fight in Missouri. But let me tell you God did not want you to fight. He wanted to develop a core of men 'who had offered their lives and who made as great a sacrifice as did Abraham.' Now God has found his leaders, and those of you who are called to positions who have not made that sacrifice will be required to make it hereafter" (Joseph Smith, *History of The Church* 2:182).

There is the recorded testimony of Wilford Woodruff and John Taylor, who described the Kirtland Temple experience—an outpouring so rich that some of those present honestly believed that the Millennium had come, that the era of peace had been ushered in, so filled were they with the spirit of blessing and love. The Prophet arose in that setting and said: "Brethren, this is the Lord that is with us, but trials lie ahead. Brethren [he was speaking now to the Twelve], God will feel after you, and he will wrench your very heartstrings. If you cannot stand it, you will not be fit for the kingdom of God." All too prophetic was that statement. Half of the original Council of Twelve later, as the Prophet put it, "lifted

234

up the heel" against him and against Christ. Four others were at least temporarily disaffected. Only two, Brigham Young and Heber C. Kimball, did not buckle under the pressure, and they were tried, too.

Let us look at the implications for now. We live in a time when many are saying we need commitment, a total kind of commitment, a "risk-everything" kind of commitment. On that subject many contemporary writers are eloquent. But on the question, To what does one commit? vagueness and often vagaries are all that are offered. Someone asked me once, "What is the definition of a fanatic?" I answered in Santayana's phrase, "A fanatic is a person who doubles his speed when he has lost his direction." But what then is the name of a person who doubles and quadruples his effort when he has found his direction? That is commitment.

It is a mistake to suppose that Abraham acted in total ignorance—that his leap was a leap in the dark. If you consult the Inspired Version or even the King James, it is apparent that Abraham saw in vision the Son of Man (with a capital *M* meaning Man of Holiness, the Eternal Father). He saw him; he saw his day; and he rejoiced. (See Genesis 15:12; John 8:56.) He received promises and accepted them. He was told, as our Pearl of Great Price reminds us, that he stood, even before mortality, among the mighty, the noble, and the great; that he was one of them; that he was chosen (which is more than simply called) before he was born; and, therefore, that there lingered in him a residual power of response to Christ that came out mightily in the hour of need (Abraham 3:22–24).

We have been told that we are of Abraham. We are his children. We have been taught that those of us who have joined the Church by conversion are just as much so as those of us who are born under the covenant. (See D&C 84:33–34.) We have been taught that the spiritual process that is to occur within us is not just a matter of changing names. It is a process whereby the blood itself is somehow purged, purified, and we literally become the seed of Abraham (Joseph Smith, *Teachings* [1938], 149–150). But those who are Abraham's descendants must also bear the responsibility of Abraham (D&C 132:30–32).

We live in the time when everybody is willing to talk about rights—civil rights, other rights—and when it is rare to hear the words *duty* and *civil duty*. There never was a right, I submit, that did not have a corresponding duty. There never was a duty that did not also eventually entail a right.

We talk often as if the priesthood is solely a privilege. It is also a burden, and many who have lived long in this Church know there are times, sometimes lengthy times, when the priesthood is much duty and very little right.

This leads to the statement allegedly made by the quotable J. Golden Kimball. Someone asked him how he accounted for the call of a certain brother to a certain position. He is supposed to have replied, "The Lord must have called him; no one else would have thought of him."

Someone else was also complaining about how difficult it was to follow a certain leader. (You see, it is not just a matter of following the request to give a spectacular amount. What if you are called to give less than you can give? What if you are called not to be called? What if you are told only to wait for a decision and be patient?) In answer to this complaint, J. Golden, says the legend, replied, "Well, some of them are sent to lead us and some of them are sent to try us." After the laughter and delight of that statement passes, the truth of it becomes apparent. All of us are sent to lead and to try each other. And the priesthood is given to try us to the *core*.

May I speak only for a moment, out of the abstractions, about some modern examples. We have a historian who has recently been through eight hundred journals and diaries of our early forefathers. Two sentences leaped at me. One from John Pulsipher, who was on an Indian mission, reads, "A man can be happy in a cave if it is his duty to be there." The other is an entry in the diary of John Bushman. He was on the Little Colorado, where water was the source of all life and where irrigation was the critical survival factor. Again and again they would build a dam, and just as often he recorded that the dam broke. On one occasion he said only that the dam broke again, and recorded, "We are not discouraged" (Bitton, *Mormon Diaries*, 51, 284).

What about the Stegner article titled "Ordeal by Handcart"? You are aware that the Donner party, under the terror of their trauma, lapsed into cannibalism. Not so with these modern human yet superhuman Mormon saints. Some of them died in each other's arms. Some died with their hands frozen to the crossbar, always with their faces west.

Then there were the three young men—Brother Huntington, Brother Grant, Brother Kimball—all only eighteen years of age, who went with the relief party the "second thousand miles" to help the Martin handcart company. On this trip they faced a stream that was swollen with ice and snow. Have you ever walked, even to the knee level, through such water? The pioneers almost hopelessly stood back, unable to go through in their weakened and emaciated condition. Those three boys carried every one of the company across and then crossed back, sometimes in water up to their waists. All three later died from exposure. When Brother Brigham heard of their heroic act, he wept and then rose in the majesty of his spirit and said, "God will exalt those three young men in the celestial kingdom of God."

What about Brother Helaman Pratt, who had been in four states—driven from all—and who now had a toehold within an adobe house in the Salt Lake Valley. Brother Brigham called him in and said: "Brother Pratt, we are calling you to colonize in Mexico. You will be released when you die. God bless you." Brother Pratt went. He was released when he died.

There are sacrifices. But the prophets again and again insist that we ought to use a different word. How can it be called a sacrifice to yield up a handful of dust when what is promised is a whole earth? But we think we know better than God. We think that what we want for us is greater than what he wants for us. Then we simply violate the first commandment, which is to love God first and over all. The moment that pattern is followed he seeks in us the one thing that we do not *really* want to give up. No, we do not respond. Many of us will say that we do not have that kind of faith. I submit to you that you do not have that kind of faith until you pass that test.

Now we are back to the statement, the wise statement, of Elder Brown: "Abraham needed to learn something about Abraham." What did he learn? He learned that he did love God unconditionally, that God could now bless him unconditionally. Do you think his prayers had a different temper and tone after that? Do you think he could pray in faith saying, "Lord, you know my heart," and the echo would say, "And *I* know it"? John Taylor said that the Prophet taught that if God could have found a deeper way to test Abraham he would have used that (Young, *Journal of Discourses* 24:264). As Paul looked back and wondered how Abraham could have his willingness account for righteousness, his conviction was that Abraham believed Jehovah could raise his son from the dead if necessary in order to fulfill the promise which that sacrifice scene contradicts. That is what God did ultimately with his own Son (Hebrews 11:19).

All about us there are quibblings, demeanings, oppositions, negations, shrinkings. But I, as one who has feet of clay that go all the way to my groin, bear testimony this morning that it is the love of God that cries out for us to prove our love for him. He cannot bless us until we have been proved, cannot even pull out of us the giant spirit in us unless we let him. If we come offering what we think he wants, without having testimony that we are doing what he really does want, we are not yet prepared. I bear testimony that in the record there is also evidence that joy can attend us even in the midst of such sacrifice. It is a sweeter, perhaps a bitter, sweeter joy. But it comes when we know that we are acting under the will of Christ. There is also the testimony that when we thus respond he delights, he rejoices, with a power that is born of his own descent into pain.

Abraham was called the friend of God, the son of God, the father of the faithful. Modern revelation tells us that now he is a little higher than the angels. Abraham, says the revelation, sits with Isaac and Jacob on thrones, "because they did none other things than that which they were commanded" (D&C 132:37). They are not angels but are gods and have entered into their exaltation.

May I make a personal reflection. Years ago, there was a moment when I became intoxicated with the idea that I could become a Rhodes Scholar. It did not take me long to become convinced that that was also what God wanted for me. The greatest shock of my life to that point was when, after passing certain of the preliminaries with the committee, I sat down and heard the committee announce two other names as going to Oxford. I was baffled. "You must be kidding," I thought. "Don't you understand? This is for me." But they did not make a mistake.

I remember giving a talk in a local ward the following Sunday—I am afraid a hypocritical talk—on prayer, where I announced that one of the great principles we had been taught is that when we pray we must always say, "Thy will be done," and then listen for it—that half of prayer was listening. As I said that, I heard something, a kind of an imp on my shoulder saying: "You're a fine one to talk that way. You've been saying, 'Thy will be done as long as it's my will' for months. Now you're bitter, bitter as gall." Suddenly, without any introduction that the audience could have understood, I said, "I prophesy [strange thing for me to say, for I had never done that before] that the thing that I had expected and wanted but which has been denied this week will somehow be made up to me—that what I am to do (and I don't know what that is) will somehow be better than what I was to do." And then, quite confused at what I had heard, I sat down.

I forgot that completely until the time came when, in circumstances I cannot here relate, it became clear that I could do graduate studies at Harvard in New England. I had forgotten any relevance in that until the hour came (thirty-five years earlier than I had hoped) that I was called to be a missionary again, and a mission president in New England. I know there are those who will say: "You might just as well have gone to England and to Oxford, had you been able to cut the mustard. It is only a coincidence." I am here this morning to say that I am convinced in my soul that what was intended for me was not old England but New. When I prayed the bitterness out and the lingering peace of the Savior in, I had nothing but gratitude.

Today we need Abrahams, Isaacs, and Jacobs. We need those who are willing to stand and who, having done all, *stand*. We have people now, and need more, who can listen to the *living* word and the *present* commitment of the Lord Jesus Christ through his prophets and stand. May God help us to respond and become sons of Abraham.

Chapter Six

CONSCIENCE AND CONSCIOUSNESS

"Conscience is a will-o-the-wisp."

"Psychologists just don't credit conscience these days."

"*Conscience* is merely the name of moral rules we learned in childhood."

These three utterances, common among students of human behavior, are more or less widely believed today. And if behavioral scientists find traditional theories of conscience unreliable, slippery, and misleading, so do many analytic philosophers. There are variations on the theme, but the chorus maintains a kind of harmony: conscience or "moral sense" is reducible to the "no-no's" of one's childhood, a somewhat accidental collection of the mores and customs of those around us, the husk in which we grew. The conclusion that is often drawn is that we may safely—

Address prepared for the Commissioner's Lecture Series, Church Educational System, and delivered in 1973 at the LDS Institutes of Religion at Weber State College, Ricks College, and the Church College of Hawaii.

and even wisely—ignore these moralistic trappings. At least we must not take them too seriously.

The purpose of this talk is to question both the premises and the conclusions of this outlook. And to recommend an inlook, a push toward origins that are adequate to the phenomenon of conscience, which, for me at least, is phenomenal. This is not, then, a defense of conscience but rather of the notion that at root it needs no defense.

But immediately an objection is raised: What is meant by *conscience?* Does not the word mean all things to all men? In the name of "conscience" has not every form of human behavior (for example, murder, theft, betrayal—and their opposites—and everything in between) been justified by men? And is there anything that has ever been praised that has not also been condemned by someone's conscience? And has not every theory of conscience been seriously opposed?

A beginning point is needed. Let me begin, then, with a seemingly uncritical and careless thesis, though I am convinced it is the best way to be critical and careful on the subject. That is to assume that all of us already have an awareness, indeed a haunting awareness, of what the word *conscience* signifies. Analytic definition would, if there were any need of it, be too late. To approach conscience without distorting it we must let it be, let it speak for itself, and in its own way. There may be need to remove semantic scales from our blurry eyes, but that is mainly because we have become adept at throwing dust. What is needed is less preoccupation with paralyzing definition and more with living introspection—with open, honest, uncluttered scrutiny of what is there below the layers of convention and cover-up. In the end, to demand a definition for conscience is analogous to demanding proof for one's own existence. In order to ask the question seriously, one must suppress the thing he demands.

If that analogy seems far-fetched, hear me out anyway.

Much discussion in the history of western ideas has focused less on what conscience is than on what it seems to say. And in response to this question, three main kinds of answers are given:

First, some maintain that conscience is a kind of rule-bank that prompts ethical and perhaps also legal and social maxims without applying them to specific cases. On this view what we "hear" when conscience speaks is such an imperative as, "You ought always to keep your promises," or, as W. D. Ross also insists, "You ought always to maximize the good." In the same line John Stuart Mill maintained that the idea of the greatest good of the greatest number—the principle of utility—is both given and assured by conscience.

A second view is that conscience is silent with respect to rules but takes situations or cases one by one. In the actual, practical, work-a-day world, conscience tells a man what is and what is not appropriate behavior. Often this caution is cast in negative terms. Socrates, for example, claimed that his inner voice or "daemon" warned him of the wrong course of action but did not speak on the right. On this view one cannot arrive at guiding principles through his conscience. Conscience only speaks to one when he is in the real—or in some cases the imaginatively confronted—world of decision and conduct.

A third view is that conscience offers neither rules nor concrete guidance. Conscience is rather the measure of ideal persons. On this view we have a kind of moral sense or intuition by which we can recognize, admire, and seek to emulate the qualities of character or goodness in other men—conscience is a kind of hero-chooser after whom our life may be modeled. It is in this form conceived as a "guide" only in the sense that it provides ideal types of personal worth.

In my judgement all three of these views have hold of something authentic. But such accounts only magnify the intriguing question of origins. How came such remarkable insights; how explain their binding power even, it seems, in those who deny them binding power? In the final reckoning, does it make much sense to say that such perceptions and judgements are merely childhood "no-no's"?[1]

---

1. I have nothing against childhood "no-no's." Many of them were, and remain, profoundly wise.

243

So much for a start.

Let us try now to come closer to the world of conscience itself, our own data. And let us question at the outset the stereotype that seems to dominate much of our common sense and conversation.

On this popular notion conscience is a combination policeman, judge, and prison warden. When we run afoul of a rule or commit an impropriety, conscience summons us to judgement—always after the fact—always in retrospect. We are hauled into court, and swinging a gavel that echoes in our spongy doubts and fears, the judge says, "Guilty, guilty, guilty!" Thus one finds it plausible to identify conscience with arbitrary parents, unkind peer group members, and authority figures in general. Anything to put the problem "out there" where we can do some arresting, summoning, and sentencing of our own.

But clearly it isn't "out there." And, whatever our motives, even a little self-scrutiny will show how much this portrait misses.

What is offered here as a nudge toward such scrutiny is personal, subjective and, many will say, whimsical. But if conscience does indeed speak and behave in any of these ways, then to find out you need simply close your eyes and sweep inwardly. For me there are elements here that are, introspectively speaking, irrefutable, however clumsy the formulation.

But my case does not depend on total agreement of details. It depends only on the acknowledgement that conscience is more that the "nothing but" of the theories.

How *much* more is the question.

To begin with, there is something uncanny in the fact that conscience not only judges in retrospect but in prospect. Long before action or even deliberation it throbs its commendation or withdraws it. Technically, each of our moral dilemmas, like every event of life, is unique. Such change and relativity is often urged against the validity of conscience or of any moral system. After all, we ourselves are changing physically, mentally, emotionally; the world environment is changing; institutions and laws are changing. Conclusion? Conscience is outgrown, outmoded, outflanked.[2] Yet conscience seems to me to cross all bridges before we come to them—and even to challenge the profession of bridge building. It seems both up-to-date and ahead of itself. In the long run does it not shed our more foolish misreadings and, regardless of change, refuse to be silent?

Then again, the stereotype misses the positive ring of conscience. Our language contains many conscience words that are negative in connotation: *uneasiness, twinge, bother, pang, smiting, gnawing, fever,* and the like. We even say, "My conscience is killing me."[3] Yet there is such a thing as a "clear conscience," and from the same source, it seems, there come purrings, approvals, rejoicings, and, as it were, songs of peace. Does not conscience kiss as well as bite?

Third, conscience is concerned with more than acts. One of its amazing but also maddening traits is that it just won't keep its

---

2. From the Stoics to Aquinas there have been attempts to construct a theory of "natural law"—a law of human nature—which is unequivocal and exceptionless; and to derive absolute moral judgments from it. This speech is not intended to resolve that issue. My own guess is that the phenomenon of conscience—what Kant called "the moral law within"—has given the theory of natural law whatever plausibility it has enjoyed. But the power of conscience to change, to grow, and to become increasingly intense and to adapt to novel circumstances gives it a special role which no finite formulation of exceptionless law can do. Moreover, it is conscience, or something closely related to it, that helps us past the conflicts that arise between fixed obligations; for example, the promise to lend a gun, and, in the meanwhile, the recognition that the borrower intends to use it to commit a crime. "Natural Law" theories always lead to such conflicts. Only by maintaining that man has only one obligation to which all other considerations are to be subserved, can they avoid the clash of competing principles. And no theory that I know of has ever made good the claim to a "one only" obligation.

Mormonism is pluralistic in its obligation-claims. And therefore, it acknowledges the constant possibility of conflict. These can only finally be resolved by a higher, present, and living decision. It follows that Mormonism can never be reduced to a set of moral laws-even to the proclamation of eternal and unchanging laws. Its essence requires indispensable living adaptation to changing circumstance: living prophets, not simply rule books; living conscience, not simply habitual discipline; and above all a living Christ, who speaks to the present, not simply a set of sentences spoken about him, or even by him, in the past.

3. Of course, it is not conscience but the violation of it that does the killing. The wages of sin, not conscience, is death.

nose out of anything. It takes on our motives, our thoughts, our feelings, our attitudes, including our motives, thoughts, feelings, and attitudes toward it. It is fussy and finicky enough to strain at a gnat; for example, the slight edge of voice I let slip into a sentence spoken to a child. But it also claims vast and presiding awareness of the sort of person I may be way down the road, and it tells me to get on with it.

That leads to its reflexive, whole-self character. A policeman, a judge, a warden enter our lives and claim authority over us for a specified time. But conscience claims authority over us all the time. And not only the actual us, but the potential us, that much-smothered and momentous self that is somewhere beyond our present achievement or reach. At this level, conscience is a kind of rider with spurs, sometimes gently, sometimes ruthlessly, prodding. Parents are often taught to judge and reprove a part of a child, his hand or his mouth or his present temper tantrum. But conscience, if I mistake not, has no such scruples. It holds one accountable for himself—all of himself. It acknowledges conditioning and extenuating circumstances and forgives you when you really can't help or hinder certain forces. But it insists you are a cause—*the* cause—of the way you respond to the bombardment. Conscience can *never* be converted to fatalism or determinism.

For this reason it is superficial to identify conscience and guilt. Even in the person comparatively guilt-free, conscience is at work sponsoring projects and related concerns. One is given only so much rope and time to celebrate any particular achievement (and if it is an easy thing, less than one is capable of, no time at all) before there begins a buildup of inner striving which eventually reaches concert pitch: "Become more!" If this is so, it unmasks the cliché which suggests that conscience surfaces only when we are facing crises or imminent death, at which point "our whole life goes before us." There is indeed—who of us does not know it—a fantastic compounding of consciousness in that split second when we fall overboard or hear a screech just before a crash on the freeway. It is a stark regaining of what one thought he had forgotten. ("What will my mother think?" said a Chicago gangland youth as

246

he fell to the pavement after a fatal stabbing.) But is conscience ever so tardy? To our reproach or defense, "Why didn't you tell me sooner?" doesn't it say, "I did!" or more precisely, "I always have!" or more precisely still, "I am the you you've been hiding from!"? One can hide only from what he knows—or at least suspects—is there.

Nor is guilt always a negative. And here we approach one of the paradoxes of conscience. The very intensity of one's guilt about his life and himself is double-edged. On the one hand it tells him something is wrong; and the more terrible the guilt, the more terrible the wrong. But it is not only diagnosis, it is also therapy. For it tells him that something is marvelously right; that something within him—I repeat, *within* him—cannot be muffled or denied. In which case, the guiltier he is, the more worthy, sensitive, and enlightened. If there were not this better-judging self, guilt could not occur. Pigs, one writer has observed, do not have psychoses; chickens do not hang their heads in shame. Man is distinguished from other entities, animate or inanimate, in his capacity for the fever of unresolved guilt. And conscience is clear on *how* to resolve it. How powerful this can become and how utterly independent it often is of conventional ethnic or social mores can be shown in some extreme cases.

It is reported, for example, that in some prison camps in Vietnam and elsewhere, sadistic guards have continued their grisly and vicious careers for years—then, one day, they have thrown down their steel whips, screaming: "I can't do it! I can't do it!" Why not?

In the same manner, some psychotherapists allege that regardless of how deranged or hallucinatory a person may be, one touch with reality remains with startling clarity. It is the recognition of the genuine as distinct from the pretended concern of the doctor or nurse. In other words, even the sickest of men recognize a deceitful personality from a genuine and loving one. One wonders if, similarly, they recognize these distinctions inside themselves.

And then there are "incorrigible" murderers on death row. If we can trust Capote's interviews, they have a remarkable pattern in common. Most prisoners can recall details of the events preceding their violence, but at the point where the actual crime began they "blank." They say, over and over, that they cannot believe they were actually there. It was "someone else" or, they insist, they were "not themselves." This apparently is more than the legal resort of temporary insanity. It is the insistence that they cannot recall responsible action. The forgetfulness is analogous to the tendency of our memories to refuse us recollection of deep horror or trauma. But if the criminal is "hardened," why should his murder be traumatic? Do we have here a failure of conscience or a witness of its power? Nietzsche summed it up shrewdly: " 'I did that,' says my memory. 'I could not have done that,' says my conscience. Eventually the memory yields."[4]

Again, the stress we often place on guilt and on fear leaves out of the picture another element of conscience—its promising power. It not only commends and commands a way of life for us but also promises fulfillment. Far from being a tartan that knows only the language of duty, responsibility, and sacrifice, does not conscience speak eloquently about satisfaction, completion, gratification, and even glorification; and how mean and trivial we are to postpone them? Hamlet observed correctly that a troubled conscience may make cowards of us all. But so it may make dynamos. Reinhold Niebuhr once listened to a committee who were ambivalent about accepting Rockefeller's endowment of the New York Center for Columbia University. "He didn't do it because he believes in education," they said, "but because of a guilty conscience." Niebuhr replied, "What's wrong with a guilty conscience?" Indeed, what is? Conscience reenthrones our neglected hold on the things that matter most.

Implicit in all this is what conscience seems to imply, in fact, to presuppose about itself. It seems completely at home with infinity, with time and space, with truth and beauty. It presupposes a

---

4. But not completely. For we shall have "a perfect knowledge of all our guilt . . . and the righteous shall have a perfect knowledge of their enjoyment" (2 Nephi 9:14; compare Alma 11:43).

whole cosmology and psychology—both what I really do want and what I really ought to want; and more amazing—how they may one day converge. Its horizon is never limited to present preoccupations. Perhaps this is why Heidegger is so impressed that conscience is all the time reminding us that time is passing and pleading that we act under the sense of the totality—the farthest limit being death. And whether conscience is equally insistent on its own indestructibility and mine—it seems to assume that here is something I cannot outsmart, outgrow, outlive, or outdie. Future reckoning is inescapable.

Everything for future reference, it seems—but also for future reverence. And now appears the most remarkable thing of all, which perhaps only the religious-minded will follow. How many times do we have to tell conscience—in how many situations—"This has nothing to do with God." Remorselessly it urges the contrary, "It has everything to do with God." The message recurrent, and somehow strangely reminiscent—against which I for one have never been able to provide insulation—is that every deliberate wrong or shoddy performance of mine is a form of blasphemy, that sin is ingratitude, that every abuse of my potential—and of others'—is a concession to ugliness and a hurt to the Divine. In short, conscience generates in me (and in so many of those I talk to) a permeating sense of the sacred. And in its resistance to darkness and its insistence on light, one would think at times it is almost omniscient.

A phenomenal phenomenon, then. Will you grant me that much? How to explain it?

Carl Jung takes a step toward adequacy. After several decades with patients in consulting rooms, he theorized that you and I have access to much, much more than has been written on us during our singular lifetime. Somehow, by the mysteries of inheritance, we possess, he claims, a racial memory. Below, as it were, our own individual subconscious, there is the "collective unconscious," a treasure-house of experience which undergirds our cognitive gropings and affects every impulse and judgement. Jung's interpreters have sometimes called this a "symbol-making factory," for it even conditions our selections of word usage and our preferences for symbolic expression—our desire, for example, to close an unfinished circle or to add a note to a musical phrase. This realm, Jung concluded, is properly called "religious." And for him the source of much human maladjustment is failure to give it proper sway in our lives.

So we can theorize that the race is somehow in us. But then how do we account for what, seemingly from the earliest traceable outset, is in the race? The question takes us a step further and puts meaning in four breathtaking sentences of modern revelation:

> Man was also in the beginning with God. . . .
>
> Behold, here is the agency of man, and here is the condemnation of man; because that which was from the beginning is plainly manifest unto them, and they receive not the light.
>
> And every man whose spirit receiveth not the light is under condemnation.
>
> For man is spirit. (D&C 93:29, 31–33)

Only something of such magnitude, I submit, can account for the full phenomenon and power of conscience. What is "plainly manifest" to us, which is to say, within us, is an intimate and infinite relationship. This implies that in God's environment, but also in ours, there was conscious, vital, personal nurture through epochs that can be measured only in light years. And though presently a veil is drawn over specific images of that realm—we do not now recall our name, rank, and serial number—there is built in us and not quite hidden a "collective unconscious" that is superracial in character, a pool of such vivid effect, such residual power in us, that our finite learnings and recoveries are at best a tiny aftermath. "Man is spirit"—this spirit. And it breathes in us with a cumulative, crystal consciousness.

Thus opens up a whole new dimension of awareness and responsibility. Conscience at this level may be subsumed under law—for what we are derived from is the essence of what we are akin to. As a candle flame leaps to another candle flame or as a stream finds a river, so "intelligence cleaveth unto intelligence," says the revelation. And likewise "wisdom receiveth wisdom"; "truth embraceth truth"; virtue loves virtue; light, light; and mercy, mercy (D&C 88:40). There are matching antipathies to deception, to hate, to vice, to unforgiving domination. Clearly conscience and the light which is in us and which comes afresh from God and his Christ are not identical. Yet one is the record or testimony of the other and all, as the revelation says, "plainly manifest" (D&C 93:31). How plainly and how manifest will differ for each of us as we give full expression to our hidden possibilities. But the Prophet Joseph once suggested how the impress is nonsensuous, "given," he said, "as though we had no bodies at all"[5]—and yet so persistently sensible. If it is short of perfect knowledge it is nevertheless the knowledge of perfecting. It is that cluster of assurances that linger in us like the warming impressions of a departed friend, giving thirst and thrust toward reunion.

One implication of all this can now be put in the form of an imperative: Give your conscience its way—protect, cherish and measure it with the light—and you will eventually see the hand and handiwork of God and goodness everywhere, most of all in yourself. Flout, abuse, betray, repress it, and you will eventually see his hand nowhere, not even in yourself. That is how moral conscience and religious consciousness interact and become one.

The two processes are vividly at work in a man who is thoroughly contemporary, though he lived seventy-four years before Christ. He is all the more persuasive because he really has a purchase, in each of his arguments and protests, on the truth. Sometimes what he affirms is true, but what he denies false. Sometimes he pushes his affirmations and denials to irrelevant extremes. But he is no strawman. Nor is he shut up safely within the thirtieth chapter of Alma. He and his arguments are in all of

---

5. All things whatsoever God in his infinite wisdom has seen fit and proper to reveal to us, while we are dwelling in mortality, in regard to our mortal bodies are revealed to us in the abstract, and independent of affinity of this mortal tabernacle, but are revealed to our spirits precisely as though we had no bodies at all" (Joseph Smith, *Teachings* [1938], 355).

us. So much so that I am giving them fashionable contemporary labels. They come along, as the high priest said Korihor came along, to "interrupt our rejoicings" (Alma 30:22). Look at the nine-point conscience-cover he advocates.

First, positivism, the insistence on the senses. "Ye cannot know of things which ye do not see" (Alma 30:15). This is splendid methodology for science, though even scientists with their precise instruments cannot "see" electrons. In contrast, one must often close one's eyes in order to "see" his conscience. Of course, by one definition one cannot "see" one's past, one's guilt, nor the pain (or peace) of conscience. It does not follow that he cannot know them. Will we not acknowledge that sometimes night pillows know more of our depths than the noonday sun because that is when we are left alone without the balm of distracting objects? "But," persists the argument, "only an infinite series of observations could tell us for sure that this mass of data is not illusory." To which one answer is that an infinite series is what we have already had and are already responsible for.

Second, psychologism. Conscience is not "objective." "Behold, it is the effect of a frenzied mind" (Alma 30:16). The question may be asked, Who is more frenzied, one who honors conscience or one who abdicates it? Frenzy can give fuel to disbeliefs as well as to beliefs. And it is protective discoloration to hold that all who condemn us or approve us, including our unoriginated inner voice, are "sick, sick, sick." In truth, the outcry of conscience may, for the moment, be the only healthy thing left in us.

Third, environmentalism. "It's just a matter of custom." "And this derangement of your minds comes because of the traditions of your fathers, which lead you away into a belief of things which are not so" (Alma 30:16). By using antiquity as a club and modernity as ploy, Korihor conceals the antiquity (eternality?) of his own position. Conscience knows that neither is to the point. Wisdom does not become folly the moment we call it "tradition," or "the establishment," or the "local provincialism." How often, for example, we ask, "Were you born into your religion?" "Yes." "Uh huh!" we reply, as if that explains everything. The assumption is that one can no more choose his religion than he can choose his parents. But what if, in the light of spirit-sweeping vision we embraced and now reembrace both? It is often said that if you had been born to someone else you would have a different set of values, a different potential. Perhaps so. If only we hadn't been born of God.

Fourth, the power-ethic, the argument of self-sufficiency. "There [can] be no atonement made for the sins of men, but every man fare[s] in this life according to the management of the creature; therefore every man proper[s] according to his genius, and . . . every man conquer[s] according to his strength" (Alma 30:17). Shades of Darwin and Nietzsche. And a bright half-truth—the fittest *do* survive. In what sense was Christ "fit" and in what senses did he survive? True religion expands life-power until it matches that of God himself, which is the only genuine and final survival. His power is always used to expand, not exploit, his creatures. But power over one's enslaved and enslaving weaknesses and over all the varieties of death and all the consequences of our acts requires help. And no one can, in good conscience, deny his need of help. We argue incessantly over which is the more important, Christ's influence or our own. That is a strange pastime when in truth both are indispensable. But, worlds without end, Christ cannot help us until we let him. Isn't that what conscience says?

Fifth, relativism and nihilism. Anything goes, and anyway it all comes to nothing. "Whatsoever a man [does is] no crime" (Alma 30:17). "When a man [is] dead, that [is] the end thereof" (Alma 30:18). The ancient death wish. "Who can say what is right or wrong?" The nerve of the argument is, again, irrelevant. What comfort can I gain from learning that people who reinforce conscience are gone or that other people want other things? And why assume that conscience would be reliable only if it said exactly the same thing to everyone? It does not follow logically. We try to make it follow psychologically. But it won't be forced. The extreme of this position, often held today, is that we ourselves create all the reality and all the meaning there is. But the argument so often begins and ends in despair. Conscience will tell you that reality is neither that flexible nor that ignorable.

Sixth, the freedom argument. "They durst not look up with boldness, . . . they durst not enjoy their rights and privileges" (Alma 30:27)."Why do ye yoke yourselves with such foolish things?" (Alma 30:13). "Behold, I say that a child is not guilty because of its parents" (Alma 30:25). The edge of this protest is sharp and at times deserved. There *is* pseudo-guilt as there is also pseudo-forgiveness. And how often the churches have merchandised by creating the very guilt they claim to relieve. ("You are utterly depraved, therefore guilty.") And how many moderns have profited by saying for a large fee the reverse. ("Your guilt is only a product of infantile trauma and not genuine at all.") Each assists us to adjust to our sicknesses instead of healing them. In the long run conscience will not stand for either of these inducements. How redeeming the revealed insight—a doctrine of original righteousness—"every spirit of man was innocent in the beginning" (D&C 93:38).

As for the "yoke," some (said a recent counselor) "will absolutely destroy themselves to prove they have a right to do it." But whom besides themselves are they trying to convince? Are they that much beholden to others? How constant our will to misunderstand the "bounds and conditions" of law and to oppose freedom to law! Law does not tell us what we *must* do. It tells us the inevitable consequences of what we *choose* to do. Conscience adapts and applies law. It does not—and cannot—destroy it. And only when we seek to vindicate our conscience do we dare "look up" to God with a boldness based on revelation—the revelation of ourselves—rather than with the many faces of deception. Korihor, you remember, was "causing them to lift up their heads in their wickedness" (Alma 30:18).

Seventh, antiritualism. Korihor attacks "the foolish ordinances and performances which are laid down by ancient priests, to usurp power and authority over them, to keep them in ignorance, that they may not lift up their heads" (Alma 30:23). Sometimes true; but how shabby and circular the stance. Sin creates an antipathy to life, especially spiritual life. Then we stay away from the banquet because we have deeply betrayed the host. (Atheists don't find God for the same reason thieves don't find policemen.) We eat husks instead and then claim that the husks are the only food. It takes a little boy, like conscience, to observe that, just as the emperor had no clothes, we have no food. And it shows. The sacramental approach to life and the life-giving power of ordinances and sacraments are apparent to all who attend the banquet. We may indeed partake foolishly. But not to partake is worse than foolish. It is death.

Eighth, the hypocrisy charge. Sooner or later, but usually sooner, things get personal—and so does Korihor. "According to your own desires; and ye keep them down, even as it were in bondage, that ye may glut yourselves with the labors of their hands. . . . lest they should offend their priests" (Alma 30:27, 28). Here is another irrelevant half-truth. No word comes more frequently to our lips in self-defense than "hypocrite." And how we straitjacket the word so its arms cannot touch us. Brought to its full fighting weight, our charge would mean that no one has the right to recommend or to rebuke a way of life unless he himself has achieved (or avoided) it. That would bind and also gag just about everyone—except Christ. Does anyone else need "room to talk"—to underwrite our conscience? As to the rest of us, supposedly smitten to silence, what a strange restriction. Really, now! A drunkard who has paid through the nose for what he imbibes through his mouth is now told he can salvage honor and credibility only if he shuts both! But no one on earth is more entitled to speak against alcoholism than the victim thereof; more, not less, when he is hopelessly addicted. If we could prove (to whom?) that the world, and especially our most vocal leaders, are full of hypocrisy, what then? The compulsive hope that we can get off the hook by tarring them with the same brush is itself hypocritical in the self-deceptive (not just other-deceptive) way Christ exposes.

Ninth, atheism masked as agnosticism. "By their traditions and their dreams and their whims and their visions and their pretended mysteries . . . they . . . offend some unknown being who they say is God . . ." (Alma 30:28). "I do not deny the existence of a God, but I do not believe that there is a God" (Alma 30:48). This is an intellectual cover for the blind faith of militant atheism. An unknown God has the same advantage as a nonexistent one; neither can get in your hair. We may hammer at others, "Do not say you know when you don't." That may bury alive the whisper of our own conscience saying, "Do not say you don't know when you do." Earlier Korihor has shown us the extent of his rejection. "God—a being who never has been seen or known, who never was nor ever will be" (Alma 30:28). This is not agnosticism but dogmatism, a vast negative faith. And shortly he claims to propose the acid test. "I will believe only if I see a sign."

The request is doubly dishonest, first because he would accept no sign as convincing, and second because he had seen signs. "Thou hast had signs enough," Alma replies. And so have we all. How many times must a man suffer before he admits that pain hurts? Why do we go on acting as if nothing up to this moment counts as evidence for God when we have been illumined innumerable times? To the man who finally cooperates with conscience (and Alma had earlier suffered in sin until his guilt led him to wish for extinction), "all things denote there is a God" (Alma 30:44). To the man who shouts it down, nothing does. But now comes Korihor's admission, the pathetic confession, the acknowledged contradiction.

Korihor pours out his story. He has been a rebel with a cause. He has had his own kind of dream, whim, and vision. And did he ever suspect who was giving him his orders? "Go and reclaim this people," he was told by the very voice of an angel. "They have all gone astray after an unknown God" (Alma 30:53). And why were such words so overpowering and why did he obey them? "Because they were pleasing unto the carnal mind" (Alma 30:53). But how did he arrange to argue away the spiritual-minded impulses in himself? "I had much success, insomuch that I verily believed that they [his denials] were true." Thus strangely he accepted his followers' word as more valid than his own. Now he acknowledges that in the very midst of his campaign of disparagement, "I also knew that there was a God." Even this admission diminishes the scope of his knowing, for Alma's inspired words to him—"I know that thou believest"—demonstrate that Korihor could truthfully have acknowledged, "I *always* knew that there was a God" (Alma 30:52). Always? Even when, as he says, he "verily believed" that his denials were true? Yes. But isn't that a contradiction? Yes. A more than logical self-contradiction into which all of us frequently fall. "And now when he had said this, he besought that Alma should pray unto God, that the curse might be taken from him" (Alma 30:54). His objections were swept away—the truths, even the profound truths he mixed with his distortions, now useless in giving him relief or justification. In their place came the agonized cry for help, and the self-condemning[6] request that Alma do the praying.

Is conscience, then, a will-o-the-wisp, something to grow out of? I have offered a portrait that seems to me to render that sort of "explanation" an inadequate "explaining away" and to suggest instead that conscience at its best is something to grow into. In addition, I have illustrated how conscience, when flouted, diminishes consciousness; as, when honored, it invincibly expands it. Neither our ill-willed parodies of conscience nor the highly sophisticated rejection of ideas which we suppose will destroy it work out. In the best and the worst of us it is still there. It is one of the things—dare we put it so strongly?—that we cannot, here or hereafter, disbelieve. At its most illumined it becomes the will of the god within us, and the god of the will to become.

But how can anyone know without knowing he knows?

Just so. How can he?

---

6. "A man is his own tormenter and condemner," said the Prophet Joseph Smith. "Hence the saying, They shall go away into the lake that burns with fire and brimstone. The torment of disappointment in the mind of man is as exquisite as a lake of burning with fire and brimstone. I say, so is the torment of man" (Joseph Smith, *Teachings* [1938], 357).

Chapter Seven

THE INTIMATE
TOUCH OF PRAYER

Åll of us need deeper understanding in prayer. All of us reach. All of us speak. But none of us have perfected the process and all of us need encouragement. Here is a portrait of the prayer life of the Prophet Joseph Smith. I'm convinced that as we feel our way into his life we will receive glimpses that are more vivid and helpful than if we simply read statements about what we ought to do—the Prophet's life gives us clear insight into what we *can* do.

There is a letter in the Prophet's handwriting written in 1832—only a few months after one of the most remarkable revelations he received. The record of that revelation is now section 46 of the Doctrine and Covenants. Joseph is writing to his wife, Emma.

"My situation is a very unpleasant one, although I will endeavor to be contented, the Lord assisting me. I have visited a grove which is just back of the town, almost every day, where I can be secluded from the eyes of any mortal, and there give vent to all the feelings of my heart in meditation and prayers. I have called to mind all the past moments of my life, and am left to mourn and shed tears of sorrow for my folly in suffering the adversary of my soul to have so much power over me, as he has had in times past. But God is merciful and has forgiven my sins, and I rejoice that he sendeth forth His Comforter unto as many as believe and humble themselves before Him" (Jessee, *Personal Writings,* 238. Spelling and punctuation standardized).

Now, that one paragraph is enough to tell us that he was struggling—blessed and magnified though he was—just as we are struggling with the weight of life, with the difficulties and weaknesses that are in us, and with the constant desire to receive of the Lord.

Some have asked in my hearing, "How is it that the Prophet Joseph Smith, age fourteen, could go into a grove, never before having prayed vocally (according to his own account, implying that he had prayed before in his heart), and that in that first prayer he received great and marvelous blessings—transcendent blessings? Does that mean that he simply had far greater faith than any of the rest of us?

One possible response to that is that the answer the Prophet Joseph Smith received wasn't just to his own prayer. I submit that it was to the prayers of literally millions, maybe those even beyond the veil who had been seeking and reaching for generations for the restoration of the gospel and the reestablishment of the kingdom of God on the earth. That suggests that you and I do not pray alone. We pray as part of a great modern movement, and we are united in that very process. I sometimes think that therefore we have some advantages that are not shared by others who have not yet found the gospel, found the authorities and gifts and blessings of the Holy Ghost, and found the crowning blessing of the priesthood.

Let me ask some elementary questions about Joseph Smith's prayer life to help us feel even closer to him, as his experience overlaps our own. Did the Prophet pray long or short? Was he, as we judge prayers, inclined to multiply words or was he inclined to be brief? The answer to that question is yes. There were times when the Prophet prayed briefly; there also were times when he stayed on his knees in prayer for a long time. Of the first, an example is an experience at Kirtland. The table has been set, and there is little to eat. He stands at the table and says, "Lord, we thank thee for this johnnycake and ask thee to send us something better. Amen." Shortly, someone knocks on the door, and there stands a man with a ham and some flour. The Prophet jumps to his feet and says to Emma, "I knew the Lord would answer my prayer." Well, that's a telegram prayer—that's very brief (see Madsen, *Joseph Smith,* 32).

On the other hand Mary Elizabeth Rollins Lightner, a convert to the Church, only fourteen years of age at the time of the experience, describes coming with her mother to the Prophet's home, sharing in a small meeting where he set up a box or two and put a board across them to make room for people to sit. Now he spoke with great power. One of her comments is that his face, to her at least, "turned so white he seemed perfectly transparent." A great outpouring of the Spirit. But then he asked them to kneel. And he prayed. Such a prayer, she says, "I never heard before or since." So much did this prolong the meeting that some on the hard floor stood up, rubbed their knees a bit, and then knelt down again. It was long (see Hyrum L. Andrus and Helen Mae Andrus, *They Knew,* 23–24).

Did the Prophet address the Lord as *Father,* or did he have a special manner of address? Most frequently, the Prophet prayed "Our Father" or simply, "Father," or "O Lord," and was not inclined, as are some in our midst, to add adjectives and flowery phrases to that. I'm not saying that making such additions is wrong, but I note that he was intimate in prayer and that a simple "Father" was sufficient.

In counseling some missionaries he once said, "Make short prayers and short sermons." And he said on another occasion, "Be plain and simple, and ask for what you want, just like you would go to a neighbor and say, 'I want to borrow your horse to go to the mill'" (Hyrum L. Andrus and Helen Mae Andrus, *They Knew,*

100). That's plain. That's simple. And that's honest. So were his prayers.

There were times in sacred circumstances when the Prophet prayed in a formal way. I have in mind especially the unique situation of dedicating temples. Some people were upset and even left the Church through the experiences of the temple, either because so little occurred in their own experience or because so *much* did. The Prophet read the dedicatory prayer for the Kirtland Temple and announced that it had been given him by revelation. We have it recorded in section 109 of the Doctrine and Covenants. That prayer has become the model, the archetype, if you will, for all subsequent temple dedication prayers. Some members were disturbed at that. First of all, they'd been taught that we don't have set prayers in our midst. The truth is that we have some. The Lord has not permitted us to modify the sacramental prayers—not by one word. They are set. And so also with the baptismal prayer.

Second, they were troubled that here was a man who had apparently been given these words to say by the Lord to whom he was to say them. That struck them as circular. But the Prophet elsewhere has taught us that, as President J. Reuben Clark put it, one of the things we should most often pray for is to know what we should most often pray for. At least half of the prayer process is our bringing our souls into receptivity so that we know what we ought to pray; we listen. There are direct statements in modern revelation, for example, about being given all things.

> He that is ordained of God and sent forth, the same is appointed to be the greatest, notwithstanding he is the least and the servant of all.
>
> Wherefore, he is possessor of all things; for all things are subject unto him, both in heaven and on the earth, the life and the light, the Spirit and the power. . . .
>
> But no man is possessor of all things except he be purified and cleansed from all sin.
>
> And if ye are purified and cleansed from all sin, ye shall ask whatsoever you will in the name of Jesus and it shall be done.

Then: "But know this, it shall be given you what ye shall ask" (D&C 50:26–30). A sensitive, developing spiritual-minded person becomes more and more attentive and responsive to the Spirit and is able, therefore, to pray as the Prophet did. The Lord also said: "He that asketh in the Spirit asketh according to the will of God; wherefore it is done even as he asketh" (D&C 46:30). Thus we ought to follow the Prophet's lead, to listen and to pray with the Spirit; then the Spirit will prompt us both as to how we should pray and what we should say as we pray.

I've asked myself, "Did the Prophet sometimes pray for things never given or for guidance not allowed, or for privileges denied him?" He did. Like us, he sometimes struggled, and the Lord simply left that problem without solving it.

Two examples. The Prophet earnestly desired to know the time of the Savior's second coming. We've been taught no man knows the day nor the hour; but still, get a group of Mormons together, and after they admit that premise they say, "But, what do you think?" Well, the Prophet also wondered. He prayed very fervently to know, and the Lord's answer wasn't really an answer, except, "I won't tell you." It was: "Joseph, my son, if thou livest until thou art eighty-five years old, thou shalt see the face of the Son of Man; therefore let this suffice, and trouble me no more on this matter" (D&C 130:15). Joseph first assumed that that meant Christ would come in fifty-six years, which would have been when he, Joseph, would become eighty-five. But he realized that wasn't what he'd been told. He'd been told that if *he* lived to be eighty-five *he* would see the face of the Lord, and that might mean after dying. So he put down the only conclusion he could come to. "I believe the coming of the Son of Man will not be any sooner than that time" (see D&C 130:14–17; see also Huntington, Diary, 129).

God simply doesn't want us to know the timing of the Second Coming. He wants us to go on living, I suggest to you, as if it were going to happen tomorrow. Spiritually speaking, that's what He wants from us—to be prepared. As He says, "I come quickly" (Revelation 22:20). But He also wants us to live our lives in a long-range way with inspiration and not in an unauthentic way, which some of our young people seem to follow. They say, "It's all going to blow up in our faces in five years, so why should I plan to go away to school?" That's not in keeping with the Lord's will.

On one occasion the Prophet was praying to know why our people had to suffer so in Missouri. A sorrowful letter he wrote them says, "He will not show [it] unto me" (Joseph Smith, *Teachings* [1938], 34). There was at least one time earlier when he begged the Lord for what the Lord had told him He wouldn't give him. As we all do, the Prophet fell into the practice sometimes of saying, "Are you sure, Lord? Really, do you understand, Lord?" "I heard you, and the answer seems to be no, but are you sure?"

We remember the instance of Martin Harris. Twice the Prophet prayed asking for permission to lend Martin the manuscript. Twice the Lord said no. When the Prophet asked the third time, we might suppose he said or thought things like "But Lord, don't you understand, his wife is pushing him, Lord. What harm can it do? She needs to see something. She needs to have some reassurance." Well, there's a passage that says, "Seek not to counsel your God" (D&C 22:4).

Mother Smith recalled how Martin came to the house, paced up and down in front, hesitant to open the door to tell the truth. The Prophet saw him out the window. Finally he entered the house. "Martin, have you lost . . . ?" (See Lucy Mack Smith, *History*, 127–29.)

For two weeks, the Prophet could not be comforted. He felt he had betrayed the Lord. And no one can conceive the joy that entered his heart when the revelation came, "Behold, . . . repent of that which thou hast done . . . and thou . . . art again called to the work" (D&C 3:9–10). He said thereafter, and I think this was a summary of his experience, "I made this my rule: When the Lord commands, do it" (Joseph Smith, *History of the Church* 2:170). Well, he learned that, but he learned the hard way.

Did the Prophet practice family prayer? The answer is yes. During one period of the Prophet's life Eliza R. Snow served as a kind of baby-sitter in his home, and she wrote a poem called "Narcissa to Narcissus." She described how she admired the Prophet in public—that she saw him for what he was. But when she was in his home and though, knowing his greatness, saw him, as she puts it, as humble and unassuming as a child, kneeling in family prayer, she could not withhold her heart, and she loved his soul. The phrase "Narcissa to Narcissus," I believe, suggests that to see him, as with the mythological lad who looked in the water and saw his own reflection, enabled her to see herself. She came to a deeper sense of prayer in beholding him.

A brother who had never met the Prophet or his family came and was about to knock on the door, but hesitated because he heard singing. Sister Emma was leading the family and the guests, who were always numerous, in a kind of preparatory worship service. And then the Prophet prayed. (See Hyrum L. Andrus and Helen Mae Andrus, *They Knew,* 147.) He prayed three times a day with his family. And though in our lives it's difficult to get together once and overlap everyone, I nevertheless recommend that principle. Morning, noon, and night they had a kind of family prayer—beautiful!

Joseph once said, citing the book of Daniel, "You must make yourselves acquainted with those men who like Daniel pray three times a day toward the House of the Lord" (Joseph Smith, *Teachings* [1938], 161). What's the significance of facing the temple? Apparently it can help recall both the promises the Lord has made to us in the temple and the promises we have made to Him—covenants in the House of the Lord. When President Wilford Woodruff dedicated the Salt Lake Temple he offered a specific prayer that people who had there committed their lives to the Lord Jesus Christ and were now assailed with temptation or trouble but were unable to get to the temple to supplicate the Lord might face the temple as they prayed, and that the Lord would honor their prayers. (See Lundwall, *Temples,* 127.)

The Prophet, even in his own household, was templeminded both at Kirtland and at Nauvoo. The temple has been designated by the Lord himself as "a house of prayer" (D&C 88:119).

Did the Prophet pray when he was in desperate circumstances? Someone has said, intending it to be critical, that for some of us religion is like a spare tire—we never really put it on until we are in trouble. The Lord did indicate in a modern scripture that many in the day of peace and comparative well-being "esteemed lightly my counsel; but, in the day of their trouble, of necessity they feel after me." But He adds, "I will remember mercy" (D&C 101:8, 9).

Well, the Prophet was in circumstances that were hard and difficult. Brigham Young once said of him: "Joseph could not have been perfected . . . if he had received no persecution. If he had lived a thousand years, and led this people, and preached the Gospel without persecution, he would not have been perfected as well as he was at the age of thirty-nine years" (Young, *Journal of Discourses* 2:7).

In one dramatic situation he was hauled out of his bed by four men one night and dragged on the ground, beaten, stripped, tarred and feathered. They attempted to poison him—because he clenched his teeth they failed to get the poison into his mouth, but it subsequently fell onto the grass and killed it. It was aqua fortis. A quack doctor who had his tools had threatened that he would emasculate the Prophet. He didn't. Even as they were at him like fiends, the Prophet vocally prayed to the Lord for deliverance. He did pray in extremity. My personal conviction is that the last words he spoke in this life were not, as some have supposed, a distress signal, but were a prayer: "O Lord, my God." These words, a few minutes later, Willard Richards repeated with hands uplifted as he thought of the condition of the Church in the loss of the Prophet.

Yes, Joseph prayed in extremity but he also prayed in great gratitude. And here is another insight. He taught the Saints that they should practice virtue and holiness, but that they should give thanks unto God in the Spirit for whatsoever blessing they were blessed with. In my own life, years have gone by, I'm sure, when I have offered prayers yet never spent an entire prayer simply to thank the Lord. My prayers have always had an element of asking, asking, asking. But Joseph taught the Saints that if they would

265

learn to be thankful in all things—simply be thankful—they would be made glorious, and their prayers would take on a deeper, richer spirit.

The sin of ingratitude is one of the things that prevent us from as rich a prayer life as he had. He seemed to have an innate and deep capacity for gratitude, even for the slightest favor, from the Lord as from his fellowmen. And I have wept at times while reading that in his journal he sometimes wrote a kind of prayer for a brother. "Bless Brother So-and-So, Father, who gave me $1.35 today to help with such-and-such a project." Even the smallest favor called forth his warmth and gratitude.

Was the Prophet effective in silent prayers, did he commend that or even command it? I note with interest eight different places where the Lord, through the Prophet, says, "pray always." That's a strong imperative. How can we? If "pray always" means vocally, then none of us do it—none of us can. But if "pray always" includes the kind of prayer that is from the heart and wordless, we're getting closer to a possibility. And if it means, even more profoundly, that we are to be in the spirit of prayer regardless of what we may be doing, then all of us can pray always.

The Prophet gave us a better rendering of a New Testament verse about prayer. It is Romans 8:26. The King James Version of the Bible has Paul saying (speaking of how the Spirit can assist us in prayer), "The Spirit itself maketh intercession for us with *groanings* which cannot be uttered." The Prophet's version is, "The Spirit maketh intercession for us with *striving* which cannot be expressed (Joseph Smith, *Teachings* [1938], 278). I think he is saying that when we have enough confidence in the discerning power of the Spirit, we stop worrying so much about the words we use and are concerned more simply to open up what is really deep in us—even things that we cannot find words for. Strivings are different than groanings—you can groan in discouragement and despondency and it can all be turned down instead of turned up, but strivings are upreaching. We can take our strivings—even those that we cannot express—and know that as we silently think and pour out our feelings, the Spirit will translate those and perfectly transmit them to the Lord. And in turn, the Spirit can respond from the Lord to us. A great confidence and a great freedom can come when we trust the Spirit for that.

The Prophet, as we know, became a learned man. He didn't begin so, but I occasionally wince a little when I hear people say, "Well, he was just an unlearned boy." How does one become learned? We say "go to school." What's a school? It's a place where there are teachers. Well, who were the Prophet's teachers? Not just the local schoolmarm or two in Palmyra. The Prophet Joseph Smith was taught face to face by some "minor" pedagogues like Moroni, Peter, James, and John, the ancient Apostles and prophets; and, if that weren't enough, the Father and the Son. It is not true to say that he was unlearned. He had the learning and wisdom of heaven. Who knows more about the epistles of Paul—professors who teach in graduate schools, or Paul?

We help ourselves in prayer by speaking aloud. It helps our minds stay on track. But there are advantages also to silent prayers and some kinds of mind wandering—letting the mind go in the direction that it seems to be impressed to go.

Now, just a word about the remarkable pattern the Prophet taught in the presence of priesthood brethren. This was a special kind of prayer circumstance in the Kirtland Temple. Here are his exact words: "I labored with each of these quorums [High Priests, Seventies, Elders] for some time to bring them to the order which God had shown to me, which is as follows: "The first part to be spent in solemn prayer before God, without any talking or confusion." (I take that to mean solemn, silent prayer.) "And the conclusion with a sealing prayer by President Rigdon" (that is, one man would then pray vocally with and for the group), "when all the quorums were to shout with one accord a solemn hosanna to God and the Lamb with an Amen, Amen, and Amen."

Notice, in passing, that we're warned by the Lord against vain repetition, but we are not warned against repetition. There are things we not only can but should repeat in our lives. And it is not correct to suppose that after you say something once, you mustn't ever say it again. Vain repetition is the kind of vanity of repeating

267

without genuine concern, just supposing that saying a thing over and over from the neck up without any feeling is acceptable. No. But the Hosanna Shout, itself, is a repetition—three times we say hosanna, hosanna, hosanna. And three times we say amen. To continue: "Then all take seats and lift up their hearts in silent prayer to God, and if any obtain a prophecy or vision, to rise and speak that all may be edified and rejoice together."

Now, that is a special set of instructions, but the spirit of it, it seems to me, applies even to our own private prayers. Note that there is first a concentration, not confused but silent, then a vocal prayer, then a giving of gratitude, and then waiting upon the Lord with our hearts sensitive, and speaking, or at least, in private life, knowing what comes by the Spirit. Did that happen, that aftermath? Yes. The Prophet says in his journal: "The quorum of the Seventy enjoyed a great flow of the Holy Spirit. Many arose and spoke, testifying that they were filled with the Holy Ghost, which was like fire in their bones, so that they could not hold their peace, but were constrained to cry hosanna to God and the Lamb, and glory in the highest" (Joseph Smith, *History of the Church* 2:391–92).

Of a similar occasion a few days before this one, Joseph said: "After these quorums were dismissed, I retired to my home, filled with the Spirit, and my soul cried hosanna to God and the Lamb, through the silent watches of the night; and while my eyes were closed in sleep, the visions of the Lord were sweet unto me, and His glory was round about me" (Joseph Smith, *History of the Church* 2:387). Much can be learned from that.

Half a century later, when forty years had passed since construction had begun on the Salt Lake Temple, the pattern the Prophet taught was used as Elder Lorenzo Snow led the Saints—some forty thousand of them—in the glorious privilege of uniting their voices in praise of the Lord that they had been able to reach the capstone. Forty thousand, and the shout was a *shout!* It echoed through the mountains. Can you imagine forty years of struggle and patience bursting out in joy as they did so! Well, that's acceptable to the Lord.

Another kind of shouting the Prophet rebuked. Let me in passing mention it. One time, Father Johnson asked a convert who had been a Methodist exhorter to pray in the family's evening worship. He hadn't overcome his habits. The exhorters in that old-time pattern were men who learned to throw their voice in a kind of falsetto quality. When the wind was right, they could be heard a mile away, some claim. This man began, literally, hallooing that way in prayer, and "alarmed the whole village." The Prophet was one of those who came running to the scene. In essence, he said, "Brother, don't pray like that again. You don't have to bray like a jackass to be heard of the Lord." (See Young, *Journal of Discourses* 2:214.) Well, George A. Smith indicates that that brother left the Church. Now, if you're sincere, there's no problem. But there's something false and inconsistent about supposing that the Lord cannot hear you unless you halloo. He can hear the quietest turning of your own sacred conscience and knows the thoughts and intents of your heart.

The Prophet taught repeatedly that the Saints should be one in prayer, that when a group comes together in fasting and prayer, united in the petition of their hearts, that makes a greater difference somehow than if anyone alone had done so. The revelations say, "Be agreed as touching all things whatsoever ye ask of me" (D&C 27:18). Be one in your prayers, for "if ye are not one ye are not mine" (D&C 38:27). One of the sisters, the wife of George A. Smith, recalled the Prophet's statement to her. "He said that we did not know how to pray to have our prayers answered." But she added that when she and her husband received their endowments in the temple, they understood what he meant. (See Hyrum L. Andrus and Helen Mae Andrus, *They Knew,* 123.) The Lord instructed the Prophet to teach several of the brethren the keys whereby they might ask in prayer and receive an answer (see D&C 124:95, 97). Well, there is much about the privilege of the sanctuary that we cannot say outside the temple, but may I simply report that Brigham Young, who learned to pray listening to the Prophet, said repeatedly to the Saints that when someone prays in a congregation we should be saying in our minds what he or she is saying with the lips. We should repeat the very words in our minds, and then when we say amen we know what we're saying amen to. Without that repetition, sometimes we do not. Why is it important? So that the Saints may be one. Truly the effectual, fervent power of united prayer cannot be overestimated.

Later comment has to do with the original problem—the problem of guilt, the problem of sin. Here is the Prophet himself writing to his wife, saying, "I have called to mind all the past moments of my life and am left to mourn and shed tears of sorrow for my folly."

If we study them closely we find that all the Saints have had their struggles. Nephi, just to name one, writes with such strength in those first and early chapters that you wonder if he ever doubted or murmured or had a setback. The contrast between his attitude and even that of his own parents is startling. But in the fourth chapter of 2 Nephi, you will notice, he opens his soul and levels with us. And even though he has been struggling with the burden of leadership, he says, "When I desire to rejoice, my heart groaneth because of my sins." Then he prays with a power that reminds one of David in the Psalms, "O Lord, wilt thou encircle me around in the robe of thy righteousness . . . make a way for mine escape."

A homely illustration of the same point is the story about the two farmers talking, and there's a horse pulling the plow, but on his right flank every time he pulls, the strap rubs what has become an open gaping sore. The observer says, "Pretty tough on that horse to make him pull when he's got a gaping sore." The other farmer replies, "Yes, plumb tough, but I reckon we wouldn't get much work done in this world if we waited until everyone was plumb fit." And that's true in the Church. We wouldn't get any work done in the Church if we waited until all of us were perfect. The Lord wouldn't be able to call anyone to any position in the Church if he waited until we were all fully worthy.

If I may be personal for a moment, when I was called to be a mission president, the call was made by President Henry D. Moyle. I was taken aback by it, and surprised that he didn't ask any hard questions. I reminded him of that. "You haven't asked any questions of worthiness." He said, "Well, when one responds as you have, we don't have many questions." That didn't satisfy me. I said, "But President Moyle, I love the Church, but I have some problems." He came around the desk, put his arm around me, and said, "Brother Madsen, the Lord has to show a lot of mercy to let *any* of us work in His Church." That's true. But what does one do when he feels, as Lorenzo Snow put it, "that the heavens are as brass over his head" (see *Juvenile Instructor* 22:22). That though he ought to pray, he doesn't feel like praying. And when he does feel like praying, he is so ashamed that he hardly can. What then? My response is this glimpse from the Prophet.

The period just prior to the dedication of the Kirtland Temple saw an outpouring of the Spirit. Many of the brethren saw glorious visions, and the Prophet himself had a manifestation in which he saw, in panoramic vision, the lives of the Brethren of the Twelve—saw them in their strugglings, their flounderings, saw them preaching the gospel, saw them eventually brought back into the celestial kingdom. Interestingly, he saw them together—a group of them at least—as he recorded it, "in foreign lands." He didn't say England, but that's where they eventually went. He saw them, standing in a circle, beaten, tattered, their feet swollen, and clearly discouraged. Now, there are different levels of discouragement; we can be disturbed a bit, we can be worried, we can then be despondent, and there are moments in life for some of us when we ask, "What is the use?" And when we sink that far, we're almost to the point of wishing we could cease to be.

Well, the Prophet didn't indicate that it had gone that far with the Twelve, but they were looking down in their discouragement. Yet standing above them in the air was the Lord Jesus Christ. And it was made known to the Prophet that He yearned to show himself to them—to reach down and lift them—but they did not see Him. And the Savior looked upon them and wept. (See Joseph Smith, *History of the Church* 2:381.) We're told by three of the Brethren who heard the Prophet rehearse that vision that he could never speak of it without himself weeping. Why? Why would he be so touched? Because he knew that Christ willingly came into the world and took upon himself the pains and sicknesses of His people so that He might be filled with compassion so that all the Father's family could come to Him, if to no one else—and sometimes there is no one else—could come to Him, knowing that He knows what is taking place in us when we sin, or suffer affliction, or are discouraged. The great tragedy of life is that, loving us and having paid that awful price of suffering, in the moment when He is now prepared to reach down and help us we won't let Him. We look down instead of up, accepting the adversary's promptings that we must not pray; we cannot pray; we are not worthy to pray. But, says Nephi in response to that, "I say to you that ye must pray always, and not faint" (2 Nephi 32:8–9).

There may be things that we are unworthy to do at times in our life, but there is one thing we are *never* unworthy to do, and that is pray. I have a testimony about this. The Prophet Joseph Smith not only taught it, but exemplified it. You *go* to the Lord regardless of the condition of your soul, and He will respond. He *never* closes the door against you. You may close it against Him, but if so that is your initiative, not His. We should call upon Him when we need Him most, and that's usually when we feel least worthy, and then He can respond.

In the modern prophet Joseph Smith we have an example of living, breathing prayer—the kind that changes life. His early successes with prayer were the foundation of a pattern that brought him progressively closer to God. If prayer had no other function than to help us concentrate on the deepest concerns of our life— even to reveal ourselves to ourselves—it would be worth doing. But beyond that the Prophet illustrates for all time that prayer isn't just subjective, it isn't just self-hypnosis. Rather, it is a plan and pattern whereby we do in fact break through the veil and receive at the living hand of the living God through His Christ.

Chapter Eight

HOUSE OF GLORY

I begin with a story that goes back to the dedication of the Salt Lake Temple, which took forty years to build. President David O. McKay used to tell of a man who didn't have money enough even to buy shoes to attend a conference in the Tabernacle. During the conference Brigham Young arose and pleaded with the brethren that there needed to be more granite brought for the temple from the quarry about fifteen miles south. It was hauled mostly by ox team. A man came out from this conference and saw another man on the street with a team of oxen. "Why weren't you in there, Brother?"

"Uh, my feet. I didn't feel right about going in."

"Well, Brother Brigham pleaded for more people to get granite."

"All right," said the man, "I'll go. Wo, hah, Buck!" And he started.

President McKay's eyes filled with tears as he related that simple incident. The reason why his name and his image come to mind whenever I think of temples is that it was President McKay who performed the wedding ceremony for my wife, Ann, and myself, and that high privilege was possible for us in part because he had done the same for Ann's parents. That morning, very early on a June day, he came in his white suit, a white tie, and white hair. There was majesty in his personality. Somehow we knew then, had we ever doubted it, that no one could speak properly if he spoke evil of the temple, for there before us stood its product.

John the Revelator, John the Beloved, visioning the city Jerusalem in glorified state, said "And I saw no temple therein: for the Lord God Almighty and the Lamb are the temple of it" (Revelation 21:22). And then he added that not only would the Lamb reign forever, as we sing, but we, having by then been glorified like unto Him, would likewise reign forever and ever (see Revelation 22:5).

The Salt Lake Temple was dedicated with a sense of sacrifice and gratitude that maybe we moderns have not reached. Forty years! Forty thousand people gathered just to see the laying of the capstone! And Lorenzo Snow, then one of the Twelve, led them in the Hosanna Shout. And then Wilford Woodruff, who had had a dream years before that he would somehow be involved in the dedication of that temple (and he was by now the President of the Church), promised that a strict reading of the requirements of worthiness would not be imposed on the members attending the dedicatory services provided they come feasting and repenting. (That was not a slip of the lip, because the Lord defines fasting and prayer in modern revelation—granting it has its negative side of mourning in some places—as rejoicing and prayer (see D&C 59:13–14). Fasting is feasting on the Spirit, and somehow not partaking of physical food isn't quite enough. Fasting is a kind of concentration, a kind of pulling ourselves together.)

Well, during a twenty-three-day period of dedicatory services averaging two thousand each session, some eighty thousand people were regenerated. President Woodruff's entry in his journal at the end of that year was: "The greatest event of the year [1893] is the dedication of the Salt Lake Temple. Great power was manifest on that occasion." (Cowley, *Woodruff,* 584).

The scriptural phrase that brings all that into a theme is that we are to receive in temples, through temples, from temples, "power from on high" (D&C 95:8). Christ is the source of that power. The temple is His. Every symbol in and out of that sacred structure points toward Him and, as a cup carries water, transmits the Holy Spirit.

Now to be specific in terms of needs that all of us feel strongly about in our time. It is a characteristic fact that the Lord has commanded the sacrifice of temple building at the times when apparently our people were least able to build them; and the sacrifice has been immense. But sacrifice "brings forth blessings."

In the 1830s the Brethren kept inquiring. They didn't have our heritage, and they didn't understand even what the word *temple* meant. They kept asking, What is it we are doing? Well, we build a temple. What for? And Joseph Smith told them on one occasion, "nor could Gabriel explain it to [your] understanding." But prepare, he told them, for great blessings will come. (See Joseph Smith, *Teachings* [1938], 91.)

Yet in a preparatory revelation (see D&C 88) the purposes of the temple are outlined. It's called "a house of prayer, a house of fasting, a house of faith, a house of learning, a house of glory, . . . a house of God." Prepare yourselves, it says, "sanctify yourselves . . . and [God] . . . will unveil his face unto you" (D&C 88:68, 119).

Let's discuss each of those purposes.

A house of prayer. "Make yourselves acquainted," said the Prophet, "with those men who like Daniel pray three times a day toward the House of the Lord" (Joseph Smith, *Teachings* [1938], 161). There is a true principle involved in literally facing the house of God as one prays and as one praises the Lord. The Prophet, as he led a group of faithful Saints through the Nauvoo Temple not yet finished (he did not live to see that day), said to them, "You do not know how to pray to have your prayers answered." But, as the sister who recorded that brief statement testifies, she and her husband received their temple blessings, and then came to understand what he meant. (See Hyrum L. Andrus and Helen Mae Andrus, *They Knew*, 123.)

A modern Apostle, Elder Melvin J. Ballard, said once to a

275

group of young people about solving their problems: "Study it out in your own minds, reach a conclusion, and then go to the Lord with it and he will give you an answer by that inward burning, and if you don't get your answer I will tell you where to go; go to the House of the Lord. Go with your hearts full of desire to do your duty. When in the sacred walls of these buildings, where you are entitled to the Spirit of the Lord, and in the silent moments, the answer will come" (*Utah Genealogical and Historical Magazine,* October 1932, 147).

For clues to personal experiences behind that statement we note that in Elder Ballard's boyhood he often looked up at the Logan Temple and its spires, was inspired by those spires, and wanted to enter the temple worthily regardless of the costs. That meant, for one thing, that he never was even tempted to break the Word of Wisdom, because he knew that might prevent him from entering that building. His later experiences, many having to do with his ministry, were a derivative often of what he felt, experienced, tasted within the walls of the sanctuary.

On a personal note, I myself, in a critical year away from home and at school, drove at times to the place in Los Angeles where we had been told there would one day be a temple, just in the feeling that the place might be an added strength to me in prayer. And it proved to be so.

"A house of prayer, a house of fasting, a house of faith, a house of learning." One of the men who touched my life was Elder John A. Widtsoe of the Council of the Twelve, a man who graduated summa cum laude from Harvard after three instead of the usual four years, who was given in that last year an award for the greatest depth of specializing in his field (which was chemistry); but they also gave an award that year for the student who had shown the greatest breadth of interests, which he also received. Elder Widtsoe wrote perceptively about the temple and temple worship. I heard him say in sacred circumstances that the promise was given him by a patriarch when he was a mere boy in Norway, "Thou shalt have great faith in the ordinances of the Lord's House." And so he did. I heard him say that the temple is so freighted with depth of understanding, so loaded with symbolic grasp of life and its eternal significance, that only a fool would attempt in mere prosaic restatement to give it in a comprehensive way.

I heard him say that the temple is a place of revelation. And he did not divorce that concept from the recognition that the problems we have are very practical, very realistic, down-to-earth problems. He often said, "I would rather take my practical problems to the house of the Lord than anywhere else." In his book *In a Sunlit Land* he describes a day when, having been frustrated for months in trying to pull together a mass of data he had compiled to come up with a formula, he took his companion, his wife, to the Logan Temple to forget his failure. And in one of the rooms of that structure there came, in light, the very answer he had previously failed to find. Two books on agrarian chemistry grew out of that single insight—a revelation in the temple of God.

The temple is not just a union of heaven and earth. It is the key to our mastery of the earth. It is the Lord's graduate course in subduing the earth, which, as only Latter-day Saints understand, ultimately will be heaven—this earth glorified.

A house of learning? Yes, and we learn more than about the earth. We learn *ourselves.* We come to comprehend more deeply, in an environment that surrounds one like a cloak, our own identity, something of the roots that we can't quite reach through memory but which nevertheless are built cumulatively into our deepest selves—an infinite memory of conditions that predate memory. The temple is the catalyst whereby the self is revealed to the self.

There was a period when I was required as an officer in the Ensign Stake to go every Friday to the temple. It was not a burden, as I had thought it would be. It became instead my joy. Slowly, because of that regularity, I was trusted with certain assignments in the temple. This meant that I could walk into the temple annex and they would all say, "Good morning, Brother Madsen"; and I wouldn't even have to show my recommend. Not only that, but I had the privilege to sit for hours in the chapel of the annex or elsewhere, contemplative, reading occasionally, but trying to absorb, trying to breathe the air that is heavier than air in that place. There I would meditate about my critical problems, which had to do with decisions about my life's work, decisions about the girl I should marry, and other struggles in how to cope. There were times when I learned something about me; there were times when peace came in a decision, and I knew that that peace was of God.

The temple is a house of learning. And it is intended that therein we not simply learn *of* or *about* Christ, but that we come to *know Him.* It has always impressed me that in the Joseph Smith Translation the classic passage about the hereafter when many will say, "Lord, Lord, did we not do this and that?" is rendered more fittingly. The King James Version says that Christ will respond, "I never knew you." The Joseph Smith Translation renders it, "You never knew me" (Matthew 7:23; JST, Matthew 7:33).

This is the gospel of Jesus Christ. This is the restored Church of Jesus Christ. This is the church that teaches us that we can have a direct and immediate living relationship with the living Christ. And we inscribe on temples, "Holiness to the Lord," "The House of the Lord." He told us, and He didn't qualify it, that as regards our preparation, "all the pure in heart that come into it shall see God" (D&C 97:16). Elder Orson Pratt points out that this promise specifically relates to a temple not yet built, a temple to be erected in the center city, the New Jerusalem, wherein someday Christ actually will dwell; and wherein, therefore, any who enter will meet Him. But again, Elders John A. Widtsoe, George F. Richards, Joseph Fielding Smith, and others have borne witness that the promise is more extensive than that; that it applies now. It is a promise that we may have a wonderfully rich *communion* with Him. *Communion!* That is to say that we are not simply learning propositions *about,* but that we are in a participative awareness *with.*

Occasionally we struggle in amateur research in Church history to understand what kind of a portrait, in terms of sheer physical appearance, one could draw of Christ if we simply utilized what modern witnesses have said about their glimpses of Him. It's an impressive portrait. But one thing perhaps we sometimes neglect in that curiosity is an awareness or a seeking for an awareness of His personality, of those subtler realities that we already recognize in other persons in all variations but which have been perfected in Him. What would it be like to be in His presence, not simply in terms of what you would see but what you would feel? To give us one clue, He says, "Listen to him . . . who is pleading your cause before [the Father], saying: Father, behold the sufferings and death of him who did no sin [that is to say, committed none, but he knows sins, for he experienced temptation to do them all], in whom thou wast well pleased; behold the blood of thy Son which was shed, . . . wherefore, Father, spare these my brethren" (D&C 45:3–5). That's a glimpse of the compassion that one comes to feel in communion—the feeling with, the feeling for, that He has. He is the one personality of whom it cannot truthfully be said: "You don't know me. You don't understand me. You don't care about me." Because of what He went through, He does know, He does understand, He does care. And He has had us sacrifice to build sacred houses where the linkage of His heart, His "bowels of compassion," can merge with ours.

The temple is a place of learning to know Him.

And now the phrase "a house of glory, a house of God." One of the most tender moments of my spiritual life was the day that Rose Wallace Bennett, an author I knew, told me that as a little girl she was present in the dedicatory services of the Salt Lake Temple. She described also the day Wilford Woodruff had a birthday, his ninetieth, when it was a little girl's privilege to take forward to him in the Tabernacle ninety roses in a setting of some eight thousand children between the ages of eight and twelve, all dressed in white. They had gathered to honor him; and then as he had come into the building (under some pretense that there was need of an organ repair), they arose and sang, "We Thank Thee, O God, for a Prophet." She could not talk about what it felt like to see his tears, or again, what it was like to be in the temple, without herself weeping. But what she said to me was: "Young man, my father brought me to the edge of City Creek Canyon where we could look down on the temple. I testify to you that there was a light around the temple, and it was not due to electricity."

There are such phrases in all the authentic literature that has to do with temple dedications: "light," "glory," "power." Even some who were not members of the Church at Kirtland came running, wondering what had happened. They wondered if the building was on fire. It was; but with what the Prophet called "celestial burnings," the downflow of the power of the living God, like encircling flame as on the day of Pentecost. A prayer for that had been offered by the Prophet and by his father, and it was fulfilled. (See D&C 109:36–37; Joseph Smith, *History of the Church* 2:428; Tullidge, *Women,* 101.)

What is glory? Well, it is many things in the scriptures. One strand of meaning is often neglected. If we can trust one Hebrew student, the Hebrew word equivalent to glory, *kabod,* refers in some of its strands to physical presence. Just as a person says in common parlance today, "he was there in all his glory," so the Old Testament often uses this word for God. In the Psalm that refers to the glory (Psalm 8) there are two changes that are crucial. The King James Version reads, "Thou hast made [man] a little lower than the angels, and hast crowned him with glory and honour." Probably what that verse said originally was, "Thou hast made [man] a little lower than the Gods, and hath crowned him with a *physical body* and with honor." This is the truth. The body is a step *up* in the scales of progression, not a step down. God is God because He is gloriously embodied; and were He not so embodied, He would be less than God.

The privilege of attending the house of God is in effect to have our physical beings brought into harmony with our spirit personalities. And I have read, but cannot quote perfectly, can only paraphrase, the testimony of President Lorenzo Snow to the effect that participating in the temple ceremonies is the only way that the knowledge locked in one's spirit can become part of this flesh; thus occurs that inseparable union, that blending, which makes possible a celestial resurrection. It is as if, if I may mix the figure,

280

we are given in the house of God a patriarchal blessing to every organ and attribute and power of our being, a blessing that is to be fulfilled in this world and the next, keys and insights that can enable us to live a godly life in a very worldly world, protected— yes, even insulated—from the poisons and distortions that are everywhere.

That is the temple. And the glory of God, His ultimate perfection, is in His house duplicated in us, provided we go there with a susceptible attitude.

Let me briefly discuss the "how" of susceptibility. Listening once in Los Angeles to the plea of President David O. McKay, stake president after stake president pledged contributions to make possible the building of the Los Angeles Temple. They made a commitment. Then he arose and delivered a masterful discourse, maybe the greatest I have ever heard on the subject of temples. In shorthand I jotted down one paragraph which I'm going to quote, but before I do so, let me give this explanation. He told of a girl— a girl, I found later, who was his niece and therefore felt confident in confiding in him. Earlier that year she had been initiated in a sorority, and not long thereafter she had "gone through the temple" (as we say); I wish that verb could be improved—"going through the temple." I wish we could somehow speak of the temple going through *us*. I wish that my children had not been confused—it's my fault that they were—when my wife and I used to say to them, "We are going to *do* sealings." They thought that we would take a stepladder and a bucket. It's a kind of Mormon activism to talk about "temple work." There is a sense, of course, in which it is work; but too rarely do we speak of "temple worship," which can send us back to our work changed.

Well, on the occasion in Los Angeles, President McKay stopped everyone by saying: "This young lady came to me. She had had both experiences, but said she had been far more impressed with her sorority." We gasped.

President McKay was a master of the pause. He let that wait for several seconds and then said: "Brothers and sisters, she was disappointed in the temple. Brothers and sisters, I was disappointed in the temple." Then he finished his sentence: "And so were you." Then no one gasped. He had us.

"Why were we?" he asked. And then he named some of the things. We were not prepared. How could we be, fully? We had stereotypes in our minds, faulty expectations. We were unable to distinguish the symbol from the symbolized. We were not worthy enough. We were too inclined quickly to respond negatively, critically. And we had not yet seasoned spiritually. Those are my words, but they cover approximately what he said. I will give you the quotation verbatim.

This was a man, at that time eighty years of age, who had been in the temple every week for some fifty years, which gave him, I thought, some right to speak. He said: "I believe there are few, even temple workers, who comprehend the full meaning and power of the temple endowment. Seen for what it is, it is the step-by-step ascent into the Eternal Presence. If our young people could but glimpse it, it would be the most powerful spiritual motivation of their lives."

When he said that, I felt it. I had myself been a critic; had made up my mind that some things were trivial, offensive. But that day the Lord touched me, and I decided that I would not speak again against the house of the Lord. I would not assume I knew better than the prophets. I would listen. And I would repent. And I would hope that someday I could testify as did that noble man. In time there was far more opened up to me than I had ever dreamed.

But there were three things amiss in me, and I dare to suppose these may apply to some others. First, I hadn't even carefully read the scriptures about the temple. It had not occurred to me that there are over three hundred verses, by my count, in the Doctrine and Covenants alone that talk about the temple and the "hows," if you will, of preparation. I had not read what the Brethren had said to help us—I was unaware of those statements. Today we are well supplied with informative material in books such as *The House of the Lord,* by Elder James E. Talmage; The *Holy Temple,* by Elder Boyd K. Packer; and several articles in the *Encyclopedia of Mormonism,* volume 4.

Second, I was, I am afraid, afflicted with various kinds of unworthiness and not too anxious to change all that. Oh, we talk of it and we aspire. We want change, but we don't want it enough. We are (and I don't laugh at poor Augustine for saying this) like Augustine, who said in a prayer, "Oh God, make me clean, but not yet." We talk of sacrifice. The one the Lord asks of *us now* is the sacrifice of our sins—the hardest thing in the world to give up. There's still a certain bittersweet enjoyment. But His promise is crystal clear. "If you will purify yourselves, sanctify yourselves, I will bless you" (see D&C 88:74). And I'm afraid the postscript is: "And if you don't, I can't."

The third point is that I had a built-in hostility to ritual and to symbolism. I was taught by people both in and out of the Church—with good intention, I have no doubt—that we don't believe in pagan ceremony; we don't believe in all these procedures and routines; that's what they did in the ancient apostate church: we've outgrown all that. Well, that in effect is throwing out the baby with the bath water. We're not against ordinances. God has revealed them anew. And I suspect they are as eternal as are what we often call eternal laws. There are certain patterns or programs, certain chains of transmission, which are eternal. Ordinances tie in with those, if they are not identical with them. God has so decreed, but that decree is based upon the very ultimate nature of reality. You *cannot* receive the powers of godliness, says the scripture, except through the ordinances (see D&C 84:20). Well, that hadn't ever entered my soul. I thought our sacraments were a bit of an embarrassment and that sometime we could do away with them. One day it suddenly became clear to me—this is the Lord's pattern of our nourishment. We need spiritual transformation. We can eat, if you will, receive, drink (the Lord uses all those images) the Living Fountain through ordinances. Well, I pray that we will reach out for what is written, reach out for repentance, and reach out in the recognition that the ordinances are channels of living power.

The dedicatory prayers for temples have from the beginning been given by revelation, and that fact has been puzzling to some.

283

How can the Lord reveal a prayer to offer to Him who has revealed it? Well, there's nothing contradictory in that. One cannot know fully what to pray until he receives guidance from the Lord. "He that asketh in the Spirit," says modern revelation, "asketh according to the will of God" (D&C 46:30). You must listen in order to know what to say. And prayers that are all ask and no listen lack something in effectiveness.

The temple is the place where we can come to understand what the Lord would have us ask. And it is the place where we can ask in silence, in joy, in earnestness.

Years ago I was involved in the Ensign Stake Genealogical Committee. We held a series of firesides. The climactic one of six was given by President Joseph Fielding Smith. The last lecture was given on temple marriage. But the week before that I had been asked to speak on vital temple purposes. I struggled with that. I was talking to young people. What was most remarkable came toward the end of what I said. I wanted somehow to let them know that my own assurance about marriage had come within the walls of the temple.

But I didn't want to acknowledge publicly that I was going to marry this girl. That had not yet been said in private, and therefore I didn't think it should be said in public. But there came down on me that night (and I have a tape-recording that tells the story) such a witness that I announced, "The Lord has made known to me that I am to be married, and to whom." She was on the front row, sitting next to my father. It came as a bit of a surprise to him, too. There was much salt water spilled. Have you heard Pasternak's phrase, "Be so close to those you love that when they weep you taste salt"? I did. I gasped, though, at what I had said and wanted somehow to alter, qualify, call back, change. That was shown in several seconds of silence. Then at last all I could do was say, "In the name of the Lord, amen," and sit down.

For all of us there is something about the temple that can change our lives. We need to reach for it, to honor it, if need be to sacrifice for it, even our sins. Some of us have fought against that, as I fought against it, because it means change, maybe some painful change. But that change is the Spirit of God working on the soul and it will come to each one of us. We will honor the promptings and let the Lord take over in our lives.

The Lord *is* in His temples, where He ministers personally and manifests himself to the faithful therein. With the power of Christ in His sanctuary, it is intended that all of us drink deeply, receive powerfully, and then testify worthily of that glorious truth. In this way we will come to share in the joys and blessings of the radiant life.

THE
RADIANT
LIFE

Chapter One

SOULS AFLAME

There is a legend about a grandfather, a holy man, who, caring for his grandson, sent him out to play. Shortly the boy returned, sobbing as if his heart would break. He explained: "I have been playing hide-and-seek with my friends. I went and hid and waited, but no one came for me." The grandfather embraced him and said: "Now you know how God feels. He hides, and no one comes for Him."

This church does not have a collection of what in classical terms is called devotional literature, nor again an official manual, which is a set of spiritual exercises. What we do have is a pool of experience, rich experience. Here I would like to select from it some bits and pieces that I believe will draw us closer to them and, through them, to the Lord.

There are religions in the world which in effect develop prayer practices after the preconceptions of their theology are taken into account. We have an opposite heritage. Our theology has been derived from prayer—this is safer, sounder, and saner, I believe. But first may I mention two hard reflective hang-ups that occur in the discussion of prayer and that have not only been resolved but also dissolved for us if we only will accept this.

First is the notion that God, being all-powerful and all-knowing, is therefore unchanging. And that since He knows all that will occur—having, it is said, absolute foreknowledge— prayer is pointless. For if God knew yesterday what is happening today, including all that I am going to do, then it is pointless to ask that it be changed. Though one can insist that His foreknowledge is not a cause, one can still ask, "But am I a cause, truly, if in fact the eventuations could not have been otherwise?"

The heritage of prayer in this church teaches us that, whether or not we settle the question of foreknowledge, there is point in reaching up to that personage who is himself free and has used His freedom to forbid to himself the use of force. He is not a computer, not a thing, I am grateful to report. He is a conscious being, and it is the relationship of our freedom to His freedom that does make a difference.

Our history is filled with instances in which what seemed to be inevitable was prevented from happening by the intervention of our prayers and God's response.

A second cause of confusion is the notion that God, being God, must know what is best for us; and that therefore if we pray and ask Him to change His mind, He would hardly be wise to answer yes. If we pray to our own hurt, a loving God would do well to answer no. And if we are simply praying to remind Him of what He already intends, why pray at all? There is a kind of intellectual lockjaw that comes from such reflection, but in truth again, the Restoration makes it clear that we have a need and that so does He, and that He needs us to listen as well as to ask. It is said among the Jews that, God preferring prayer to mere silence and not receiving it, caused great affliction among the Israelites of the Exodus, so they would at least cry out from their pain.

We do need Him and He does need us, and one would almost gather from diaries and journals which report firsthand experience that His will can be swayed—in part because the very prayer process changes us, and God can respond to the change; and in part because, in the two-way relationship that exists, we learn and grow through His response.

I turn now to questions that are more soulful and reply with experience. There is, some insist, a circularity in faith itself. Faith, the child once said in a Sunday School class, "means believing what you know darn well isn't so." Faith is sometimes thought to be in the religious world a substitute for reason, and in fact a form of credulity. It is thought to be faith that something is or isn't. But the first principle of the gospel of Jesus Christ is not such faith. It is faith in a person about whom we already have some knowledge. Faith is not exerted in vacuo. Trust in a person is based upon acquaintance with the person, or at least belief about the person that begins secondhand. But the whole point of the gospel is to make it firsthand. So He who counsels us, "Pray always," is asking that we come to Him in confidence.

Second, it is said that prayer is a crutch. After all, mature people are supposed to stand on their own two feet; they don't have to pray. Prayer is a form of wishful thinking, a kind of wanting pie in the sky. Well, as to that, first of all there is nothing wrong with crutches for people who need them. There is nothing wrong with escalators and elevators. But speaking of crutches, agnosticism is a kind of crutch. It is a perennial postponement of decision, and it assumes that postponement is safer than commitment. Atheism is a pair of iron braces. It claims to know more than can be known. Someone has said that atheists don't find God for the same reason that bank robbers don't find policemen. They work very hard to avoid Him. But throughout the Doctrine and Covenants is the admonition, "Seek and ye shall find." The implication is, don't seek and you likely won't find.

But it is said: "I don't pray because I have doubts. I doubt things about myself, about the gospel, and even about God." It is truly said that doubt and faith do not coexist in the same person at the same time, but they can exist within a second of each other. Witness Heber C. Kimball's standing by the door while Brigham Young was lying on what appeared to be his deathbed. Said Heber, "I doubt very much if Brigham ever rises from that bed."

291

However, "he had no sooner uttered the words, than he spoke up, as with another voice, and said, 'He *shall* live, and shall start upon this mission with me tomorrow morning.' And they did start the very next morning, on their mission to England" (Whitney, *Heber C. Kimball,* 434). He was right the second time. From doubt to faith.

On another occasion he stood in the Bowery in Salt Lake City and announced to threadbare and barely surviving people, "States goods will soon sell in Salt Lake City for less than they sell for in New York. In the name of the Lord. Amen." And as he returned to his seat from the pulpit, he said he "had missed it this time." Someone on the stand said, "I don't believe a word of it." And Brigham Young said, "Let it stand." It did stand. When the California gold rush came, the prophecy was actually and completely fulfilled. Elder Kimball was right the first time and he went from faith to doubt. (See Whitney, *Heber C. Kimball,* 389–90.)

It is an honest prayer to say: "Lord, I believe. Help thou mine unbelief." And it was, after all, a prophet of God, Joseph Smith, who said—and he was a man of faith—"If I had not experienced what I have, I could not have believed it myself" (Joseph Smith, *Teachings* [1976], 361).

But it is said: "I don't pray because I am not good with words. I would rather someone else would do the talking." Fair enough, but our history is filled with instances of people who had mind-boggling verbal gifts and of others who did not. There have been many, like Moses, who needed an Aaron. And there are in our midst today those who are both deaf and dumb, whose lips are sealed but who yet may pray from their core wordlessly. Joseph Smith offered a better rendering of the King James Version's line by Paul that says "the Spirit maketh intercession for us with groanings which cannot be uttered" (Romans 8:26). The Prophet's version is "with striving which cannot be expressed"—meaning, in words (see Joseph Smith, *Teachings* [1976], 278). But if a person does have trust in the living God, he can from his core reach upward, put an arrow on those imprisoned needs, and they will be carried by the Spirit, perfectly communicated and responded to. And what relief when we do it!

But it is said, "I do not pray because my prayers have not been answered." Answered, we mean, do we, not heard? Ah, but they have been heard and recorded. We are taught that one day we will have a perfect, bright recollection of all that has been in our lives here, but what of all that has been before that? The historian B.H. Roberts thought long and hard on the record, and he pursued this subject so often and so deeply, trying to account for the radical differences he perceived among those who have received the gospel in this dispensation. Seeing that some seemed almost to be born with it, and had responses to the gospel and its powers far beyond anything they could have learned in the short space of mortality, he concluded that they did bring it with them. Thus his summary was "Faith is trust in what the spirit learned eons ago." We do come here bringing, though they are locked under amnesia, the residual powers, the distillation of a long experience. And to those of us who see the hand of the Lord everywhere and to those who see it nowhere the same promise is made: The day will come when we shall know that we have seen Him, and that He is the light that is in us, without which we could not abound (see D&C 88:50). There is locked in all of us as there was in Enos— and I understand Enos to say he was surprised that it was there— more faith than we presently know. We are heard, but the response of God may not be what we would here and now wish. Yet haven't we lived long enough to say to the Lord, "Disregard previous memo," to thank him that He answered no, and to ask that He erase some of the requests that we now realize were foolish or hasty or even perverse?

Now may I take slices from autobiographical accounts. Are we to pray in practical terms or specific terms? It is said that on one occasion Brigham Young, hung up on a sand bar crossing a river on the plains, had a companion who said, "Let's pray." To which Brigham is supposed to have replied: "Pray? I prayed this morning. Let's get out and push." There is a time for total concentration in prayer and a time for answering prayer with one's own muscles and initiative.

This is the same man who was specific enough to bring to the Lord concrete and urgent feelings, even hostile ones. It is said he left his prize saddle once, in the proper place, but someone misplaced it or didn't hang it properly and the horse trampled it into shreds. He rebuked the man who had shown the neglect, and then made a beeline for the bedroom, where he said (someone overheard him), "Down, Brigham!" Then he knelt and said: "Lord, I am sorry. I was angry. Take my anger away and help me to do better next time." "When I am angry," said a friend of his, "the first thing I do is pray." Some of us have been taught that should be the last thing we do, that we should soak our head in a bucket and then pray. "I am never so angry but what I can pray," said Heber C. Kimball (Young, *Journal of Discourses* 3:231). The same goes for related emotions.

In the same spirit, Brigham Young once said: "I do not recollect that I have seen five minutes since I was baptized that I have not been ready to preach a funeral sermon, lay hands on the sick, or pray in private or in public." Think of that. Then he added: "I will tell you the secret of this. . . . If you commit an overt act, repent of that immediately and call upon God to . . . give you the light of His Spirit" (Young, *Journal of Discourses* 12:103). Why spend a week rationalizing and defending what you have done amiss or have not done aright?

Can we pray when there is really hardly the heart for it? Lorenzo Snow leaves us the glimpse that after he was, as he felt, stillborn into the Church, nothing really significant happened in and after his baptism and confirmation. He kept praying for the witness of the Spirit. It didn't come. Not only not feeling as he was wont, but feeling that the heavens were as brass over him, he nevertheless went to an accustomed place to pray. He had no sooner opened his lips than the Spirit descended upon him in a marvelous way. He described it as like the sound of rustling silken robes—they did not have the word electricity then. This experience was more tangible in its effect upon every part of his body than being surrounded by water in baptism. He was filled, though praying when he didn't want to pray. (See *Juvenile Instructor* 22:22.)

But are we not to bring a certain proper reverence to prayer, and if we are out of that, should we not repent and wait? Listen to Heber C. Kimball. He is praying with his family and in the midst of the prayer says, "Father, bless Brother So-and-So." Then he bursts into a loud laugh. I can imagine the heads of his children popping up and their eyes opening. There is a slight pause, and then he says, "Lord, it makes me laugh to pray about some people," and he goes on with his prayer. (See Whitney, *Heber C. Kimball,* 427.) I leave you to say whether that is lightmindedness or profound intimacy with the Lord. He knows. We have a funny bone. He gave it to us.

My father taught me this ancient legend about Adam and Eve. As they were departing from the garden, there was a solemn farewell, the Father recognizing far more clearly than they did what they, as vanguard pioneers in the real world, were going to face. They said good-bye, but just before the couple disappeared in the mist the Father couldn't stand it. He called them back and gave them a sense of humor.

We are admonished not to betray the sacred. That is lightmindedness. "Remember that that which cometh from above is sacred, and must be spoken with care, and by constraint of the Spirit; and in this there is no condemnation, and ye receive the Spirit through prayer; wherefore, without this there remaineth condemnation" (D&C 63:64).

But we are also blessed that we should have a glad heart and a cheerful countenance. If you cannot laugh at yourself and even at some of the absurdities of this world, you take yourself too seriously. Prayer can manifest that phase of one's core with divine approval.

But again, there is the problem of method. Do you have to say it a certain way? Do you have to have an appropriate technique? We may say: "I don't know whether I am sincere or not. I don't know whether I want to pray or not." In the right circumstances this is an acceptable prayer.

But can you cry out of affliction with any hope of help? Of course. It was Joseph Smith in the dungeon at Liberty Jail who asked the questions we all sooner or later will: "O God, where art thou?" And the second question, "How long, O Lord?" To the first question, the answer was, "I am here," and to the second, "Not long, but a small moment, Joseph." Note that it was the Lord's definition of time. "If thou endure it well and art faithful, thou shalt triumph" (see D&C 121:1–2, 7–8). I am impressed with the number of miracles of overcoming, of solving problems, but I give it as my testimony that equally impressive are those divine blessings that enabled people to endure what they could not overcome, to hold on, to wait and wait and wait.

But can one pray for the impossible? There is in certain traditions about omnipotence the inferential notion that one could ask that a friend who had been killed in a foreign war the day before should yet live. That God, having command of time, could actually answer the prayer with yes. Not so, I submit. There are laws. There are conditions. And God himself cannot change them. "Yes," we cry out, "He could and sometimes does prevent this or that." But He could not prevent it and still accomplish other of his multiple purposes. It must be rough to be the Father of everyone.

Is there a name that we are most often to use, which He prefers? Good question. It is answered in the life of Christ, who chose almost without exception one word—Abba. In Hebrew it means "Father," but it means a shade more than that. It means as a child would whisper it, "Daddy." Intimate. We are all given names after we are born, and the Lord wills to give us a name after we are reborn. We take it upon us, willingly and by covenant. It is His name. And through it and with it we are equipped to pray more powerfully than if we prayed only in our own name. In my imagination, I wonder if when the personage said, "Joseph, this is my beloved," He might also have said, "Beloved, this is our Joseph." Or, if it might have been that they stood in visitation—which is more than vision, and must have been bewildering at least at the outset—and could have said, "Remember us?" We are to use the name of Him who descended below all things.

From the above slices I come to a focus and a conclusion. There are levels beyond levels of prayer. There are heights beyond heights. There are promises in modern revelation that in due time, after we have proved that we are determined to serve the Lord at all hazards, then we may receive keys whereby we may ask with the assurance of an answer.

Said Joseph Smith to Brigham Young on an occasion, "You have passed certain bounds and conditions, Brother Brigham," and Brigham explains, "he passed certain bounds before certain revelations were given" (Young, *Manuscript History* 4:19). Brigham passed the same keys to others, including Wilford Woodruff. Wilford Woodruff is the one who said at the dedication of the Salt Lake Temple that it had been made known to him by revelation that the reason a representative of the Woodruff family had been called to preside was that "the Lord could not find a weaker vessel" (Salt Lake Temple Dedication Notes, April 1893, 125).

Our whole history teaches that out of weakness we can be made strong. Why does the Lord choose the weak? Among other reasons, it is because they can be taught and influenced, whereas He has to use a jackhammer on the proud. Further, because they are transparently weak, those who have eyes to see are not confused on where the power really comes from.

There are levels beyond levels, gifts beyond gifts. I summarize them with this glimpse. It was in a school of instruction, the school of prophets—and prophetesses, too. The first thing the Smith brothers thought on a day of rich spiritual outpouring in that room above the Newell K. Whitney store was, "Where is mother?" They sent a messenger in great haste, who brought her to participate. (See Lucy Mack Smith, *History,* 224.)

In such a setting the Prophet asked that each in turn speak; that, as the revelation says, all might not speak at once, but that everyone might have an equal privilege (see D&C 88:122). The subject was faith. Scriptures were quoted. The last man to speak, as it happened, was Heber C. Kimball, who told of an experience in his own family. His daughter, Helen Mar, was standing by a table on which dishes were stacked. Her mother warned the child as she left the house: "Stay away from those dishes. If you break one of them I will whip you." Vilate left, and Helen Mar did what little children do when they are told not to do it. To her dismay, she let a table leaf fall, and several dishes were broken. What now? She went out, as she had watched her parents do, and near a tree she prayed that her mother's heart would be softened. We don't know just what she said, but no doubt it was simple enough, such as, "Bless my mother that she won't whip me." When her mother returned, she saw the situation. She flared. She took the girl by the hand into the bedroom, intending to administer the promised punishment. But she couldn't do it. We can imagine the scene—the arms of her daughter around her neck and the child saying, "Oh, Mother, I prayed that you wouldn't. I'm sorry, I'm sorry."

When Brother Heber had finished telling the story, every man in the room, including Joseph, was in tears. And Joseph said—to those grown-up, strong, independent, willful, intelligent men— "Brethren, that is the kind of faith we need. The faith of a little child going in humility to its parent." (See Whitney, *Heber C. Kimball,* 69.) That sums it up.

This verse is a fitting conclusion: "Pray always and I will pour out my Spirit upon you, and great shall be your blessing—yea, even more than if you should obtain treasures of earth and corruptibleness to the extent thereof. Behold, canst thou read this without rejoicing and lifting up thy heart for gladness? Or canst thou run about longer as a blind guide? Or canst thou be humble and meek, and conduct thyself wisely before me? Yea, come unto me thy Savior" (D&C 19:38–41).

Chapter Two

IN A PLACE
CALLED GETHSEMANE

A prophecy uttered by the Prophet Joseph Smith in 1841 is in fact being fulfilled before our very eyes: "Jerusalem must be rebuilt and the temple, and water come out from under the temple, and the waters of the Dead Sea be healed" (Joseph Smith, *Teachings* [1976], 286), and all this before the coming of the Son of Man. When my wife, Ann, and I first touched that ground with our feet I had a prejudice that the setting of the Savior's life really was not significant; the meaning of His words was what mattered, and the environment and circumstances of the time were not crucial. After many visits since, for we have both visited and lived there, I am of the contrary opinion. I believe that He cared very much about the setting, and that meaning is lodged still in the very rocks, in the very mountains, in the very trees of Israel.

On many of our trips to Israel we had groups mostly of persons we would consider young, but on one trip there was a woman past eighty-two, who had to prepare for it at length—had to exercise and get constant reassurances from her physician as to whether she could endure the rigors. We were touched that as we walked away from a church that has been built near (and some say over) the ancient site of Gethsemane, she who had come so far and lived so long was on her knees near the place where tradition says Jesus knelt.

North of Jerusalem is the Galilee. And in visiting there I am struck that the location of Caesarea Philippi is at the mount called Hermon. Some possibility assigns it as the Mount of Transfiguration, but it is in any case at the headwaters of the Jordan, which then feed the Galilee and then flow south and are literally the nourishment of all Israel. It was there, and I think Jesus chose the place carefully, that He announced to Peter, after Peter's confession, that He would build His church as on a rock. I think it is significant that there is there still a huge faced rock, and below it and in it a cave; and out of that cave, at the time Jesus stood there, there flowed water. Not so since—an earthquake changed all that. But was Jesus therefore saying to Peter, whom He knew by revelation was to be His presiding Apostle, and of Peter, who by revelation had recognized Him, "Upon this flowing rock I will build my church"? (Matthew 16:18). Well, such are the suggestions of the setting. Is it also, one may ask, only happenstance that He chose to be baptized near the waters called dead at the lowest point of the earth—1200 feet below sea level—descending thus even physically below all things?

There are trees in Israel, and we are taught from the record that each in a way was significant in the Savior's ministry: palm trees, fig trees, oak trees, but most of all olive trees. Even to this day the process of planting, cultivating, pruning, and harvesting from olive trees is a laborious one. And the process of then taking the olives, which at first are bitter and useless, and going through another step of hard labor and pressure to produce ripe, mellow olive oil—that too is done today. In the time of the Master olives and olive oil and the olive mash that resulted from the crushing were the very essence of life. All that comes clearly to mind as one stands there.

Religious literature is permeated with the notion that a tree of

300

life is representative of eternal life. It is planted in a goodly land, some traditions say on the very navel of the earth, the highest point of the earth; which, symbolically at least, is the temple mount in Jerusalem. A tree planted and watered by the waters of life whose fruit is the most precious. Our own Book of Mormon says further of that fruit that it is sweet, that it is pure, even that it is white (see 1 Nephi 8:11; 11:8). And there are even now, incidentally, in Hebron, in Israel, magnificent vineyards where the very fruit itself is white, almost transparent. These happen to be the sweetest and the purest of the grapes. The imagery that it was so precious impressed Nephi after he was given the blessing of recapitulating the vision of his own father, Lehi. And he said it when asked—yes, precious, I beheld precious. But even that superlative didn't satisfy the angel, the narrator of the vision, who said, "Yea, and the most joyous to the soul" (see 1 Nephi 11:9, 23).

Well, the tree of life has been utilized through sacred history as the symbol both of Israel and of the Redeemer of Israel. And there are traditions that in due time that tree, from which the branches had been broken off and dispersed, would somehow be planted anew, and graftings and gatherings take place anew, until the tree was again productive.

The olive tree is not deciduous. Its leaves never fall off. They are rejuvenated and stay. It is in that sense evergreen or ever olive-colored. It is a wild thing if not cultivated. But after long and patient cultivation, usually eight to ten years, it becomes productive; more than that, it continues to be with age. And there are trees today—for new shoots come forth from apparently dead roots—that are known by actual horticultural study to be eighteen hundred years old. Some trees on the Mount of Olives may be older than that. One could almost say of the olive tree, "It is immortal."

Olive oil is used by many today in the Middle East as a condiment for salads or as a cooking oil. But in the Savior's day olive oil was the very substance of light and heat in Israel. An olive lamp, into which one poured the pure oil and then lighted it at one end, provided light even in a darkened room, enough light to fill

301

the room. Moreover, the mash provided fuel and burned long. And the balming influence, the soothing, salving influence of olive oil, was well known in the Middle East. The tradition of the balm of Gilead and the soothing even of troubled waters was well known in Jesus' own day.

We speak today of the olive branch as a symbol of peace and forgiveness. Paul even refers to "the oil of gladness" (Hebrews 1:9). It is in that sense also symbolic of joy.

Did Jesus know all this? Surely He did. Was there then something significant in His choice of the mount known as the Mount of Olives? And was it true then, as now, that Mount Oilvet was symbolic and sacred, all of it? Let me remind you that on that mount four holinesses came together in a remarkable way. I speak first of the place. It was eastward from the temple, a temple which by now had been desecrated, the temple which He first called on a day of cleansing "my Father's house," but which later He spoke of as "my house" (John 2:16; Mark 11:17). In that house was a Holy of Holies. Two olivewood pillars stood as entrances, and they were in fact connected to the menorah, the perpetual lamp, and from them came two kinds of tubes, into which were poured olive oil; then it burned.

A Jewish tradition says that when Adam, close to the time of his own death, was debilitated, he sent Eve and his son Seth back to the garden for the healing oil. But at the threshold they were met by an angel who said there would be no oil again until the meridian of time when the Messiah would come, and then the oil would be that of the olive tree.

Another tradition, based on a scripture in Leviticus, says Moses was commanded to teach the children of Israel to bring to him for the tabernacle olive oil, "pure olive oil beaten for the light" (Leviticus 24:2). The tradition says that such oil was burning in the time of Jesus; but it had lost its sacred significance, or had not yet received its sacred fulfillment.

Jesus went on the mount overlooking the temple mount, as, says the scripture, "he was wont" (Luke 22:39). Luke even says that in the last days of His life He lodged there, He "abode there" at night (see Luke 21:37). On that hill was a garden, but the more proper word is vineyard. A vineyard of olive trees? Yes. That same word is used in the parable or allegory of the tame and wild olive tree as related in the book of Jacob. The Lord of the vineyard, Dr. Sidney B. Sperry believed, was the Father of us all. The servant in the vineyard was the Messiah. His task, the weightiest in all history.

It is called Gethsemane. *Geth* or *gat* means "press," and *shemen* in Hebrew means "oil." The place of the olive press. You can see such presses still in Israel, for after the processes of salt and vinegar and pressure came the time when they gathered the olives, placed them in a bag, and then with a huge crushing rock (to push it usually required an animal) they crushed those olives until the oil flowed. The place of the olive press.

Another holiness was the week of Pesach, Passover. Ann and I have been privileged to attend that still kept and honored, sacrosanct celebration—Passover. Since the destruction of the temple it has been modified. At the time of Jesus they brought the lamb, the faultless lamb (and, by the way, down that very mount), to the altar, and it was slain and the blood sprinkled on the altar. That was the season—the time.

As for the person, this was Yeshua Massiach, Jesus the Messiah, a stem of Jesse, so Isaiah prophesied, from the stump or the root of the house of David (see Isaiah 11:1). He who had been the Revealer to Abraham, Isaac, and Jacob. He who had not only approached but sat upon Jacob's well, and to a despised woman announced, for the first time on record: "I am He. I am He from whom shall flow living waters" (see John 4:14, 26). It was He who had been prophesied. The word *messiah*, as it appears today in the King James Version in Daniel 9:25–26, has roots of "the anointed one." Now came the night when He would become the anointing one.

Further, the word *messias,* as it is used in the Gospel of John, has another root: *tsahar,* meaning to glow with light as one glistens when one is anointed. To earn the name, the holiness of the name, He had to tread the press. That image is used by Isaiah, but the Lord himself uses it in our own time, in that remarkable summation revelation the Prophet Joseph gave us of that glorious vision recorded in section 76 of the Doctrine and Covenants. "I have trodden the press" (in this case the wine-press, but the two merge). "I have . . . trodden the wine-press alone, even the winepress of the fierceness of the wrath of Almighty God" (D&C 76:107).

Having spoken of the holy place, the holy time, the holy person, and the holy name, may I offer a glimpse of what must have gone through Him and of what He must have gone through. "Mine hour," He had said often, "has not yet come," but now it had. After the Last Supper the record says, "and it was night" (John 13:30). Thus an explanation—I think we need no other—for why the three Apostles couldn't stay awake even though He pleaded.

Somewhere, somewhere on that mountain, He knelt.

I have witnessed the effort of the most pious of Jews as they stand—they do not kneel—at the place that is but a remnant of the wall below the ancient walls of the temple mount. Rhythmically, they throw their whole bodies into their prayer. They are sometimes ridiculed for this. They say: "We are fighting distraction. We want to concentrate. Movement helps." Well, the movement of that night, I suggest, was internal, not external, and somehow the bitterness was as bitter as gall. Not just the family of our Father who dwell upon this earth were affected, but, as we have been taught by the Prophet Joseph Smith, those of other earths also (see McConkie, *Mormon Doctrine*, 65–66). So the atonement of Jesus Christ is intergalactic in its effect. That burden, that bitterness, He vicariously took within. "How?" we cry out. But a child can understand. Pain hurts. Even the presence of it hurts those of us who merely stand detached and observe. The Savior, who is supersensitive and did not take a backward step from the will of the Father, could and did feel for and with us. The pressure worked upon Him. Somewhere on the road between the north and the south, He cried out, anticipating, "Father, save me from this hour." We don't know how long was the interim between that sentence and prayer and the next, but He then cried: "but for this cause came I unto this hour. Father, glorify thy name." And the voice said, "I have both glorified it, and will glorify it again" (John 12:27–28).

Luke, who tradition says was a physician, recorded that great drops of blood came from the Savior's pores (Luke 22:44). The bitterness oozed. It is not a spectacle one wishes to recall, but we have been commanded, and weekly we memorialize it in an ordinance called the sacrament. Even then, all His preparation and all that He could summon from His own strength was not sufficient. And more earnestly, says the record, He prayed, and an angel came, strengthening Him (see Luke 22:43–44). Strengthening, but not delivering. What is it like to have the power to summon legions of angels to end the ordeal yet not to summon them? During that same night He was betrayed. He was taken prisoner. He was broken into, pierced by scourging; and a merciful reading of Pilate's motives suggests that he hoped this would suffice for those who were crying out against Jesus. It did not. The weight, I submit, had begun there on the mount, a much greater weight than the weight of the cross that He was then to bear.

Now, what conclusions can we draw from all this? First, hereafter when we speak or hear the words, "I anoint you with this consecrated oil," let us remember what the consecration cost.

As we sit—but in our spirits as we kneel during the sacrament service—and are asked to remember His body, recall that it was the veritable tree and olive beaten for the light, and that there flows from that mount unto this whole earth, and beyond, the redemptive power of healing and soothing and ministering to the needy.

In the hours of gladness, should our cup run o'er, let us remember that to make that possible a cup—the bitterest of cups—must have been drunk.

On that day when our life, the life of attempted faithfulness, is bludgeoned and becomes wearing and wearying, may we remember that no great and good fruits come easily, that we are the olive plants who were supposedly planted anew in Him, and that only time and suffering and endurance can produce the peaceable fruit which He yearns for us to have. He does not deliver until the perfect work has done its work.

Finally as we go into the days of affliction which have on every level and through all the prophets been promised us, hard days, let us remember that from that mount, in what most would have thought was the most tragic event of history, has come the source and power of purification and life. One day He will honor it again, this time descending in His glory. And when His foot touches it, this whole earth will know it. The mount itself shall separate, be shaken, and an earthquake will follow. The earth itself will be purged and cleansed and will eventually shine with celestial light. We are promised we may be there, either to descend with Him or to ascend to meet Him, and either of those is glorious. Over and over He spoke of himself as the bridegroom preparing His own for a feast. In our own Doctrine and Covenants we have been promised that feast, when all worthies who have been made worthy will gather (see 58:3–11). In the beginning of this dispensation, this revelation was given: "Wherefore, be faithful, praying always, having your lamps trimmed [that means full] and burning [that means alight and afire] and oil with you, that you may be ready at the coming of the Bridegroom" (D&C 33:17).

I bear witness that Jesus is the Messiah and that He could not have known, according to the flesh, how to succor His people according to their infirmities unless He had gone through in Gethsemane what He went through. I bear testimony that the knowledge He has today, what one of the prophets calls "the bowels of mercy," reaches out unto the Father, who grieves that any tree in His vineyard should be lost. He pleads even now for more time, for you and for me, until we too have been purged and can sing the song of redeeming love.

Chapter Three

MAN ILLUMINED

The sum of this chapter can be put in one word: *Light.* We see with and through light; but we rarely examine light itself. Yet continually why and what and how questions are put to me which, I am convinced, are less questions than they are questings, questings for Light.

No theme is more central to modern revelation than light "which lighteth every man that cometh into the world" (John 1:9). The Church itself came "out of obscurity and darkness" into the light, and the light of modern revelation centers in Christ. Consider the following excerpts:

That which is of God is light. (D&C 50:24)

That which doth not edify [lift, inspire, enliven] is not of God, and is darkness. (D&C 50:23)

He that ascended up on high, as also he descended below all things, in that he comprehended all things, that he might be in all and through all things, the light of truth. (D&C 88:6)

And the light which shineth, which giveth you light, is through him who enlighteneth your eyes, which is the same light that quickeneth your understandings. (D&C 88:11)

Truth embraceth truth; virtue loveth virtue; light cleaveth unto light [as darkness cleaveth unto darkness]. (D&C 88:40)

Light and truth forsake [detect and withdraw from] that evil one. (D&C 93:37)

[Christ's light] is *in* all things, giveth life to all things ["maketh alive all things" (Moses 6:61)] . . . is through all things [surrounds, envelops, permeates] . . . is the law by which all things are governed. (D&C 88:13, 41)

And if your eye be single [constantly upreaching and outreaching] to my glory, your whole bodies shall be filled with light, and there shall be no darkness in you; and that body which is filled with light comprehendeth all things. (D&C 88:67)

Then shall ye know that ye have seen me [Christ (indirectly in the light of sun, moon, and stars, but directly in a former condition of glory in his presence)], that I am, and that I am the true light that is in you, and that you are in me; otherwise ye could not abound [that is, live, grow, flourish]. (D&C 88:50)

Every man whose spirit receiveth not the light is under condemnation. For man is spirit. (D&C 93:32–33)

That which was from the beginning is plainly manifest unto them, and they receive not the light. (D&C 93:31)

He that keepeth his commandments receiveth truth and light, until he is glorified in truth and knoweth all things. (D&C 93:28)

He that receiveth light, and continueth in God, receiveth more light; and that light groweth brighter and brighter until the perfect day [the day of perfect light, the light of the perfect day]. (D&C 50:24)

From these revelatory and sweeping insights into the nature of light and the light of nature, one senses the beginnings of the whole cosmology, a prodigious and unifying key to the secrets of the vast universe. I select only those themes that apply to man himself, his makeup, his comprehension, his life fulfillment.

LIGHT AS THE REAL

These revelations suggest that man is more than a receptacle of degrees of light; he is somehow in his very primal makeup composed of light. One associate of the Prophet Joseph Smith understood him to say "that light or spirit, and matter, are the two great primary principles of the universe, or of Being; that they are self-existent, co-existent, indestructible and eternal and from these two elements, both our spirits and our bodies were formulated."

It is implicit in this statement that "pure light" (if that means unembodied light) is somehow less advanced than the living light that comes in the complex organization of spirit bodies and physical bodies—could we say "light magnified"?

Yet the Prophet added: "Light and heat . . . fill the immensity of space, and permeate with latent life, and heat, every particle of which all works are composed" (Letter from Benjamin F. Johnson to George Gibbs, 7).

Light and heat are, even in their grosser forms, refining and welding influences. But the light and heat in the fusion of realities that is man transcend somehow the lesser and grosser forms of light.

LIGHT AS TRUTH

If, then, light is interfused with man's spirit and physical bodies, we may see how fitting it is to say that light is truth. The glorified Christ says, "I *am* the Truth." Elsewhere He speaks of himself as "the Spirit of Truth" and in the same vein "the light of truth." And again as "Intelligence, or the light of truth," and says, "I am more intelligent than they all" (Abraham 3:19), more intelligent, that is, than all other intelligences.

Truth in one sense is, as our hymn says, "the sum of existence." It is another name for reality, that which is. But in a second sense, "truth is knowledge" (D&C 93:24), the accurate perception of that which is. Christ himself has become the truth in both senses. First, He is the fulness of personality: He is the sum of human existence. Second, He illumines the truth for us. By experiencing the struggle toward perfection, He "descended below all things" into darkness that "comprehended him not" (D&C 88:6; 45:7). Thus He received a fulness of the glory of the Father, which is a fulness of the light of God. And having made that light His own, He is for us the source of "the life and the light, the spirit and the power, sent forth by the will of the Father" (D&C 50:27).

In mortality the more light one receives, the more he can receive. We grow and glow not just by addition but by multiplication. Hence the promise, "For unto him that receiveth it shall be given more abundantly, even power" (D&C 71:6), and its correlative warning, "But whosoever continueth not to receive, from him shall be taken away even that he hath" (JST, Matthew 13:11). The more a person increases in light, the more he gains access to truth and acquires intelligent consciousness of all that light penetrates—on the one hand the immensity of space and, on the other hand the immensity of time, "things as they are, and as they were, and as they are to come" (D&C 93:24). Eventually he may receive the fulness of light that circumscribes all truth.

Said Brigham Young:

It is not the optic nerve alone that gives the knowledge of surrounding objects to the mind, but it is that which God has placed in man—a system of intelligence that attracts knowledge, as light cleaves to light, intelligence to intelligence, and truth to truth. It is this which lays in man a proper foundation for all education (Young, *Discourses,* 257).

When we are told, "If ye receive not the Spirit ye shall not teach" (D&C 42:14), it means more than that we should not. We cannot. More—without it, we cannot even understand. "Why is it," the Lord asks, "that ye cannot understand and know, that he that receiveth the word by the Spirit of truth receiveth it as it is preached by the Spirit of truth? Wherefore, he that preacheth and he that receiveth, understand one another, and both are edified and rejoice together" (D&C 50:21–22). Teaching any truth, even the most elemental or simple facts, is exciting to both teacher and student. Touched by the light, they tend to see the infusion, the "hand of God," as it were, everywhere.

And I have felt
A presence that disturbs me with the joy
Of elevated thoughts; a sense sublime
Of something far more deeply interfused.
(Wordsworth, "Tintern Abbey.")

But one who has yet to respond needs what the Prophet once referred to as a rebirth of one's eyes or a change of heart before he can see any difference between the kingdom of God and the kingdom of the world (see Ehat and Cook, *Words of Joseph Smith*, 256). Such a one moves about unaware of any light. Just as 20–20 vision is helpless without light, so, in the wider world of the spirit, the "eyes of the understanding" must be quickened.

Quickened carries at least three strands of meaning—"to enliven, to hasten, to permeate." Careful introspection will show that there is no mental process that is not intensified by the subtle enlightening process described by the Prophet—"when you feel pure intelligence flowing into you" (Joseph Smith, *Teachings* [1976], 151). Not only are there "sudden strokes of ideas," the "first intimations," but also a brightening effect that enables us to see what we saw before, but now in quite literally a new light. The effects extend to the person as a whole—even his balance, coordination, and motor skills. In the understanding, light has to do with the clarifying of concepts and judgments (more than analytic proficiency), with the heightening of imagination (more than aimless fantasy), with the recovery and interweaving of memories (more than chance deliverances of the subconscious), and with the strivings and inspirings of creativity. These phenomena take a person beyond the "light barriers." His mental life is "brighter."

The teaching that our "whole bodies" can be full of light (D&C 88:67) suggests that what we call I.Q. is a clumsy and misleading "measure" of man's cognitive powers. Genuine intelligence, or the conscious "light of truth," is the light that recognizes and absorbs or "cleaves" to truth, and it involves the whole person. Intelligence, in short, is a kind of light-susceptibility. Hence the Prophet needed a Urim and Thummim until he himself became one. We

311

have a glimpse of that level of light and burning in the Prophet as he emerged with Sidney Rigdon from his chamber, after they had written "while yet in the Spirit" a portion of what they had together beheld in the vision of the degrees of glory (D&C 76). His statement is: "My whole body was full of light and I could see even out at the ends of my fingers and toes" (Lundwall, *Vision,* 11).

We are reaching toward this awareness when we say, "I know with every fiber of my being. . . ." The scriptures are replete with testimony that the capacities, the hidden potential, the lava of our inner responses to truth far exceed any plaudits ever offered for the "genius." We can no more "drink up the ocean" than we can learn all truth "line by line." But "that body which is filled with light comprehendeth all things" (D&C 88:67), and the ocean, indeed all oceans, are subject to the rays that proceed from and return to Him who is "glorified in truth" (D&C 93:28) and "knoweth all things" (D&C 38:2).

The principle "truth embraceth truth; virtue loveth virtue; light cleaveth unto light" (D&C 88:40) helps us explain many of the experiences of the religious struggle. For example:

• How five minutes is sufficient to bring vibrant and total trust for one person, and fifty years not long enough for another, though the "evidence" or record is the same for both.

• How the most intense sympathy, empathy, and social feelings emerge in settings of light and spiritual experience, a mutual kinship out of mutual kindling.

• How enslaving habits and degenerate compulsions in the flesh, which stand like an impenetrable shield between the spirit of man and the Spirit of God, can be purged and purified—burned out—by a light-power that heals and redeems. And why the statement "you can't change human nature" is simply *false* if "you" includes your spirit and Christ's Spirit power.

• How light can be glaring and unpleasant, even blinding, when first we are subjected to it, but then the increasing intensities and heats become more than endurable; they render our former condition repugnant.

312

• How grosser light stops with surfaces and casts shadows, but the higher light can be in us and through us.

• How we "receive the Spirit through prayer" (D&C 63:64), but also we need to improve our prayer pattern until we pray with the Spirit and "in the Spirit" (D&C 46:28–30).

• How there are two kinds of burning in us; one a burning of conscience, urging and lifting us to become what we have in us to become (and accumulating guilt in postponement), and second a burning of approval and peace when we set about repenting.

• How negative feelings can restrain the peace and power of light as it flows down, yet the flow of the Spirit can melt away all such dross if we will permit our spirits to take the lead.

LIGHT AS THE GOOD

If light is somehow the substratum of all reality and also of all intelligent awareness of reality, it is only another step to say that light is the foundation of good. In few, if any, ancient or modern cultures has "light" become symbolic of evil, "dark" of good. Instead, light tends to be identified with the good, the valuable, the blessed, the sacred. But it is more than a symbol or a ritual. The scriptures teach that the light of Christ is given to every man that comes into the world, but that it enlightens "through the world" all those that hearken (D&C 84:46). Light edifies, lifts, and "that which does not edify is not of God and is darkness" (D&C 50:23). That is the bound and condition of all law, physical and moral, the "law by which all things are governed" (D&C 88:13). Light is not just the test of good; it is the nature of all that is judged truly good. Alma, who in earlier years had emerged from guilt-ridden darkness that made his own extinction seem desirable, wrote, "Whatsoever is light is good, because it is discernible" (Alma 32:35).

In the realm of the good, as elsewhere, light is the "bound and condition" of all preferred ways of life. And these bounds and conditions are inexorable and exceptionless, not because they tell us what our choices must be but because they tell us what the *results* of our choices will be. Of course, one can attempt to "become a law unto [himself]" (D&C 88:35), but only at the cost of diminishing the light. Every minute of every day we are increasing or decreasing in our receptivity to light, and there is no way to escape the inevitability of that consequence in our thoughts, our acts, our very breath. One can look upon the law of light either as the enemy of freedom or as freedom's guarantee, which "is preserved by law and sanctified by the same" (D&C 88:34). One can abide the law only as one can abide the light, and vice versa.

An unconditional imperative can be derived from this: Seek the increase of Christ's light. And all commandments are instrumental to this end, which is an intrinsic value. If it is said (as it is fashionable to say) that such an imperative is only binding upon me if I make it so, that if I find it unappealing, or meaningless, or even absurd, then it is not mine and therefore is not binding at all, one reply is that a measure of light itself is essential even to such a denial of the light. Christ is the true light that is in us, even when we turn our backs on Him. He himself became God by abiding in the light. And even God is bound by the law.

LIGHT AS BEAUTY

From the understanding that light is the root of reality, of truth, and of goodness, the next step is to recognize that light is the foundation of beauty. And, again, not only does light enhance the beautiful—light itself is beautiful.

The scriptures, and notably the Book of Mormon, teem with Hebraic symbols for the beautiful and the lovely, revolving around light, brightness, fire, and whiteness. Thus of the vision of the tree of life that Lehi and Nephi beheld, it is written: "The beauty thereof was far beyond, yea, exceeding of all beauty, and the whiteness thereof did exceed the whiteness of the driven snow" (1 Nephi 11:8).

Similarly one can feel the ancient writers straining for superlatives in their descriptions of white fruit, "to exceed all the whiteness that I had ever seen" (1 Nephi 8:11), of white robes or clothing, "nothing upon earth so white" (3 Nephi 19:25), and of the white virgin, "exceedingly fair and white . . . most beautiful and fair above all other virgins" (1 Nephi 11:13–15).

Artists have often depicted this recognition of light as divine beauty by the halo, the nimbus, and the golden circle above the head. But that is at best a token of the promise and the actuality. For "whole bodies" are promised illumination, and the light not only hovers over but also surrounds and engulfs the entire personality until it is gloriously beautiful. It was, after all, every one of the multitude, and all of each of them, even the seams of their clothing, that became scintillant with white light in the presence of Christ during that "ineffable outpouring of prayer," as Elder James E. Talmage calls it, in the 3 Nephi narrative (see 3 Nephi 19:25). Modern men and women of God who have witnessed such radiance of soul say it is "like a search light turned on within." It is "the same glorious spirit," the Prophet once wrote, "gives them the likeness of glory and bloom. . . . No man can describe it to you—no man can write it" (Joseph Smith, *Teachings* [1976], 368). Aesthetic delight, then, whatever else it is, is delight in light. And it is surely significant that the whole color spectrum, every vivid color of the rainbow, harmonizes in white light which, in turn, harmonizes in Christ.

At the everyday level there are the light-variations in the human face, almost infinitely intimate and animated. "You will always discover in the first glance of a man, in the outlines of his features, something of his mind," said the Prophet Joseph (Joseph Smith, *Teachings* [1976], 299). Particularly around the eyes ("the light of the body is the eye" [Matthew 6:22]) the forehead, and the lips one sees recorded a person's past and present encounters with light. It has nothing to do with fairness of complexion, with age, with cosmetic skill, with habitual patterns of facial set or mood, or even with the features we are accustomed to identify as "attractive." One must remember Isaiah's telling—should we say warning?—prophecy of the Messiah: "there is no beauty that we should desire him" (Isaiah 53:2). Later Christ could see through the rough and rugged exterior of John the Baptist and call him "a burning and a shining light" (John 5:35). And John the Beloved could say of Christ that "in him is no darkness at all" (1 John 1:5). The true beauty "in the eye of the beholder" is also in the eye of the beheld, and the glory of both. It is the divine light of beauty, as also the beauty of divine enlightenment, and it comes from above before it comes from within. Not all who are handsome or beautiful in the conventional sense are illumined. But all who are illumined, though conventionally "plain" or even "ugly," are beautiful.

The face may also reflect darkness. It is no abuse of terms to say that in some faces, and in all of ours at times, there is an "aura of darkness" that is disagreeable and unbeautiful, encircling in its gloom. Darkness here is not just a metaphor for attitude. It is an apparent absence of light that prefers and reflects "works of darkness" and finds the presence of light too much. No artifice successfully conceals it, not even a perpetual and mannerly smile. Seeking to become appealing, which is the ultimate testimony that light is good and beautiful, the adversary himself "transformeth himself nigh unto an angel of light" (2 Nephi 9:9). But his is "dark light"; and as the Master warned us, "If therefore the light that is in thee be darkness, how great is that darkness!" (Matthew 6:23). Having fallen from a condition of brilliant light, having flouted the inner light, Satan and those he seals his own in "outer darkness" are in deliberate darkness that cleaves to and surrounds them like a self-imposed cloak.

LIGHT AS LIFE

In mankind, the true, the good, the beautiful are not only reflected but come to life. And again the scriptures teach of the inseparable connection—in fact, the eventual union in their highest forms—of light and life. "In [Christ] was life; and the life was the light of men" (John 1:4). And it is His light that "giveth life to all things" (D&C 88:13). And in man the inclusive *all* refers to the life of the mind and all the creative and responsive forces that are interwoven in him. A modern revelation speaks not only of the classic symbol "eternal life" but also of "eternal lives" (D&C 132:22–25), the plural emphasizing expansion and intensification of the lives within the whole person.

316

As the flourishing of plant life depends upon the light-nourishment traceable to the sun in the process of photosynthesis, so the light of the sun depends upon the Son of God. "He is in the sun, and the light of the sun, and the power thereof by which it was made" (D&C 88:7). In fact, one man records that the Prophet once said, "There is no light, except the Father and the Son" (Young, A. D., Diary, 5). The nourishing that leads to the flowering of the soul—the crucial need of the soul—is His, and through Him ours. "I am come that they might have life, and that they might have it more abundantly" (John 10:10). Without Him we could not "abound," which is to say live, draw breath, survive. But to abound is to abide in Him, and to abide in Him, as vine to root, is to live abundantly.

When we are instrumental in transmitting this life-renewing power, we can be so drained that, like the Master or his modern prophets, our very "virtue" goes out and we are left visibly pale. "I became weak," said the Prophet after blessing nineteen children, "from which I have not yet recovered" (Joseph Smith, *Teachings* [1976], 281). But when we are recipients of this power, it is the very "renewing of [our] bodies" (D&C 84:33), the reversal of all forms of distress, disease, disability, and degeneration, and the rekindling of our emotional life. In such times the effect in us is not only the opposite of darkness; it is the opposite of heaviness or burdensomeness. It is the essence of spiritual and physical buoyancy. "My burden is light" (Matthew 11:30).

In contrast, the soul-shrinking that occurs in the absence or withdrawal of light inevitably has to do with the heart's definition of life: love, and with love, joy and peace. It was John who recognized, as have few in history, that to hate is to be in darkness, and that conversely to love is to walk in the light (see 1 John 2:10–11). "Your minds in times past have been darkened," says a modern revelation, "because of . . . vanity and unbelief" (D&C 84:54–55). And vanity and unbelief are both ways of cutting ourselves from love, even from enlightened love of ourselves. The resulting condemnation is diminution of light, which blinds and numbs our capacities for the calm excitement of inspired love, the relish of joy, and the serenity of inner peace. We become, as Nephi told his brothers, "past feeling" (1 Nephi 17:45), and "the love of the Father shall not continue with [us]" (D&C 95:12). This, as the scripture earlier says, is the equivalent of "walking in darkness at noonday" (D&C 95:6), or, more technically, walking in noonday light, but afflicted with a darkness "that comprehendeth it not" (D&C 6:21). We literally die a little.

EVEN TEMPLES

We began by saying that the universe is a combination of matter and of light or spirit, and that man himself is a microscopic universe. The Lord applies to us a more majestic word: *temples* (D&C 93:35). By divine design the temple is a microscopic man and man is a temple all alive. Standing on Mt. Scopus, northeast of Jerusalem, I was swept into a montage of images of temples— temples of Solomon, of Herod, of modern Kirtland and Nauvoo. I saw them built by the song of worthy sacrifice, endowed with encircling light and fire, and then violently desecrated, their veils ripped and trampled. Just so man, the living temple of God, can be a harmony of radiance or a divided shambles of darkness. In his vision of the future inhabitants of the holy city, John wrote:

> And I saw no temple therein; for the Lord God Almighty and the Lamb are the temple of it.
>
> And the city had no need of the sun, neither of the moon, to shine in it; for the glory of God did lighten it, and the Lamb is the light thereof. . . .
>
> For the Lord God giveth them light; and they shall reign forever and ever. (Revelation 21:22–23; 22:5)

To be light-magnified and light-purified is to have a foretaste of that temple of celestial personality: to begin to see as we are now seen by Him, and to know as we are now known by Him. And to enter that temple is to see God, the God of lights, born in us, the lightened god that is us. And as the temple is the fusion of all of heaven and earth, so within us the real, the true, the good,

318

and the beautiful are to be blended in the prism of perfected personality. In Christ and through Christ, the singular sheen of saintliness will be swallowed up in the "eternal burnings" of godliness.

Chapter Four

FORGIVENESS

The experience I relate first is well known in the Church. I want to share a few extra glimpses.

The one who had the experience was in the Quorum of the Twelve. As a junior member of that quorum he sat in a meeting in which the President of the Church (then John Taylor) asked his brethren for their vote to readmit into the Church a man who earlier had disgraced the Church. It is a complicated story. The man had not only committed a grievous sin but also, when confronted with it in the presence of the Twelve, had vehemently denied it. When finally he buckled and acknowledged his sin, he was excommunicated.

Considerable time had passed since then, and President Taylor now felt this man should have the privilege of beginning over. He asked his brethren. At first there was some feeling of "Oh no, is he really ready?" But over time, eventually, all the Quorum members except Heber J. Grant said yes. He alone said no.

In one of the later meetings at which this issue was discussed, President Taylor said to Elder Grant, "Why, Heber, why?" In substance, their exchange was as follows:

Elder Grant replied, "Because he stood up and lied!" That seemed to him almost more vicious than the sin.

Then President Taylor said: "But Heber, how will you feel when you stand before the Lord Jesus Christ hereafter, and it is clear that you were responsible for keeping this man outside the Church?"

That didn't slow Elder Grant down at all. He said: "Why, I will look Him in the eye and say: I *am* responsible for keeping that man out of the Church!"

President Taylor smiled and said: "Well, Heber, stay with your convictions! Stay right with them!"

When Elder Grant went home that day, while waiting for lunch he opened the Doctrine and Covenants, as it happened turning to section 64. He read: "I, the Lord, will forgive whom I will forgive, but of you it is required to forgive all men" (D&C 64:10).

That's tough enough. *All* is an inclusive word, isn't it? There is no exception. But the revelation also says, "he that forgiveth not his brother his trespasses standeth condemned before the Lord; for there remaineth in him the greater sin" (D&C 64:9).

My first question on this is "Greater than what?" Are we to say, for example, that a woman who refuses to forgive her husband of adultery has committed a more serious sin than adultery? The sin of this man, who lied about it, was that, a moral sin; and yet, taken at its face value, the above verse seems to say, "It's worse not to forgive."

Well, one of the great things about Elder Grant was that when he knew he was wrong, he was wrong; and he was a practitioner of what Brigham Young called instant repentance. He brought his hand down hard on the book—so characteristic of him—and said aloud so his wife could hear: "Well, that settles it. If the devil himself repents, I'll baptize him!"

Now the sequence. He went right back down to the Church Office Building. He had to see President Taylor. He explained to him that he had changed his mind and wanted this man baptized into the Church. President Taylor was pleased. He laughed his

Lancashire British Santa Claus laugh and then asked, "Heber, what happened?"

Elder Grant told him. He had opened the Doctrine and Covenants accidentally to that passage. Now we are getting to the psychological.

"Heber, how did you feel this morning at the meeting?" (where he alone stood up in opposition). "How did you feel about this brother?"

He said: "I felt like I wanted to go out and knock him down!"

"That's right, you did. Now Heber, how do you feel now?"

Elder Grant started to weep. "To tell the truth" (and I think it was a little bit of a surprise to him) "To tell the truth, President Taylor, I hope the Lord will forgive the man."

President Taylor said: "Heber, I put it to the vote so that you"— and I think he mentioned one or two others—"might learn what you have here learned today. This morning you did not have the Spirit of the Lord Jesus Christ. This afternoon you do. Never forget that, Heber!"

Elder Grant learned to forgive essentially because it was a commandment. It is in the scriptures. He had always sustained the scriptures. They said we should forgive everyone. He did it. That's not quite the same as learning to forgive *because you profoundly need forgiveness yourself.*

The problem with being as good a man and as righteous a man as Heber J. Grant is that one tends to lack compassion for those who have all kinds of problems with doing what to oneself is easy. But he later learned that; he had condemned one of his own brethren, accused him, and in effect said, "You are not doing what you ought to do in this matter." Then he came to realize that it was he and not the other man who wasn't doing what he should. And then he went in abject humility, threw his arms around the man, and pleaded for his forgiveness, and asked for his encouragement and help in repenting. Heber J. Grant was a more compassionate man after that.

It is implicit in Elder Grant's final reaction that even though he complied out of a sense of "I will obey because I am commanded," in the moment he did it, it sank into him; it changed him.

I recall the essence of a statement made years ago by Elder Jeffrey Holland in a Young Special Interest Multi-Regional Conference. He started by saying that forgiving others is the hardest thing required of us by the gospel of Jesus Christ. But we ought not to feel particularly sorry for ourselves that it is hard. He went on to say in a way I cannot duplicate that when some Roman had driven the spikes at the Crucifixion, of all the things Jesus the Christ might have thought or said, either in prayer or in outreach through others, the least likely from a mortal point of view is that the expression of His thought and heart would be to plead for forgiveness for the crucifiers. That is Christlike in the ultimate sense! The miracle is that we have the power—we, mere men and women—to do that. But this doing isn't exactly an act—it's an inward doing that changes everything.

Now, may I digress for a minute with a few implications and then come back to our whole concern, which is, How can we do more to help our loved ones and ourselves become forgiving, as well as forgiven, in the recognition that somehow these two are inseparably linked?

First, a philosophical implication. People used to come to Joseph Smith and ask questions, and I would that someone had been around with a tape recorder. In the Nauvoo period some came and asked him a hard question. The controversy was between egoism and altruism. In its ultimate form egoism maintains that what we all are doing, when you get down to the basics, is seeking our own satisfaction! This view, psychological egoism, holds that no one ever acted in the interest of others. If he seemed to, that was all on the surface; at root, all motives are self-serving.

The opposite view is altruism, which means that at least *some* of our acts—and there are those who maintain it is possible that *all* of them—are not in the end self-serving but are other-serving, so that even those things that appear to be the mere gratification of self—eating, drinking, sleeping, whatever—and all the separate complications of those, turn out in the end to be an effort to help others.

Now, what these brethren wanted to know from the Prophet was, Is it wrong to seek your own satisfaction? Is the principle of self-aggrandizement wrong? The classic answer, one of the most illuminating things I have ever read in Mormon literature, is the Prophet's reply, according to Oliver B. Huntington, who was there. It is this:

Joseph acknowledged "that some people entirely denounce the principle of self-aggrandizement as wrong," but "it is a correct principle," But it—that is our concern that we have accomplished something for our own ultimate glory—"may be indulged upon only one rule or plan—and that is to elevate, benefit and bless others first." That's one version. Another version, not quite that strong, is "seek to elevate and enoble others also." "If you will elevate others, the very work itself will exalt you. Upon no other plan can a man justly and permanently aggrandize himself." Those two adverbs suggest to me that it is possible temporarily and unjustly to aggrandize yourself; but permanently, no. (See Hyrum L. Andrus and Helen Mae Andrus, *They Knew,* 61.)

It seems to me that many of us suppose that all absolutes are obsolete! Under pressure, I would personally defend as an absolute law what I have just said. You can rephrase it as you wish, but it would come down to something like this: "It is impossible, worlds without end, to achieve your own fulfillment without the explicit and conscious inclusion of others. If you ignore, reject, or trample down others, in the long run you will absolutely and always fail." That's the gospel of Jesus Christ.

Now, a theological version of that. Does not the Lord's Prayer say that we are to pray: "Forgive us our debts, as we forgive our debtors"? (Matthew 6:12). Have you ever wondered about that linkage? Why didn't he simply tell us to pray and ask to have our *own* debts forgiven? He asks us to pray in such terms that we could almost put it in this negative way: "Father, forgive us to that degree and only to that degree that we forgive others." That's a prayer which, if answered at all, would in some cases evoke a negative answer. The positive way is: "Father, because I have reached that point in my life where I have a broken heart and a contrite spirit, because I have seen my weaknesses and my need I yearn to forgive all others! Including my enemies"—and the point is reached where it isn't just "including; it is *especially* my enemies." Why? Because they are the ones that are bearing the heaviest burdens of unforgiveness.

Christ did set that pattern. He is our paradigm. It has always interested me that the reason the woman taken in adultery isn't stoned is that Jesus appeals to the conscience of those around Him: "Who among you is really justified?" That is what He is saying, and it interests me psychologically that He didn't stand up and put His chin up, saying: "Which one of you dares to throw a rock!" That's probably the way some of us might have done it. He wasn't even facing them. He was stooping down, writing in the sand. Some people think He was writing the Ten Commandments at the same time and then saying: "Which of you would say that you have. . . ." But their faces and their attitudes were not in His vision. They could slink away one by one and not have to question whether they were defying His defiance. I think the Master was a Master.

So only He was left with her. "Woman, where are thine accusers?" He said, so as to underline, "I do not condemn thee, go thy way and sin no more." The actual sequence of events, I think, is not that she first made radical restitution, proving what we all like to talk about, the four or five or six R's of repentance, and then having paid the full price, she is confronted by Jesus, who says: "You're off the hook now. You paid." Not exactly that. It's as if He forgives her *first* as the *foundation* for her repentance. The Joseph Smith Translation says: "And the woman glorified God from that hour, and believed on his name" (JST, John 8:11). It seems that from the moment she tasted the power of divine forgiveness, she repented.

Now, the reason I don't want to dwell on that is that it may be out of phase, that may not be quite the way the Lord wants us to understand the sequence. So as far as His forgiveness is concerned, we are taught, He went through it *all* to earn the right and to have the power to forgive. So far as *our* forgiveness is concerned, He keeps saying we have to forgive everybody. Everybody.

How much do we have to forgive?

Everything.

For how long do we have to forgive?

Just all the time.

After we clean the slate and get up to today, what if people go on deliberately, maliciously repeating the transgressions against us?

Answer: Continue to forgive.

The Prophet Joseph Smith said once in a sermon: "We have not yet forgiven [some people] seventy times seven, as our Savior directed; perhaps we have not forgiven them once" (Joseph Smith, *Teachings* [1976], 238).

I turn to the really important issue and I have to bear testimony to the truth of our own need and of the impact this can have in seeking the health and wholeness of those around us. It is remarkable that we are told not to forgive is a serious transgression. It is remarkable further that, in a way, sons of perdition, sons of darkness, are those who have *deliberately* and *knowingly* rejected Christ. How much do they really know? The Prophet said the symbol of that is standing out in the noonday sun saying the sun is not shining. To put this even more concretely, he said a person cannot commit the unpardonable sin unless he knows absolutely what he is doing. "He has got to deny the Holy Ghost when the heavens have been opened unto him" (Joseph Smith, *Teachings* [1976], 358). Now, that indeed is a slamming of the door against God with a permanence and a depth of understanding that defies our present comprehension.

In section 132 of the Doctrine and Covenants the question is raised, What is unpardonable? The answer: "Wherein ye shed innocent blood" (v. 27). Now we have the explanation of what that phrase means. Whose blood? Jesus Christ's! But how could one do that? He has lived and died in this mortal time. "You assent," says the verse. "You assent [you agree with, you consent] unto my death." Elsewhere in the scriptures that is called "crucifying the Son of God unto themselves" (see D&C 76:35). In this case it isn't just a matter of killing a body, which is all the Romans saw. It is, in effect, wanting to render null and void, so far as you are concerned, what He did as to body, spirit, and mind or intelligence. It is, in effect, to say: "I prefer to serve Master Mahan, and I refuse to accept what you have done." Now, notice that this is not an act but *is* a sin, a most horrifying sin of the mind. It is something one does inside. My suggestion for our thoughts and prayers is, Isn't radical unforgiveness of others of the same caliber of sin?

If one commits murder in an act of passion, that may take five minutes; but if twenty-four hours a day, waking and sleeping, you go on holding grudges, harboring hostile feelings, this is a kind of self-contradiction. You may have reached that point of desperation in your own life when you have prayed and yearned to have the monkey off your back—your guilt and your sin—and maybe you sense that a half-measure of forgiveness has come from the Lord. But then you turn and say: "But not him! Don't you forgive him! I'm not going to; he doesn't deserve it!" Thus you then close the channel of love and compassion and revelation from the Lord. It is like triple plate steel against water. It cannot get through to us.

Now, seriously, how soon can you say to yourself: "Your unforgiveness is worse than your husband's (or wife's) sin"; or, "Your attitudes towards your father built up over thirty years are really more soul-shrinking than anything he ever did or didn't do."

That's strong, but it's right! I submit that it's true! We alone are responsible for allowing into our hearts the poison of unforgiveness. We have power that moment, gloriously, to see that this person we have thought of as the cause of our sins is himself suffering. We take on that glorious attitude of the Master.

A simple illustration is the story told of Lord Byron. He's walking down the street, and here's a bully beating a smaller man until the welts rise, apparently just to be doing it. People are around, watching, some of them with alarm and some of them with a kind of strangely satisfying fascination. And the man goes on and on with it.

Byron comes to the man and says, "How long are you going to go on beating him?"

The bully turns and says, "What's that to you?"

He replies with tears in his eyes, "Because if you will let him go, I will take the rest of it."

The story of a woman I know illustrates all that I have been trying to convey. She hated her husband, but by counseling she was able to come to see what he was going through; this was not yet forgiveness, but the concern to somehow relieve him came to her like a wave. Jesus said we are to forgive our enemies, and we have been unaware that often our enemies are our loved ones. Categories get mixed, and the person we love the most we hate the most. But when we deeply forgive others we throw it all off and say, "No more will I nurse and brood that poison in any degree." The magnificent change in us is that then, sometimes for the first time, we believe and feel *we* have been forgiven.

We then belong to the family of the Lord Jesus Christ. In a sense we take on burdens similar to His. He didn't deserve it! He didn't have it coming! He had every right to say to mankind: "What right have you . . . ?" Similarly, in many cases we do not deserve what we get at the hands of others in this world of pain and affliction. But that is beside the point. The point is that whatever has happened, we must forgive; and the law is, when we do we will feel a blessed forgiveness of ourselves from the Lord himself.

Faith and testimony tell us it is worth everything to go on seeking, to cleanse and purify our lives, to repent. I submit that the core of that is the power to forgive; that the core of that is the power to receive forgiveness. And the proper word at the end of that is *grace*. As we progressively keep God's commandments we "shall receive grace for grace" (D&C 93:20). One meaning of that is that we will receive as much grace—free, unearned, unmerited blessedness from the Lord Jesus Christ—as we are willing to give to others. Grace for grace. May God help us to catch that vision, to recognize that love day by day cannot endure—I don't think it can last a day—unless there is forgiveness, reciprocal forgiveness.

There comes to my mind the punch line from the movie *Love Story,* which was not a real love story. Part of the line is "Loving is not having to say you are sorry." Perhaps that has an occasional application, but my own conviction is different. With all my soul I say it is precisely the opposite. When you really love, you instantly say "I'm sorry" when you have hurt the beloved.

I once thought the Atonement was over. Of course, in one important sense it is. It happened, it is locked in the New Testament era. Jesus did say on the cross "It is finished." But as I read the scriptures we cannot say that at that moment Jesus' suffering ceased forever. In one way His suffering has increased since the Garden of Gethsemane. That one way is obvious to any of us. After having paid that terrible price in an agony that is beyond our power to comprehend, He now must face the sorrow of God's children being heartless, cold, calculating, and indifferent. He sees us with His own compassion and knows how desperately we need mercy; yet He has to bear the burden of knowing that the reason mercy is not operative in our lives is that we ourselves lock it out. "All eternity is pained" (D&C 38:12). All eternity is embodied in Jesus Christ, and even now He suffers. But I know of no place in scripture where He announces that because of that He is giving up, or that because our sins have become so extreme He will refuse forgiveness to the penitent. He promises that forgiveness is always there, and this is a joyous thought. But along with the joys both here and hereafter there will always be a measure of sorrow.

Yes, in worlds ahead all of the righteous will experience a measure of pain and sorrow for the sins of the world. It will be part of our destiny, as with the three Nephites (see 3 Nephi 28:9). But that very sorrow can lead to mercy and forgiveness and redemptive love.

Chapter Five

THE GOSPEL
AND THE SABBATH

The decision to write on this topic really goes back to many visits that my wife, Ann, and I have had in the homes of Orthodox Jewish people—mostly while we were in Israel. We noted how they observed the Sabbath, especially Shabbat Eve. That triggered in me a great interest in searching their lore for the roots of Sabbath observance.

I want to discuss first the origins of these sacred rites, and then four mighty metaphors. They are more than that to the Jew; they are mighty meanings of the Sabbath in their lives. Then we'll talk about startling parallels between what they teach and practice and what we in the Church teach and practice on this count. Then I'll share two or three powerful stories about the Sabbath. Then finally, I'll give a description of how the Jews actually bring into focus these great traditions.

Two cautions at the outset. The Jews do not agree on anything. They, themselves, have a saying: "Two Jews, three opinions." Also, it is important to know that though there is even today among the Orthodox a most scrupulous observance of the Sabbath day, they are by no means in the majority, even in Israel. What I am therefore describing applies to less than a majority in the contemporary world.

The other caution has to do with our understanding the difficulty the Master had in His own period among the Jews. One of these difficulties arose from a too strict, too rulish, too self-destroying approach to the Sabbath. He had to say more than once that the Sabbath was made for man, not man for the Sabbath. Yet we can err in supposing that because, as we like to say, that is simply a relic of the law of Moses; we have somehow outgrown it. The truth may be that we are farther down the mountain than they in the full application of what is intended.

Let me start then with a reference to one of the classics in all Jewish literature, by Abraham Joshua Heschel. The title is simply *The Sabbath.* Heschel points out that the origin of the Sabbath is not, as some suppose, the commandment—namely, the fourth— in the Decalogue. It is in the creation narration itself. It is first clear from the records, he points out, that the use of the word *holy* does not occur in the creation narrative for any of the six days of creation. Each of them and what was done, the Lord pronounced to be good.

But on the seventh, and only then, does the word *kaddish,* meaning "holy," occur. There it says God himself sanctified the day. It also suggests, and we have other sources for this view, that somehow God or the gods themselves observe the Sabbath. Observe in the sense of keep, that is. And the commandment "Remember," as in "Remember the Sabbath day," is a Jewish phrase which doesn't exactly mean retain in your memory. It means, more accurately, "memorialize" this day. On the Jewish view (if there is an agreed one), God himself did some creating even on the seventh day. Namely, He created Menohah, which is approximately "tranquility." He left some things behind in terms of labor and creative work, but on the seventh day He created tranquility. Then, say they, so must we.

Some have supposed that to say this day was sanctified or

needs to be shows that in the divine plan there is something crucial about time and timing. Does it really matter? The question, of
course, is raised most prominently in our generation by the
Seventh Day Adventists. Does the exact time one designates for
Shabbat really matter? Or does it only matter that in any given
series of seven days one be a Sabbath?

Let me point out that we have reason to know that the Lord
does care about time and timing. To illustrate this, Doctrine and
Covenants section 77 (an interesting number in the present
context) clearly teaches that just as there are seven days in our
week, which we call twenty-four-hour periods, so in the Lord's
economy there are seven one-thousand-year periods. Six of those
will constitute the more or less man-controlled history of this
earth, but the seventh, as Joseph Smith put it once, will be tried
by the Lord himself (see Joseph Smith, *Teachings* [1976], 252).

The Millennium is a day—a one-thousand-year day, following
six others of the same duration. If we had unerringly kept the cal-
endar from the beginning, we would know exactly when the
Messiah—for us, the Lord Jesus Christ—will come. He will come
at the beginning of the seventh thousand-year period. It is expedi-
ent that we not know exactly when that is, but it will be then as
He has announced.

The Jewish conclusion follows from this sort of reasoning. It is
that, far from the Sabbath being a day of strict injunctions, which
are joyless duties imposed on duties of the prior day; the Sabbath
is the reward for, the outcome of, indeed the climax of all other
preparatory creations. It is not an imposed stoppage. It is what all
the preparation was designed for, and therefore it has great value.
It was, indeed, made for man.

Some have pointed out that even one's ability to work on the
six days is enhanced by not working on the seventh. The Jews
have a tradition that Moses put that argument to the pharaoh and
convinced him; and that therefore the children of Israel in bondage
were permitted, on sheer economic grounds, to have one day in
seven off. But for mainline Judaism that is beside the real point.

To make a man forget that he is the son of a king, said the Jews, is the worst thing the evil of the universe can achieve. The Sabbath is a day when every man is a king and every woman a queen.

One could argue that the things that might well have destroyed the Jews failed to do so because, if for no other reason, they kept the Sabbath—even in a small degree. They themselves say it isn't the case that the Jews have kept the Sabbath; rather, the Sabbath has kept the Jews. What could have destroyed them? Well, their last prophet, in their own view, was Moses, so they speak of all the others as lesser, and of the end of prophecy. With the loss of a living prophet they lost someone in charge—what we would refer to as a priesthood bearer. No rabbi claims to have the ancient priesthood. They lost their kingdom—they lost the privilege of which David is to them the highest symbol, of having a king who was somehow both a spiritual and a temporal exemplar. They lost their temple—it was destroyed and crushed—and finally even lost their land and were dispersed in a hundred countries in the world. They almost lost their language. How have they survived? Well, many think it is because, even in the dispersion, they have retained this tradition of keeping the Sabbath.

A beautiful myth says that on the Sabbath day, in addition to your own soul, a second soul possesses your body—a good or better soul. And this is a symbolic way of saying that in every man and every woman there are two kinds of inclinations, good and bad. But on the Sabbath, somehow God sees fit to send an extra spirit, if you will, which lifts a man above his ordinary evil inclinations and spells peace.

They also have a story that whenever a Jew returns home from synagogue on Shabbat Eve, two angels follow him—one bad, one good. If when they reach his home all is prepared—the table set, the candles lit—then the good angel prays and says, "May this be the way the Sabbath will be in this home every week." The other angel, against his will, says amen. But if the man returns home and it's just as it always is, more or less in chaos and no effort has been made toward the Sabbath, then the evil angel prays that this may be the way it always is in this home; and the other angel, against his will, says amen.

They go farther in saying that the Sabbath outweighs all other commandments. In some of their literature, to keep the Sabbath is to keep the whole law and to break it is to break the whole law.

I turn now to more on what I call the metaphors. Note that nothing I say will list things you ought to stop doing or start doing on your own Sabbath. What I hope to do is to stir a new attitude, a new feeling, whatever you do. For the Jew, to miss the feeling is to miss it all, and some of us Latter-day Saints are missing it all. Here are four ways in which they teach by metaphor.

First, as I've indicated, they see the Sabbath as a sanctuary in time. Now, it's true they have strict requirements, and even now in Israel there are hospitals which are so prepared, organized, and planned, that they keep the Sabbath. If you care enough, it can be done. But all that discipline—all that "thou shalt not"—is seen as an instrument to joy. A disciplined joy, indeed, but nevertheless joy and celebration. Mind, says one of the great rabbis, is established by joy; by melancholy it is driven into exile. It is a sin, according to Judaism, to be sad on the Sabbath. If that's startling language, I'll startle you further. The Talmud says that we will be held personally accountable before the judgment of God for every legitimate Sabbath pleasure we did not enjoy. We are *commanded* to have joy. To miss the joy is to miss it all.

This joyous note is marked among them by special things: by special dress, by a special tablecloth in the evening, by special food—sumptuous food, in fact. Then there are the twisted loaves. One tradition says the two loaves wrapped in one symbolize the word for "remember the Sabbath" and also the word for "keep the Sabbath." Others say it symbolizes the law and the prophets. There may be other possibilities, but all point to exhilaration. Except in certain offshoot groups of Jewish tradition, there is nothing we can find that is puritanical—if by puritanical we mean with H. L. Mencken that a Puritan lives in mortal dread that somewhere, sometime, somebody is enjoying himself. The Jews talk about the joy of the commandment. This is in their hearts. This is on their lips. And if I can put it in modern language, they make a production out of it.

334

Second, they speak of the Sabbath as a feast. And they remind themselves over and over that when Moses had the children of Israel in the wilderness a double portion of manna was given just before the Sabbath, but none on the Sabbath, so that the day was recognizable in two ways—by what was absent and what was present. Jews serve the most beautiful meal of the week on Shabbat Eve. The mother often has to prepare for as much as two days before, and one of the traditional dishes is a kind of stew which stays simmering all night long the night before the Sabbath and then needs only to be served. The feast is itself a form of ritual, and it requires special preparations and special activities. It is, to quote one writer, a palace in time. Something of the same spirit attends America's Thanksgiving dinner. It involves, for one thing, the bringing in of the stranger or of the poor. (This is why Ann and I had such firsthand and close experiences. We were foreigners, and were invited for that very reason.) "Come and share our Shabbat." It is a feast even for the poorest man in the poorest ghetto. Why? Well, because even if he is poor and cannot afford the twisted loaves and a little wine and the meat and the fish and the candles, the synagogue in that area will see that he has them. That's a requirement. So on that particular day even a poor man is rich.

The third metaphor has roots in the Jews' mystical tradition, but it has biblical precedent. They talk about the Sabbath as heaven on earth; as—if you want to be specific and mathematical—one-sixtieth of paradise. You have a foretaste of paradise. The seventh day, some legends say, is the reflection of the seventh heaven, the highest heaven. By the way, they also say having dreams is one-sixtieth of being a prophet. They believe that this is cosmic, that nature herself celebrates the Sabbath. In the Church we have a hymn titled "Come Away to the Sunday School." One of the lines is "Nature breathes her sweetest fragrance on the holy Sabbath day." That's the Jews' feeling. Even the rivers don't work on the Sabbath. They are accustomed to throw up rocks and dirt, so they may be very calm on the Sabbath. Even hell celebrates the Sabbath. People who have been tormented in hell are, for purposes of the Sabbath day, released. The hosts of heaven celebrate the Sabbath. They gather and they sing and they feel tranquility.

All the miracles of the six days of creation, say the Jews, are somehow available to us, or should be, on the seventh day. And all creation "resolves itself into melody if we have ears to hear."

Finally, they speak of the Sabbath as a queen, as a bride. How did that get started? Well, here are two traditions. According to Rabbi Simeon, the Sabbath said unto the Holy One (their word for *Adoni,* the Lord) "O master of the universe, every living thing created has its mate, and each day has its companion, except me [this is the Sabbath speaking]. I am alone." The Holy One replied, "Israel will be your mate." So, on their view, Israel cries out to the queen or the bride and says, "Come, holy Sabbath." He who prays on the eve of the Sabbath and recites the verses that begin, "The heavens and the earth were finished"—the scriptures say he is become a partner with the Holy One in creation.

Now, the tradition goes further. The Sabbath is meaningful to God. The world would not be complete if the six days did not culminate at the Sabbath, but they compare this to a king who has made a bridal chamber, has plastered it, painted it, adorned it. Now what does the chamber lack? Obviously, a bride. What did the universe still lack? The Sabbath. Imagine a king who made a ring. What did it lack? A signet. What did the universe lack? A Sabbath. So the Sabbath is a bride. Its celebration is like a wedding, and the bride is to come lovely and bedecked and perfumed.

There's a subheading to their argument: sanctification. We're taught that the Lord sanctified the Sabbath (Genesis 2:3; Moses 3:3; D&C 77:128); and in Jewish thought, sanctification is associated with marriage. The symbolism is clear. Why do the typical celebrants of the Sabbath among the Hasidic Jews link myrtle with the Sabbath? When going out to invite friends to a wedding, the groom carries myrtle. What is myrtle? Well, the poet Judah Halevi makes the point that *hadas,* the Hebrew word for myrtle, was the original name of Esther, whose beauty was legendary.

An overhead awning of myrtle is erected for the bride during the canopy ceremony of marriage. The old man who in a Jewish story was running at twilight to welcome the Sabbath and carrying two bunches of myrtle was asked why. He's supposed to have replied, "One is for remember and one is for keep." I don't know how close the Greeks are to the Jews on this, but in Greek mythology myrtle was Aphrodite's tree—a special plant and a symbol of love.

On one point there is tremendous overlap. Most traditions about God and creation hold that He did it, finished it, and in effect abandoned it. There was no more creative work for God to do. Sometimes in Jewish parlance, you ask what God has been doing since He finished the creation. They answer, "making marriages." For most Christians, it's all over. Yet Jews speak of continual creation for God. So do we Latter-day Saints, do we not?

Just lift one sentence from the New Testament: "I go to prepare a place for you" (John 14:2). That is further labor. We overlap on the notion that even heaven will involve work, problems, and—dare I say it?—yes, busyness of a kind. It was a great surprise to Wilford Woodruff, in one of his frequent glimpses of the spirit world, to have a conversation with the Prophet Joseph Smith. The Prophet said he was in a hurry. It troubled Elder Woodruff, so he asked the Prophet why. "I expected my hurry would be over when I got [to the Spirit world]." The Prophet explained: "We are the last dispensation and so much work has to be done [to prepare to go to earth with the Savior], and we need to be in a hurry in order to accomplish it" (Durham, *Discourses of Wilford Woodruff*, 288–89). Yet there is a kind of rest—peace and joy—that can occur even in the midst of such concern. Hence the one kind of work that Orthodox Jewry will permit its rabbis to do on the Sabbath is work for God. None other.

On the idea of the Sabbath as bride, I have a letter from a friend—a Jewish mother—who visited my wife and me and mentioned that she'd had chats with the rabbi out of the campaigns for what a woman should or should not be doing, and that she'd been completely satisfied with what he taught her. So I asked her, "What does it mean in your tradition for the woman to be the queen of the Sabbath?" Here are a few sentences from her reply. "The mother is responsible for the atmosphere of piety and reverence and for the teaching of Jewish ideals. She prepares the Shabbat dinner" (by the way, the men are encouraged to help and we've seen them do it), "and gathers her children around while she pronounces the blessing over the lights. The woman prepares the home for each festival. She creates the mood of joy. She is general counselor. The Talmud says no matter how short your wife is, lean down and take her advice. And for husbands—another Talmudic statement—but how can a man be assured of having a blessed home? Answer: By respecting his wife." (I love all these old sayings, subtle stories, and yiddish theater.) Then she goes on. "The woman sets the spiritual tone. She is the most responsible for her children. It is an enormous responsibility and a joy to have." Well, that's from a Jewish mother. The Jewish mother has great influence and power in the home.

Now I shift to some parallels. Be honest about the kinds of predicament we frequently are in when the Sabbath begins, and you can ask how anyone can really let go wholeheartedly. We have read together, Ann and I, a famous novel by Herman Wouk, *The Caine Mutiny,* and more recently his two books which have been compared to Tolstoy, *War and Remembrance* and *The Winds of War.* Herman Wouk is a playwright and therefore on Friday has often been in that situation which characterizes Broadway opening plays—rehearsals; the play tottering toward probable disaster, and so on. But at the first sign of a star (the Jewish Sabbath begins when you can see two stars in the evening) he abandons his play and as an Orthodox Jew goes home, where he finds his children (whom he hasn't been noticing lately) in their best bib and tucker, finds his wife with everything prepared. He describes it as like coming home from the wars. He knows that from sundown to sundown it is "time out," and no one who respects him can get to him—the telephone is off, so is the television; nothing mechanical is supposed to be utilized in a strict Orthodox home. One of his friends, a producer, said to him one day after this had been repeated many times, "I do not envy you your religion, but I do envy you your Sabbath."

Let's consider some of the pressures that are upon us just as we enter the Sabbath, and show how both Judaism and, I suggest, Mormonism have a response. Suppose you are poor. Well, as I've said, in Judaism the poor are invited in, and if they lack, they are provided with the essentials of Sabbath devotion. In several places in the Doctrine and Covenants, Latter-day Saints are taught not to be so concerned about riches per se. "He that hath eternal life is rich. Seek not for riches but for wisdom" (D&C 6:7; 11:7). The Sabbath is the day when wisdom can be reenthroned. Suppose you have failed or had setbacks during the week. The Jewish teaching is that the Sabbath will renew your perspective, and your failure will seem somewhat trivial in relationship to the ultimate plans and purposes and promises of God.

But suppose you are sinful. Judaism says that the Sabbath is not a day for confession and for mourning.

There we split a little. We have in section 59 of the Doctrine and Covenants a commandment—the whole section has the flavor of Sabbath observance—to confess our sins one to another and before the Lord. That has come to mean not detailing our actual transgressions, but the acknowledgment of need, and that we are sinful (and just by coming to church we acknowledge it). Well, presumably if you are mourning for your own sins or for the loss of a loved one you should keep that private on Sunday, because you are to have a glad heart on that day. We are so commanded. If we do this, says section 59, "with a glad heart and a cheerful countenance—not with much laughter, for this is sin—but with a glad heart," then are the promises fulfilled. I know people who have occasionally tried to impress others with how sad they look because they have fasted all that time, but our revelation says that fasting and prayer are "rejoicing and prayer." That comes as news to most children. But the intent is the same, I believe, as the Jewish intent that fasting ought to be feasting on the Spirit. Going without food combined with a prayerful heart is supposed to contribute to that kind of feasting. If it doesn't, you have missed the joy and have missed it all.

But suppose you are condemned. Well, in their tradition you're out of prison for that day, and even in prison the glory can surround you. But suppose your soul is itself deeply wounded. Join the club. We're commanded to come to church with a broken heart and a contrite spirit. If you trace the roots of that phrase, you will find they are, in one word, "buffeted." Come, acknowledging it if you've been beaten down this week. You always have, but if you'll come with a proper spirit you will be healed and renourished.

But suppose you are rushed, and there are projects and pressures and commitments and so on. The Jewish view is to stop, slow down, be quiet, and you'll have greater strength to carry on. Our version of that—it's also an Old Testament phrase—is "Be still and know that I am God" (D&C 101:16). We can't really know that when the din is as strong in our ears as it usually is. I sometimes think that the very volume of some contemporary music— and I hesitate to use the word *music* for what I'm describing—is exactly designed to quiet and muffle the scream of our inner world and our life and conscience. As if we could drown it out with the noise.

But suppose we are at war? In Jewish thinking, war justifies bending the Sabbath. The Jews have been taken advantage of occasionally by enemies who said: "Ah-ha! we know how to get to the Jews. We'll attack, and they won't fight on Shabbat." So they do fight. And they do fight if necessary on Yom Kippur, as the Egyptians found out some years ago. But their commitment arises from the conviction that there are emergencies. Nevertheless, much of their Sabbath celebration, in the past, has been in the midst of crisis. Ann and I have been to Israel many times. Hardly a time, prior to the time we departed, have we not been counseled by friends: "Don't go! This is the worst possible time. There's a crisis over there." Of course, they're always right. In Israel they live in the midst of such crisis, but they keep the Sabbath. It would not be wrong to say they keep it precisely in part because it is a crisis world in which they live, and on the

Sabbath they close out that world—the jungle, the bombs, the guns. They pull the drapes and it is not proper to talk about war or politics, even to think about them, during the time of rejoicing.

But suppose all of your machines have broken down? The mechanical ox is in the mire? Well, one of the blessings they claim of the Sabbath is that you get back to the simple elements of life for God's earth as it is and for the most elemental way of living.

What if you are filled with anger? Their answer: You shall kindle no fire, and that, of course, is literal fire; but they go on, not even the fire of righteous indignation. Peace. And so we have been counseled, "Renounce war and proclaim peace" (D&C 98:16), especially on the day of peace.

But suppose you are bitter and unforgiving. Come to the sweets and taste and forgive. We have done that as a church. There is a jubilee year in traditional Jewry when whoever is imprisoned or has debts and so on is forgiven and released. By the way, no interest is charged on the Sabbath in strict Jewish reckoning.

But what if your animals are in need? Their answer is, let them rest.

An offshoot group, not strictly the Orthodox, going back to the fifteenth century are convinced that joy is the giant cure-all; that if you can be enthusiastically happy, then all evils somehow are walked under your feet. If you can't, then no other solution will ultimately do. Two men from this group were arguing about who was the greatest miracle worker among the rabbis, and one of them had a rabbi who, he thought, qualified. This rabbi was going along a highway when a storm gathered. He had clothing on that he wanted preserved, and also he didn't want to drown; so by use of his great power he caused that, though there was rain to the right of him and rain to the left of him, where he was traveling there was no rain.

The other man was not impressed. "That's nothing," he said. "My rabbi was on the way to a distant town on Friday, which he thought he could reach before sundown (when the Sabbath began). But the driver had miscalculated, and now, suddenly, dusk was falling. He saw he was in danger, God forbid, of violating the

341

Sabbath; whereupon, he performed his miracle. He put forth his hands, and behold it was Sabbath to the right of him and Sabbath to the left of him, but in the center there was no Sabbath—it was the middle of the week."

A second story: A poor man was the Sabbath guest of a rich one. He ate so voraciously and with such vigor that perspiration streamed down his face. "My friend," said his host, "why do you work so hard?" "Because," he replied, "I'm trying to fulfill the commandment 'in the sweat of thy face shalt thou eat thy bread.'"

Then there is the delightful story of a maker of books whose name, allegorically, was Shabbati. His family and he were so poor that they did not have anything for the Sabbath, but they were too proud to go to their neighbors, who would have been under obligation either to invite them or to provide them with the essentials. He went home late from the synagogue so nobody could even inquire of his situation.

When he arrived home, there was the Sabbath table fully prepared—everything in order; the candles lighted, and his wife looking fresh and delightful. How did it happen? Well, his wife had found an old garment and also some gold buttons. She had hastened to the market and turned in the buttons for their worth in money and had prepared the Sabbath meal. He was so delighted at this that he took his wife in his arms. (This is how he reported it in confessing to his rabbi). "Master, I could not contain myself. Tears fell from my eyes. I praised the Lord. I praised Him again and again. We began to sing. I forgot the majesty of the Sabbath. I took my wife by the hand, led her out, and we danced in our little house. Then we sat down to eat, but I was so overcome with the fish course that I jumped up, took her in my arms, and danced again. Then we ate the soup. I danced a third time, and cried for happiness. But oh, Master, it came to me afterwards that perhaps our dancing and laughter had disturbed the sublimity of God's Sabbath. If we have sinned, we have come to ask for penance."

What did the rabbi reply? "Know that all the hierarchy of heaven sang and laughed and was joyful and danced hand in hand with this aged man and his wife when they were happy on the

Sabbath Eve. And when you heard my laughter"—the rabbi had laughed three times himself, to the great shock of many—"it was because I was with them in spirit when they went out to dance, and I danced and sang with them."

That's not a Puritan Sabbath. But you may find such celebration and rejoicing in the Nauvoo period of Mormon history.

Now finally, how is it done in practice? Ann and I were invited into many Jewish homes, and I'll give you a description that's mostly of one home. Let me just say as the preface that most of the Christian writers I have read tend to suppose that heaven is an effortless place, and usually their descriptions of hell are far more interesting. But these persons we visited had put in great labor and preparation to make the Sabbath a creative experience. In the home of an Orthodox rabbi who had four lovely daughters and whose synagogue we had earlier attended, we saw the essential components—his wife, his children, the lights, the twisted loaves, the meat, and the *gefilt,* fish. We saw the *kipah* or *kipot* (the latter would be the plural). These are the little skull caps, which an Orthodox Jew wears everywhere but which others wear in synagogue and on sacred occasions. We were given our own. If it seems strange to you that a person would cover his head in reverence rather than uncover it, just think a little more deeply about your own experience in the temple.

After the evening had come—the two stars could be seen—we witnessed the tablecloth, the beautiful *chollah.* We learned that there had been a ritual bath for some family members, not just a usual bath but a Shabbat bath. We listened to their songs. Some do not sing well, but they make a joyful noise. We thought we could detect certain overtones of Russian music and Eastern European music, and that's understandable because the majority who escaped the Holocaust and came to Israel have such roots. It sounded almost like a Russian cossack chorus. Their music is the kind that leads you to respond to the rhythm, to clap, to motion. For them the ultimate outcome of good music is dance. We witnessed the prayers, the ceremonial lighting of the candles (in one other home we attended, they sang a transition hymn that starts on a worldly level and then moves into a reverent attitude). We partook of each of the cups of wine, which in our case was grape juice. This has to be a product of the vine, but it can be raisin juice or grape juice or wine—any of the three. With each of these came a certain ceremonial prayer.

As he broke the bread, the father, who was also a rabbi, handed it to us. You have to somehow be in touch as he is in touch. We saw the use of the ritual salt, based on Leviticus—"With all thine offerings thou shalt offer salt." We saw how very congenial was the discussion between parents and children. It's the children's day; they know they have their parents on this day, if on no other. On this particular evening we did not hear the reading of Proverb 31, but in another home we did, and that's often a ritual—the famous verses about who can find a virtuous woman, who is more precious than rubies. In one home I was asked to read that, and in the presence of the woman to whom these passages were applied I was moved more than I can describe. There are Jewish mothers, I'm told, who resent the reading of those words because they think it is sop, as it were, of comfort after neglect and hostility all week; then suddenly the husband waxes poetic and gives them their just due.

There is an intimacy we observed even in their feeling for the divine, though they're very careful, out of long philosophical tradition, to keep God distant. And yet some rabbis do not feel bad about referring to God as Daddy; and they're not talking about big daddy or Daddy Warbucks. It's a matter of the intimate warmth of filial love. In one home we witnessed a blessing pronounced upon the youngest son, and this is also ceremonial and traditional. And the blessings were of *Ephraim* and *Manasseh*. Latter-day Saints will recognize that. The blessings of Ephraim and Manasseh! A Jew pronouncing such a blessing upon his youngest son or grandson? Yes. That's a tradition.

In one home we heard the hymn that is used at the end of the Sabbath, on Saturday night. It's a prayer for the immediate return of Elijah. Their tradition is that Elijah can't come on Friday because everybody's too busy preparing for the Sabbath. He can't come on the Sabbath because that's a day of rest. But the tradition is that he will come on the day after Shabbat. Just for interest, if you'll read Doctrine and Covenants section 110 and check the date you'll find it was April 3, 1836, when Elijah came to the Kirtland Temple. That was a Passover Sunday, the day after the Jewish Shabbat.

At the end of the day, the Jews have a little ceremony—you taste something special, you smell something special. And now the Sabbath queen leaves and you're back to the work week.

All this moved us. Through the warp and weft of my comments you see that there's a creative idea here—an act of creation is involved in making the Sabbath what the Sabbath ought to be. If a person doesn't do this, for him the day is not a Sabbath at all. Also, through what I've described, there emerges a balance of solemnity on the one hand and pleasure on the other—even very worldly pleasure, if you want to say it that way. Should we be embarrassed by that or troubled by it? Not, I think, if you read section 59, which promises not only blessings from above and revelations in their time—which you would expect from Sabbath observance—but also, on the condition that we do it in rejoicing, very earthly blessings. The promise, precisely worded, is "the fulness of the earth is yours." It names houses, gardens, barns, orchards, vineyards. Those are all temporal, down-to-earth realities. And then the senses—to strengthen the body, to enliven the soul, to please the eye, to gladden the heart, for taste and for smell, and so forth. All these are physical, yet they have spiritual counterparts. The wholeness of Sabbath worship is holiness. It involves all of man—body and spirit—and that insight is in authentic Judaism.

It's not uncommon among us, I'm afraid, to think of the Sabbath in a negative way, as a set of tough requirements—perhaps to avoid desecrating it. What I would hope has emerged here is the other side—the beautiful, joyful, happiness-giving effect of sanctifying the day as partners with the Creator. I think it is common to think that if we don't do certain things, there will be positive rewards—that we will be rewarded for sacrifice, for suffering, for service—but very uncommon to think that God will reward us for rejoicing, for enjoying, and for feeling pleasure. The Jewish tradition is, I repeat, that God will in fact reward and compound the very pleasures of the Sabbath. Otherwise it would be as if, beaten and tattered, invited in from afar to a magnificent feast, one refuses to partake of it.

A parable puts it thus: A man who has earned seven coins and is carrying them along the streets sees a poor beggar and out of compassion gives him six coins. Then as he continues walking down the street, he discovers that the beggar has followed him and stolen the seventh one. God has given us six days for labor. It is a terrible mistake to steal the seventh day, which is both His and ours—the very climax and meaning of what has gone before.

I submit that the Sabbath is a time whose idea has come.

Chapter Six

THE AWESOME POWER
OF MARRIED LOVE

These days we see around us an increasing disintegration not only of such family solidarity as once existed, but even in the rejection of the idea of family. Articles are published that say the family is long gone. It is outmoded. But it is interesting to contemplate this fact: that though divorce has never been more frequent, remarriage has never been more frequent; and that people who have struggled and felt that they have failed, and have been estranged and divorced, are trying again and again, suggesting that for all the propaganda to the contrary there is a strong, lasting thirst for the fulfillments that marriage promised. And I am convinced that in the Church—though there is so much anguish and in many marriages struggle—we at least have a greater vision of the possibilities and a greater set of helps to reach toward them than any people in the world.

Now the opening question: What is love? "The awesome power of love" is a phrase from an anthropologist named Ashley Montague. He tells of an orphanage, a foundling home in New

347

York, where orphaned children were taken. Their mortality rate—just the sheer life-and-death struggle—was appalling; two out of three died before the end of the first year.

But then a flourishing contrast was noticed in one particular section of the orphanage: none of the children there seemed to have the struggles to live that the others did. And so, as scientists will, the authorities began various sorts of observation, asking themselves questions as they went along. What could be the reason? Were they eating something different? Were they getting a different kind of nurturing? What was the story?

Well, by accident, which often happens in science (they call it serendipity) they discovered the explanation. There was on that particular wing of the orphanage-hospital a scrub woman whom everyone knew as Old Anna. Her task was to clean the floors. She was as big as a streetcar, but she loved little children. Though she had been forbidden to do it, when no one was looking she would pick them up and hold them. She would sometimes even strap them two at a time on her big hips, and then as she worked on the floor she would lean over and talk to them. She loved them. Those children lived. They ate more. They slept better. They were healthier. And the mortality rate in that wing was well down.

The next question was how to clone Old Anna. They couldn't, of course. But this story underlines that love, whatever it is, is powerful. And after much reading and much talking with knowledgeable people, I have concluded that Paul's definition is the one that does the most to help us understand the nature of love—it is a "fruit of the Spirit" (Galatians 5:22). But I would even go so far as to say that love is the Spirit; that the very love that God has for us is manifested most powerfully through the Spirit. I have always believed this, but let me share by paraphrase something that says it better than I could.

Elder Parley P. Pratt describes the effect of his spending several days with the Prophet in Philadelphia, which is, interestingly, the City of Love. He says the Prophet "lifted a corner of the veil and [gave] me a single glance into eternity."

During these days, Elder Pratt recorded, "[the Prophet] taught me many great and glorious principles. . . . I received from him the first idea of eternal family organization. . . . It was from him that I learned that the wife of my bosom might be secured to me for time and all eternity; and that the refined sympathies and affections which endeared us to each other emanated from the fountain of divine eternal love" (Pratt, *Autobiography,* 297).

In clarifying this important subject, the Prophet in effect inverted everything Parley P. Pratt and other early converts had believed about marriage and family when they joined the Church. That the Fall, for example, was really Eve's betrayal of Adam. That's a standard view still in the wider Christian world. This erroneous concept labels women as inferior. That's just for openers. They also believed that the body, being matter, was intrinsically evil, so using two bodies in the procreative act, using them as instruments, had to be wrong—in any case an embarrassment. Why hadn't God arranged it so that children could be brought into the world in some other way? Third, there was the belief that marriage was of the earth, earthy, and perhaps a compromise with the devil. And finally, in the life to come all earthly marriage relationships would be done away.

What Joseph Smith did was to invert or turn around, not just contradict, all four of those. Number one, the Fall was in fact a knowing and *wise* decision of both Eve and Adam in order to make possible the very conditions that would build and perpetuate family. Number two, the body is not intrinsically evil, but is— and this is one of the most sacred words in our vocabulary—a temple. Yes, it can be abused and distorted, but as God intends it to be, it can be glorified and hallowed.

Third, marriage, far from being a compromise of the world and of the devil, is properly the highest ordinance of the kingdom of God, reserved for the highest sanctuary room in the temple—the sealing room. And finally, far from its all being done away hereafter, only for the righteous and the sanctified will the privilege of everlasting marriage and family be granted. The others will be the lonely and the estranged, at least in the full sense of their possibilities. Having been taught by the Prophet, Parley P. Pratt wrote: "I had loved before, but I knew not why. . . . I could now love with the spirit and with the understanding also." That is the blessing of the Restoration. If we can only begin to glimpse that, it gives us the bearings upon which to shape our course.

On one occasion Brigham Young was approached by two women who were asking for a divorce, and he gave an idealistic response. He said to them: "If that dissatisfied wife would behold the transcendent beauty of person, the Godlike qualities of the resurrected husband she now despises, her love for him would be unbounded and unutterable. Instead of despising him, she would feel like worshipping him. He is so holy, so pure, so perfect, so filled with God in his resurrected body. There will be no dissatisfaction of this kind in the resurrection of the just. The faithful elders will have then proved themselves worthy of their wives, and are prepared then to be crowned gods, to be filled with all the attributes of the gods that dwell in eternity. Could the dissatisfied ones see a vision of the future glorified state of their husbands, love for them would immediately spring up within you, and no circumstance could prevail upon you to forsake them" (Church Historical Department document Ms/d/1234 box 49/FD8). Now, it also works the other way around, that if the husband could only see his wife in her glorified condition, he would be so moved he would feel to worship. You might pause and say, "Wait, wait, wait. We are talking idolatry. We are not supposed to worship each other." In the ultimate scheme of things we will feel to do so when the person is worthy of it.

But Brother Brigham was also practical—he had one foot in this world and one in the next. It is said that a woman came to him one day and said, "Brother Brigham, my husband told me to go to hell," and Brigham said, "Sister, don't go."

We live in a world where there is much clamor and struggle and anguish respecting the role of woman. I heard of a man who literally dragged his wife, I mean bodily dragged her, into a stake president's office, sat her down, and said, "Now, President So-and-So, you tell my wife to honor my priesthood, and then our problems will be solved." This good stake president had his scriptures ready. He opened them to Doctrine and Covenants section 121, verse 37, and said, "Brother, according to what I read here, you have no priesthood."

Elder James E. Talmage wrote: "In the restored Church of Jesus Christ, the Holy Priesthood is conferred, as an individual bestowal, upon men only, and this in accordance with Divine requirement. It is not given to woman to exercise the authority of the Priesthood independently; nevertheless, in the sacred endowments associated with the ordinances pertaining to the House of the Lord, woman shares with man the blessings of the Priesthood. When the frailties and imperfections of mortality are left behind, in the glorified state of the blessed hereafter, husband and wife will administer in their respective stations, seeing and understanding alike"—oh, hasten the day!—"and co-operating to the full in the government of their family kingdom. Then shall woman be recompensed in rich measure for all the injustice that womanhood has endured in mortality. Then shall woman reign by Divine right, a queen in the resplendent realm of her glorified state, even as exalted man shall stand, priest and king unto the Most High God." And then he adds in full confirmation of what Brother Brigham said: "Mortal eye cannot see nor mind comprehend the beauty, glory, and majesty of a righteous woman made perfect in the celestial kingdom of God" (In *Young Woman's Journal,* October 1914, 602–3).

Now, some are going to say, "I don't quite understand, because we are taught, aren't we, that the spirit we leave this life with we will have in the next life, and everything we take there by the way of failure and sin is going to be perpetuated. So what you're saying sounds like it's sort of a magical cure-all."

This quotation does not say that it is all automatic. According to Elder Bruce R. McConkie there is a fallacy in the Church, and that is that in order for us to be worthy of a celestial resurrection we must be perfect before we leave this life. It is false. While each of us is expected to make all the progress possible in mortality, we cannot be fully perfected in this world. There will be more to be done in the spirit world, but in the glorious celestial resurrection much improvement will take place. And that vision—that really it is going to happen and if we live consistently it will happen—can make a lot of difference during the hours of discouragement and despair. There are problems in some marriages and in some families that will not all be resolved here, and it is pointless to hope that they will. But it is not pointless to have long-range faith that as you continue doing your all, they will be resolved, and that's the promise that these prophets have given us.

Latter-day Saints who have really embarked in the service of God have a celestial homesickness. The words of the hymn "O My Father" turn out to be the most requested words of all the mail that has ever come to Temple Square in Salt Lake City. Even in the secular world—people out there who have never heard of the understanding of the family that we have—even they sense in those words something poignantly nostalgic, "Father, Mother, let me come and dwell with thee." Eliza R. Snow wrote the words to this hymn, of course. Zina Diantha Huntington, who at age eighteen lost her mother under very trying circumstances in Nauvoo, went to the Prophet and expressed an ultimate concern: "Will I know my mother as my mother when I get over on the other side?" And the Prophet replied: "Certainly you will. More than that, you will meet and become acquainted with your eternal Mother, the wife of your Father in Heaven." Such an idea had never entered her head, and she burst out, "And have I, then, a Mother in Heaven?" He replied: "You assuredly have. How could a Father claim His title unless there were also a Mother to share that parenthood?" The record continues: "It was about this time that Sister Snow learned the same glorious truth from the same inspired lips, and at once she was moved to express her own great joy and gratitude in the moving words of the hymn, 'O My Father'" (Gates, in *History of the Young Ladies MIA,* 16).

We don't know how extensive and detailed the organization of the family was in the premortal life, but we were family there. We *were a family.* And according to George Q. Cannon (see *Utah Genealogical and Historical Magazine* 21:124) and Orson F. Whitney (see *Improvement Era* 13:100–101), who gave this a lot of thought, it may well be that some of the kinships we feel for each other here are but the trailing of the impressions and expressions of those former associations.

I once had the opportunity to ask a related question to Elder Joseph Fielding Smith. I was at the Church offices doing some research when I ran into his wife. Since she was going into his office, which was then in the Historical Department, she took me with her. "Let's go see Daddy," she said. I knew who Daddy was. As the great Church scripturalist, he overawed me. He looked up with a smile and said, "Brother Madsen, you can have one question." So I asked, "Brother Smith, do you think marriages are made in heaven?" Well, I had him over a barrel—his wife was standing right there. And he hesitated, so she kind of punched him. "Daddy, Daddy, don't you think our marriage was made in heaven?" Now, he had to be honest. So he said, "Well, it's in heaven now."

The Church has never given sanction to the idea that somehow all Latter-day Saint marriages were predetermined in heaven, but there is an interesting Jewish tradition that answers the question "What has God been doing since the creation?" with "Making marriages."

In this church we know, as others in the religious world don't know, that we didn't begin our existence or our family consciousness in this world.

Many of us have heard the statement made—and ascribed to either Joseph Smith or Brigham Young—to the effect that if a person could see the glory of the telestial kingdom he would commit suicide to get there. If only we could get the fundamental doctrines across to Church members as rapidly as we get across rumors, everyone would be saved. Am I saying that's a rumor? Well, I am saying this, that over a period of many years I have combed everything Joseph Smith said and wrote, and I can't find it. Hugh Nibley has done the same with Brigham Young's words, and he can't find it. It is hard to prove a negative, of course. What I can say is that we have found a statement from Joseph via Wilford Woodruff that says something else that is close, and I suspect it is the origin of the alleged statement (see Walker, Diary, August 1837). Elder Woodruff said the Prophet taught this, roughly: that if we could see what is beyond the veil we couldn't stand to stay here in mortality for five minutes. And I suggest from the context that he was not talking about the telestial kingdom. He was talking about what it was like to be in the presence of God and the family.

Speaking of homesickness, the Lord's anesthesia is our amnesia. We would not stand this operation except for the fact that the curtain has been drawn over our past. So we do not know our name and rank and serial number. We have no specific memories of our premortal lives. Patriarchs give us a glimpse under inspiration. We have forgotten so we will stay here and tough out the spook alley. That is not a bad metaphor, because there was complete understanding before we got into this tunnel of why and what it would lead to. That's why we had the courage to shout for joy at the prospect (see Job 39:7), which in light of present circumstances is astonishing. We were able to envision what it could lead to because there we were in the presence of it. We would come back, should we be so blessed, and be like our Father and our Mother.

For some years now I have been much involved in studying Jewish lore, and for a semester I taught at Haifa University. It has been exciting to find specific instances of the fact that we in the Church have much in common with the great mainstream tradition of Judaism respecting the family. The Jews speak of some kind of premortal arrangements. They speak of the fall of man in positive terms, as we do. Yes, it brought bitter conditions, but as the language of Genesis says, the curse is "for [our] sake" (3:17). And yes, we have the promise of difficulty and pain in childbirth, but says the promise, "they shall be saved in child-bearing" (JST, 1 Timothy 2:15). Not easy, but fruitful.

Further, the Jews say that somehow Adam was originally two bodies, and the Lord took off one to make Eve. They say that Abraham was promised above all else that he would have a posterity that was not just as numerous as the stars but also would shine like the stars—not just quantity but quality too. Abraham's willingness to go on Mount Moriah and offer his only son—they call that the *akeda*. That means the binding. Their legend says that Isaac asked to be bound, so that he would not involuntarily prevent his father from sinking a knife. They say that Abraham's and Isaac's response was the greatest willingness and sacrifice in history, and therefore the place which had been flat before became a mountain after; God exalted the place. They say that Sarah didn't date her life until after the birth of Isaac. They say that every line in her face disappeared after Isaac was born. They say that the reason why murder is so wrong is that it destroys not just a life but a race. They say that the notion that somehow marriage is against the will of God is contrary to the truth; that getting married is one of the chief things God wants us to do, and that the heavens rejoice over a marriage where there is a genuine exchange of love. Finally, in their traditions, it is not inappropriate to call the Lord what I mentioned Jesse Evans called her husband—not just Father, but Daddy. That's what *Abba* means in Hebrew.

Well, some of that has echoes in our hearts. Yet I was quoting not from Mormon sources but Jewish ones.

Now, one other glimpse far beyond in an exchange of letters between Heber C. Kimball and his wife, Vilate, that reflects love at their mature level, after they had been through all that occurred from New York to Nauvoo. She was writing to him while he was away on the next to last of his several missions. (It is a paradox that this marvelous church that is so inclined to glorify and celebrate family has often required that members leave the immediate family to go and serve the wider family.) She wrote in part: "Let your heart be comforted, and if you never more behold my face in time, let this be my last covenant and testimony unto you: that I am yours in time and throughout all eternity. This blessing has been sealed upon us by the Holy Spirit of promise, and cannot be broken only through transgression, or committing a grosser crime than your heart or mine is capable of."

Heber was so moved that he wrote a reply which became a prayer. It asked that they could live together and die together because, said he, "Thou, O God, knowest we love each other with pure hearts" (Whitney, *Heber C. Kimball,* 334–35).

The last prophecy Heber C. Kimball uttered was made as he walked along behind Vilate's casket and said, "I shall not be long after her." And he wasn't.

One of the consequences of such unifying love under the power of the Holy Spirit is that it makes separation almost like amputation. Yet in the vision of what ultimately can be and will be, and in the knowledge that there is yet to be some relationship in the spirit world, we can abide here in love and hope.

President Spencer W. Kimball, himself a great example in this matter, taught the Church much. Let me say that I once sat with him in a ticklish situation of marriage counseling. He drew two overlapping figures that were somewhat like circles, but the overlap in the center was a larger area than the two ends that didn't overlap. And his point was that differences—man, woman, husband, wife—maybe are no-man's-lands or no-woman's-lands. These he and Camilla just never entered and learned not to try to. We should acknowledge that. That's an individual problem. Perhaps it will be resolved eventually, but when you find out that there are some areas in which you just are not overlapping, then endure them.

For example, I know a man who insists on making pancakes on Saturday morning. Maybe his wife wants to suggest the proper bowl, and perhaps a little less flour, or some other idea that might improve the pancakes. He almost drives her out with a hatchet. "Now, now—this is mine!" So she has learned to just sleep a little longer and then come down and eat the pancakes. That's a non-overlap area.

On the other hand, in every marriage there are happy places where the two overlap, and those are to be cherished.

President Kimball enunciated three principles in this connection. One is *humor. Forgiveness* is next—a hard one. And he also talked a lot about coping and overcoming selfishness, about developing *unselfishness!* He said that giant strides could be made in most households if we would really cultivate these three qualities.

First, then, humor. It is one of the most powerful ways of stimulating thinking. Think of that. But that's not the reason why I am recommending it. I am recommending it as the oil that smooths the frictions of life, and especially in the home. I am not talking about the humor that portrays something sacred. We have been warned against that. If you laugh at sacred things, make light of them, you will lose the Spirit. I am talking about the humor that laughs at oneself, that acknowledges one's foibles and finds them funny instead of tragic.

One of the best examples I know is President Hugh B. Brown, to whom I was close in his last years. His dear wife was post-stroke paralyzed in those years and at the final stages could not even speak. They had a nurse in the home during the last year or so. One day in his late eighties, after taking a bath (his annual bath, he jested) President Brown climbed out and began to work on the ring around the tub. Suddenly he got a stitch in his back; he couldn't stand up. Problem: Should he call the nurse? He tried several things. Nothing worked. And then it occurred to him that if he crawled on his hands and knees, he could perhaps roll onto the bed. So he started crawling. As he did so, it became clear to him what he might look like from the point of view of a spectator. He started to laugh, and that made his back hurt more. Now, I suppose that you could tell that story and get people to weep if you left out the humor. They would see it as a tragic situation—that *poor old man*. But he handled it with humor.

He was sometimes delightfully clever even in those late years. On one occasion Elder Boyd K. Packer took him by the arm as he was struggling with those bad legs. "Brother Brown, can I be your cane?" He replied quickly, "Yes, if I am Abel."

He was walking down the aisle with an aged sister when she said, "Oh, President Brown, I have always wanted you to speak at my funeral." He responded, "Sister, if you want me to speak at your funeral, you'd better hurry."

Some might think: Wait a minute; can a person laugh about something as serious as death? Yes. There he was in bed (this really happened, his daughter told me the story); he had had a kind of stroke, and the doctor summoned the family, suggesting that he probably wouldn't make it through the night. So there they were gathered solemnly around his bed. But at about 5:00 A.M. he started to rally. He got better! Still better! Finally he opened an eye, only one, and he surveyed the situation. They saw a slight curl on his lip, and he said, "I fooled you, didn't I?"

What's wrong with that? Nothing, that is *joie de vivre,* and only one who has spirituality and vision can have that kind of sweet, self-deprecating humor.

Let me say to the men, instead of getting rigid and defensive when you've made a foolish mistake, laugh at yourself, acknowledge it. Your wife will agree with you. It's wholesome. It blows the pretenses away. It cleans out the carburetor in your life. You laugh with each other. I am not talking about pointing a finger at her and laughing at her. That's wrong. Don't do that in public or in private. But laugh at yourself.

We all catch ourselves in stupidities at times. They occur frequently in my house. My children all know that I am supposed to be able to put a lecture together, but nevertheless I make language mistakes. Sometimes I fluff a whole line—really mess it up. For instance, "The queen showed up with a twenty-one-sun galute and wore her gownless evening strap." So my daughter always says, "All right, Dad, get out of that one," and then I try. They know what's going on, and they laugh and then I laugh. And of course, that lubricates. Now, in our families we need more of it. Is that compatible with spirituality? It is, and maybe good, clean humor and true spirituality require each other.

Let me suggest an even closer example of this. I wish I knew it was true. It's an apocryphal story, I'm afraid, but I want it to be true. It goes as follows: A young man goes one day to see Elder Harold B. Lee when he is President of the Church. He walks in and solemnly announces: "I have had a revelation for the Church, and I am here to tell it to you so you will tell the Church. It is that the Church is mistaken in asking converts to wait a year before receiving the temple endowment. Now you know." How would you handle that if you were the President? In our story, President

358

Lee says: "I am not going to question your religious experience, but I have noticed something since you came in. You haven't smiled once. And anyone who takes himself that seriously is not likely to be receiving much revelation."

Think about it. It is the case that humor enables us to have a proper perspective and to acknowledge our finitudes and our failures and get past them. But being rigid and solemn and unyielding—that is the way to a dreary life and an early grave.

Elder LeGrand Richards was proof of what I am saying. The man's face was almost frozen in a smile before he was gone. What a delightful human being! Somebody asked him how he accounted for his longevity. (By the way, he attended the fiftieth wedding anniversary of his daughter. Figure that out. "Why don't we invite the folks over for our fiftieth wedding anniversary?") "Brother Richards, how have you managed to live so long?" He said, "I've never worried." Think of that. We all worry. Some people don't worry because they just don't know what's going on. Elder Richards didn't worry because he *did* know what was going on. Testimony, faith, insight, prophetic glimpses—he could cope, therefore, in ways that others couldn't, and he laughed at himself. Delightful! So cultivate humor; restore it to your home if it's been lost.

About forgiveness. A tough line from the Doctrine and Covenants talks about patiently bearing attacks from one's enemies (see D&C 98:23–24). You say: "Wait a minute, we're talking about the home. We don't have any enemies at home." Is that so? Sometimes our hardest struggles to eliminate friction are with the people we love or are trying to love. And though the revelation was given in the context of the brutal persecutions the Saints endured during the Missouri period, surely the spirit of it must carry over to all situations of potential hostility. Bear it patiently, the scripture says, even if the person who is hurting you hasn't shown the first sign of repentance. Now the exact language. Suppose you don't do that. Suppose you seek revenge for the hurt, even slightly in the tone of your voice or whatever? What then? The suffering you are going through "shall be accounted unto you

359

as being meted out as a just measure unto you." What? The wrongs this person has done to me for forty years are going to be accounted a just judgment unless I've borne it patiently? That's what it says. Think of it.

It isn't an easy thing to do, but the commandment of the scriptures is that we are to forgive everyone—even those who are still hurting us. The opposite of it is to keep a laundry list of grievances and in the high pitch of an argument to bring them all up in serial form. That is not Christlike. Further, the person who will suffer the most is the person who does not forgive (see D&C 64:9). That is a law. So forgive. The person may or may not deserve it. Forgive anyway. How? Well, the scriptures give us one clue. Jesus said, "Pray *for* your enemies" (3 Nephi 12:44). I have italicized the *for*. It's easy enough to pray against, as in "Lord, come down in judgment on this fiend and let there not be a grease spot left." That's not praying for. That's seeking vengeance. We must pray for, and the more we pray for, the more we find ourselves feeling forgiving. And then a special blessing comes to us. We accept that *we* are forgiven of the Lord. Otherwise, we cannot be. I submit that it is psychologically impossible to really believe that you are forgiven of the living God if you are still nurturing unforgiveness toward others. And that's what the Lord's Prayer says. I am going to put it negatively, so it will strike you. "Father, don't forgive me one inch more than I am willing to forgive others." That's what it says. Forgive us as we forgive others. If that's how much forgiveness we are going to receive, some of us are in trouble. As Joseph said, we haven't forgiven seventy times seven; perhaps we haven't even forgiven once (see Joseph Smith, *Teachings* [1976], 238).

Third point. President Kimball talks about selfishness. Selfishness? What is that? Well, partly because of our culture, partly because of human nature, we suppose that we are entitled to more than we're getting. That's the real bottom line for a Latter-day Saint. It isn't just that we are all frustrated—all of us are. Perhaps no one in this world receives enough love. But it isn't just that, it's that we feel in our heart of hearts that we are entitled to more, and that hurts. Promises of the scriptures are constantly before us: If you do this and this, then this will be the result. Perhaps it doesn't seem to be working for us. Instead of getting better, it is getting worse. So we say, "I'm entitled." President Kimball's point is that we have to learn there is meaning even in suffering; and we have to learn to care enough for blessedness that we postpone some kinds of happiness. But isn't blessedness happiness? Of a sort, yes, but we learn by the example of Jesus Christ that to bring about the happiness of others one must sometimes go through lots of unpleasant experiences. And we aspire to be Christlike. Well, is there a meaning in suffering?

A convert to the Church named Benjamin Crue was for a time at the City of Hope Hospital in Duarte, California, as the head of their chronic pain center. Fifteen different experts focused on one patient each time—psychiatrists, surgeons, neurologists, pharmacologists, even people whose training was in physiological psychology. Here were patients for whom no effort to reduce or remove pain had worked.

Benjamin Crue told me they learned something fundamental from their observations. They learned that when a person has chronic pain, unless he has at least one "significant other" in his life (a term used for someone about whom he cares and who cares about him), nothing we do really helps much with the pain. He told me this because of a sentence in my book that says love is the lasting therapy; a thing I believe, but had no evidence for. Now he gave me the evidence. He said that on the other hand, if there is such a person, even if it is only one—the person really cares about the sufferer and vice versa—then either he can cope with the pain or there can be substantial reduction in it. That's the power of love.

What is unbearable in life, I think, is the sense that what we are doing and suffering is meaningless—that there will be no adequate outcome from it, only more pain; that it all somehow is ended at death. But the gospel teaches us that, depending on us and our relationship with the Lord, even our worst struggles can be sanctifying, glorifying, and perfecting. It is a strange thing, is it not, that the same phenomenon—namely, pain—can have opposite effects, depending on one's attitudes and responses. For some it can lead to bitterness, the shriveling of the soul, hostility, and shaking the fist at God and all men; and to others it can lead to deeper love, deeper compassion, a more radiant exposure and expression, and eventually exaltation. Said Joseph Smith, "Men have to suffer that they may come upon Mount Zion and be exalted above the heavens" (*Teachings* [1976], 323). Now, you may say, "Didn't Jesus Christ suffer so we wouldn't have to?" Yes, certain kinds of suffering He tempered or removed, including the suffering for sin. But once we take upon us His name our problems aren't all over. They are only beginning, for we are counseled to lose ourselves. And that's not selfish.

The question is frequently asked, Is marriage for procreation only? Answers come from the prophets. Let me read three. Joseph F. Smith speaking: "The relationship of man and wife is not only the sole means of race perpetuation, but for the development of the higher faculties and nobler traits of human nature, which the love-inspired companionship of a man and a woman can alone insure" (*Improvement Era* 20:739). Elsewhere the same prophet: "Sexual union is lawful in wedlock, and if participated in with right intent is honorable and *sanctifying*" (*Gospel Doctrine*, 309). Parley P. Pratt: "The union of the sexes is . . . also for mutual affection and cultivation of those eternal principles of never-ending charity and benevolence which are inspired by the Eternal Spirit; also for mutual comfort and assistance in this world of toil and sorrow and for mutual duties toward their offspring" (*Science of Theology*, 105). The Doctrine and Covenants says of such a marriage as we are here describing, "It shall be visited with blessings and not cursings, and with my power, saith the Lord, and shall be without condemnation on earth and in heaven" (D&C 132:48). What a glorious truth! The giving of love by each partner in a marriage can itself be sanctifying to both the giver and the receiver. And what a glorious principle it is that ultimately we will be capacitated to give in fullness and receive in fullness!

That leads me to another glimpse beyond. The season of the dedication of the Kirtland Temple saw a great outpouring of the

Spirit. In a Thursday fast meeting a man and a woman, apparently not husband and wife, stood up spontaneously, sang together a song in tongues, and then sat down; a song that they had never heard before so far as they knew, and words they did not fully understand. An interpretation was given by the gift of the Spirit. (See Tullidge, *Women,* 208–9.) Think just for a moment of such a harmony of soul that two people who did not know each other until that situation, at least not in any depth, are literally transformed and are symphonically one. What a glimpse of possibilities!

Now, a few things about how love can find a way.

I had an uncle who had Parkinson's disease—he was in constant motion. His wife had arthritis and insomnia. When they climbed in bed at night he put his hand under her neck—a perfect vibrator—and slowly she relaxed and went to sleep. Then he pulled his hand over, and he went to sleep and the jiggle stopped. Love finds a way.

Many years ago President David O. McKay was being wheeled by President Tanner from his room in the hotel around to the elevators. When they reached the elevators he said, "Oh, I'm sorry, we must go back." President Tanner asked no questions and immediately pushed him back. What was the problem? He hadn't kissed Emma Ray good-bye. He was then ninety-three. Still some sizzle at ninety-three. Love finds a way.

Two other examples. In a ward I was in was a woman who had two children. Both were boys, and after age two both developed a rare disease in which every life process somehow reverses. I was asked to give a blessing to the second child, who had by that time lived to be twenty-one but was nothing but skin and bones—not even enough muscle left for lungs—and he shortly died. Because of the care her sons needed she hardly left that house, or even that room, for twenty-one years; and yet she and her husband were the most exciting youth leaders in the stake, had the most radiant kinds of personality, and were full of fun and games as well as wisdom. Love finds a way.

Years ago Elder Charles A. Callis went down to the southern states to organize the first stake there. With him was Elder Harold B.

Lee, who also was a member of the Twelve. Elder Callis said of the first location that he could stay in a motel but would prefer to go back to a little old chapel-home where he and his wife had been accustomed to stay. This was one of those inseparable links after some fifty years, his wife having died. So he slept there while Brother Lee slept in a motel. The next day they came together. Traveling in a car, they had stopped and were waiting for a traffic light to change when Elder Callis turned and said, "Brother Lee, last night my wife came to me" and his head went down and he was gone from this life. Brother Lee organized the stake; then he gathered together Brother Callis's personal effects. And as he was walking out of that chapel-home he heard Brother Callis's voice say, "Well done, my boy." I heard Brother Lee say that the power of such love is what the gospel is all about. And he shook my lapels once when I was an aspiring young bishop, and said, "Brother Madsen, the most important work the Lord has given you to do is in the walls of your own home, and don't you forget it."

I recall a meeting at which Elder A. Theodore Tuttle was presiding. It was a big meeting—regional meeting, conference, priesthood meeting, I don't remember which. At about five minutes to nine, Elder Tuttle said: "Brethren, let's have closing prayer and adjourn. There are other things to consider, but let's adjourn, because one of you may have a date with your wife to go out and get a malt, and nothing we can do here is more important than that." The gospel teaches that the Church is the instrument to the glorification of the family, not the other way around. And we all need to keep that in mind.

It is a deep conviction of mine that the vision of eternal family life that has been revealed through the Prophet Joseph Smith is true. When President Kimball gave an address in which he talked about how difficult marriage is—he spoke for sixty minutes on how tough the drudgery and the diapers and the rest can be—he tried to alert those young people who were thinking in terms of "butterfly wings and honey" that once you get the woman off the pedestal and on the budget, reality sets in. He warned them they were wrong if they expected that just the initial *flash* of romance and love would somehow perpetuate their marriage for the rest of their lives. No, they were going to have to go and get more and more of love, and then bring it home. And where do you get that? In the temple, for one place, and by serving each other and receiving the Spirit; the more you increase in the Spirit, the more you increase your power to love and be loved. Nevertheless, having talked mainly in warning terms, even negative ones, about the realities, he uttered this sublime, positive sentence: "Marriage can be more an exultant ecstasy than the human mind can conceive" (*BYU Speeches of the Year,* 1976, 146).

Ecstasy is a strong word. I suspect most of us, in this world, only taste it, but that is the word. The Lord promises us a fulness of the glory of the Father, which is equivalent to the fulness of joy, and that is worth giving everything for.

I have already mentioned that remarkable man Brother LeGrand Richards. I wrote him because I didn't believe the story. (It was subsequently published in his biography.) I now have a letter which I will preserve to the end of my days. It tells of his proposal to Ina, made after his first mission. He was walking along with her, and everything was well between them, when he said, "Ina, there is someone who will always come before you." She gasped. She cried out, and she ran. She bolted, as women do to cover the tears. When LeGrand caught up with her, he stopped her and said: "Wait, wait, you don't understand. On my mission there were times when the Lord was so close that I felt I could almost reach out and touch Him. He has to be the foundation of our lives; but, Ina, if you want to be second, I want to marry you." Now, I ask my female readers, is that an ideal proposal? Is that a highly romantic way to go about proposing to a girl? A girl said to me once, "I want a boy to say to me some day 'I love you so much I would go to *hell* for you.' " I couldn't resist saying, 'What about going to heaven?' "

The truth is that love should be triangular. If both partners, husband and wife, are really committed to the Lord Jesus Christ, then the love across the bottom of that triangle will flow powerfully. If either one of them or both is not, there will be problems. That's why the temple marriage is so different from eloping to Reno. The temple requires that you first make unconditional covenants with Christ, and then you can be trusted to kneel down and make unconditional covenants with each other. That is not required in Reno. Sometimes young people ask why, really what difference does it make? So much stress on going to that one building; why can't we go somewhere else? (By the way, President Lee taught that if you do have to go somewhere else, the second most sacred place on earth is . . . what? You don't go to the chapel or the reception center; you go to the home. That's the second most sacred place.)

Now, what I have testified over and over to young people is this: that it isn't *just* that when you go to the house of the Lord for your wedding certain things are said about forever; that's important, all-important, but that's talking about the *quantity* of the relationship. If it isn't of sufficient *quality,* however, there won't be that quantity. The temple ceremony is designed to give you the keys and powers of the transforming quality of love that will make that love worth perpetuating forever. You may say, "Just going through a ceremony surely doesn't do that." It does. I am troubled with people who disparage ceremony. The ceremony in this case is a channel, and all that precedes it—the whole temple ceremony, Elder Eldred G. Smith has said—is a temple *wedding* ceremony. Everything that precedes it and up through it is there to give to you divine powers, or at least to bestow them in the embryonic stage. And yes, returning and returning to the temple increases and increases those powers and one's understanding and perception of them. To deny these things is like saying you don't think that just taking an ordinary man and putting your hands on his head and saying a few words is going to make any difference in his life. The answer is, it does. There is a tangible mantle that goes with ordination and receiving the Holy Ghost and being called to positions of responsibility, and there is a tangible power from the Almighty God that is supposed to come to us through His temples to powerfully enrich our marriages. If you lack this conviction or feel that it has diminished, then I plead with you to do the things that

366

will restore it and increase it. And if you say, "I don't love him or her anymore," then do the things that will cultivate love. They are clearly set out in the gospel of Jesus Christ.

The Lord who lives and loves is a Father and is not companionless. And His concern, His work and His glory, is that we should share in the fulness of eternal life that He enjoys.

Chapter Seven

ELIJAH AND THE TURNING OF HEARTS

There is something in the scriptures about an offering to be offered up one day by some specific persons, namely the sons of Levi. Puzzlement. Who are they? What is the offering?

In early 1847 Brigham Young was ill at a place called Winter Quarters. He had been prayerful and his feelings were mixed. He still was deeply grieved at the loss of his closest earthly friend, Joseph Smith, and was burdened heavily with the kingdom and its leadership. He was puzzled over the question of adoption. Some of the Saints whose own literal forebears showed a lack of interest or even deep hostility regarding the Church wished they could be grafted into a faithful family. Some such ordinances were performed. Now Brother Brigham was praying about it.

He had a dream in which he saw the Prophet Joseph Smith. Some beautiful passages demonstrate that Brother Brigham wanted to join the Prophet. If you think that wasn't sincere and lasting, you should know that his last words on earth, thirty years later, would be one word three times repeated—"Joseph, Joseph, Joseph."

After this 1847 interchange and the assurance the Prophet there gave him that he must live on, Brigham inquired about adoption and the Prophet replied. In the account there are seven different ways in which he says, "Tell the people to get and keep the Spirit of the Lord."

There is a marvelous statement about how we know the spirit received is the Spirit of the Lord, for Joseph says at one point, "They can tell the Spirit of the Lord from all other spirits; it will whisper peace and joy to their souls; it will take malice, hatred, strife and all evil from their hearts; and their whole desire will be to do good, bring forth righteousness and build up the kingdom of God." Then the interesting conclusion: "Be sure to tell the people to keep the Spirit of the Lord; and if they will they will find themselves just as they were organized by our Father in Heaven before they came into the world. Our Father in Heaven organized the human family [in the premortal councils], but they are all disorganized and in great confusion" (Young, *Manuscript History,* 23 February 1847). So much for Brigham Young's glimpse of the crucial nature of the Spirit in finding ourselves united in a family relationship.

But now to the scriptures for a moment. It could be said that the earliest and latest revelations in the Doctrine and Covenants touch on this theme, the first being section two (which was actually given before section one). That is the revelation or statement of Moroni to the Prophet Joseph Smith in 1823. It says that Elijah will be sent. And what for? To "plant in the hearts of the children the promises made to the fathers, and the hearts of the children shall turn to their fathers" (Joseph Smith—History 1:39). Elijah will be among those who participate in the most glorious family reunion in all history. It could be called a sacramental wedding breakfast to be held following the Lord's second coming. (See D&C 27:5–14.)

Elijah did come. He came to the Kirtland Temple on April 3, 1836 (see D&C 110:13–16). Jewish literature is replete with the promise and expectation of Elijah's coming. That is the last promise of the Old Testament, in the last verses of Malachi. And it is Jewish tradition that on the second night of Passover they must leave open the door and place at the table head an empty chair and a goblet full of wine in the expectation that Elijah may come. It is interesting, especially in light of that Jewish tradition, that April 3, 1836, was the second day of Passover. The symbolism is beautiful. Elijah comes, as they expect, to a home. He comes to a goblet of wine—the sacramental wine. He comes to turn hearts, which is more than changing minds—he turns hearts to hearts. He somehow bridges some gap, some alienation, some separation that has occurred in the human family.

No subject preoccupied the Prophet Joseph Smith more than this one. In his later years he spoke at least eight times pleading with the Saints to ponder and pray over this principle. We ordinarily say that Elijah did something pertaining to the dead or work for the dead. A half truth. In the first place, no one is really dead. Those who are in the spirit world are, as we are taught by the prophets, more alive than some of us here. Elder Melvin J. Ballard used to say that they have "every feeling intensified" spiritually. And as for their being dead and gone, no, they are not gone either. The prophets teach us that the spirit world is not in some remote galaxy; it is here, it is near. And as the Prophet put it, speaking of their feelings for us, those who are bound to us somehow by the anxieties of their forebearing, "their bowels yearn over us" (Joseph Smith, *Teachings* [1976], 159). He said they "are not idle spectators" in the last days (Joseph Smith, *Teachings* [1976], 232). He explained, "Enveloped in flaming fire, they are not far from us, and know and understand our thoughts, feelings, and motions [one account says emotions], and are often pained therewith" (Joseph Smith, *Teachings* [1976], 326). And he could have added, "rejoiced therewith." When the scriptures say, "All eternity is pained," that is, I take it, a metaphor for the pain of these spirits. Similarly when they say, "the heavens weep for joy."

So Elijah does have something to do with them. But the Prophet taught that he also has something to do with us, with the living. Had he not come, the whole earth would be cursed; or in another version, the earth would be utterly wasted at Christ's coming. Wasted, I take it, means at least two things. It would be in a sense a waste if this earth, created by our Father and His Son as the dwelling place of their family, turned out to be a house barren. Not a home. Not a place of genuine familial love. In that sense it would have been a waste to create it. But second, were there not a family welded and united and full of love for Christ, it would be the case that all mankind, unable to endure His presence, would be laid waste at His coming. Thank God for the restoration of the power to prepare such a family. That conferral came through Elijah.

The Prophet said, speaking of this, "How shall God come to the rescue of this generation?" And he answered, "He will send Elijah" (Joseph Smith, *Teachings* [1976], 323).

Well, that generation may have been a difficult one, but this generation in which you and I live is in some ways a worse one. Constantly students ask me around the country, "Do you think the world is getting better or worse?" And I always answer, "Yes." The wheat is getting "wheatier" and the tares are getting "tarier"—and rapidly.

How can a mere prophet change a whole generation, and an ancient prophet at that? Well, we can know a few things about him. Know that his name is interesting—El-i-yah: literally, in Hebrew, "My God is Jehovah." But more than that, it symbolizes the sealing or the union of father and son. Know that he conferred keys, and we understand, if only dimly, that means authority— priesthood authority. There are men on the earth today who hold those keys by direct line of ordination. Every marriage in this Church that is binding both here and hereafter has been performed under those keys and their delegated authorities. Second, Elijah had a revelatory function. There is a spirit that is somehow emanating through him and his work and ministry which has reached out far beyond the bounds of this Church, turning hearts and not just heads. And one account says that it was his function to reveal to us "the covenants of the fathers in relation to the children, and

the covenants of the children in relation to the fathers"—perhaps
pointing to something that happened prior to mortality. Elijah is
also an exemplar of what is his mission, for it is not yet over. As a
translated being, one not yet subject to death, he had the unique
privilege of ministering to the Master and the three Apostles on
the Mount of Transfiguration (see Matthew 17:1–8) in an experience which we are told we cannot yet fully understand, the fulness of the account having been reserved for the future. A Jewish
apocalyptic tradition says that those two prophets who are to one
day testify in the streets of Jerusalem to prepare the hearts of the
Jews to be turned to the prophets (see D&C 98:16–17), and are
then to literally be killed and lie in the streets—martyrs just prior
to the coming of the Messiah—are Elijah and Enoch. Elijah has
been patient through millennia awaiting the opportunity to bring
earth and heaven back together, to tie together the old and new
worlds, to take the estranged and the alienated and the embittered
and somehow transform their hearts, and to prepare all of the
family who will to be family, welding them indissolubly in order
to greet the Christ.

Let us draw a few personal and emotional implications from
this. Feeling, after all, centers in the heart, and the role here is not
one of mere intellect. It is a matter of feeling something inside. The
Prophet said on one occasion to the Relief Society that he grieved
that they were not exhibiting greater union of feeling among them.
And he went on to say, "By union of feeling we obtain power with
God" (Joseph Smith, *History of the Church* 5:23). When he introduced the ordinance of the washing of feet in Kirtland among the
brethren, he taught them that this ordinance—an essential one—
was to enhance the union of feeling and affection among them, that
their faith might be strong (see Joseph Smith, *History of the
Church* 2:309). And repeatedly the Lord has said in modern revelation that He reveals himself by His Spirit to the mind and the
heart. "Behold, I will tell you in your mind and in your heart by
the Holy Ghost which shall come upon you and which shall dwell
in your heart" (D&C 8:2), an impressive blending of intellect and
sentiment.

Now, we need not dwell on the point that in our culture the family is coming unglued. There are those who hold that the great wave of the future, a better future as they see it, is to totally abandon the notion of united families—and they recommend it. One can call attention to devastating statistics outside the Church, but I want to talk strictly about inside it. One of our statistics, and I am only approximating, is that there are well over 600,000 children in this Church who are being raised by a single parent. There are delinquent fathers. There are delinquent children. Just from conversation in my own office over the years on the BYU campus I have heard sentences that tell it all. For example, "My mother gave me five hundred dollars and told me to go away." Or: "I couldn't possibly tell my father. He would kill me." Or again, "My mother has been divorced three times." Or again, "No one in my family cares anything for the Church." Or again, "Just before I left for my mission my father threatened to take my life." Or again, "I don't dare go home."

Robert Frost saw it clearly on the home. He said, "Home is where, when you get there, they have to take you in." Would that it were so. Many who are joining the Church in this generation are doing so at the cost of never being permitted through that door of home again. My own great-grandfather wrote a letter from Nauvoo. He was a squire—a kind of amateur attorney—who had loved the Mormon people but had never joined them. And his motivation was elementary: he had a wife and a son, and both of them said that if he ever did, that would be the end; they would never speak to him again. The letter to Brigham Young says, "Is this what the Lord requires of me?" And Brigham Young's answer, in a word, was "yes." My great-grandfather joined the Church, and his wife and his son kept their word.

Yes, we are in a real world. And the alienation, the pain, the hostility, the torment, the trauma, even in some Latter-day Saint homes, is a long distance from Elijah, who said he would turn hearts toward and not away. Is there hope? There is.

Let's discuss now not what one needs to do but what one needs to feel. First there is forgiveness. We are glib, I think, in quoting the passages that talk about our needing to forgive, and even to forgive all people. They are there. One of the strongest passages is in the context of the Prophet Joseph and his own weaknesses, his pleading with his brethren to forgive him, pleading as the revelation does; and then going on to say that if they don't, there remaineth in them the greater sin (see D&C 64:9). Strong language, saying that one's refusal to forgive a sinner is a worse sin than whatever sin the sinner has committed. Well, forgiveness is the very nature of Christ's way. I suggest that it may be difficult to forgive your enemies, but it is even more so to forgive your loved ones who have sometimes manifested hate—and you have too, in response. It is harder to forgive your loved ones because you care about them and you have to go on living with them, or struggling to, and they can go on hurting you over the years and the decades. But our hearts will never turn to our fathers in the way this spirit of which we have been testifying motivates us to do unless we forgive.

You see, we have inherited all kinds of things. There is a standard procedure for students with bad report cards. They can go home and say: "Look, Mom," or "Look, Dad." "Which do you think it is, heredity or environment?" And their parents can say, "Neither of the above." The fact is that we willingly chose to come into the world, likely in this time and circumstance. And when a young person says to his parents in deepest animosity, "I didn't ask to be born," if they give the proper, prophetic answer they will say: "Oh yes, you did. You not only asked for it, you prepared for it, trained for it, were reserved for it." I am saying that both he and they are mutually involved.

And by the way, that's a snarl word in our generation. *Involved.* No one wants to get involved, in anything. Do your own thing. Be yourself. But you and I and all of us are involved. It was collusion. And therefore, as you look back at the seventy or so forebears— and that's what it would take at fifty years each, only seventy to get you back to Abraham—you might recognize that you have inherited the blood of generations. And *blood* may be not a correct word scientifically, but it stands in the scriptures for *seed,* which is

374

specifically the heredity, the inheritance of tendencies, and all of us have them. And so you have the blood of this generation, from which we must become clean—"clean from the blood of this generation" (D&C 88:85). If you are, you will be clean from the blood of every generation, because it is compounded and accumulated into now. And that includes the blood of some degeneration.

So perhaps you do have problems that you can blame on ancestors, and if you forgive that and choose to stand close to the Lord in the process of purifying your life, that will affect your whole family in both directions. You are not alone. There is no way you can regain solitary and neutral ground. You are in it—in involvement. And this, I take it, is one of the profound meanings of that long, laborious allegory in the book of Jacob, the allegory of the tame and wild olive trees. If you take a wild branch and graft it in to a tame one, if the branch is strong enough it will eventually corrupt and spoil the tree all the way to the roots. But if you take a tame branch and graft it in to a wild tree, in due time, if that branch is strong enough, it will heal and regenerate to the very roots. You will then have been an instrument in the sanctification even of your forebears.

Do these considerations ever sober us in moments when we suppose either that no one cares for us or that whether they care or not, our life makes no difference? To be that kind of branch and achieve that kind of transformation backward and forward is perhaps the greatest achievement of this world. But to do it one must be great, one must be linked, bound to the Lord Jesus Christ. One must be mighty. One must be something of a savior. And that is exactly what the Prophet Joseph Smith said we are—"saviors on Mount Zion" (Joseph Smith, *Teachings* [1976], 330). And how are we to be saviors on Mount Zion? he asked once in a discourse. He answered by saying that we do so by (first building then) going into the temples of the Lord, and in our own first person presence, going through all the temple ordinances for and in behalf of loved ones who have passed on. This can "redeem them that they . . . may be exalted to thrones of glory." And it will help "fulfill the

375

mission of Elijah" (Joseph Smith, *Teachings* [1976], 330). Yes, saviors, redeemers of our families.

We have many examples in our history. I chose this one not because it is exceptional but because it isn't. Erastus Snow, given a blessing by the Prophet Joseph Smith, was told in effect: "Brother Erastus, your father knows nothing of the gospel of Jesus Christ, but the Lord God will be your Father and He will watch over you. And if you will walk in the full path of righteousness, the time will come when you will save all of your kindred flesh; and in due time, if you are worthy, these blessings which I pronounce upon you will be confirmed upon you by your own father. And then your joy will be full."

The capacity to forgive comes only through the capacity for loving the Lord Jesus Christ. And He taught us how. He said, "Pray for your enemies." That's different, I remind you, than praying against your enemies. If you want to know how you can turn feelings of hostility into feelings of forgiveness and love, that's the how. You pray for them. You may choke in the effort, but as you keep going, the time comes when you mean it. And then you not only mean that you want to forgive, and feel it, but you even find yourself praying that He will forgive. And you look with compassion instead of spite at the whole traditional mix that has made you what you are and to some degree what you aren't. So much for forgiveness.

Now, the other is even harder. The word is *sacrifice*. And we know that the family of man was taught from Adam down to make external sacrifice with the firstlings, the firstborn. These were consumed, burned on an altar, all to typify and prepare for the coming of the living sacrifice, who was Christ himself. We now know that when the Lord appeared to the Nephites He said, in substance: "No longer will I accept burnt offerings. From now on I will accept only your hearts. You must bring to me the sacrifice of a broken heart and a contrite spirit." (See 3 Nephi 9:19–20.) We use the term "broken heart" to mean radically frustrated in a romance. That meaning is accepted, but in the scriptural usage a broken heart is a malleable, meltable, moveable heart, and a contrite spirit is an honest, acknowledging spirit that says, "I am, in fact, dependent on what I am in fact dependent on." There is not self-deprecation here, only honesty: "I need help." And when that is acknowledged, help comes.

I suggest that one sacrifice the sons of Levi and the daughters of Levi are to offer in the end is the willingness to give themselves in the cause of saviorhood and to care more about family and the preservation and intensification of family than they care about anything else in this world. That has costs. Some things have to be given up. Some things have to be postponed. And the focus is sacrifice. I have to say honestly, I believe it is painful. I have to say I believe that there are many among us who are easily pulled in other directions. And I have to say I consider that a tragedy. I occasionally hear housewives say that they are "mere house-wives." What have you done in the last twenty years? Oh, nothing—just fed my family three meals a day and more or less kept them together. Is that all? President Lorenzo Snow said with power on one occasion that if a woman raised a righteous family she would be exalted in the celestial kingdom (cited by Leroy C. Snow in a Snow family reunion program). Our generation is making attractive every other thing but. That is not the gospel of Jesus Christ.

So I plead with you, be forgiving and be sacrificial.

Flying in from the Far East some time ago, I found on the plane a young man obviously recognizable as a Mormon Elder. We chatted. I didn't at first tell him who I was or that I really already did think the Mormon church was great. But I soon learned that there were three things a little unusual about him. First, his father had died while he was on his mission. When I was myself a mission president, I prayed every night and every morning for two things. One, that I would not have to send any missionary—male or female—home in disgrace. And two, that I would not have to send an Elder or a Sister home dead. In a way that's an unfair prayer, because I suspect that, with tens of thousands of young people out in the real world, in the long run there is no way to avoid some lapsings. But I so prayed. I had not foreseen another difficulty, and

377

that was to have to call in a missionary and tell him that one or the other of his parents—or in one case both—were gone.

Well, this Elder on the plane had lost his father. His father had not been particularly faithful in the Church. His mother had taken up the burden, and of course, as required, had sent the monthly check. The second thing was that he had let his mother know he was coming home, but he hadn't told her when. And the third thing was that he hoped to go to BYU. As I got off the plane, and I was first off, I saw a face and something told me that this was his mother. I restrained myself from telling her that her son was on the plane. I went to a position where I could see both her face and his. He got off and walked along a bit casually, carrying cameras and briefcase. And then he saw her. There was recognition, gratitude, forgiveness for whatever may have been amiss in the past, and a total royal embrace. That's it. That's everything.

It is precisely that kind of embrace and reunion which you and I were sent into the world to make possible with loved ones in a future existence. It will not be possible except we are repentant and have faith in the Lord Jesus Christ sufficient to enable us to forgive and to sacrifice. That is our mission and our commission.

Occasionally when I have been in Jerusalem I have tried to picture in my weakness what He promises us will happen there one day. Mount Olivet, or the Mount of Olives, is the place from which He ascended. It is the place of His greatest suffering. It is the place where there was a garden, *Gat shemen;* in Hebrew, Garden of Oil Press, where, as it were, He trod the olive press to produce the oil of healing, the balm, the peace. That place today, if you study it carefully, is a place of everything except reunion. It is a place of destruction. Graves are everywhere. Shattered things are everywhere. Barbed wire, glass, the droppings of animals, everything you can name. And hostility and bitterness is symbolized on that very mount in the fact that different faiths, each with its own claim, build churches, build basilicas, and then each refuses to acknowledge the existence of the other. There are machine gun remnants. There is a monument to a place where paratroopers in the Six-Day War were gunned down by the dozens. War is what is symbolized there.

Yet the promise of the Lord Jesus Christ is that He will descend to that mount (see D&C 45:48). His foot will touch it. It will then cleave in twain, and there will be an earthquake. Dramatic, but true—an earthquake covering the whole earth. And there will be a transformation of the earth, preparing it for its terrestrial condition. As He descends with His worthy hosts, the privilege will also be given to those who remain here to be caught up together to meet Him. We will not have to simply remain and wait, but as in every genuine effect of true love, we will want to take our own steps toward the full embrace.

Thus it is our privilege and calling to become in our own limited way redemptors of the human family, ours and His. It is impossible to love Him truly and not love what is His; and God assigned Him all of us. And it is not possible for us to really love ourselves unless we love what is truly us, and that is the whole house of Israel in which we belong. As we learn to do this and accordingly act as saviors, we will be helping to fulfill the great mission of Elijah.

BIBLIOGRAPHY

Aiken, Henry D. *Reason and Conduct.* New York: Alfred A. Knopf, 1962.

Alder, Alfred. *The Practice and Theory of Individual Psychology.* London: Routledge, 1955.

Alston, William P. and George Nakhnikian, eds. *Readings in Twentieth Century Philosophy.* New York: Free Press of Glencoe, 1963.

Andrus, Hyrum L., and Helen Mae Andrus, comp. *They Knew the Prophet.* Salt Lake City: Bookcraft, 1974.

Appleton, Robert. *Catholic Encyclopedia.* New York: Robert Appleton Company, 1908.

Barrett, William. *Irrational Man.* Garden City, N.Y.: Doubleday, 1958.

Basic Writings of St. Augustine. New York: Random House, 1948.

Bergson, Henri. *The Two Sources of Morality and Religion.* Trans. R. Ashley Audra and Cloudeley Brereton. New York: Holt and Company, 1935.

Bitton, Davis. *Guide to Mormon Diaries and Autobiographies.* Provo, Utah: Brigham Young University Press, 1977.

Blakney, Raymond B., trans. *Meister Eckhart.* New York: Harper Torchbook, 1957.

Blanshard, Brand. "The Case for Determinism." In *Determinism and*

Freedom in the Age of Modern Science. Ed. Sidney Hook. New York: Collier Books, 1961.

Bohme, Jakob. *Personal Christianity.* New York: Ungar, 1957.

Bokser, Ben Zion. *The Legacy of Maimonides.* New York: Philosophical Library, 1950.

Brightman, Edgar Sheffield. *A Philosophy of Religion.* New York: Prentice-Hall, 1940.

Buber, Martin. *I and Thou.* Trans. R. G. Smith. New York: Scribner, 1958.

Bultmann, Rudolph. *Kerygma and Myth.* Ed. H. W. Bartschr. London: S.P.C.K., 1953.

BYU Devotional Speeches of the Year. 1976.

Calvin, Jean. *Calvin: Theological Treatises.* Philadelphia: Westminster Press, 1954.

Castell, Alburey. *An Introduction to Modern Philosophy.* New York: Macmillan, 1943.

Chardin, Tielhard. *The Phenomenon of Man.* New York: Harper Torch, 1959.

Clark, James M. *The Great German Mystics.* Oxford: Blackwell, 1949.

Collins, James. *The Existentialists.* Chicago: Regnery, 1959.

Cowley, Matthias. *Wilford Woodruff.* Salt Lake City: Deseret News Press, 1909.

D'Arcy, M. C. Introduction. *St. John of the Cross, Poems.* Baltimore: Penguin Classics, 1960.

Davidson, Robert F., ed. *The Search for Meaning in Life.* New York: Holt, 1962.

Desan, Wilfrid. *The Tragic Finale.* Cambridge: Harvard University Press, 1954.

Dillenberger, John and Claude Welch, eds. *Protestant Christianity.* New York: Scribner, 1954.

Durham, G. Homer, ed. *Discourses of Wilford Woodruff.* Salt Lake City: Bookcraft, 1969.

Eddington, Arthur S. *The Nature of the Physical World.* Cambridge: Cambridge University Press, 1953.

Ehat, Andrew F. and Lyndon W. Cook, eds. *The Words of Joseph Smith.*

Provo, Utah: Brigham Young University Religious Studies Center, 1980.

Eliade, Mircea. *The Sacred and the Profane.* New York: Harper and Row, 1961.

Emmet, Dorothy. *The Nature of Metaphysical Thinking.* London: Macmillan, 1949.

Feuerbach, Ludwig. *The Essence of Christianity.* Trans. George Elliot. New York: Harper, 1957.

Flew, Anthony and Alasdair MacIntyre, eds. *New Essays in Philosophical Theology.* New York: Macmillan, 1955.

"Flowers." *Juvenile Instructor* 27 (15 January 1892): 41–43.

Frankl, Viktor E. *Man's Search for Meaning.* New York: Washington Square Press, 1963.

Freud, Sigmund. *The Future of an Illusion.* [New York]: Liveright, 1953.

Fromm, Erich. *Marx's Concept of Man.* New York: Ungar, 1961.

Gates, Susa Young. Recollection. In *History of the Young Ladies Mutual Improvement Association of The Church of Jesus Christ of Latter-day Saints.* Salt Lake City: Deseret News Press, 1911.

Geertz, Clifford. "Religion as a Cultural System." In *Anthropological Approaches to the Study of Religion.* Ed. Michael Banton. Conference on New Approaches to Social Anthropology. New York: F.A. Praeger, 1966.

Ghandi, Mahatma. *Ghandi's Autobiography.* Washington: Public Affairs Press, 1960.

Gilson, Étienne. *Elements of Christian Philosophy.* Garden City, N.Y.: Doubleday, 1963.

Grant, Heber J. *Gospel Standards.* Comp. G. Homer Durham. Salt Lake City: Improvement Era, 1941.

Grattan, C. Hartley. *The Three Jameses.* London: Longmans, Green and Co., 1932.

Guthrie, W. K. C. *History of Greek Philosophy.* Vol. 1. Cambridge University Press, 1962.

Happold, F. C. "Coinherence of Spirit and Matter." In *Mysticism.* Baltimore: Pelican Books, 1963.

383

Hepburn, Ronald W. *Christianity and Paradox.* London: Watts and Company, 1957.

Holy Scriptures, The. Containing the Old and New Testaments. An Inspired Revision of the Authorized Version, by Joseph Smith Jr. A new corrected edition. Published by the Reorganized Church of Jesus Christ of Latter Day Saints. Independence, Missouri: Herald Publishing House, 1944 and subsequent printings.

Hook, Sidney, ed. *Religious Experience and Truth.* New York: New York University Press, 1961.

Hospers, John and Wilfred Sellars, eds. *Readings in Ethical Theory.* New York: Appleton, 1952.

"How He Became a Mormon: from Lorenzo Snow's Journal." *Juvenile Instructor* 22 (15 January 1887): 22.

Huntington, Oliver B. Diary, 1843–1932. The Church of Jesus Christ of Latter-day Saints Historical Department.

Huxley, Julian. *Religion without Revelation.* New York: Mentor Books, 1964.

James, William. *Principles of Psychology.* Vol. 1. New York: Holt and Company, 1890.

Jenson, Andrew. *Latter-day Saint Biographical Encyclopedia.* Salt Lake City: Andrew Jenson History Co., 1901.

Jessee, Dean C., ed. *The Personal Writings of Joseph Smith.* Salt Lake City: Deseret Book, 1984.

Johnson, Benjamin F. to George Gibbs. Letter. The Church of Jesus Christ of Latter-day Saints Historical Department.

Jones, Rufus. *A Call to What Is Vital.* New York: Macmillan, 1948.

Journal of Discourses. Liverpool: F. D. Richards, 1856.

Jung, Carl B. *Modern Man in Search of a Soul.* New York: Harcourt Brace, 1934.

———. *The Undiscovered Self.* New York: Mentor, 1964.

Kegley, Charles W. and Robert W. Bretall, eds. *Reinhold Niebuhr.* New York: Macmillan, 1956.

Lamont, Corliss. *Humanism as a Philosophy.* New York: Philosophical Library, 1949.

———. *The Illusion of Immortality.* New York: G. P. Putnam and Sons, 1935.

Laub, George. Journal, 1845–1857. Provo, UT: Brigham Young
University, 1938.

Lee, Harold B. *Youth and the Church.* Salt Lake City: Deseret Book,
1953.

Leibnitz, G. W. *Theodicy.* London: Routledge & Kegan Paul, 1951.

Lewis, C. S. *The Problem of Pain.* New York: Macmillan, 1962.

———. *The Weight of Glory.* Grand Rapids, Mich.: William B.
Eerdmans Publishing, 1949.

Lundwall, N. B., comp. *Temples of the Most High.* Salt Lake City:
Bookcraft, 1966.

———. *The Vision.* Salt Lake City: Bookcraft, n.d.

Macquarrie, John. *Twentieth Century Religious Thought.* New York:
Harper and Row, 1963.

Madsen, Truman G. "The Contribution of Existentialism." *Brigham
Young University Studies* 1 (winter 1959): 9–20.

———. *Fables on Foibles, For This Time of Your Life.* Amherst, Mass.:
New England Youth Conference, The Church of Jesus Christ of
Latter-day Saints, August 1964.

———. *Joseph Smith the Prophet.* Salt Lake City: Bookcraft, 1989.

———. "Whence Cometh Man?" *The Instructor* 98 (June 1963):
204–6, 208.

Marcel, Gabriel. *The Philosophy of Existentialism.* New York: Citadel
Press, 1962.

McConkie, Bruce R. *Mormon Doctrine,* 2nd ed. Salt Lake City:
Bookcraft, 1966.

McKay, Llewelyn R. *Home Memories.* Salt Lake City: Deseret Book,
1956.

Menninger, Karl and Seward Hiltner, eds. *Constructive Aspects of
Anxiety.* New York: Abingdon Press, 1963.

Montague, William Peperell. *Belief Unbound.* New Haven: Yale
University Press, 1930.

Morgenbesser, Sidney and James Walsh, eds. *Free Will.* Englewood
Cliffs, N. J.: Prentice-Hall, 1962.

Nietzsche, Friedrich Wilhelm. *Basic Writings of Nietzsche.* Ed. Walter
Kaufmann. New York: Modern Library, 1968.

Otto, Rudolph. *Idea of the Holy.* London: Oxford University Press, 1923.

Pegis, Anton C., ed. *Introduction to Saint Thomas Aquinas.* New York: Modern Library, 1948.

Pratt, Parley P. *Autobiography of Parley P. Pratt,* 3rd. ed. Salt Lake City: Deseret Book, 1938.

———. *Key to the Science of Theology,* 7th ed. Salt Lake City: Deseret News Press, 1915. Deseret Book, 1978.

"Recollections of the Prophet Joseph Smith." *The Juvenile Instructor* 27 (15 March 1892): 173.

Reinhardt, Kurt. *The Existentialist Revolt.* Milwaukee: Bruce Publishing Company, 1952.

Richards, Samuel Whitney. Diary, 1846–1886. Typescript. Provo, UT: Brigham Young University Library, 1946.

Roberts, B. H. *Comprehensive History of the Church.* Salt Lake City: Deseret News Press, 1930.

———. *Seventy's Year Book.* Salt Lake City: Skelton Publishing Company, 1912.

———. *The Gospel.* Salt Lake City: Deseret Book, 1950.

———. "The Immortality of Man." In *Improvement Era* 10 (April 1907): 419.

Robinson, John A. T. *Honest To God.* Philadelphia: Westminister Press, 1963.

Robison, Parker, ed. *Writings of Parley P. Pratt.* Salt Lake City: Deseret News Press, 1952.

Rogers, Carl. *Counseling and Psychotherapy.* New York: Houghton Mifflin, 1942.

Ross, W. D. "Determinism and Indeterminism." In *Foundations of Ethics.* Oxford: Clarendon Press, 1939.

Russell, Bertrand. *Mysticism and Logic.* New York: Doubleday Anchor, 1957.

———. *Why I Am Not a Christian.* New York: Simon & Schuster, 1957.

Ryle, Gilbert. *The Concept of Mind.* London: Hutchinson, 1949.

Salt Lake Temple Dedication Notes. April 1893. The Church of Jesus Christ of Latter-day Saints Historical Department.

Sartre, Jean Paul. *L'Etre et le Neant.* Paris: Libr. Gallimard, 1949.

Schipp, Paul Arthur. *The Philosophy of Bertrand Russell.* Evanston, Ill.: Library of Living Philosophers, 1946.

Schweitzer, Albert. *Out of My Life and Thought.* New York: Mentor, 1960.

Seminar on the Prophet Joseph Smith. Provo, Utah: Brigham Young University Extension Publications, 1961.

Seminar on the Prophet Joseph Smith. Provo, Utah: Brigham Young University Extension Publications, 1962.

Shedd, William Greenough Thayer. *History of Christian Doctrine.* New York: C. Scribner and Sons, 1863.

Sheed, F. J., comp. *The Mary Book.* London: Sheed and Ward, 1950.

Smith, Joseph. *History of The Church of Jesus Christ of Latter-day Saints,* 2nd. ed., 7 vols. Salt Lake City: Deseret Book, 1948.

Smith, Joseph F. *Gospel Doctrine,* 12th ed. Salt Lake City: Deseret Book, 1961.

————. "Unchastity: The Dominant Evil of the Age." In *Improvement Era* 20 (June 1917): 739.

Smith, Joseph Fielding, comp. *Teachings of the Prophet Joseph Smith.* Salt Lake City: Deseret News Press, 1938. Deseret Book, 1976.

Smith, Lucy Mack. *History of Joseph Smith by His Mother.* Salt Lake City: Stevens & Wallis, 1945.

Smith, N. Kemp. *New Studies in the Philosophy of Descartes.* New York: Macmillan, 1952.

Snow, Eliza R. *Biography and Family Record of Lorenzo Snow.* Salt Lake City: Deseret News Press, 1884.

Snow, Lorenzo. Journal, 1840–1901. The Church of Jesus Christ of Latter-day Saints Historical Department.

Stace, Walter T. *Time and Eternity.* Princeton: University Press, 1952.

Talmage, James E. "Were They Crickets or Locusts, and When Did They Come?" *Improvement Era* 13 (December 1909): 100–101.

Tillich, Paul. *Biblical Religion and the Search for Ultimate Reality.* Chicago: University of Chicago Press, 1955.

————. *Love, Power, and Justice.* New York: Oxford University Press, 1960.

———. *Systematic Theology.* Vol. 2. Chicago: University of Chicago Press, 1958.

Tullidge, Edward W. *Women of Mormondom.* New York: Tullidge & Crandall, 1877.

Wald, George. "The Origin of Life." In *The Physics and Chemistry of Life.* New York: Simon and Schuster, 1955.

Walker, Charles C. Diary, August 1837. The Church of Jesus Christ of Latter-day Saints Historical Department.

Weigel, Gustave. "Myth, Symbol, and Analogy." In *Religion and Culture.* New York: Harper's, 1959.

Whale, J. S. *Christian Doctrine.* London: Cambridge University Press, 1963.

Whitehead, Alfred North. *Religion in the Making.* New York: Macmillan, 1926.

Whitney, Orson F. *Life of Heber C. Kimball.* Salt Lake City: Bookcraft, 1967.

Wild, John. *The Challenge of Existentialism.* Indiana: Bloomington, 1955.

Wisdom, John. *Philosophy and Psychoanalysis.* Oxford: Blackwell, 1953.

Wordsworth, William. "Tintern Abbey." In *Complete Poetical Works.* London: Macmillan, 1890.

Young, Alfred Douglas. Diary. The Church of Jesus Christ of Latter-day Saints Historical Department.

Young, Brigham. *Discourses of Brigham Young.* Comp. John A. Widtsoe. Salt Lake City: Deseret Book, 1946.

———. *Manuscript History of Brigham Young.* Ed. Elden J. Watson. Salt Lake City: E. J. Watson, 1971.

INDEX

357–62; purpose of, 362–63; finds a way despite trials, 363–64; after initial romance, 364–65; ecstasy possible in, 365; how to increase, 365

Marx, 30

Mathematics, nature of, 220

Matter, 309, 318, 349

McConkie, Bruce R., on worthiness for celestial resurrection, 351–52

McKay, David O.: on love, 93; exemplifies the language of love, 104–6; disappointment of, in temple endowment, 157–58, 281–82; on comprehending meaning of temple, 282; still in love at ninety-three, 363

Mechanist, 12, 55n. 1

Membership, 212–13, 228, 240

Memory, 64, 66, 161, 224

Mencken, H. L., 334

Menninger, 42

Mental illness, 101

Mercy, 329

Mill, John Stuart, on conscience, 243

Millenium, 332

Milton, John, 30

Mind, 38, 41

Mind-body, problem of, 8, 10–11

Miscommunication between the genders, 100, 102

Missionaries, sacrifices of, 271, 377–78

Montague, Ashley, 347

Montague, William Peperell, 24

Morris, 39

Mortality: willingly chosen, 12, 374; veil drawn at birth, 13; purpose of, 121; of Christ, 132–33

Mother in Heaven, 352, 354

Mount Moriah, 233

Mount of Olives, 302–3, 378–79

Mount of Transfiguration, 215

Moyle, Henry D., 270

Murder, 355

Music, 340, 363: spiritual nature of, 155–56; of Jewish Sabbath, 343–44

Myrtle, 336–37

Mystics, 39

Name of Christ, taking the, 168–69

Names of deity, 296

"Narcissa to Narcissus," (poem by Eliza R. Snow), 264

Natural, definition of, 93–94

Nature celebrates the Sabbath, 335

Nauvoo Temple, 275

Nephi (son of Lehi), 270, 301, 314–15

Nibley, Hugh, 210, 353

Niebhur, Reinhold, 15, 32, 196; on conscience, 248

Nietzsche, R., 40, 56, 118; on conscience, 191, 248

Nihilism, 12, 23, 253–54

"O My Father" (hymn), 35, 156, 352

Obedience, 263

Objectivity, 76–77

Occult, danger of, 229

Oil, 211. *See also* Olive oil

Olive branch, 302, 375

Olive oil, 301–2, 302–4, 378

Olive tree: symbolism of, 300–303, 305–6; allegory of tame and wild, 303, 375

Opposition, 112–13, 160–61, 198. *See also* Trials

Ordinances: anti, attitude, 221, 254–55; has same root as *ordained, order, ordinary,* 222; ordinary made extraordinary through, 223; beautiful and true combined through, 224; infinite memory unlocked through, 224; not to be altered, 226; as a form of prayer, 226; community in, 230–31; Christ manifested through, 231; pattern of

nourishment from, 255, 283;
eternal nature of, 283
Ordinances (power of): full of godly
power, 78–79; unifying power of,
224, 230–31; 229; two worlds
connected through, 225; power of
godliness manifested in, 226;
power to withstand Satan through,
229
Ordinances (symbolic nature of): as
metaphors of the universe, 220; as
signs of God and Christ, 222; as
signs of reality, 222;
understanding of, 223; archetypal,
225
Ordinations, performing, 152
Organisms, one-celled, 24
Original sin, 41–42, 42n. 23
Otto, Rudolph, 14, 62–63, 357

Pain: redeemed by love, 80; limits to,
121; does not compound, 122; of
spirits at our conduct, 370; as part
of the world, 373; love is therapy
for, 631. See also Trials; Suffering
Parenthood, Divine, 34–35
Parents, 106–7
Pascal, 22
Passion, 94–95. See also Love,
romantic or phsycial
Passover, 303
Patience with enemies, 359–60
Patriarchal blessings, 15, 151, 354
Paul: on Abraham, 238; on Spirit
assisting us in prayer, 266; taught
Joseph Smith, 267; definition of
love, 348
Peace, 302, 317, 369
Perfection: suffering necessary for,
49, 265; commanded to attain,
191; of the Atonement, 194; not
required for Church callings,
270–71
Persecution, 359
Personality: of the Divine, 32–23;

celestial, 43; of Christ, 73, 129;
three kinds of, 214–15; hard to
measure, 220
Perspective: renewed on Sabbath,
339; toward mortality from
preexistence, 352–53; and worry,
359; toward pain and trials,
361–62
Perspective theory of evil, 46–47,
115–16
Pessimist, 23
Peter, 267, 300
Physicalism, 37–38, 39, 40
Planting and harvesting, image of in
D&C, 211
Plato, 220: on knowledge by
recollection, 64n. 5; on learning as
recollection, 207; on preexistence
of soul, 207
Plotinus, 38
Polanyi, M., on knowing, 219
Positivism, 252
Power: prophetic, based on love, 84;
of light, 312; of married love,
347–67; temple wedding a
channel to receive, 366–67;
obtained from union of feeling,
372
Power-ethic, 253
Praise, use of, 106
Pratt, Helaman, call to Mexico, 237
Pratt, Orson, 122: on love, 166; on
every spirit having seen Christ in
preexistence, 207; on no man
being without a gift, 208; on
future temple in Jerusalem, 278
Pratt, Parley P.: on threefold nature of
man, 40n. 15; on loving, 81; on
"natural" affections, 93–94; on
conscience, 156; on innate feeling
to kindred spirits, 206; learned of
eternal family from Prophet,
348–50; on purposes of marriage,
362
Prayer: flashes of, 66; yearning,

143–44; man not alone in, 259; gratitude expressed during, 265–66; in extremity, 265; constant, 266–67; worthiness and, 270–72; purpose of, 272; temple a house of, 275–77; LDS theology a result of, 289–97; Spirit assists in, 292–93, 313, 261–62; for enemies, 360, 376

Prayer (elements of): how to, 145–46; as a dialogue, 150; honesty in, 212; addressing the Father in, 260; language and length of, 260; formal versus informal, 260–61; discerning the Lord's Spirit and one's own desires, 261–62; lack of answers to, 262–63, 293; frequency of, 264; facing temple during, 264, 275; structure of, 267–68; vocal, 267, 269; be one in, 269

Prayers (specific): sacrament, 167–70; of Christ in new world, 180; of Joseph Smith in sacred grove, 259; revealed, 261–62, 284; family, 263–64; quorum, in Kirtland temple, 267–68; of Christ at Gethsemane, 304–5; and fasting, 339–40

Predestination, 60n. 14

Predestinationists, 12, 55n. 1

Premortal existence: belief in, 12; memories of, 13–14; intimations of, 65–66; Christ with us in, 131–32; exquisite condition of man in, 205; personal ties before earth life in, 206; purpose of preparation there, 206; man's choice to come to earth, 206, 374; memory of, to be restored, 208; organization of human family in, 352–53, 369; Jewish tradition on arrangements in, 354

Pride, 58, 297

Priesthood: duty and burden of, 236; to try men, 236; and marriage relationship, 351; blessings, 366; keys of sealing power, 371

Privation theory of evil, 46, 116–17

Procreation and marriage, 349, 362

Progression of God and Christ, 48

Prophecy, spirit of, 155

Prophets, 193; on pre-existence, 14–15

Psychologism, 8, 15, 33, 252: on Fatherhood of God, 29–30; on nature of self, 43; views on conscience, 156

Pulsipher, John, on duty, 236

Punishment, Divine, 47, 114–15

Purification, 42

Puritanism, 334, 343

Queen: Sabbath as, 336–37; woman in exalted state, 337, 344, 350–51

Questioning faith, 136–38, 148–49

Quickened, 211–12, 311

Rabbi Simeon, 336

Racial memory, 219–20, 249

Random Harvest, James Hilton (film version), 203

Rasmussen, Ellis, 233

Reality, 253–54

Rebirth, 211

Rebuke of others, 79

Red China, 201–2

Relativism, 253–54

Religious consciousness, 62–65

Remembering, 165, 168

Repentance: completed, 128; not required before we forgive, 216, 359; immediate, 294; burning of approval within, 311; woman taken in adultery and, 325; the Sabbath and, 339, 341

Repetition, vain vs. acceptable, 267–68

Responsibility, relationship to freedom, 58–59

Restoration, the, 259, 350

117–20, 122–23; should not be wished for, 120–21; innocent, 121; necessary to develop compassion, 215, 272; meaning in, 361–62. *See also* Trials
Suicide, 20, 23, 153
Sun, light of the, 317
Survival of the fittest, 253
Sustaining the Brethren, 213
Symbols, 218, 220, 275

Talmage, James E., 228, on woman as celestial being, 351
Talmud, 338
Tarski, A., on mathematics, 220
Taylor, John, 82, 228, 320–22; on testing of Abraham, 238
Taylor, William, on love between Joseph and Hyrum, 83
Teacher training program, 213
Teaching, 213, 223, 310
Temple (blessings of): gives insights on love, 92; link between heaven and earth, 210; channel of power from on high, 274–75; communion with Christ possible in, 275; key to mastery of the earth, 277; place of self-knowledge, 277; harmonization of spirit and body in, 280–81; all aspects of man's nature blessed in, 281; wife shares priesthood blessings of, 351
Temple (function of): as house of Jesus Christ, 210; all symbols of, point to Christ, 275; house of prayer, 275–77; house of learning, 277–79; house of glory, 279–81; house of God, 279–81; purposes of, 284–85
Temple (response to): engenders sense of the sacred, 157; David O. McKay and endowment, 157–58, 281–82; comprehending meaning of, 158, 282; criticism of, should

be reserved, 281–82; preparation for, 282–83
Temple, body is a living, 318–19
Temple ordinances: "doing names," 214; dedicatory prayer, 261; marriage, 349, 365–67; washing of feet, 372
Temptation, in the heart, 164
Test, 232. *See also* Trials; Suffering
Testimony, 152–53, 159
Thankfulness, 265–66. *See also* Gratitude in prayer
Third Nephi, book of, 72–73, 159, 171–82
Thomas, 39
Thoughts, evil, 163–66
Tillich, Paul, 23, 32, 63n. 1
Time, 26, 296, 310, 331–32
Tongues, singing in, 363
Tranquility on the Sabbath, 331, 335–36
Translating as learning process, 72
Transubstantiation, 169
Tree of life, vision of, 301
Trees, 300–301. *See also* Olive tree
Trials: purpose of, 199, 232, 265; can hasten growth toward perfection, 265, 305–6; of Joseph Smith, 296; result of Fall, 354; attitude of entitlement, 360–61. *See also* Suffering
Trinitarianism, 192
Tritheism, 192
Truth, necessary to love, 76–77, 309–12
Tuttle, A. Theodore, 364

Unity: of body and spirit, 41; being one, 180; in prayer, 259, 269–70, 270; of feeling among Saints, 372
Unselfishness in marriage. *See* Marriage
Urim and Thummim, 208, 311

Vain repetition. *See* Repetition
Veil: over preexistence memories, 13;

Keep the Faith !

Stand-up & be
counted for righteous
things. Help others in
their needs when
possible !

Be kind to yourself
and others –

Learn to laugh at
yourself

Learn something new
often.

Keep the faith
always ↑↑!

Be generous with
others.

Tell the you loved
ones you love +
appreciate them – often

cultivate humor
throyour home 359

page
355

Abraham promises
354-355

see:
p. 154 our church has
Judaism common